Healthcare Communication

Healthcare Communication

Bruce Hugman
BA MA DipEd

International Training and Communications Consultant

Communications Consultant to the WHO Foundation Collaborating Centre
for International Drug Monitoring (the Uppsala Monitoring Centre, Sweden)
He lives in Thailand.

London • Chicago Pharmaceutical Press

Published by the Pharmaceutical Press
An imprint of RPS Publishing

1 Lambeth High Street, London SE1 7JN, UK
100 South Atkinson Road, Suite 200, Grayslake, IL 60030-7820, USA

RPS Publishing is the publishing organisation of the Royal Pharmaceutical Society of Great Britain

First published 2009

Typeset by J&L Composition Ltd, Scarborough, North Yorkshire
Printed in Italy by L.E.G.O. S.p.A.

ISBN 978 0 85369 749 7

A catalogue record for this book is available from the British Library.

No one ever found wisdom without also being a fool. Writers, alas, have to be fools in public, while the rest of the human race can cover its tracks.

Erica Jong

For additional and new materials:
Online Resources at www.pharmpress.com
For individual reaction to the book:
author@brucehugman.com
For reader forum and author blog:
www.brucehugman.com

Contents

Preface

This is a personal note from the author to you, that most important of people, my reader, to explain a few things about me and the book.

I was born in the UK in the final months of the second world war, and am, therefore, (a) very old, and (b) a child of the era of universal, free healthcare for all, as it was embodied in the British National Health Service (NHS). I believe in healthcare as a right for all, not as a commodity for purchase, or a privilege for developed countries, or a grudging and tight-fisted concession for the poor. In that sense, I am a dreamer.

However, I am also hard-headed enough to know that we do not live in an ideal or idealistic world, and that the realities of modern healthcare around the world (including the modern NHS) are far from the aspirations of the original UK health scheme. But I also have a vision of how first-class contemporary healthcare can be delivered at the personal and local level across the globe, by healthcare professionals who are medically and technically proficient, and are thoughtful, reflective, compassionate, and experts in human relations and communications. I know that there are some places where such ideals are a living reality of daily practice but that there are far more where they are not.

This book is about the immense richness and complexity of human nature, and the intriguing challenges of being an effective professional and human being in all roles and relationships, with patients, with colleagues and beyond. While relationships with patients are constantly in mind throughout the book, and there are lots of specific examples, this is not an itemised workshop manual of advice and techniques for every patient encounter. Its aim is to nourish your knowledge and insight on a very broad front, so that you can bring greater understanding and wisdom to the whole spectrum of your work. You will find much more detailed, methodical, technical and research-based material in other excellent books, many of which are referenced in the appendixes.

To hard-pressed professionals, some of the material may seem absurd in its ambition – 'Who has time for this?' they may say. The answer is this: the fundamental wisdom of this book takes time to acquire, but living that wisdom does not so much take time, as change the way time is spent and its quality and usefulness. For those meeting patients, there may be only four or eight or eleven minutes but that time can be squandered – or richly exploited for the patient's welfare and benefit. All encounters with patients and all relationships can be enriched by greater knowledge and skill, whatever the culture, the continent or the constraints.

This book is for everyone in healthcare, especially doctors, nurses and pharmacists, in training and in practice. It is also for other medical specialists and non-medical personnel, for everyone in the healthcare team who wants to reach higher standards in patient care and greater satisfaction in work. It's about creating compassionate and coherent relationships and systems for the delivery of healthcare. It also includes many of the skills for managing essential, everyday communications activities which do not directly involve patients but which affect everyone in one way or another (writing, public presentations, dealing with complaints and many more).

I hope you will enjoy the book, be provoked to think and argue and disagree, be inspired by it, and find many things that will stimulate and intrigue you and help you to be even more effective in your important work.

Bruce Hugman
Chiang Rai, Thailand
January 2009

Disclaimer

The author, Bruce Hugman, runs a forum on healthcare communications, which you are invited to join at *www.brucehugman.com*. This forum does not express the views or concerns of the Royal Pharmaceutical Society of Great Britain or Pharmaceutical Press. Pharmaceutical Press can accept no responsibility or liability whatsoever in respect of its operation or content.

About the author

Since 1995 Bruce Hugman has been consultant in communications to the Uppsala Monitoring Centre (WHO Collaborating Centre for International Drug Monitoring), in Uppsala Sweden. He has written extensively on healthcare communications, particularly relating to pharmacovigilance and patient safety, and teaches and lectures in many parts of the world. His careers include teaching English and social studies in schools and universities, managing an agricultural smallholding, working in the criminal justice system as a probation and training officer, holding senior public relations posts in public transport operations and, for over a decade, running his own communications company in the UK before going freelance. He has published books in the fields of literary criticism, sociology, criminology and biography, and contributed to edited collections on drug safety and patient safety. He lives in Thailand.

Acknowledgements

Writing this book has been a wonderful opportunity and a big challenge, but it would not have happened at all, and would not have had half the quality I hope it has, without the direct and indirect contribution of a very large numbers of wise and kindly people.

Four people have provided particularly generous support in the shaping and writing of the book: Dr Arnold Gordon, who meticulously and tirelessly examined a late draft, offering many valuable suggestions and insights from early on; Dr Awi Curameng, who read early drafts, helped in the writing of some of the more specialist medical material, and was an enthusiast for the project from the beginning; Jeremy Lowe, whose thoughtful and supportive editing and commentary helped me along in the difficult middle stages of the book; Prof Rafe Edwards, whose friendship, support and insight in relation to life in general and to this book in particular, have inspired me over many years. To them, I am deeply indebted.

In the preparation of this book, friends, colleagues and previous strangers round the world have been extraordinarily generous and helpful with support, ideas and materials. Some of them appear in the second list below, but there are many who do not:

Alex Dodoo, Ghana
Kenneth Hartigan-Go, The Philippines
Anna Linquist, Sweden
Abida Haq, Malaysia
Anna Celén, Sweden
Ronald Meyboom, The Netherlands
William Frempong, Sweden/UK
John McEwen, Australia
Brian Edwards, UK
Anne Kiuru, Sweden
Vladimir Milashin, Russia
Elisabeth Dodds, UK
David Lelievre, UK
David Coulter, New Zealand
Philip Roddis, UK
Souad Skalli, Morocco
Lucia Turcan, Moldova
Carolina Senic, Moldova
Yang Le, China
Jayesh Pandit, Kenya
Ali Bahceci, Sweden
Pravich Tanyasittisuntorn, Thailand
Laura Hugman, UK
The Hagqvist family, Sweden
Christopher Stapleton, UK
Jirathi Srikhao, Thailand
Chi Wen Chiang, Taiwan
Kate Lloyd, UK

The content of the book, and such wisdom and insight as it may have, come from a lifetime of interest in the issues and endless reflection, reading and discussion about most of them, with hundreds of people – students, colleagues, friends, clients – over the years. They come particularly from the influence of a number of remarkable people I have had the privilege of knowing, who have influenced my life in one way or another, some of them profoundly. Many of them know, I hope, about my gratitude and affection, but this is an opportunity for me to express those feelings publicly, and to put them on record.

To these great people, some out of contact for many years, some now dead, but most still alive and well and in touch, I owe a debt of gratitude for the various ways in which they contributed to the richness and happiness and learning in my life:

Jean Morton
Jack Porter
Eric Sainsbury
Audrey Sainsbury
Christopher Ricks
Marie Lindquist
Roy Deakin
Tony Kennan
Maire Kennan
Roy Stephenson
Ian Chisholm
Rob George
Vicky Robinson
Jeremy Hawksley
Caro Hawksley
Colin Reid
Betsy Reid
David Pickup
Mike Corner
Richard West
Melvyn Hopwood
Christina Tan
Marjorie Thompson
The team of wise and remarkable staff on the James Pringle HIV/AIDS ward at the Middlesex Hospital, London, and the community and palliative care teams, in the early 1990s.
The staff and students at the Faculty of Pharmacy, Rangsit University, Pathum Thani, Thailand, whose enthusiasm for learning about healthcare communications provided the original stimulus for the writing of this book.

I am grateful to Joanne Barnes, whose knowledge of the world took me to the doors of the Pharmaceutical Press, and so to the writing of the book; and to my ever supportive brother and sister-in-law, Iain and Jenny Hugman.

Finally, a slightly romantic footnote: some of this book was written in my wooden cottage in Sweden, previously owned by that doyenne of Swedish journalism and letters, Sigrid Kahle. When she moved away, she left me the great oak desk on which she had done much of her lifetime's writing, and I am grateful for that and the inspiration it and my recent friendship with her have provided.

Thank you all!

Permissions

A number of organisations, publishers and individuals have kindly given permission for the use of their ideas or copyright material in this book:

Cohen, M R (ed.). *Medication Errors*, 2nd edn, 2007. American Pharmacists' Association.
Hargie O (ed). *The Handbook of Communication Skills*, 3rd edn, 2006. London: Routledge.
International Pharmaceutical Students Federation.
Paling J. *Helping Patients Understand Risk*, 2nd edn, 2006. The Risk Communications Institute. *www.riskcomm.com*
Silverman J, Kurtz S, Draper J. *Skills for Communicating with Patients,* 2nd edn, 2006. Oxford: Radcliffe Publishing.
Austin Health, Melbourne, Australia.
For Less Inc., Ethnicityonline.
The Plain English Campaign.

Specific quotations or material are referenced in the chapter notes and references from the page on which they occur.

Cartoons and quotations

The author hopes you will enjoy these diversions from his own thoughts and words. The quotations do not necessarily represent his point of view, but many provide important challenges and alternative perspectives to our ideas from serious writers and thinkers. Please note that the quotations have not been edited to conform with modern principles of non-discriminatory language: they appear as they were originally written or spoken). The cartoons were drawn by Richard Lear at J&L Composition.

Part A

Getting started

The first chapter sets out the purposes and principles of the book, and the second provides some suggestions about how to use it if you do not simply want to read it straight through from beginning to end.

The basic framework in the third chapter gives an overview of the intricacies in the process of any problem-solving consultation with a patient, and sets the scene for the rest of the book. Although this is based on a physician diagnostic consultation, the content and pattern are relevant to any investigative and decision-making encounter with a patient.

Note on 'HCPs'

The author dislikes acronyms and jargon but throughout the book the abbreviated form of healthcare professional (HCP) is used for economy of style and space. It is used primarily to refer to nurses, pharmacists and doctors, on whose work the book is mainly focused, but embraces all those who have therapeutic or helping relationships with patients, for whom the content of the book is also intended.

The instruction we find in books is like fire. We fetch it from our neighbours, kindle it at home, communicate it to others, and it becomes the property of all.

Voltaire

1 Introduction

If you work for patients in any role in healthcare, this book is written for you and your colleagues in the whole multi-disciplinary team. Whatever your job, this book is dedicated with admiration to you, because you are making a contribution to some of the most important activities that human beings are capable of:

- helping people to live healthy and fulfilling lives
- preventing and relieving pain and suffering
- providing comfort and support to people who are sick, injured, disabled or dying
- increasing the world's stock of compassion and hope.

Whatever your role, you have a contribution to make through the exercise of your knowledge and expertise; through your dedication and humanity; and through the quality of your communications. At the heart of the best healthcare are caring people with great skills of many kinds.

> An inquiring, analytical mind; an unquenchable thirst for new knowledge; and a heartfelt compassion for the ailing – these are prominent traits among the committed clinicians who have preserved the passion for medicine.
>
> *Lois DeBakey*

There is not one of us who cannot become more effective and fulfilled as human beings by studying ourselves and others, and through learning more about relationships and communications. This book offers that opportunity. The rewards are great: not just for our own satisfaction and happiness, but also for our value and usefulness to others in our professional and personal lives.

This book ambitiously covers a very wide range of material about human relations and communications relating to most aspects of healthcare activity, but at its heart are some very simple truths which are relevant to almost any human encounter:

- The best healthcare is provided for patients and their families by people who are experts in their field but who also have equal measures of compassion and generosity, and an exceptional capacity to relate and communicate effectively.
- The best healthcare grows from the ideal of service to patients, their families and carers, based on an unfailing determination to understand what they need and want, to explain options and consequences, to protect their safety, and to collaborate with them in achieving agreed goals.
- To have a vivid and accurate insight into what life is really like for other people transforms how we see the world, and how we think, feel, behave and communicate.
- To study and understand ourselves, our own strengths and weaknesses, our foibles and prejudices, our motivation and our aspirations is the basis for confidence and sensitivity and true usefulness to others.

This book provides material of two main types:

- Analysis and discussion designed to lead to a deeper knowledge and understanding of relationships and communications.
- Examples and suggestions of what to do and how to do it in healthcare relationships.

You will also find much more on the publisher's website in Online Resources at www.pharmpress.com.

Box 1.1 Major focus on patient safety

As this book goes to press, major reform in regulation of the medical and healthcare professions is under way in the UK. Following publication of the White Paper, *Trust Assurance and Safety: the regulation of health professionals*,[1] and the Government's response to reports from the Shipman and other malpractice enquiries,[2] professional competence and patient safety are under intense scrutiny as major changes are planned and implemented.[3] The General Medical Council[4] and other professional bodies are also working hard in these areas.

Among the many issues at stake is regular revalidation of healthcare professionals, including, among much else, evaluation of communications effectiveness and patient satisfaction.[5] This book exemplifies many of the new standards in these areas.

The World Health Organization's World Patient Safety Alliance (2004),[6] the US Joint Commission's award-winning 'Speak Up' patient safety campaign (2002),[7] and other initiatives across the world are also focusing on many of the same issues.

The values, principles and skills described in this book are perfectly in line with the new legislative and regulatory vision in many countries, which, more than ever before, draws attention to the necessity of active partnership between all stakeholders, especially between healthcare professionals and their patients.

The author's assumption is that once you have mastered material of the first level (and perhaps read a great deal elsewhere too), how to approach patients, and what to do and how to do it will be much clearer to you. It is impossible to provide a reference manual of techniques for each of the vast variety of patients whom you will meet, but once you understand the theory and the principles, what you need to do becomes much easier and more obvious.

The darker aspects of professional life: the constraints and the limitations; the ever-tightening budgets; the shortages of time and resources; the pressures for productivity and narrow cost-effectiveness; inequity of access; the impact of bureaucracy, politics and litigation – all so familiar – do cast a shadow on the ideal vision of excellent healthcare for all. But, in truth, the tougher the environment, the greater is the need for expert and humane relationships within it, and for communications that are as open, honest, supportive, effective and inclusive as possible.

War is what happens when language fails.

Margaret Atwood

Above all, this book assumes that we can all improve our knowledge and skills, and continue doing so as long as we live. No matter how repetitious some relationships and experiences may seem, no two are ever the same, and there are always new things to be learnt about ourselves and others. The author and publisher hope you will enjoy this foray into the fascinating territory that is communication, and that it will, in some measure, change how you see the world, and, of course, help you to become more effective, fulfilled and useful in your work.

Learning from you

One of the repeated messages in this book is that good communication is always genuinely interactive, and that listening is usually more important than talking.

A book makes personal interaction with readers and listening to them quite difficult, but the author is keen to hear from you about your reactions, thoughts, criticisms or objections in relation to the material in this book. We will learn things from you, and the second edition will be a much better book if it includes some of your thoughts and experiences. We need to hear from those of you who want to point out the shortcomings of the book as much as from those who approve of it.

Especially valuable will be examples of communications challenges and solutions in real healthcare situations that you have experienced.

Please email author@brucehugman.com with your feedback or go to www.brucehugman.com for a readers' forum.

The Pharmaceutical Press also has a website, www.pharmpress.com, where you can find new material and further discussion of the issues in this book in Online Resources.

Please let's hear from you and make your reading of the book and your response to it into an active communication between us and other readers throughout the world.

2 Signposts for the journey through this book

To find out what is in this book . . .

If you are in a hurry with 15 minutes to spare:

- Skim the contents pages.
- Read the introduction at the beginning of each major section (blue pages).

If you are under pressure but have 30 minutes:

- Skim the contents pages.
- Read the introductions at the beginning of each major section.
- Read the summary at the beginning of each chapter.

If you need help thinking about a particular issue or problem:

- Check out the contents and index pages.

If you have got just a few spare moments:

- Browse the cartoons and quotations . . .
  otherwise . . .
- read any chapter or
- start at the beginning and keep going!

For direct practice communication issues: Chapters 3 and 9–21; Appendix 3.

For analysis of the nature of communication and the profound influences of human psychology: Chapters 4, 5, 9 and 10.

For discussion of communication, vision and ethics in healthcare: Chapters 6–8.

For many kinds of everyday communication activities not involving face-to-face relationships with patients: Chapters 22–26.

For a large collection of references to books, websites and other sources on all topics: Appendices 1 and 2.

For more serious readers, alone or in groups or teams, there is a selection of discussion issues and practical challenges at the end of each major section of the book. They invite critical thinking and debate about many of the issues in the book, and beyond. Commentary on many of these can be found in Online Resources at www.pharmpress.com.

3 The basic framework for working with patients

Table 3.1 is a skeleton framework of activities and tasks, which is relevant to every encounter between every HCP and patient. It is only details (such as diagnosis and prescribing) that are confined to particular roles; the other elements of perception, assessment, decision making and so on apply across the board.

It is presented as a bird's-eye view of the whole process, which you can refer to when you're immersed in the detail of the book. It is far from comprehensive, but it highlights the major elements of any professional encounter with a patient, and particularly the extent to which communication is inextricably involved in almost every aspect of an effective healthcare relationship. Although it looks elaborate when laid out step by step, this process, or something very similar to it, is what happens in all the best problem-solving encounters with patients. With experience, it will become spontaneous and rapid.

This framework is based on activities and tasks, whereas the material of the book is presented mainly by topics (knowledge and skills), many of which are applicable at any stage throughout a consultation or relationship to most or all of the activities and tasks.

Here you can see the broad picture at a relatively high level. When you have read the book,

you will have a richer and more knowledgeable appreciation of all the issues recorded here, and many, many more.

The fundamental question to ask in all health-care relationships is: 'How can I understand the needs of my patients and help them solve their problems?'

It is much more important to know what sort of a patient has a disease than what sort of a disease a patient has.

William Osler

For another methodical, and much more advanced analysis of consultation skills, see Appendix 3, p. 291.

Table 3.1 A basic skeleton framework of activities and tasks relevant to every encounter between HCP and patient

Key questions	Key issues	Key attitudes, knowledge and skills	Key areas for effective medical/technical knowledge, skills and expertise	Key areas for effective communication skills	Commentary
1. What is the nature of this situation and what is required of me?	Appraisal of the setting in which one is confronted with the patient; the needs, the priorities, available resources, timescales	Wide field of perception, rapid collection and processing of facts and evidence, questioning of others and gathering information	✓	✓	Primarily applicable in unusual situations, such as accidents, emergencies or natural disasters, or when standing in for others, but useful even in familiar settings
2. Do I like this patient?	Assessing spontaneous first impressions and feelings; ensuring just and fair treatment	Self-awareness; honesty; ability to restrain negative or overly positive reactions and compensate for them; awareness and control of non-verbal behaviour		✓	Unrecognised strong first impressions may skew an entire relationship and cloud perception of reality to the detriment of understanding a patient, diagnostic accuracy and the best possible therapy
3. Who is this patient?	Attempt to glimpse the whole person through their words, feelings, behaviour, personal history and in their social and family environment. Who are the significant others in this patient's life? What is their reaction to their current situation and to me? Evidence accumulates throughout even the shortest consultation.	Unprejudiced openness to human diversity; establishing rapport and trust; empathy, listening, questioning, observation, including non-verbal behaviour; discovery and interpretation of patient's psychology; understanding of relationships and major influences in patient's life; perceiving and taking account of patient's response to HCP and situation		✓	Underlying everything – care, concern and compassion; an intense concentration on trying to grasp the essence of the whole person beyond their symptoms and disease, even in the shortest encounter; grasping the context and quality of the patient's life beyond healthcare
4. What is this patient's problem? Is this patient sick?	Listening to and interpreting the patient's story and symptoms and attempting diagnosis of the problem as a joint enterprise	Medical/technical knowledge, experience and diagnostic and thinking skills; taking medical and medication history; open-mindedness; empathy, listening, observation, exceptional questioning skills; avoiding hasty judgements; sceptical (questioning) approach to solutions; attention to intuition	✓	✓	The problem or problems may not be what they first appear to be, nor what the patient thinks; they may have medical, psychological or social components; they may be simple, complex or uncertain; they may not be what the records suggest

Table 3.1 A basic skeleton framework of activities and tasks relevant to every encounter between HCP and patient *(continued)*

Key questions	Key issues	Key attitudes, knowledge and skills	Key areas for effective medical/technical knowledge, skills and expertise	Key areas for effective communication skills	Commentary
5. What further tests or procedures (if any) are necessary to reach a diagnosis?	Identifying and communicating next steps (if any); eliciting patient's reactions; setting timescale and making plans	Explanation and reassurance; joint planning; managing patient's reactions and feelings	✓	✓	Patient may be disappointed at postponement of diagnosis; may be anxious or alarmed about tests or procedures; may have practical problems about more appointments
6. What is the patient's reaction to the diagnosis or lack of diagnosis?	Accurate understanding of the meaning of the diagnosis or lack of diagnosis for the patient and their life	Empathy, listening, observation, questioning; showing support, concern, compassion as appropriate		✓	Whether relief, despair, shame, anger, or many other emotions, the reaction must be acknowledged and dealt with. The slow, painstaking process of complex diagnoses may need explaining
7. What resources do I have available to help this patient solve their problem?	HCP's silent, internal considerations: assessment of extent or limitation of: • time • technical/medical/ medication/other resources • expertise	Comprehensive factual knowledge within and beyond healthcare; imaginative grasp of resources that may be relevant to meeting this patient's needs; 'gateway' thinking to provide access to other resources	✓		Situational assessment: availability or limitation of resources will vary from location to location; there may be time but no technical resources; technical resources but little time, and so on. HCPs work within what they have and what is available beyond them
8. Within those resource options what resources are available for this patient?	HCP's silent, internal considerations: identification of likely best options to solve this patient's problem within constraints of time/medical and other resources/expertise/patient and healthcare finances	Careful matching of options to patient's symptoms, disease and situation. Honest consideration of the possibility that you are not the best person to handle this patient's problems without additional expert consultation. Should you refer the patient to another HCP or other non-medical experts or resources?	✓		Secondary situational assessment: first, making choices of best solutions; second, ruling out those not practically or financially possible (but not necessarily excluding them from discussion with the patient). Resisting pressure to solve everything here and now if it is not the best option

Table 3.1 A basic skeleton framework of activities and tasks relevant to every encounter between HCP and patient *(continued)*

Key questions	Key issues	Key attitudes, knowledge and skills	Key areas for effective medical/technical knowledge, skills and expertise	Key areas for effective communication skills	Commentary
9. What is the patient's view of the options and their consequences?	Full explanation of identified options, their rationale, risks and benefits, and consequences; exploration of the patient's views and feelings; review of options not available to this patient and reasons	Empathy, explanation, listening, questioning, answering questions, communicating risk; using visual aids or other communications resources; dealing with disappointment or anger (when options are limited or distressing)	✓	✓	Exceptionally demanding when explaining often complex matters in ways which make sense to the patient; poor levels of health literacy a major obstacle; potentially large emotional content in reaction to this stage as well as diagnosis
10. What therapy or course of action can we jointly agree?	Discussion, negotiation and informed consent	Empathy, listening, proposing, negotiating, questioning, explaining; taking the patient's view seriously; overcoming obstacles; managing consent (or refusal)	✓	✓	Great skill needed in exploring options, making genuinely joint decisions and reaching informed choice
11. What needs to be done by me, other HCPs, others in or beyond healthcare, and by the patient and others in their family or social environment?	Planning overall strategy, including tests and referrals, liaison, support services and so on; agreeing action and change in patient's life; keeping good records of everything	Joint planning, negotiation, review of requirements and options; structure and clarity; empathy, listening, observation, questioning, explaining; reaching joint commitment to the plan; providing supporting resources (notes, charts, pill-boxes, etc)	✓	✓	Great clarity of mind required to see the whole picture and then present it to the patient in a way that makes sense and can be remembered and followed
12. How can risks be minimised, safety enhanced and adherence encouraged?	Anticipation and discussion of risks (maybe for the second time); following best practice (e.g. in dispensing); explanation and support for adherence; medication counselling	Explanation, seeking feedback, checking understanding, listening, questioning; communicating risk; motivating and providing personal and practical support	✓	✓	Vital stage of consultation which needs to have adequate time planned for it; may require ingenuity and creativity to achieve its aims and empower the patient to take effective responsibility for therapy

Table 3.1 A basic skeleton framework of activities and tasks relevant to every encounter between HCP and patient *(continued)*

Key questions	Key issues	Key attitudes, knowledge and skills	Key areas for effective medical/technical knowledge, skills and expertise	Key areas for effective communication skills	Commentary
13. What plans need to be made for future contingencies and contact?	Ensuring that future personal and medical needs (including the unexpected) are discussed, anticipated and provided for; continuity of care and contact is offered and planned; names and contact numbers provided	Empathy, questioning, listening, explanation; providing reassurance and sense of continuity of care and concern; for hospitals, coherent and effective discharge counselling and resources	✓	✓	It is too easy for a patient to feel abandoned once the primary consultation or activity (surgery or whatever) has been completed. Careful plans need to be made, even if only for optional contact should the patient want it
14. What else is concerning the patient?	Ensuring the patient is leaving with current questions and concerns adequately dealt with	Empathy, questioning, listening, observation; silence, waiting for thoughts to develop		✓	Because consultations are often concluded at the end of the obvious agenda, many patients leave with questions and concerns unanswered. Some patients declare their primary worries only as they are leaving or when they are asked
15. Is the patient leaving with a clear grasp of the main issues?	Final review and check of primary information and decisions agreed	Summarising, checking understanding, seeking feedback, reinforcing messages, encouraging and motivating	✓	✓	Repetition and checking of primary messages and requirements are essential if patients are to understand and remember them

Communication knowledge and skills are critical for almost every aspect of any healthcare consultation. That is the fundamental message of this book: without excellent, interactive communications with patients, no amount of medical or technical brilliance will reach their potential for providing the very best patient care.

Part B

The nature and importance of communication

Communication is one of those taken-for-granted, everyday activities to which we tend to pay little conscious attention. Although everyone can communicate at some level, we can learn to do it much better and put it to good use at work. Part B examines the nature of effective communication, the needs and urges that drive people to communicate, and the current revolution that is taking place in every corner of the globe. It concludes with a chapter arguing and demonstrating that effective communications are fundamental to the delivery of the best healthcare, because only communications can address many of the fundamental problems.

Be careful about reading health books. You may die of a misprint.

4 What is effective communication?

Effective communication is a reciprocal, interactive process in which sender and recipient have responsibilities to ensure that a message has been received and understood. A communication is not complete until the loop has been closed: the sender has evidence from the recipient that the message has been received and made sense of. In healthcare, HCPs have a special responsibility to ensure that messages are tailored exactly to the personality, needs and abilities of the patient, to encourage the engagement of the patient, to verify that the message has been received and completely understood, and has the best possible chance of supporting agreed action or change.[8]

The basics

Communication is the sending and receiving of:

- a message
- a signal
- information
- data.

In this book, *message* is the term used to encompass all four.

All living organisms communicate in one way or another – whales, bees, flowers, cells – and, of course, people.

Much behaviour in nature is genetically programmed and some is learnt (including, for example, feeding, nest-building and mating rituals). Although it is all intentional (that is, has a purpose), relatively little of it is consciously or voluntarily intentional, unlike some, but by no means all, human communication and behaviour.

Communication may be made with spoken or printed words, pictures, objects (working models, for example), diagrams, toys, music, theatre and the whole range of electronic media, or any combination of them. It may be face-to-face, individually or with a group or crowd; voice only or at a distance in other ways. The principles apply to all

Box 4.1 A complete and effective, intentional, human communication is an exchange that involves:

- sending of a message (transmission)
- receipt of a message
- confirmation of receipt and interpretation
- a purposeful reaction (which may or may not include the reaction, change or result intended by the sender)
- feedback about the process (see Box 4.2).

Figure 4.1 An effective completed communication. This is the simplest possible model of the communications loop, which always needs completion. The initial formulation of the message should be influenced by feedback from previous communications and research into the audience, and any follow up to the message itself must be equally influenced by how recipients have responded in the first instance.

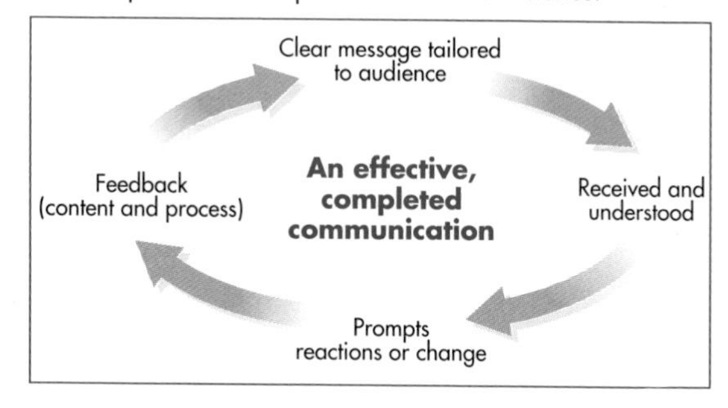

methods and circumstances, including informal social relationships.

At the end of an effective communication, both (or all) parties feel that mutual needs have been met (both utilitarian and emotional) and that an agreed goal of some kind has been achieved as far as possible. They may also feel satisfaction and pleasure in the process and the outcome.

The most important thing in communication is hearing what isn't said.

Peter Drucker

Effective communication is not simply transmission (sending). The sender is responsible for ensuring the communication loop is completed. The recipient has a reciprocal responsibility for seeing that the loop is completed, but the primary responsibility is the sender's. These principles apply to any form of communication, whether face-to-face, a mass mailing, a personal email or a patient information leaflet. It applies to every method of communication: pictures, sound, objects, films, diagrams and charts. Did the communication reach the chosen individual recipient or recipients within the intended audience, and what effect did it have on each of them?

Box 4.2 Process

All human communications involve *content* and *process*: that is, what is being communicated and also the multiple variables (often feelings) influencing how the content is sent, what the recipient feels about the content and the method and so on. The simplest message (content) may be compromised by the process: for example, if the recipient is upset by the tone or form or timing of a message. A brilliantly formulated message from a source that is not trusted may not only not get through, but also have a negative effect. Meetings often fail to achieve goals because the process – the feelings of the participants – are not recognised and managed. See also Chapter 25, p. 253).

Isn't one of your first exercises in learning how to communicate to write a description of how to tie your shoelaces? The point being that it's basically impossible to use text to show that.

Donald Norman

We also continuously communicate messages that we may not consciously intend: the entire range of our non-verbal behaviour (everything except the actual meaning or content of the words themselves – our facial expressions, tone of voice, style and tone of writing, the clothes we wear, the physical state of our office) all send information about our state of mind, attitudes, feelings towards anyone who encounters them, either in person (face-to-face) or at a distance (in a meeting or across a ward, through a memo, letter or email, for example). This behaviour accounts for more than half of the impact of all our communications.[9–11] This, again, highlights the difference between explicit, intended verbal *content*, *non-verbal communication* and *process*. (See Chapter 10 for a detailed account of non-verbal communication.)

Effective communication is 20% what you know and 80% how you feel about what you know.

Jim Rohn

Box 4.3 'But I sent her an email . . .'

This is a poor excuse for failure to get someone to attend a meeting because:

- the email may have gone astray
- there may have been an error in the email address
- she may have been on holiday
- she may have misunderstood the message
- there may have been an error in the typing of the time or the date.

It is not a communication until it is clear that none of these potential failures has occurred: that is until you have positive confirmation of its safe delivery and a response from the recipient confirming reading of the message as sent and intended.

Requesting an email delivery confirmation or read-receipt is an important first step, but that does not confirm that the message was actually read, nor provide information about what sense the recipient made of the message nor what they felt about it. Only when there is active feedback, does any transmission (sending an email, SMS, letter, memo, putting up a notice) become a *communication* seriously worthy of the name.

Interaction

Effective communication takes place only when there is interaction between the parties, when the sender seeks a response and the recipient is actively engaged. However clear the message may appear to be, its effectiveness is determined by the behaviour of the recipient, face-to-face or at a distance, who may:

- be distracted, day-dream or sleep
- ignore the message
- make no response
- listen attentively or intermittently
- understand partially or wholly, or misunderstand
- feel or express disapproval of the sender
- disagree with the intention of the message
- comment or ask questions
- confirm understanding and express willingness to comply with the message
- have a positive or adverse reaction to the tone, content, form or timing of the message (irritation or resentment, for example)
- interpret the message in terms of their own framework and not that of the sender.

Only if the sender understands these and other possible variables, anticipates them, plans the message to take account of them, then listens, observes and asks what is going on in the recipient's mind, does the message have a good chance of being successful.

Only if the recipient is actively involved, will they be sure to make good sense of the message; only by comments and questions will they get the information they need and will the sender know what progress is being made. Both senders and recipients need to be assertive in their collaboration to make a communication effective, and there needs to be motivation on both sides to make the communication work. There will be rare times, of course, when a patient or other recipient is so uncooperative or recalcitrant, and no amount of effort will succeed. HCPs can do only so much!

Traditional lectures – the transmission of lengthy and complex messages – are not really communications at all, because there is rarely any interaction or active feedback, even if the recipients are awake and appear to be listening (see also Chapter 26). Notices, some meetings and mass-mailings can also be ineffective in their one-directional broadcasting of information. Traditional top-down, paternalistic communications are similarly fragile.

The revolution we cannot ignore

The message of this chapter is as true for the simplest and most traditional of communications (say, a handwritten memo or letter) as it is for the sophisticated personal, commercial and mass communications of the 21st century. In the past, it has often been possible for someone who is lazy to get away with ineffective communications, because public demands and expectations were low. In recent years, the revolution in communications, driven particularly by developments such as activity on the internet, has revolutionised expectations. The old, top-down model of expert authority and knowledge transmission is losing its predominance as more people discover the authority of their own experience and the richness of resources among their peers, and question the 'infallible' reliability of experts.

Among these busy internet communities are many exclusive to patients, who are discovering new ways of understanding and managing disease. The move from pedagogy to andragogy in education (from passive learning to the interactive development of critical minds) has also had a major impact in many parts of the world and continues to do so as old patterns begin to fade.

Box 4.4 Traditional and radical

> *Encyclopedia Britannica*, in its printed form, and Wikipedia stand as icons of the old and the new: the former a kind of revered depository of wisdom promulgated by experts, in which readers are simply recipients not partners; the latter a living, organic, evolving resource of great richness, with its subject matter chosen by users and written, debated, developed and refined by them as a community. This is not to enter the debate about their relative merits, but to point out that audiences, who were previously passive recipients or consumers of expert information, are increasingly taking responsibility for their own knowledge and learning – and, consequently, are radically more critical and demanding in relation to the quality and credibility of communications they will take seriously.

Box 4.5 Wikipedia

> In 2008 Wikipedia claimed to have 683 million annual visitors, viewing or editing 10 million documents in 253 languages.[12]

Top-down was never truly satisfactory and empowering, and always liable to corruption, but is was accepted for millennia as the only way,[13] and it does remain relevant in some aspects of life. We have to understand the fundamental principles of effective communications in their own right, and, at the same time, recognise that the communications revolution that is taking place everywhere around us will leave us powerless if we do not employ the very best contemporary wisdom and skills in everything we do and say.

Box 4.6 Exceptions

> There are several kinds of communications that do not fall within the scope of this discussion of reciprocal, partnership relationships, particularly those resulting from the exercise of power or authority: legislation or government edicts; the opinions and pronouncements of judges; the disciplinary interview or discipline in the classroom, for example. Although many common communications skills may be part of these processes (empathy, listening, questioning, explaining), the purpose of such communications is not necessarily mutual agreement and collaboration, but rather the imposition of rules, decisions, behaviour, with or without consent. That authoritarian model has played a large part in the history of healthcare relationships, and is still present in some places even today.

The essentials in healthcare

In social relationships, all of us – senders and recipients – have a responsibility to make sure messages are effective, but in healthcare, the responsibility is primarily for the HCP to make sure the message is received, understood and has the intended effect. In an ideal future, when patients know more about medicine, when they have the knowledge and confidence to be full partners in their therapy, the responsibility will be shared to a greater extent. (They would know what questions to ask, and have the confidence to ask them, for example). For now – and for the foreseeable future – it is our job to ensure our communications really do work (at the point of consent for therapy or dispensing are prime examples).

The sender's basic tasks

The sender's basic tasks for any kind of effective communication are:

- Research and understand your audience, whether an individual or a crowd.
- Formulate the message clearly.
- Identify the highest priority elements of the message.
- Tailor (target) the message to the abilities and knowledge of the recipient, including using appropriate language and breaking it into digestible pieces.
- Choose the most appropriate channels/methods for the recipient for primary and supportive delivery (face-to-face, words, leaflets, pictures, diagrams, charts, emails, text messages, meetings, internet sources, video, etc.).
- Present and transmit visual or aural messages clearly and attractively (i.e. to get attention, to stand comparison with contemporary standards, to look or sound smart).
- Check that the message has been received.
- Check that the message has been interpreted and understood as intended.
- Seek and deal with questions, uncertainties, objections.
- Negotiate alternatives, if necessary.
- Restate or reformulate the message.
- Check understanding of the revised message.
- Check the change or action the recipient intends.
- Review outcome and agreement.
- Repeat the message.
- Get feedback about the process (was it effective, productive, clear, helpful and so on?) (There is more on several of these topics in Chapter 22.)

A recipient's basic tasks

- Pay careful attention to the message.
- Check or question facts, uncertainties or ambiguities.
- Confirm understanding of the message.
- Offer or negotiate alternatives, if relevant.
- Confirm the change or action intended.
- State terms of agreed outcome.
- Give feedback about the process.

Should it be evident to you that a patient is not responding carefully in the ways suggested, then you have to be even more active in seeking feedback to compensate for their lack of attention – by asking for a repetition of the message, for example, along with the other basic tasks listed above (see also Chapter 11, 'Checking understanding and seeking feedback' section).

Box 4.7 Checking the message

An HCP has just explained a patient's medication.

HCP: 'OK. Do you think all that's clear?'

P: 'Yes, thanks.'

HCP: 'Can you just tell me what you think I've said, so I can be sure I've not left anything out?'

P: 'Umm. Take two of these [drug name] three times a day after eating. One of these [drug name] before going to bed. Stop taking the herbal stuff I've been using – what's it called?'

HCP: 'St John's wort.'

P: 'Yes. OK. Come back and see you if I get bad headaches or feel sick. Finish the course.'

HCP: 'Yes, and drink plenty of water throughout the day. You should feel fine, but if anything worries you, come back straightaway.'

Asking for a repetition to check the HCP's performance ('Did I get it right?'), rather than seeming to check up on the patient's attention or intelligence, is an effective and diplomatic technique.

Every day, lots of HCPs and patients fail to meet up on time or in the right place because the process isn't conducted efficiently: checking the details (exactly where?); checking the time (exactly when?); confirming the day and date, especially if it is some time ahead. Problems of clarity and understanding occur in what appear to be the simplest possible communications; the risks of their happening in more complex communications, like most of those in healthcare, are enormous if the basic tasks are not understood and meticulously executed on every occasion. Many adverse drug reactions and medication errors, for example, arise from weaknesses in this process (see also Chapter 17).

To me the ideal doctor would be a man endowed with profound knowledge of life and of the soul, intuitively divining any suffering or disorder of whatever kind, and restoring peace by his mere presence.

Henri Amiel

Different planets

Communication of all kinds (spoken, written, printed, electronic) uses symbols and conventions to represent and convey meaning – letters of an alphabet (in many languages), words, idioms, linguistic structure, punctuation, numbers, graphics and so on. Serious communication can take place only between those who share the same symbols and conventions. At the most basic level, a shared language is a prerequisite, but:

- Even those sharing the same language will not necessarily share the same vocabulary, idioms or linguistic structures.
- Blind or partially sighted people will not see the symbols.
- Deaf people will not hear them.
- Poorly educated people will not be able to interpret them.
- Native and non-native speakers may be confused by them (very large numbers of people cannot read, for example, or have very limited vocabulary).
- Health literacy is a major issue in all countries (and quite separate from the usual questions of literacy and numeracy).

Furthermore, the specialised world of medicine has an entire vocabulary of its own, which may be completely obscure to most ordinary people if it is not translated into everyday language.[14–17]

Box 4.8 'I can't understand this medical jargon'

A despairing patient writes to netdoctor.co.uk to ask the meaning of what he has been told following a bladder cystoscopy: squamous metaplasia of the trigone; bladder mucosa generally injected; petechial haemorrhages; trabeculation; chronic stromal inflammation.[18]

Can you put these into everyday language that a patient would understand?

Who ever thought up the word 'Mammogram?' Every time I hear it, I think I'm supposed to put my breast in an envelope and send it to someone.

Jan King

The sender's responsibility, mentioned above, to 'tailor the message to the abilities and knowledge of the recipient' thus takes on an entirely new dimension. Communication becomes a highly refined, expert activity, which must be applied individually and uniquely to every encounter with another human being.

The challenge in healthcare relationships is all the greater because, unlike most relationships between friends and peers, HCPs and their patients often belong to different personal, social and psychological worlds: bridging the distances requires great skill, often under considerable pressure of time.

Many of these issues will be explored in detail in this book, with practical guidance about how to tackle the challenges. The next chapter discusses the great range of purposes that human communication serves and the different skills needed for different purposes.

The single biggest problem in communication is the illusion that it has taken place.

George Bernard Shaw

5 Why do we communicate?

There is an enormous range of practical communication purposes and activities in which we all engage in our personal and professional lives, all of which require particular skills and techniques, which can be analysed, learnt and practised. The basic social urge may have a deeper influence on our motivation and behaviour than we realise. Understanding these basic issues is essential to conducting good health-care relationships.

The purposes of communication

We have discussed what communication *is*, and how challenging it is; now we need to review what it is *for*. It may seem obvious, but it is not, because when we communicate, we may be pursuing any one or more of many different conscious or unrecognised purposes, as well as expressing feelings and meeting more basic human needs. Each distinct purpose requires different skills, behaviour and techniques to achieve it, and self-awareness to avoid the pitfalls. In our private lives we do all this more or less spontaneously (and more or less well), without much reflection. In our professional lives we need a greater degree of awareness of how to approach it and the processes and skills involved.

All the purposes of communication apply equally to our personal as well as our professional lives. With patients, you may need to:

- *Investigate* their medical and medication history and health problems.
- *Inform and explain* (educate, teach) about therapy, risk and medicines.
- *Influence, motivate* to adhere to a regimen or to change some aspect of habits or lifestyle.
- *Explore, explain, negotiate* and *make decisions* about therapeutic and other options.

Box 5.1 Why do we communicate?

Here are some of the broad kinds of communication purposes in medicine and in life in general:

- to inform, educate, teach, train, counsel
- to influence, persuade, change
- to research, investigate, explore
- to solve problems, negotiate, make decisions
- to collaborate, build teams, raise morale
- to motivate, inspire
- to manage, supervise, control
- to offer support, concern, compassion
- to build relationships
- to seek friendship and affection
- to seek intimacy and sexual opportunities
- to entertain.

- *Collaborate and manage* a complex regimen of therapy, procedures, consultations, tests and check-ups.
- *Express support and concern.*
- *Build trusting relationships* and much more.

Each of these is a distinct part of the complex process of human relationships; each must be tailored to the particular individual patient; and each can be done effectively or badly.

Subversive purposes

There are also many disreputable purposes that can be pursued through good communication –

activities that we see every day around the world from people who seek to oppress and diminish others, to:

- manipulate or coerce
- maintain secrecy, limit knowledge and freedom
- mislead and confuse
- convert and enslave
- exploit and abuse.

These unethical purposes can be pursued with brilliant and effective communications (and often are). Although we may repudiate the aims, we can, nevertheless, always learn from the methods. Ethical purposes, on the other hand, can be pursued unethically (supporting or helping people in order to gain some leverage over them, for example). (For more on ethics in communication, see Chapter 8; for more on hidden motivation in communication, see Chapter 9.)

Men make use of their illnesses at least as much as they are made use of by them.

Aldous Huxley

The social urge

Communication serves a wide variety of practical, utilitarian purposes, as described earlier – to achieve specific, identifiable aims. But the urge to communicate is so fundamental a characteristic of human beings that we are driven to do it whether or not there's some particular, evident purpose. We are social beings – drawn to spend time with others and in groups – and communication is one of the basic means through which we express and fulfil ourselves.

In our personal and social lives, we seek relationships of all kinds, at varying levels of intensity, because it is our nature to do so. Most people seek a small number of intimate relationships, in which they are loved in the broadest sense. These are the relationships with partners and closest friends that provide some of the richest rewards of existence, and the strength and security to face the challenges of the outside world. To live without such relationships is a painful burden and a disabling obstacle to the chances of finding happiness. That is a burden suffered by many people whose social skills and psychology have prevented them from finding love and friendship. Patients in this category need special attention. (See Chapter 13 for more on social disability.)

Underlying everything we do, in every aspect of our lives, however disturbed or self-defeating our behaviour, is this urge for good relationships and approval. For only the few, including genuine social isolates and some of the most mentally damaged, is this not true.

The purpose of life is not to be happy – but to matter, to be productive, to be useful, to have it make some difference that you have lived at all.

Leo Rosten

What's going on?

This is all important information for any professional to understand, so that they can be aware of and make sense of their own behaviour and the behaviour of others. For example, a lonely patient may unconsciously be seeking rewards and comfort in this basic area of human need at the same time as they are presenting symptoms for attention; the symptoms may even, in one way or another, be created to provide the opportunity for making contact with healthcare and may be relatively unimportant to the patient. Willingness to recover and cease contact may be impeded by fear of the ending of the special attention that healthcare offers. For isolated, shy or lonely people, HCPs provide an important social opportunity, without many of the usual hazards and complications of spontaneous relationships.

I reckon being ill as one of the great pleasures of life, provided one is not too ill and is not obliged to work till one is better.

Samuel Butler, The Way of All Flesh, *1903*

The sexual urge is another driving element of basic human nature, of human biology, of course, and also has a part in our general, social motivation, perhaps more than we would feel comfortable admitting. In our first, spontaneous, instinctive responses to many people of either gender or any age, there is almost certainly an element of sexual appreciation and assessment (positive or negative), whether or not we allow it into consciousness and recognise it. Such reactions can have a powerful positive or negative effect on how we respond to people, how much attention we give them, unless we are aware of how our behaviour is being skewed and, in our professional lives, remedy such distortions. (This is why the question, 'Do I like this patient?' is one of the first we need to answer, as proposed in the basic framework at the beginning of this book.)

Communication has explicit, practical purposes, which serve professional and many other useful ends; but underlying all communication and all relationships, are the urges for approval, attachment and intimacy. Under control by the mature, secure professional, these urges may enrich and energise relationships; but they carry the risk of derailing and exploiting relationships with patients for those professionals whose self-awareness and control are weak, or who are unaware of the unconscious or conscious, purposeful or manipulative games some of their patients may be playing.

Box 5.2 Feeling good in a group

> Similar effects of acceptance, confidence, confirmation and fulfilment as come from a great friendship may also be found in a group where personal relationships are much less intense and/or intimate.
>
> Groups of friends, housewives, teenagers or elderly people meeting for sport, work, travel, chat, music making, whatever, can make members feel good about themselves through the simple fact of belonging and the acceptance and recognition it provides.
>
> Groups can be an important resource in healthcare, too, when a patient can feel more like a normal person, sharing their life with similar others, and getting a different and much broader kind of support for their problems – hypertension, HIV, diabetes, stroke and so on – than any HCP can ever give.

What are we all looking for?

What are the benefits, rewards and pleasures people are looking for in their relationships? How does this affect our understanding of relationships with patients?

The positive energy and life-enhancing effects of socially attractive and popular people can be described as 'healing' – they offer encouragement and a sense of wellbeing and hope to others; at their best, they can repair and uplift the mind and the spirit. Few, if any, things are more important in healthcare, where we know how closely patient morale, confidence and optimism are related to physical health and the capacity to manage illness. HCPs have a direct impact on the whole person, not just the symptoms and the body.

> There are some people who have the quality of richness and joy in them and they communicate it to everything they touch. It is first of all a physical quality; then it is a quality of the spirit.
>
> *Tom Wolfe*

Earlier, we discussed the basic social urge and its power in bringing people together and stimulating communication. Ideally, consciously or unconsciously, we seek relationships that are:

- safe – in which we shall not be hurt, or rejected or ridiculed
- affirming – in which we feel valued and appreciated for who we are and what we can do
- empowering – which give us strength and confidence to live our lives and meet its challenges
- open and trusting – in which we can expose ourselves, declare who we are without fear (this is often critical in the development of intimacy, which, in its usual non-sexual sense, is on the very borders of healthcare relationships)
- reciprocal – in which both parties feel and enjoy the benefits of knowing each other; complementarity
- affectionate – where there is genuine liking, and care and commitment.

What is interesting about the list above is that the best healthcare relationships will offer patients the same spectrum of qualities. The difference from personal relationships is that HCPs are not seeking the same level of personal rewards through their patients as through their colleagues and friends; they are offering the same qualities to patients, but limiting their own needs and demands and the scope of the relationship. Patients in general do not want personal intimacy with their HCPs, but they do want to feel that relationships have those qualities which would, in other circumstances, permit intimacy – the qualities that stimulate trust, confidence, openness and healing. Healthcare relationships do not demand affection, nor even liking for patients, but this must not undermine the offering of an effective helping relationship, particularly establishing trust and confidence in the patient.

Most of us are probably not able to put into words everything about a person that attracts us or repels us, because relationships often have mystery at their heart. Consider, for example, those individuals who have serial relationships in which they are repeatedly hurt or damaged. What we seek is not always good for us.

Conclusion

This chapter has reviewed the purposes and motivation underlying human communication, discussed how complex the issues are, and suggested how clear-headed we must be to understand and manage all the variables in relationships with patients. It has examined some of the basic human needs that direct and shape relationships and communications and what we can learn from them about relationships in healthcare.

The next chapter looks at the special place of communications in healthcare.

6 Communications at the heart of healthcare

Communications affect every aspect of healthcare, for better or for worse, from the highest levels of policy making to the briefest encounter of any member of the team with patients or their families. The morale of staff in a hospital is as much a matter of the quality of communications as of anything else; quality of communications significantly influences patient welfare and outcomes – along with every other aspect of healthcare relationships and practice.

A tough life

Few human activities persistently demand as much of their workers as healthcare. From the grandest new hospital to the remotest jungle outpost, health professionals face constant and extraordinary challenges and demands every day of their lives.

The challenges are:

- medical
- scientific
- technical
- financial
- practical.

They demand enormous resources of:

- emotion
- judgement
- imagination
- creativity
- improvisation
- energy
- patience.

They also need selfless commitment to the welfare of individuals and society, and to endless and exhausting communications.

Where there is good access to healthcare and the wonders of modern drugs and procedures – still in far too small a percentage of the world – infant mortality has fallen, life-expectancy has increased, serious diseases have been controlled or eliminated, and general health and quality of life have been immeasurably improved. From the highest 'hi-tech' procedures in sophisticated clinics and hospitals to the work of barefoot doctors, traditional birth assistants and medical assistants and vendors in rural Africa, many achievements have been truly remarkable.

> Modern medicine is a negation of health. It isn't organized to serve human health, but only itself, as an institution. It makes more people sick than it heals.
>
> *Ivan Illich*

But beyond the biggest issue – universal access to quality medicines and medical care, especially for the poor in rich countries[19] as well as those elsewhere – there is a growing realisation that all is not well in healthcare, even – especially – in the most advanced locations.

- The number of people killed or injured by medicines or medical treatment is shockingly high, and much of the damage is preventable (many adverse drug reactions, medication errors and infections, for example); in some countries (the US and Australia, for example) there have recently been more and more patients seeking to sue their healthcare providers for negligence.

- Where expectations of medicine have accelerated, there are also greater levels of dissatisfaction among patients.[20]
- The effectiveness of the regulation of medicines, management of their safety and the behaviour of pharmaceutical companies have all been brought into question, from time to time.[21]
- Political and ideological conflicts are obstructing progress (in funding, immunisation programmes and access to anti-retrovirals, for example).
- Even the confident assertion above about increased longevity is under threat as certain groups in the US, especially some women, show decreased life expectancy.[22]
- As healthcare professionals are put under more and more pressure to increase outputs and reduce costs, many – especially workers in the system and patients – express the view that medicine is losing direction and purpose.

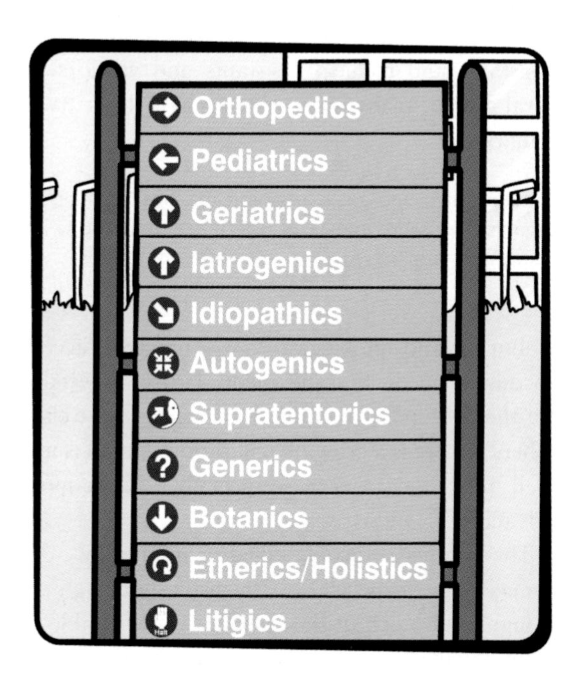

The current worldwide movement to refocus healthcare on patients – and particularly on their safety – is a consequence of how far off-course healthcare and healthcare systems have strayed.[23] Physicians admit that their practice is distorted by pressure of time and fear of litigation; nurses bemoan the lack of time they have to care for patients; pharmacists are forced to become retail entrepreneurs as the financial viability of their core business (and their true value) shrinks – the list is long – and none of it is driven by the needs of patients; indeed, much of it is hostile to the interests and safety of patients.

As a people, we have become obsessed with Health. There is something fundamentally, radically unhealthy about all this. We do not seem to be seeking more exuberance in living as much as staving off failure, putting off dying. We have lost all confidence in the human body.

Lewis Thomas, The Medusa and the Snail, *1979*

But what has this to do with communications skills? The core reasons are all related to communications:

- The priorities and economics of public and individual healthcare should be driven by the wishes and priorities of the people in general, including HCPs, and by patients in particular; those can be discovered and met only by politicians and policy-makers asking, listening and negotiating (core communication skills), by open public debate and by HCPs and patients representing their views strongly at every possible opportunity (advocacy, influencing, persuading and promoting a message).

We must stop talking about the American dream and start listening to the dreams of Americans.

Max Beerbohm

- Many of the most serious problems in healthcare result from profound failures in communication, especially lack of transparent, comprehensive and effective communication about priorities, about therapy, and risk and safety at all levels.

A range of other big issues are related largely or exclusively to communications:

- failure of management:
  - poor organisational management, morale and relationships in many regions or institutions
  - lack of explicit, relevant shared vision and priorities at national and local levels
- failure of collaboration:
  - conflicting priorities among healthcare professionals themselves, and between them and administrators, financial managers and politicians
  - lack of clear and coherent communications among complex, interdisciplinary medical teams and across support and community networks
  - status and professional rivalries
- failure of information, education and transparency
  - lack of transparent, effective regulatory information
  - absence of information or provision of inadequate information resources for patients – including opportunity and education for being informed and active partners in their own healthcare
  - lack of public education about risk and benefit of medicines and therapy, about uncertainty, and about reasonable expectations of medical intervention
  - poor grasp of the complexity of medical questions and of scientific method among journalists
  - the prevalence of superstition and irrationality in medical matters across large populations in many parts of the world
- failure in patient relationships
  - lack of will and time to ensure that patients are fully involved in the process of understanding and agreeing to their treatment, and so,
  - high levels of poor adherence to treatment régimes
  - high levels of patient dissatisfaction with the way in which they are treated by healthcare systems and providers.[24]

A new concern is the increasingly complex electronic communications and recording systems emerging in some countries, along with those that allegedly support diagnosis and treatment decisions, where lack of compatibility and portability, the mechanisation of decision making, and the potential for error are serious new issues.

All sorts of computer errors are now turning up. You'd be surprised to know the number of doctors who claim they are treating pregnant men.

Isaac Asimov

Box 6.1 Distracted by data

Although electronic systems may greatly enhance efficiency when effectively designed and managed, there can be damaging and unexpected side effects. A patient reports:

'Visits to this doctor involve minutes spent while she locates my health records on the computer, and minutes spent as she enters new data, all the while with her gaze and attention fixed on the computer rather than on me. The tap-tap of her fingers indicates that she is too busy to be taking in whatever I have to tell her, and that the electronic task has been elevated over the old-fashioned hands-on approach to clinical care.'[25]

Such perceptions and opinions need to be taken very seriously.

Asserting the need for change

Your skills as a communicator, and those of your colleagues worldwide who are committed to making things better, can profoundly affect how priorities are determined, how best practice is protected, how all these weaknesses are pinpointed, how local and national strategies are developed to resolve them and how healthcare develops in the future. Above all, and for most HCPs, along with your appreciation of the importance of communication itself in all its forms, your own skills will help ensure that patients get the greatest possible benefits from whatever healthcare resources are available, however limited, in mental, emotional and psychological terms.[26]

This book is particularly concerned with the knowledge and skills needed to establish the richest and most effective relationships with patients. It is based on the knowledge that effective

Box 6.2 Pregnancy should not be a death sentence

The article under this headline in the *Guardian*[27] reported that the death rate of mothers in childbirth in sub-Saharan Africa is 1 in 16. In the UK it is fewer than 1 in 8,000. What explains such tragic and unnecessary loss of life? Lack of interest, vision, commitment, political will, resources and communications. Communications at international, national and local levels; communications and teaching for traditional birth attendants in remote rural areas; information for mothers about how to reduce the risks. In Thailand and Bangladesh great progress has been made: why can't it be done elsewhere?

communications improve processes, relationships and outcomes of all sorts (including preventing patient complaints[28]), but also on the belief that healthcare needs vision and inspiration to tackle the obstacles to consistent achievement of best practice – and to deliver ethical and effective services.[29–33]

The greatest mistake in the treatment of diseases is that there are physicians for the body and physicians for the soul, although the two cannot be separated.

Plato

Part C presents a vision of healthcare to drive our practice and our communications, and a discussion of the question of ethics in communication.

Revision, discussion and application (1)

This is the first of eight short sections of questions and issues, which follow each of the main parts in the book. The items fall into two groups:

A. Revision and discussion

This section is for readers who would like some further stimulus to help them process and revise the ideas in the chapters in Part B and to take their thinking further and deeper. The material in this book does not necessarily provide all the answers in detail.

B. Application

Questions relating to the practical use and application of the ideas and principles are listed in this section.

Commentary on many of the questions and issues appears on the publisher's website in Online Resources at www.pharm press.com.

A. Revision and discussion

1. Why is it so important that we should examine our degree of liking for a patient before we launch into a professional relationship with them? What are some of the pitfalls if we fail to make this assessment at the very beginning?
2. Why is simple transmission of a message, without follow-up activities, so unsatisfactory? What are some of the assumptions of those (bureaucrats, teachers, HCPs) who believe that their communication task is complete when then they have simply transmitted a message? Why is abandoning the top-down, expert-driven model of communications such a challenge?
3. What is the difference between *process* and *content* in communication? Why does process have such a powerful influence on the effectiveness of communications? In planning a communication what are some of the process variables that must be considered before a message is sent?
4. What are some of the similarities and differences in terms of effect and communications content between good professional relationships and good personal relationships? Where are the boundaries of good professional relationships and what are some of the purposes and activities they should usually exclude?
5. What are some of the multiple ways in which people try to gain the approval of others or to compensate in relationships for deficiencies in their lives? What are some of the problems caused by anyone whose drive to seek approval is greater than their interest in finding the truth and solving problems? What particular problems are associated with HCPs or patients bring driven by the need for the approval of others?

6. Summarise the main arguments for the proposition: effective communication is at the heart of the best healthcare.

B. Application

1. Identify six communication activities in healthcare and specify how response and feedback mechanisms can be built into them.
2. Identify categories of patients who might benefit from participation in support groups for the meeting of their needs as patients and as whole people. What are the needs of patients which cannot always or ever be met by HCPs alone?
3. Examine all the patient communication activities and materials in your immediate environment and assess how far you think they meet the basic standards of effective communications. How far are the needs of patients really catered for in the activities and materials you have identified?
4. Examine the official and organisational communications which you experience from day to day and assess how far you think they meet the basic standards of effective communications. How far are your needs catered for? How far is process recognised as a vital element? What exactly are the virtues and deficiencies of relationships and communications in your situation?
5. What are the areas of patient ignorance or misunderstanding in healthcare issues which you most often encounter and which have a negative impact on communications and therapy? What measures can be taken in your immediate environment to provide remedy? What needs to be done at a higher level to increase patient knowledge and understanding?
6. What kinds of patient dissatisfaction are you aware of in your situation? What are some of the causes? What kinds of practical measures and improved communications might help to reduce patient dissatisfaction?

Part C

Aims and ideals in healthcare

In order that the best medical skills and most effective communications can fulfil their potential for the benefit of patients, we need to have a clear idea of the purposes of healthcare and the ideals we would strive to achieve. The first chapter in Part C examines what such a model might be, and how, even with limited time and resources, we can hold on to it as an inspiration and a guide. Communications are shown to be an essential element in the pursuit of such a vision. The second chapter examines the ethics of healthcare communications and sets out some of the principles and standards of best practice.

Wherever the art of medicine is loved, there is also a love of humanity.

Hippocrates

7 Vision at the heart of healthcare

To be ethical, effective healthcare communication must have ethical purposes, and be practised in pursuit of a clear vision, which sets out the aims and priorities of practice. A model of healthcare is offered for readers' consideration and debate: it puts healthcare at the top of political and social priorities, and the needs of patients at the top of the practice agenda. Whatever the restraints imposed by policy and limited resources, healthcare professionals have a duty to hold on to their ideal practice priorities and to pursue them with energy and dedication.

Pursuing a vision

Effective communication is a morally neutral activity – it can be used for any purpose, good or bad. The unifying characteristic of all great communicators is that they have a passionate vision of what they want to achieve. Nowhere is that clearer than in business: commercial communications (public relations, advertising and marketing) are among the most sophisticated we have, and they are driven by a radical determination to pursue profit and to dominate the market. The best are successful because they have a clear ideal, and the technical ability and the communications skills to fulfil it. The same is true of great leaders.

The purpose of communication is to achieve something, to get results. The purpose of effective communication is to increase the likelihood of good results. But what are the results we are working for in healthcare? That is where we need to have a vision for healthcare and a clear idea of why we communicate and do the important work we do.

Health is a state of complete physical, mental and social well-being, and not merely the absence of disease or infirmity.

World Health Organization, 1948

Box 7.1 A vision for healthcare

Here are some of the main aspects of a vision for healthcare that underlie this book. You might like to consider and debate these with your colleagues and see what you think is missing, or what is uncertain or controversial.

- The purpose of healthcare is to improve the health, happiness and quality of life of all individuals and societies across the world through the diagnosis, management and prevention of disease.
- The priority given to healthcare in any society and the priorities and methods within healthcare must be driven by the express will of the people in general and by the wishes of patients and patient groups.
- Healthcare priorities must relate directly to the disease patterns and social needs in every community.
- Access to healthcare should be universally available on the basis of need, and not be dependent on wealth, status, age or any other variable.
- Healthcare services should be provided swiftly and effectively to meet the medical needs of individuals and of society.

Box 7.1 *Cont.*

- Society should take responsibility for ensuring that citizens, especially children and young people, are educated in medical matters, especially in all aspects of safety.
- Decisions about therapy must be made in negotiation and partnership with patients who fully understand the risks and benefits of any option and of alternatives, and on their genuine, informed consent.
- The full benefits of healthcare will be realised only when patients are seen as whole people (that is, not disease states to be treated) and are willing and well-informed partners in the entire process.
- As far as possible, healthcare should strive to reduce dependence on itself, and encourage societies to take greater responsibility for management of their own health.
- Compassion, concern and respect are as essential to good healthcare as good medical practice.[34,35]

Achieving every aspect of this ideal is dependent on effective communications and interaction of some kind:

- Healthcare and quality of life priorities for individuals and societies as a whole are issues of profound importance which require investigation, research, social debate and some measure of consensus – a very challenging communications project. (Considerations at the social level, for example, include: access to healthcare and its costs; the range and availability and cost of approved drugs; the range of conditions falling outside priority spending; and patient groups with the highest priority for resource allocation. Considerations at the individual level, for example, include: the possible choice between *length* of life and *quality* of life; and the choice between enduring occasional distress or medicalising every symptom of psychological unease.)
- Prevention of disease: all public health matters (for example, smoking, safe sex, obesity, polio and malaria eradication, therapy for tuberculosis and HIV, and immunisation) require extremely sophisticated communications.
- 'Education in medical matters': teaching is one of the most complex of communications activities, often done less than effectively (see Chapter 26).

- The encounter between expert health professional and lay patient is among the most demanding of any communication activity in any professional life.
- 'Patients as whole persons': here there is not only a requirement for superb communications but also a fundamental respect for persons, a grasp of every individual's unique and special (and complex) reality, genuine respect and concern for them, compassion for their situation, and the ability to express and share those feelings explicitly or implicitly (the opposite of the 'find it and fix it' technical, disease model of practice).

Who wants to live to be a hundred? What's the point of it? A short life and a merry one is far better than a long life sustained by fear, caution and perpetual medical surveillance

Henry Miller

It is not surprising that most of us need help in being better communicators! Some people are naturals but most of us can learn to perform much better and, therefore, not only do our job more effectively but also play our part in the development and enrichment of healthcare's vital contribution to the welfare of the world.

The art of medicine consists of amusing the patient while nature cures the disease

Voltaire

Coping with limits

Nowhere are the pressures and dilemmas sharper than under managed care regimes, and in countries where even socialised medicine is subjected to the rigours of profit and loss accounting. The ideals of this book may seem unrealistic to professionals who are daily required to increase their productivity and reduce their costs. The sensitive and intense engagement with patients recommended here may strike them as unworkable, promoted by someone out of touch with the reality of practice.

Box 7.2 Most NHS staff say patients are not top priority

Fewer than half of the staff in NHS trusts across England think caring for patients is the top priority at their place of work, the government's health watchdog has disclosed.

The Healthcare Commission surveyed more than 150 000 nurses, doctors and ancillary staff to check whether ministers were succeeding in a campaign to create a more patient-centred health service.[36]

Each time a man stands up for an ideal, or acts to improve the lot of others, or strikes out against injustice, he sends forth a tiny ripple of hope . . . and crossing each other from a million different centers of energy and daring those ripples build a current that can sweep down the mightiest walls of oppression and resistance.

Robert F. Kennedy

The challenge for every one of us is to be clear about our vision of ideal medical practice in a healthy society, and then to shape the systems of delivery so that they both preserve the inalienable heart of good practice (the idealistic goal) and remain financially viable (the pragmatic goal). Financial viability is partly determined by the priority given to medicine (the health of the people) in social policy and national budgeting – essentially political considerations. When the pragmatic or financial concerns become dominant, at the expense of the ideals or the promised social priorities, then clearly something serious has probably gone wrong. If reform (or revolution) is needed, then it is the ideals and social consensus that should drive it and the resources that should follow. That this rarely happens is unarguable. Within restricting and pressurised systems, we can only hope that HCPs can maintain their ideals, and are able to convey the depth of their vision to everyone they meet, even if it is only through unsatisfactorily brief or symbolic gestures. (This problem is extensively discussed in Chapter 16.)

For the most part, Western medicine doctors are not healers, preventers, listeners, or educators. But they're damned good at saving a life and the other aspects kick the beam. It's about time we brought some balance back to the scale.

Claire Todae

With a vision of what healthcare is for, you can then apply your technical, professional and communication skills to working towards achieving it. If you are clear that the primary determinant of all your decisions should be the health, safety, needs and wishes of patients in general, and of *this* patient in particular, then you will uphold the most critical priority and be among the best practitioners – and your patients will say so too.

The next chapter examines the framework of values in which the vision can be pursued ethically.

We have to ask ourselves whether medicine is to remain a humanitarian and respected profession or a new but depersonalized science in the service of prolonging life rather than diminishing human suffering.

Elisabeth Kübler-Ross

8 Ethics in healthcare communication

Ethical behaviour and communications in healthcare are based on serving the best interests of the patient, in terms that they would recognise and assent to; the ethics of altruism and partnership. It also depends on taking the truth, as far as it is known, as the starting point for any communication, with extreme caution in deviating from it for any reason. Transparency – openness, disclosure, honesty about the strength of evidence and about uncertainty – is among the highest requirements of ethical communication. Although ethical practice puts patients at the very centre of all considerations, it does not imply that healthcare professionals should not take pleasure and enjoy rewards from their work, nor that they should not make demands of patients or set limits for them.[37]

The stern face of professional ethics

Ethical communication in professional life is a non-negotiable requirement of acceptable behaviour and practice:

- The primary purpose of all professional healthcare communication is to serve the expressed, known and genuine needs of patients, customers, clients, and to bring about the best possible health and quality-of-life outcomes for them and society through negotiation and partnership.

All of the positive communications purposes listed in Chapter 5 (education, counselling, negotiating and so on) can be pursued ethically – that is openly, honestly, transparently, and in the interests of the other person – or unethically:

- Information becomes propaganda when it is skewed or distorted, biased or incomplete, or when its purpose is misrepresented
  - marketing information that patients taking homeopathic medicines get better or say they feel better misleads us if we do not also see the results of responsible placebo trials (most of which suggest there is no difference between control and placebo).
- Persuasion becomes manipulation when it serves the interests of the communicator, rather than mutual interests or the primary interests of the recipient
  - an HCP keen to enrol patients in a clinical trial, may use arguments that go beyond a patient's medical needs and wishes or the potential benefits to them, by pressurising or threatening them in one way or another.
- Training becomes conditioning or brainwashing when the direction or choice of the recipient is diminished or removed
  - a senior doctor or academic may insist on absolute adherence to certain idiosyncratic ways of thinking or methods of practice, which diminish the education, development and confidence of juniors.
- Offering help and support to others becomes damaging and exploitative when it serves the

psychological needs of the giver rather than the needs of the recipient

— an HCP who is lonely, controlling, depressed or incompetent behaves in ways that may intrude on a patient's rights and privacy or compromise their autonomy.

In wartime, truth is so precious that she should always be attended by a bodyguard of lies.

Winston Churchill

Two conclusions can be drawn here:

- It is important to be alert to what your motivation and communications purposes are at any moment, and to use appropriate skills for the task in hand and for the particular individual you're relating with.
- It is important to examine your feelings, motivation and intention in any communication to make sure they are ethical (to review their ethical integrity) – that is, genuinely and primarily serving the interests of the recipient.

All these elements are common, everyday aspects of all communications of all kinds. Although social conversations and business communications will not necessarily follow healthcare (altruistic) ethics, we may expect them (certainly wish them) to follow a general ethic of truthfulness, openness and transparency. If we are not to be victims of the skilful manipulation or the lies or distortions of others, then we have to be as critical in our analysis of communications directed at us as we are of communications we offer to others.

Highest level principles

No discussion of healthcare ethics would be complete without mention of these vital aspects:

- non-maleficence (at least 'do no harm' – *primum non* (or *nil*) *nocere*)[38]
- beneficence (doing the best for the patient in their terms)
- justice and fairness
- equity (distributive justice)
- autonomy (respect for individual rights and independence).[39]

Each of these principles has a profound impact on many healthcare situations, particularly in relation to the provision, denial or withdrawal of treatment. Although communications will reveal an HCP's disposition towards these values, they are not properly the topics of a communications handbook like this. What HCPs have to do is to demonstrate their grasp of these principles and their adherence to them through their behaviour and communications. They must be the taken-for-granted basis for ethical practice.

Table 8.1 demonstrates that the ethical challenges cover both interpersonal (patient relationship) ethics, as well as much wider issues of equity, justice and fairness. (Most of the issues in the table are discussed in this book.)

Transparency

Transparency is an important term in the discussion of ethical communication for anyone in healthcare – regulators, insurance companies, pharmaceutical companies, health authorities, hospital management boards, nurses, pharmacists, doctors, porters and receptionists – everyone. It means communication where:

- The intention is explicit and clear.
- The evidence or arguments are explained, and the extent of their strength and completeness is carefully stated.
- Uncertainty is acknowledged.
- Differing or opposing views are acknowledged.
- There is no hidden agenda.
- There is no censored evidence or undeclared intention.
- The source and purpose are clear.

You don't tell deliberate lies, but sometimes you have to be evasive.

Margaret Thatcher

Here are some simple examples of unethical, non-transparent communication, which come more

Table 8.1 Top ten ethical challenges facing Canadians in healthcare[40]*

Rank	Scenario
1	Disagreement between patients/families and healthcare professionals about treatment decisions
2	Waiting lists
3	Access to needed healthcare resources for the aged, chronically ill and mentally ill
4	Shortage of family physicians or primary care teams in both rural and urban settings
5	Medical error
6	Withholding/withdrawing life sustaining treatment in the context of terminal or serious illness
7	Achieving informed consent
8	Ethical issues related to subject participation in research
9	Substitute decision making (partners, families, powers of attorney and so on)
10	The ethics of surgical innovation and incorporating new technologies for patient care

'We can reasonably assume that these issues are relevant and important in many societies and healthcare settings.'

or less down to simple deceit (lying) in the attempt to avoid responsibility or blame, or achieve some subversive, hidden intention:

- A pharmaceutical company promotes its drug as 'safe' when clinical trials have shown some ambiguous and uncertain evidence of problems in specific patient groups.
- A hospital administrator denies systematic poor hygiene practices in a hospital where there has been a major outbreak of infection.
- A nurse blames the quality of a batch of IV needles for the pain she has caused a patient, rather than her own incompetence.
- A doctor blames the inefficacy of a medicine for lack of alleviation of symptoms, rather than misdiagnosis of the disease.
- A doctor or pharmacist pushes a favoured (or economical or profitable) therapy without the patient's knowledge or against the patient's wishes, without explaining other options.
- A regulatory authority withholds information from the public about dose-related serious adverse drug reactions under pressure from the manufacturer, and later denies that the evidence was available or convincing.
- A catering officer has miscalculated meal requirements and has run out of meat and fish and is serving only vegetables, which are unpopular in the hospital. Trying to foist a vegetarian diet on reluctant patients, she says: 'Our suppliers let us down and I'm afraid there isn't anything else.'

Underlying lack of transparency is almost always the intention to deceive and, as such, it is almost always unethical (and deplorable). Withholding information from patients or their families is an ethically perilous activity too.

A lie which is half a truth is ever the blackest of lies.
Alfred Lord Tennyson

Does the truth hurt?

Many of the ethical problems in healthcare communications relate to disclosure: how much should the patient or the public or the media be told? These are typical dilemmas across the whole range, which are often managed very badly for patients, families or external audiences like journalists, where the facts may be manipulated, distorted, denied or avoided:

- incurable disease, damage, disability (What happened? Who was involved?)
- terminal illness (What is the prognosis? What quality of life?)
- risks of therapy (Were they fully explained and understood?)

- uncertainty (Were doubts and uncertainty made explicit?)
- errors and accidents (What happened? Who was involved? What's being done to prevent recurrence?)
- incompetence (Who was involved? What's being done?)
- safety profiles of drugs or procedures (Are they known and explained to patients?)
- product quality issues (Who authorised supplier/supplies? What's being done?)
- performance of individuals – surgeons, for example. (Are outcomes monitored? Are poor performers dealt with in some way?)
- competing or conflicting interests – in research, for example. (Is there adequate oversight? Are infringements punished?)
- funding sources and limitations (Where does the money come from? What are the strings attached? Who determines budgets?)

The truth has never been of any real value to any human being – it is a symbol for mathematicians and philosophers to pursue. In human relations kindness and lies are worth a thousand truths.

Graham Greene

In relation to all of these, there may be someone who puts forward arguments (perhaps very vehemently) of the following kinds:

- 'It's better for them not to know.'
- 'It's none of their business.'
- 'Disclosure will do more damage than good.'
- 'If they find out, they'll never trust us again.'
- 'We'll lose the support of XXX (collaborators, suppliers, funders, politicians and so on).'
- 'Nobody needs to know.'

Man seeks to escape himself in myth, and does so by any means at his disposal. Drugs, alcohol, or lies. Unable to withdraw into himself, he disguises himself. Lies and inaccuracy give him a few moments of comfort.

Jean Cocteau

Making choices about communicating the truth

How should you make ethical choices about how to behave, what to say? There are two responses, one idealistic, one pragmatic.

The idealistic response is: tell the truth as far as it is known. This should be the absolute starting

point for any discussion of communication and disclosure for any audience.

Every choice or step which leads down the path of threatening or compromising telling the truth needs the most thorough analysis and ethical justification: is it genuinely the case that withholding information from this person or audience at this time would protect this person or audience from knowledge that they would truly not want to have at this time, or from distress or damage that they would blame us for imposing on them at this time? Can we be certain that, in the future, when the full story is known, our decision will be approved of and respected?

Time will inevitably uncover dishonesty and lies; history has no place for them.

Norodom Sihanouk

Failing to tell the truth, more often than not, results from fear of embarrassment or criticism or exposure, but it is a habit too of those who believe they know what is best for others, without concern for any actual knowledge of the wishes and feelings of others. Such people may be authoritarian, patronising or paternalistic. Such reactions are very common, and few of us can escape their intrusion into our considerations at one time or another.

When it comes to controlling human beings, there is no better instrument than lies. Because you see, humans live by beliefs. And beliefs can be manipulated. The power to manipulate beliefs is the only thing that counts.

Michael Ende

Box 8.1 Across cultures

Different cultures do have different values in relation to disclosure in general, and to whom disclosures should be made in particular. This is true in societies where what in the West would be seen as the autonomous rights of the individual, are to an extent subsumed within the rights and expectations of the family or the social group. Respecting the autonomy of an individual (in whichever mode) is, nevertheless, an important aspect of ethical relationships in healthcare (see also Chapter 14, p. 136).

From the other perspective, the basic question is whether the choices being made primarily protect the interests of the patient or audience, or the holders of the information? If the latter, we are well into the wilderness of unethical choices.

Many situations will be more complex – where, for example, ethical disclosure may have secondary damaging effects (honest revelations about drug or vaccine injury (however small) may bring about a crisis of confidence in a programme or a manufacturer and threaten supplies of essential pharmaceuticals, or provoke mass rejection of the therapy with serious public health consequences).[41–43] The elaboration of this and the many other likely dilemmas requires a book in its own right, and here we cannot go further than declaring the basic principle which should drive all such choices: stick to the truth and never deviate from it simply for reasons of expedient self-interest. If there is any deviation, make sure it is for the soundest, ethically valid reasons, which you would defend openly and strenuously in public (as, indeed, you will almost certainly have to do at some time).

A truth that's told with bad intent / Beats all the lies you can invent.

William Blake

The pragmatic response to the problem is this: the truth will out. Sooner or later, the previously undisclosed truth will emerge, and those who hid it will be called to account for their actions. Any damage (imagined or real) that might have been feared from early disclosure is likely to be much worse as the patient or the audience asks, 'Why didn't you tell us?' There are very few reasons that will assuage the anger and indignation underlying that simple question. In spite of all the evidence that deception eventually causes problems, there seems to be a deep-seated management and political psychosis about the issue: if we are clever enough we can cover up anything. Individuals, too, make decisions about disclosure based on suspect grounds: 'It's better she shouldn't know she's dying,' or, 'Let's keep their hopes up and not tell them about the risks.'

Justice will overtake fabricators of lies and false witnesses.

Heraclitus

Healthcare ethics should be driven by the interests of the patient, their health, quality of life, relationships, autonomy, choices and emotional wellbeing. And it is the authentic interests of the patient, along with those of their families, partners or carers, as *they* would recognise them, not as we might think they are or should be. At the extreme, we would be behaving ethically if we helped patients to achieve goals (short of criminality or abuse of others) which we disagreed with or disapproved of, or took courses of action which we believed were not in their best interests, but they had freely chosen, knowing the consequences.

The ethics and problems of altruism

Healthcare ethics are altruistic, that is they require behaviour which is more concerned to serve the interests of others than it is to serve our own. That does not, as is sometimes suggested, mean to serve others at the expense of our own interests (although that may sometimes be the case), nor to deny ourselves satisfaction or reward through serving others. There is sometimes a puritanical thread in the discussion of these issues, which suggests that benefiting from helping others is disreputable, 'selfish' in the derogatory sense. It is only the pursuit of self-interest at the expense of others which is disreputable.

The doctor, surgeon, nurse or pharmacist who makes a brilliant career through research and practice, while providing the best possible service to their patients, is not in breach of any ethical code. It is only those who manipulate or deceive patients to further their own ends or careers who are to be weeded out. The individual HCP who gets great satisfaction from helping patients recover their health and strength is likely to be much more effective and respected than the one who is merely going through the motions, with little sense of pleasure or reward. Altruism does not mean selflessness.

Every major horror of history was committed in the name of an altruistic motive. Has any act of selfishness ever equaled the carnage perpetrated by disciples of altruism?

Ayn Rand

Take care of the staff

With its focus on patient-centred care and communications, this book could be read as meaning that the interests of HCPs and all staff are of little or no consequence, or should come a distant second to those of patients. That is not the intention. In order to deliver the very demanding standards of care that best practice requires, HCPs and all staff need to be content and fulfilled in their work, and their welfare and satisfaction given as much attention by their employers and managers as those of patients are by staff dealing directly with them.

All of the good communications knowledge and skills laid out for the benefit of patients are relevant to internal, organisational relationships which need to be sensitive, thoughtful, insightful, supportive – and ethical. Unsupported and unappreciated staff cannot deliver the best care, whatever their technical or communication skills. Employers and managers must apply their altruism to their staff, who, then, in their turn, will have the strength and resources to deal generously with their patients.

Altruism is about vision and loyalties: whose interests are truly the top priority? For anyone in healthcare, in whatever role or at whatever level, if that top priority is not patients, then the ethical basis of the whole enterprise is suspect. If the welfare of staff is not a very close second priority, then there is no hope of patients getting the quality of ethically sound service that is their right.

Making demands

Atruism does not imply always being undemanding or compliant. It does not imply avoiding argument or even conflict with patients. Insisting that a patient takes some degree of responsibility for their behaviour (using condoms, not smoking while pregnant, taking exercise, returning for tests, telling the truth) may be in that patient's best interests, as long as the motivation is not assertion of the HCP's authority for its own sake, and the best interests of the patient have been conscientiously reviewed and analysed.

Setting limits is another activity which can, superficially, seem hostile to a patient's interest (or can seem so to the patient), but may protect them in the long run. Limiting contact time with very demanding patients is an example: some patients would monopolise an HCP's entire day, and need to be controlled with firmly, but kindly imposed boundaries, based on the equity of protecting time for all patients. Refusing to prescribe drugs for every symptom is a further example of both ethical professional responsibility and altruism.

> The public blames the medical profession for giving too many tranquilizers and antidepressants. But what would you do? Doctors like to see healing as the result of their work. Yet today we often must be content with far less. There are so many things wrong with people's lives that even our best is only a stopgap.
>
> *Richard A. Swenson, MD*

Authority and power in healthcare relationships

The setting of such limits is an example of the exercise of an HCP's power, based on the authority of their role. An HCP's power is based on legally sanctioned rules and regulations (in relation to declaring death or prescribing narcotics, for example); on their professional role, knowledge and expertise; and on the willingness of others to concede to it, rationally or emotionally. Although an individual will not usually exercise power beyond the formal limits of their delegated authority, much of an HCP's informal power in practice and in relationships is subject to discretion and, therefore, can be exercised in ways which are ethical or not. The way in which an HCP's power is used in imposing or agreeing a course of treatment, or refusing treatment, for example, is a matter of ethical concern, and may be acceptable or not, in principle or to the patient. Some patients will be willing to accept an assertive or paternalistic exercise of power, whereas, for others, it will conflict with their habits and needs (and may be one of the elements in creating what an HCP may see as a 'difficult' patient – see Chapter 13).

Patients have power, too, of course – based on their formal rights as citizens and users of healthcare, and on their psychology and motivation. It is in the latter area that most problems occur, when a patient is bringing unacceptable pressure of one kind or another to bear and an HCP is struggling to assert or maintain control. Resolution of such conflicts usually needs to come through negotiation and collaboration, not through the unethical assertion of the HCP's power, unless the case is hopeless and the HCP states unnegotiable terms or ends the relationship.

So the ethics of altruistic, patient-centred care do not imply self-denying concessions by an HCP, nor denial of authority or diffidence in exercising power, but rather ethical negotiation in the relationship, and a commitment to the pleasures and rewards of achieving a deep understanding of patients, and of what will deliver the best results in terms of their health and wellbeing.

Part C discussed a range of important ideas and issues underlying good practice and effective communications. Part D analyses and discusses critical aspects of human psychology and behaviour which influence all relationships and communications, and in which HCPs need to be well-versed.

Revision, discussion and application (2)

A. Revision and discussion

1. Examine the box 'A vision for healthcare' in Chapter 7, and subject each element to hostile analysis, using arguments you think of yourself and those that might be deployed by those with different, less radical or more traditional ideas. Keep to the level of principle (not pragmatic considerations such as finance, political will and so on) and determine how strong and sustainable the proposed vision is against the opposition of those whose priorities are different.
2. Examine the vision item by item, and assess the extent to which you feel each element is expressed and fulfilled in your situation, or region or country. What are the achievements and deficiencies? What is missing in your real world? What are the priorities for reform? Is there anything practical that can be done locally to move forward?
3. What do you see as the major communications challenges to achieve the vision with various audiences? What messages need to be sent to whom and by what methods to try and bring about change? (Concentrate on those nearest to you – managers and administrators, colleagues, patients, the local community, but consider others as well if you wish to extend your horizons.)
4. What are some of the ethical failures in relationships and communications you see in healthcare and in the world around you? In scanning the daily news, what examples of people being deceptive with transparency and the truth can you find? Identify some of the techniques and motivation behind ethically dubious behaviour and communications.
5. What is your view about telling the absolute truth as the starting point for ethical communications in healthcare? What arguments and reasons would you put forward, personally, and in relation to your culture, to justify telling less than the truth in any healthcare situation, particularly with patients?
6. What are the situations (if any) in which an HCP has the right to assert authority against the wishes of the patient? Include situations where there is legitimate (perhaps legal) authority as well as those based on personal and professional authority. What are the ethical and communications challenges in such situations?

B. Application

1. In what situations would you regard patients as being overly dependent or unhealthily dependent on healthcare? How would you react to such patients and what would be the nature and content of your communications?
2. What kind of communication would you have with a patient who had no interest in being a partner in therapy but simply wanted you to identify a problem and solve it?

3. What would you say to a patient (a) whose diagnosis you had got wrong; (b) to whom the wrong drug had been dispensed by you; (c) whose operation had been repeatedly postponed; (d) who had been reassured that all was well before a life-threatening disease was later diagnosed; (e) whose symptoms were so vague as to be untreatable? What are the ways in which these patients could be dealt with unethically and unprofessionally?
4. Knowing that a risk-averse patient's life can be preserved only by high-risk therapy, how do you present the arguments for treatment ethically? What choices can you give the patient that respect their autonomy?
5. How should an understanding of effective, ethical communication affect relationships within a healthcare organisation or team? What principles that have been described in the book so far apply equally to professional and to patient relationships?
6. From your own experience, identify some ethical dilemmas that have been presented to you in your practice. Examine how you dealt with them (or saw them being dealt with), what was good about them, what was unsatisfactory, what could have been done better. What lessons did you learn from them?

Commentary on many of the questions and issues appears on the publisher's website, in Online Resources at www.pharmpress.com.

Part D

Behind the scenes

The next two chapters provide an introduction to some crucial aspects of human psychology which have profound effects on our relationships and communications with others, and on their relationships with us. It is about those things that drive our emotions and behaviour, and shape our experience of the world, and about the way those emotions and behaviour are expressed in healthcare and all relationships.

They review:

- our inner life: what are our primary personal characteristics and hidden urges and predispositions?
- perception: how do we see and make sense of the external world?
- non-verbal communication: how to read, understand and use this most powerful aspect of communication

Communication leads to community, that is, to understanding, intimacy and mutual valuing.

Rollo May

9 Secret life: what drives us in communications?

HCPs and all people are driven by a host of different influences, including emotions and experiences from the past, the characteristics of their personalities, their social and educational background, what they perceive, their prejudices and their purposes. Much of this influence takes place below the surface of relationships and communications, often unconsciously, but professionals need to understand and interpret at least some of what is happening within themselves and their patients in order to ensure the integrity and effectiveness of their relationships and service to patients.

The foundations

Every experience of our lives contributes in some way to the building of our personalities, and certain individual experiences or an accumulation of related experiences play a large part in determining who we are, what we do with our lives, how we perceive others and, therefore, how we communicate. What we show in our own behaviour, and what our patients show us, is never a straightforward response simply to the reality of the moment, uninfluenced by our personal history. It is much more complicated than that.

We need to understand what is going on under the surface in ourselves and in patients in order to avoid mistakes and misjudgements (in our first impressions of others, for example), and to ensure that our communications are not diverted or hijacked by unrecognised influences.

Interaction

Our responses to others are determined mainly by two categories of perception and feelings which come together in the complex inter-reaction of a relationship:

- the characteristics of the other person (age, gender, race, for example)
- our personality, motivations and disposition towards the world in general and as they are stimulated by the other person.

Box 9.1 Characteristics of others

Here are a few of the aspects of others that shape how we react to them, often unconsciously, and positively, negatively and everything in between:

Our positive or negative reaction or prejudice in relation to:

- gender
- age
- religion
- sexual orientation
- race
- lifestyle
- status

Our responses to types (perhaps stereotypes) of people, which may be irrationally positive or negative:

- parental figures
- child-like or dependent figures
- authority figures
- people of same or opposite sex
- wealthy people
- secondhand car salespeople
- doctors or teachers
- good-looking or plain people
- scruffy people, smart people.

Simultaneously, the other person is reacting to us on the same basis.

All of us react differently to different kinds of people, even differently at different times. Some of our reactions may be obvious – pleasure or unease, for example – although the causes may not be so clear, but other reactions may be hidden and still have a profound effect on the relationship. From the moment we meet a patient, we need to be examining our reactions and understanding how they are influencing the way we feel: are we leaping to unfair conclusions before we have really seen who this person is? Are we treating this person as if they were someone else whose image we have in our minds (a child, mother, previous patient, for example)?

Box 9.2 Stereotypes

The process of stereotyping attributes a set of characteristics to all members of a group, without regard to individual differences. It is based on prejudice (see Box 9.4) and prevents accurate perception of the character of individuals. 'All doctors are arrogant'; 'You can't trust Muslims'; 'Teenagers are irresponsible'; 'Gay men are promiscuous' ; 'A woman's place is in the home' – all sweeping and inaccurate judgements. If we see the world through such stereotypes, we will never see individuals clearly and, therefore, never be able to help them effectively.

Instead of being presented with stereotypes by age, sex, color, class, or religion, children must have the opportunity to learn that within each range, some people are loathsome and some are delightful.

Margaret Mead

The interplay of personal and social factors

The basic facts and characteristics of our lives and those of our patients have an immediate and profound effect on relationships. Here is a brief review of some of the main issues:

Age

- How patients relate to HCPs may be strongly influenced by their own age and their feelings about it, and their feelings about the HCP's age and people of that age in general (older patients may lack confidence in young HCPs; younger patients may feel older HCPs cannot understand them and so on). HCPs need to be aware of how they instinctively relate to patients of different ages and adjust to the reality of the person in front of them

Age is an issue of mind over matter. If you don't mind, it doesn't matter.

Mark Twain

Gender, sexuality and sexual orientation

- Being male or female is so fundamental an aspect of being, that many people may not recognise how profound an impact it has on every aspect of experience and relationships: men and women, heterosexuals and homosexuals see and experience the world from radically different perspectives; there are entirely different sets of formal and informal rules for men and women and, in some societies, strictly defined differences and limited opportunities; men and women form quite different kinds of relationships with their own and the opposite sex.
- Gender is not only a major determinant of disease patterns, but also how disease is perceived, presented and tolerated; it may cause sensitivity when dealing with HCPs of the opposite gender; pressures and conflicts associated with gender or sexual orientation may play a considerable part in patients' psychological wellbeing; disease and ageing may adversely affect patients' self-image and performance as effective or attractive men or women. All these elements may have a powerful impact on first impressions for patient and HCP alike and on the development and authenticity of subsequent relationships. (There is more on this topic in Chapter 14.)

What does the truth matter? Haven't we mothers all given our sons a taste for lies, lies which from the cradle upwards lull them, reassure them, send them to sleep: lies as soft and warm as a breast!

Georges Bernanos

Education

- One of the primary determinants of access to life's opportunities, education is far from universally available and of variable quality where it is; extraordinary numbers of people even in advanced societies are illiterate or just functionally literate, including many of high intelligence or talent who have been failed by the system; health literacy is a major problem in all societies (Box 9.3).
- Patients will generally have very little understanding of disease and therapy, and will vary greatly in their capacity to process and make sense of medical information, to weigh evidence and to evaluate opinion; if they are able to read at all, the range of ability will cover the whole spectrum from elementary to wholly competent; those who cannot read may go to elaborate lengths to disguise what they may feel to be the shameful fact.
- Level of educational ability, and self-image in relation to it, will affect patients' relationships with HCPs in many ways, including, at one extreme, defensive, evasive behaviour to avoid the revelation of ignorance or incompetence, through to the possibly know-it-all arrogance of the literate and self-confident at the other extreme. Educational achievement is not necessarily an indicator of knowledge or intelligence in relation to health and medicine.

Every act of conscious learning requires the willingness to suffer an injury to one's self-esteem. That is why young children, before they are aware of their own self-importance, learn so easily; and why older persons, especially if vain or important, cannot learn at all.

Thomas Szasz

Today's public figures can no longer write their own speeches or books, and there is some evidence that they can't read them either.

Gore Vidal

Wealth

- An individual's position in the hierarchy of wealth will have a major impact on their self-image, their opportunities in life, their state of mind and potential for happiness and fulfilment. In many places it will also absolutely determine their access to healthcare and their ability and willingness to purchase medicines and services.
- Financial status can have a deep effect on self-image and perception of self-worth, demoralising those who are poor, and leading to over-confidence in those who are comfortable or rich. The poor may greatly undervalue themselves and their rights (to attentive healthcare, for example), while the rich may demand more than their fair share.
- The disparity in wealth and status between HCPs and many of their patients may colour healthcare relationships and confidence in HCPs' understanding and judgement.

Box 9.3 Stark facts about literacy, numeracy and health literacy

The 2003 US National Assessment of Adult Literacy estimated that 30 million adult US citizens function at 'below basic' level of literacy skill, and 11 million adults are at the 'non-literate in English' level (that is, in the primary language of the country). More than half of the population are at 'basic' or 'below basic' levels in numeracy skills.[44] We can infer that the situation will be much the same, worse or much worse, in other locations.

Health literacy is defined as, 'the capacity to obtain, process and understand basic health information and services needed to make appropriate health decisions'.[45] The demands of health literacy (and numeracy) are much greater than those of basic literacy (specialised vocabulary, concepts, evidence and so on), so we can be sure that large numbers of people (perhaps well over half of even an educated population, and certainly much higher numbers elsewhere) will have difficulty in dealing with simple health information.[46]

I'm not feeling very well – I need a doctor immediately. Ring the nearest golf course.

Groucho Marx

Parenthood and coupling

- The wishes and priorities of patients who are parents will be significantly different from those who are not, and their feelings about parenthood – the pressures, the successes, failures, the risks – will influence how seriously they take their own needs and what concessions and trade-offs they are willing to make for themselves or their children.

- HCPs who are not parents, or who are single, may sometimes be under pressure to admit their lack of experience or credibility in dealing with children and family matters. In response to comments such as, 'You can't possibly understand what it's like,' HCPs need to develop strategies for demonstrating that not having a partner or not being a parent does not mean an inability to understand relationships and parenthood. Attentive, empathetic relationships with patient parents (and any parents) will nurture knowledge and confidence. Being a parent or partner does not, in any case, always mean understanding parenthood or partnership or being an authority on them in general.

Half a psychiatrist's patients see him because they are married – the other half because they're not.

Arnold H. Glasgow

Social status and occupation

- Few people are unaware of status when they meet someone else, and relationships are always shaped to some extent by perception of the differences. HCPs, being, on the whole, well-educated and of relatively high status, may prompt deference or hostility (or many other things) from those of perceived lower status, depending on how the individual relates to the world. Patients who perceive themselves to be of higher status (for whatever reason) may patronise HCPs, or bully them or expect special treatment or concessions. On the other hand, it is easy for HCPs unknowingly to favour or patronise those of higher or lower status than themselves.
- The achievement of collaborative healthcare partnerships with some patients may be very difficult, especially with those who wish to concede control to those they see as being experts of high status.

People who think they know everything are a great annoyance to those of us who do.

Isaac Asimov

Race

- Few people are uninfluenced by preconceptions or prejudices about ethnic origins and identity in relation to their own self-image and their reactions to others. In our professional relationships, we need to recognise positive or negative feelings or doubts where they exist, and struggle to ensure that they do not contaminate or distort our communications and behaviour.
- Dealing with the prejudice or negativity of others may require quiet tolerance or explicit acknowledgement of it to reduce its impact (see also Chapter 14).

First impressions

In the basic framework in Table 3.1 (p. 9), the question, 'Do I like this patient?' was proposed as an essential enquiry at the very beginning of an encounter. If you do not actively consider this question and its nuances and consequences, there is a risk of the encounter being diverted down an unrealistically positive or negative path, guided by prejudice and misapprehension about the person: at its crudest, people you instinctively like will get more attention and concern than those you don't; stereotypes you feel comfortable with will get better service than those who make you uneasy. First impressions can distort the entire process of a relationship if they are not recognised and put aside while the true picture of the person is allowed to emerge.

Once a reaction – especially a first impression – has been allowed to settle, then it will affect how the relationship proceeds, and may not change in the face of correcting evidence – because perception has been limited by the initial judgement: if I initially allow myself to feel that this patient is unreliable or disreputable, I am likely to ignore evidence that suggests anything else and even structure the encounter to exclude anything else; I am likely to interpret what I see in the light of what I have already decided.

This also applies to diagnosis: too early a conclusion about a patient's primary disease (based, perhaps, on a too-hasty review, or on inadequate questioning) may blind an HCP to subsequent, conflicting evidence which suggests something quite different. The new evidence may be obvious enough (to a third-party, for example) but not to the perception of the HCP, narrowed by a premature conclusion.

Box 9.4 Prejudice

. . . is pre-judgement – having a view or a set of feelings about something which is not truly based on evidence, especially of the immediate person or situation. Prejudice is often irrational, based on fear of difference, or undifferentiated approval, and is usually generalised to a whole category of people. Much prejudice is socially learnt, culturally specific and probably has its roots in a tribal worldview. Although some aspects of some views on some categories of people may have some basis in reason ('The English tend to be more reserved than the Americans' for example; or, 'Asian cultures tend to be more deferential than those in the West'), generally, prejudice is irrational, uncritical – and often passionate. Undifferentiating dislike of black or white people, dismissal of authority figures, mocking of women or gays – and so on – are always crude, primitive reactions based on some dark psychological purpose; worse, they always result in injustice to the individuals who suffer the effects of others' prejudice, because prejudice does not permit accurate perception of the unique instance of a particular individual, whether it is negative (the most common) or positive.

Western women have been controlled by ideals and stereotypes as much as by material constraints.

Naomi Wolf

Perception

Every diagnosis or decision an HCP makes, every relationship they form, is based on what they perceive, but perception is a highly subjective process, driven by many of the elements already discussed, and may mislead us if we do not understand it and its enormous potential unreliability and variability.

The range of what we think and do is limited by what we fail to notice. And because we fail to notice that we fail to notice, there is little we can do to change; until we notice how failing to notice shapes our thoughts and deeds.

R.D. Laing

The physical and social worlds bombard us with information, impressions and stimuli every second of our lives. Staying sane requires selecting the things we pay attention to (hence, ignoring lots of others), and focusing on what provides for our survival and comfort, and getting through our daily duties and routines. Our customary field of perception is very narrow in the midst of the vast and overwhelming nature of the world around us. (The collapse of this essential filtering mechanism is one of the characteristics of some mental disorders, leading to psychological turmoil and loss of control.)

Why are empirical questions about how the mind works so weighted down with political and moral and emotional baggage?

Steven Pinker

You would not be human if you did not have all kinds of immediate, spontaneous reactions to the

Box 9.5 A range of possible patients

Consider your natural, spontaneous reactions to this list of patients who might walk into your room, be admitted to your ward or come into your pharmacy:

- a teenage girl with wild hair, short skirt and skimpy top, heavy make-up, pierced nose and ears, leather boots
- a good-looking, 30-year-old man, well-toned body, figure hugging T-shirt and jeans, short hair, clean-shaven
- a very old woman, wrapped tightly in heavy, smelly clothes, carrying three scruffy plastic bags, sniffing loudly
- a smart, elegant, dark-skinned middle-aged woman, walking in confidently
- a woman in a burka (veil and body-length covering)
- a middle-aged man in dirty blue overalls, with grease and dirt on his hands and face, hair down to his shoulders
- a distraught, poorly dressed woman in her 30s, weeping and clutching a very small baby.

Ask yourself these questions:

- Is my immediate feeling negative or positive or something else?
- Is my immediate feeling attraction or repulsion or something else?
- Is my immediate feeling surprise, shock, pleasant anticipation or something else?
- Am I in any way reacting to this person as a stereotype?
- What is my immediate assessment of the seriousness of this patient's visit and their likely problems?

Box 9.6 The world is suddenly full of ...

A very common experience is a powerful indicator of the selectivity of perception. Someone draws your attention to something – a model of car, a new coffee shop, the name of a band, a flower, a new brand of sneakers – and, suddenly, the world is full of examples of the object which you'd hardly noticed before. The examples were always there, but they hadn't come to your attention, hadn't been brought within your field of perception. Once you've noticed them, you are amazed at the frequency of their appearance, and wonder how you could have missed them before. The explanation is simple: we don't, and can't notice everything; much of the reality of the world around us is always excluded from our perception – including 'obvious' information about the people we meet, unless we are very actively observant, critical and alert. It's significant, of course, that we tend to be at our most observant and receptive when our minds are relaxed, either naturally or through substances such as alcohol or some drugs. Tension and intensity narrow our field of perception: highly desirable though this may be during a surgical operation or the planning of therapy, it's very limiting in perceiving others accurately, or, for example, interpreting the facts about a patient's life and symptoms.

range of people listed in Box 9.5, and to the crude, superficial, *selected* characteristics which are presented in the list – characteristics that disregard most of the individual's actual reality. Depending on your tastes and sexual orientation you will respond differently to males and females; depending on your personal preferences, you'll react differently to different physical types; depending on other prejudices and preferences you'll respond differently to adolescents, elderly people or different religions – and so on, through the vast list of variables within you and within the person to whom you are reacting. Remember that, at the same time, the other person will be going through the same process of assessment of you.

It is not that we must banish partial or prejudiced responses, pretending they don't exist, but that we must be aware of them and their power, and how limiting and distorting they can be, and do everything we can to put them aside while we try to find out who this person really is. When a patient walks in, after registering our instantaneous degree of liking, our priority must be to scan the field of perception as widely as possible and ask ourselves, 'Who is this person?'

It is not surprising that smart, articulate (and perhaps wealthy) patients tend to get better treatment than poor, inarticulate patients, because many HCPs have a class prejudice: they are relaxed, trusting and confident with their own class (educated, articulate people) but uneasy with those of significantly different backgrounds, who are seen, if not as inferior, then often as strangers. Very few of us are free of similar class or caste prejudice.

Personality and motivation

We react to others on the basis of what we think we see and who we think they are, mediated through our perceptions and prejudices, which, themselves, are influenced by basic aspects of our personality. How we relate and what we are trying to achieve are driven by our personal and social motivation. Self-awareness of all these elements is essential if we are to have the best chance of escaping the limiting framework of our spontaneous, instinctive responses, and open ourselves, as far as possible, to the genuine reality of another person. This is a requirement of ethical professional relationships.

Box 9.7 Personality

Aspects of personality that influence how we see others and relate to them:

- optimism/pessimism
- religious beliefs
- degree of personal contentment
- levels of stress
- health of self and family
- success (or otherwise) in personal and sexual relationships
- job satisfaction
- financial worries
- moral stance on human behaviour and specific issues
- level of trust in others.

These characteristics may arise from formative life experiences, discussed below.

Some aspects of personality are neither good nor bad in themselves, but their expression is to be judged by their appropriateness in any given situation: mothering or parenting, consciously and thoughtfully expressed for the support of someone of any age with developmental needs for affection, care, support, approval and encouragement, are entirely admirable approaches. They become unacceptable, however, when they are an automatic response to anyone in a temporarily dependent position, expressed to meet the needs of the giver without reference to the needs of the recipient, or when applied in ways that inhibit the freedom of the recipient to become strong and independent. If you have mothering or parenting impulses, then be aware of them, value and enjoy them, but make sure they are used for the benefit of others, not primarily your own. If your natural impulses are sometimes less attractive (impatience with those who are slower or less intelligent than you, for example), be aware of them too, and manage and control them, with the ultimate hope of lessening their influence, perhaps even eradicating them.

If your emotional abilities aren't in hand, if you don't have self-awareness, if you are not able to manage your distressing emotions, if you can't have empathy and have effective relationships, then no matter how smart you are, you are not going to get very far.

Daniel Goleman

Formative experiences

We and our patients are formed by the experiences of our lives, positive and negative, and it is important and illuminating to be aware of the kinds of formative experiences enmeshed in our own lives and in those of our patients in order to understand current behaviour and emotion. Here are some of the kinds of experiences that shape us (and our patients, of course):

- the degree of care, attention, love and security in childhood
- the extent to which there was acceptance and love (unconditional love)
- the extent to which abilities, talents, imagination and creativity were recognised and encouraged

Box 9.8 Motivation

The range of known or unrecognised purposes that may drive our behaviour:

- to exert power
- to control
- to help
- to ingratiate, seek approval
- to demonstrate status or superiority
- to get others to do the work
- to manipulate
- to provoke gratitude
- to seek sexual stimulation or pleasure
- to make others dependent
- to mother or parent
- to encourage independence
- to love
- to heal
- to punish
- to amuse
- to be popular.

- the way in which sexuality was managed
- the degree of adolescent and adult sexual fulfilment or frustration
- experience of the anger of others and the management of anger
- the extent to which success, failure and boredom became settled patterns
- the commitment and effectiveness of teachers and authority figures at all levels
- experience of health, illness, injury and death
- success or failure in social relationships
- experience of relaxation and pleasure
- the extent of knowledge of and interest in the world at large
- experience of abuse, violence and betrayal.

You can see clearly how these elements might strongly influence personality and the qualities and nature of relationships. A patient who, for example, has experienced multiple failures in their life may find it very hard to approach relationships or therapy with any degree of commitment or optimism; a patient who has had previous bad experiences of healthcare may find it very hard to trust HCPs and benefit from their help and so on. Understanding such biography will greatly enhance an HCP's ability to help patients. Understanding such elements in their own biography will help HCPs develop much greater clarity about their own relationships and motivation.

The doctor's name was Sylvia. I told her she'd have a problem with me because Sylvia was my mother's name.
Paul Lynde

The underlying script

Human behaviour is complex and multi-layered; reality itself is complex and ambiguous. When someone says something, there is an apparent meaning in the words, but it is rarely as simple as it appears and there are often one or more substrata of meaning and intention, perhaps deception. A patient, for example, may be conscientious in trying to tell their HCP everything relating to their disease or problem (having correctly interpreted the HCP's wishes in that respect), but have as the principal motivation the wish to gain the approval of the (perhaps admired) HCP, rather than to facilitate the solution of their medical problems. This ingratiating motivation puts the relationship on an entirely different footing from a patient who might use exactly the same words (although presented differently non-verbally), but be motivated by a conscientious wish to be thorough and to get to the bottom of the problems. Management of two such different patients would be dramatically different, as long as the HCP had heard and understood the underlying scripts.

Box 9.9 Managing a distracting sub-script

HCP: 'I'm sorry I think we've got into a tangle here. I was not suggesting that you don't care for your children.'

Patient: 'Don't blame me for the fact that they're always sick.'

HCP: 'Really, that's not what I meant. I'm sorry I wasn't clear. I simply wanted you to bring them to see me sooner so you wouldn't worry so much and I could treat them.'

P: 'Jack always blames me when anything goes wrong.'

HCP: 'I am not blaming you. I can see you've got a lot on your plate and you're doing very well. Now, please tell me what you think the problem is.'

Here, the patient brings with her a deep expectation that everyone will blame her for everything, perhaps even believing that she is to blame, and reacts badly to the HCP, whose intentions she misinterprets. An element of the problem is that the HCP did not perceive how vulnerable the patient was and was less careful than he would otherwise have been. This short exchange reveals an immense amount about the painful inner life of the patient.

The interplay, often conflict, between what is happening on the surface and what is really driving the communication and relationship is so common that we hardly notice it.

In every human encounter or group, as we saw in Chapter 4, there is *content* and *process*: what appears to be happening on the surface (mostly the words and their meanings) and what is driving the way in which the words and meanings are being used, presented and interpreted. Sometimes these are in perfect harmony (such as old friends together, or mature, tried-and-tested teams), but

Box 9.10 What's going on?

Analyse the underlying process and meaning of this everyday encounter:

Consultant: 'Where are the notes for Mrs Johnson?'

Junior doctor: 'They're not written up yet.'

C: 'What? Why not?'

JD: 'We've had two emergency admissions and I haven't had time.'

C: 'I don't care of there's been an earthquake, I need those notes now.'

JD: 'You'll have them in an hour.'

C: 'Not good enough. I don't have time to sit around waiting for you to get your act together. Typical. Why am I surrounded by incompetence?'

often there's a huge divergence. Such divergence requires recognition and interpretation if participants are not to be locked in an unproductive cycle. If you try to engage with the words, but miss the underlying script of emotion and motives, you'll never get anywhere. The expert communicator can grasp these issues and bring them into the open.

Box 9.11 Possible indicators of professional relationships skewed by unrecognised emotions and needs

In healthcare professionals:
- spending excessive time with a patient or making clinically unnecessary or unusually frequent appointments
- failure to recognise or tackle a patient's distracting psychological needs which are complicating diagnosis and treatment
- creating dependence or inappropriately asserting authority
- seeking inappropriate information about a patient's private or sexual life or showing a degree of tenderness or concern that is ambiguous or inappropriate
- the negatives of many of the above:
  - — unreasonably limiting time or contact
  - — not seeking sufficient personal or intimate details to illuminate the clinical picture
  - — not making demands
  - — failure to show appropriate concern
  - — distance, detachment, coolness.

In patients:
- ill-defined or generalised symptoms that are not presented convincingly
- talking about general issues or failure to get to the point
- repeat visits for minor problems or issues
- symptoms that have clear psychological or social causes
- excessive deference or concession
- flirting
- evidence of loneliness, depression, failure
- assertive distancing or non-cooperation.

The influence of social and organisational values

When we consider how our perception and reactions are determined, we must take into account influences beyond our own personalities and those of patients. The extent to which we may be influenced by class or caste or racial issues is referred to in the previous discussion, and such social, cultural and political issues deeply affect how we see others and relate to them. We need to be alert to those aspects of our reactions to others and of their reactions to us.

A particular and powerful example of such influence comes from the internal culture and priorities of the systems or organisations we work in. Institutional racism and sexism are common examples. In places where such values are prevalent, there is an implicit assumption about the superiority of one ethnic type or of men, which influences perception of every kind of issue and determines behaviour and priorities in ways which are hostile towards the interests and rights of other ethnic groups or of women.

I do not think white America is committed to granting equality to the American Negro. This is a passionately racist country; it will continue to be so in the foreseeable future.

Susan Sontag

In healthcare, particularly corrupting sets of values would relate to elevating financial issues above all others or to blaming only individuals for errors or near-misses. In the first instance, the impact of decisions on patient needs is demoted to secondary consideration; in the second, the weaknesses in systems are never examined as the possible causes of problems (see also Chapter 17).

If we find ourselves perceiving patients through the distorting lens of some set of limiting, prejudicial or damaging values, personal or organisational, then we have to remove it and try, as far as possible, to achieve clear vision of both the person and our purpose in relating to them.

Conclusion

All human relationships are complex in one way or another. They are shaped by a host of internal and external influences. We need to be critically aware of those influences, controlling and moderating them when they are reducing our ability to see patients clearly and to provide them with the best possible service. We need to understand patients in the light of the multiple influences behind their behaviour and communications, so that we can provide them with communications, relationships and therapy which go beyond surfaces and engage the whole person. We need to be aware of the complexity of our own experience and motivation, protect patients from inappropriate or damaging exposure to our weaknesses, and provide them with the benefit of our strengths.

10 Beyond words: the power of non-verbal communication

The quality of all relationships is formed and maintained much more through non-verbal communication than through words, which play a relatively minor part. Becoming skilled in reading and interpreting non-verbal behaviour is essential to enhancing effectiveness in all relationships and in helping patients. Learning about our own non-verbal behaviour, and using that knowledge to influence how we relate to others will help us to see below the surface and to be more useful and successful in everything we do. Physical, non-verbal elements of the environment also contribute significantly to the messages that patients receive and to their reactions to healthcare. Blindness to non-verbal behaviour is almost complete blindness to the meaning and complexity of all communication, of who other people really are and what they are communicating or trying to conceal.[47–49]

Multiple factors beyond words

Beyond the mere words in any message, a host of other factors shape the meaning and signal the intentions of any communication:

- tone of voice (patient, kindly, impatient, assertive, persuasive, etc.)
- rhythm, speed, inflection and volume of voice (whispering and shouting at the extremes, for example)
- choice of language (simple, complex; clarifying, illuminating or mystifying, for example)
- facial expression (smile, frown, open-mouthed astonishment, anger – thousands of possibilities; vascular change, blushing, etc.)[50]
- gestures and movements (hands, arms, shoulders; tapping feet, drumming fingers, etc.)
- body posture, movement and position (relaxed, tense, protective, slumped, active; use of own and others' personal space – too close, too far, respectful, invasive, etc.)
- eye contact, movement and direction of gaze (frank and open, evasive, attentive, focused, distracted, unblinking, rapid movement, etc.)
- clothes and accessories (impressive, pretentious, normal, exhibitionist, scruffy, neat, fashionable, outdated, etc.)
- smell (pleasant, bad, subtle, sweet, overpowering, sweaty, neutral, etc.)
- overall impact of presence and being (gestalt) – (reassuring, relaxing, intimidating, welcoming, supportive, challenging, hostile, compassionate, etc.)
- behaviour (action, results, outcomes; settling a visitor comfortably, conducting a physical examination; showing a person out; moving a wheelchair or gurney, etc.)
- the combination of some or many of these in clusters. (The agitated jiggling of a foot under the table is a single piece of behaviour, perhaps resulting from the expression of feelings being eliminated from other parts of the body and so concentrated in one place; usually, however, non-verbal behaviour comes in clusters or bunches, affecting different parts of the body simultaneously).

The body never lies.

Martha Graham

All these are non-verbal elements of communication and relationships, and are part of the rich and complex, total package of signals we transmit and receive whenever we meet another person. Non-verbal behaviour may facilitate or obstruct communication. We are, inevitably, communicating signals, and processing incoming data, whether we intend to or not, and whether they are helpful or not. These are the main elements that determine instantaneous first impressions, without a word being spoken, and determine almost the entire course and outcome of an encounter with another person. These are the evident clues to the underlying script described in the previous chapter.

Box 10.1

The 53 muscles of the face offer an almost infinite range of expression, considering the number of possible combinations and the range of action in each one – from vestigial to intense.

The right word may be effective, but no word was ever as effective as a rightly timed pause.

Mark Twain

Research has shown time and time again that, in human relationships, the words alone (what you'd otherwise see on the printed page) account for less than half, down to as little as a tenth of the effect and perception of communications. Tone of voice, rhythm, volume, inflection (the paralinguistic aspects of speech), along with all aspects of body language are primary determinants of how a message is perceived. In any case, the eyes – seeing – work many times faster than the ears – hearing – and the brain faster than both.

Women seem to be very much better than men at reading non-verbal behaviour; 'women's intuition' may be as much to do with a more developed capacity to read and interpret evidence as it is to do with innate wisdom (although both are relevant). Much non-verbal communication is minuscule, microscopic, fleeting and vestigial but, nevertheless, revelatory to those who have eyes to see and ears to hear. To be effective communicators we have to develop those acute eyes and ears too.

Box 10.2 Simple examples

Everyone can recognise whether or not an apology or greeting is warm and genuine or insincere, not from the words used, but from the tone of voice:

- 'I'm sorry' can be an empty vocal gesture without positive emotional content, or a true admission of regret or guilt (or anything in between).
- 'How are you?' can be a mere formula greeting, or an expression of genuine, warm interest and concern.
- Even a cliché such as 'Have a nice day!' can be said in a way that conveys genuine goodwill.

The tone of voice will tell you what is intended; facial expression, body posture, eye contact and other behaviour will provide further powerful evidence of the intentions and emotions of the speaker.

It is impossible to make any communication without non-verbal elements being the major part of it. Although you can control aspects of non-verbal communication (we'll come to that later), usually, most of them are spontaneous or automatic – your tone of voice, body posture, facial expression and so on, simply happen as part of the total, integrated package of communication signals or messages you send out. It is obvious with any kind of strong emotion – you can see such feelings clearly exhibited by a person without any need for words – the intention and the behaviour are consistent; but it is also true for many other, less simple and obvious feelings and reactions: they are all 'written' on the face and in behaviour, however subtly, whatever the words.

The doctor may also learn more about the illness from the way the patient tells the story than from the story itself.

James B. Herrick

The richest and most complete communication takes place when all the elements are in harmony – when the thoughts, emotions and words, and the non-verbal behaviour accompanying them are a harmonious, integrated whole: you see such complete communication in people who are immensely happy, enthusiastic, depressed or angry: all the elements cohere to make a powerful, unambiguous statement. Such coherence is an important goal in professional communications, as we shall see later.

Not only is the display of non-verbal behaviour largely instinctive and spontaneous but so also is the perception and interpretation of it: when you meet someone or receive a communication from a person physically near you, your senses (sight and hearing particularly, perhaps smell) and your brain instantaneously process myriad pieces of information and come to a conclusion about the person and the meaning and intent of the message. The judgement is based on the information being sent, but it is processed through, first, perception (which may or may not be alert or accurate) and second, through existing knowledge and experience of the signals being sent.

We all know how easy it is to misinterpret what someone says or the expression on their face: we may not hear the words accurately, may mistake the tone, or misread the facial expression; this may result from a transmission which is unclear or ambiguous, or from our idiosyncratic response to the message which results from some inner angle or twist or distortion of the message as transmitted. Such misinterpretations are especially common in cross-cultural communication where non-verbal behaviour may have very different meanings for different people (see Chapter 14).

> But behavior in the human being is sometimes a defense, a way of concealing motives and thoughts, as language can be a way of hiding your thoughts and preventing communication.
>
> *Abraham Maslow*

Divergence

Because most non-verbal behaviour is largely spontaneous, it is immensely revealing – much more so than the words chosen. This is particularly clear when the non-verbal signals are in some way divergent from the verbal message. In the 'I'm sorry' example in Box 10.2, we can judge whether or not the expression of regret is sincere from the tone of voice, facial expression, body language and so on; it is clear when the non-verbal signals confirm,

compromise or contradict the verbal meaning. We can often recognise when there is a conscious effort to mask the divergence between what is actually being said and what is truly felt – when there is a certain artificiality, awkwardness or pose in the non-verbal behaviour.

The most extreme example of divergent non-verbal signals is when someone is lying directly. Here there is a fundamental struggle between the conscious intention to deceive the listener and the body's natural inclination to display real feelings non-verbally. The liar has to attempt to try to control non-verbal behaviour – against the spontaneous urges of the body – to make it look like the behaviour of someone telling the truth.

Although some people have mastered the art of lying convincingly, few of us can do it without giving something away in our non-verbal behaviour (hesitation, scratching the nose, looking away, tugging an ear; perhaps a blush, sweating or pallor) – something that an acute observer will not miss. You'll know almost every time if your child is lying – that shifting, squirming, eye-avoiding behaviour; with adults it is much the same, although subtler, less obvious and often more consciously manipulated, although vascular responses (like blushing or pallor) are almost impossible to control.

Today, human civilization is drowning in a sea of lies.
L. Neil Smith

'Non-verbal leakage' is a real fact of life: if you're angry, depressed or demoralised, or desperate to get home at the end of the day, it is very difficult to hide the feeling completely, however hard you try, whatever the content of your conversation.

Many non-verbal signals are perceived and registered in ways which the conscious brain and sense don't notice – they somehow pass into the great message-reception centre of our being, where they influence our instant reactions to a signal, and are stored in ways that will influence our future reactions and more general feelings about the person or the message. We respond in these ways not only to specific signals (a threat, or an expression of affection, or a difficult question), but also to the general quality of an encounter with someone: we may feel generally relaxed, at ease, or tense and uncomfortable in someone's company – and we may or may not have an accurate or clear understanding of why that is. The elements of the situation that give rise to these broader feelings are conveyed to us by the explicit or implicit intentions of the person we are with, and by a host of non-verbal signals which we may or may not notice consciously, but which are certainly registered by the astonishing capacity of our ever-alert communication receptors (mostly eyes, ears, nose).

Silence remains, inescapably, a form of speech.
Susan Sontag

Box 10.3 Sexual chemistry?

Insect behaviour is known to be influenced by pheromone release, but it is still uncertain whether the same process applies to human sexual attraction, in spite of the hundreds of non-regulated products on the market, claiming to provide the irresistible sexual-stimulating molecules for consumer purchase. However, it cannot be ruled out, and some of our behaviour may be determined by processes beyond our consciousness or control. What is certain is that how we smell is important in relationships, as the multi-billion dollar fragrance industry extravagantly demonstrates.

The impact of our presentation of ourselves and our response to the presentation of others is influenced by 'gestalt' – the overall impression that the many signals and the total presence of the person convey. The ease or unease we experience in another's presence may be attributable not only to individual elements of their communication and behaviour, but also to their levels of energy and what we might call personality – that co-ordinating force which makes us what we are. Someone who is depressed or happy exudes depression or happiness in ways that are hard to pin down but which have a considerable impact. The same applies to confidence, uncertainty, compassion, boredom and indifference – aspects that express deep aspects of personality, and are instantly evident to a third party.

Those who consciously manipulate the non-verbal aspects of their communication for dubious purposes may deceive some of the people some of the time, but there are almost always clues to the discrepancy between appearance and intention, if not immediately, then often subsequently when the real intention emerges unambiguously. The fixed smile for television; the earnest corporate apology; the embrace of racial inclusivity; the gesture of concern; the declaration of commitment to a patient – may appear real enough at the time (although perhaps not to a really acute observer), but later may be shown to be the deceptive face of hypocrisy. All of us use such techniques from time to time, especially in a tight corner. But, very few of can disguise completely the non-verbal clues that reveal our true intent.

Box 10.4 Bizarre contemporary phenomenon

> The transformation of serious television newscasting (the transmission of facts, analysis and information) into show business has been partly accomplished by the distracting flamboyance of newscasters' non-verbal behaviour: from the over-emphatic, emotional elements of tone of voice, to the extravagant hand gestures and mobile facial expressions, to say nothing of banal footnote commentary (nod and a wink). Intellectual communication has been turned into a kind of pseudo-intimate circus side-show, hardly to be taken seriously. Such is the corrupting influence of the need for approval (and ratings) and the power of non-verbal communication to convert serious messages into something with the weight of neighbourhood gossip.

Monitoring and moderating non-verbal behaviour

The control of non-verbal behaviour that is essential for appropriateness to the task in hand and good professional relationships is based on the ethical demand of respect for the patient and of removal of obstacles to the most effective therapy and communication. If we find that we don't like a patient, for example, or are in a state of personal euphoria, we have a duty to disguise those responses and states of mind and the clues that would reveal them. Such obstacles are likely to come from the zone of the private person, where preferences, prejudices, values and tastes may be legitimate, but from which patients need to be protected. This deviation from absolute honesty and transparency is justified on the grounds that our weaknesses and preoccupations would usually be a damaging and unethical intrusion into the relationship with a patient and a distraction from helping them: such control is part of the professional act.

- When anxious or distracted, we suppress those feelings and associated behaviour in order to focus attentively on the patient.
- When we feel disapproval or disgust at a patient's behaviour or personal hygiene (for example), we do our best to rein in and hide such reactions and deal with the person, unless there is some positive, planned reason for being frank.
- When we are shocked by a patient's revelation, we moderate or disguise the feeling, unless there is good reason not to do so.
- When we are in a bad mood or a state of exuberance, we try to find a moderate path which matches the needs of the patient and doesn't oppress them with our subjective state of mind.

- When under great pressure, we consciously slow down our physical movements and speech in order to give the patient confidence in our attention and space to express their concerns.

The physical environment

The person communicating – with all the verbal and non-verbal variables – is the most potent influence on anyone's response, but there are also many things in the immediate environment which will have an impact, some potentially very powerful. These are part of the broad category of communication beyond words.

Never go to a doctor whose office plants have died.
Erma Bombeck

In the clinic, consulting room or hospital waiting area, a host of physical, non-verbal elements send strong positive or negative messages (communicate) to patients, visitors and colleagues:

- layout and arrangement of rooms or physical space
- signage and notices
- tidiness and cleanliness
- comfort of seating
- convenience of amenities (reading material, drinking water, toilets, etc.)
- temperature, humidity and freshness of atmosphere
- lighting levels, colour schemes, decorative elements (such as plants and pictures)
- privacy
- interruptions.

Although there may be no conscious recognition of any of these elements, impressions will very rapidly be received and registered in the brain, and will significantly affect feelings. Relationships with patients will be eased and enhanced, confidence and trust will be stimulated in an environment that is welcoming, comfortable and attractive – where, at least, some thought has been given to the issues and some trouble taken.

I was going to have cosmetic surgery until I noticed that the doctor's office was full of portraits by Picasso.
Rita Rudner

Managing and using non-verbal communication

First you must become expert in reading the non-verbal communication of others and in being alert to the hundreds of elements in the environment that influence what people think and feel about you and your organisation.

Reading others is something you do all the time, but it is a skill that needs refining and deepening if you are to become the first-class communicator that good healthcare requires you to be. The details will differ from region to region and from culture to culture, but the principles are exactly the same.

Box 10.5 Fieldwork

Observe and study people all the time; turn down the sound on your television; see how much you can tell about people when you see only their behaviour. When you are out and about, observe the environment in shops or airports or restaurants – how do the non-verbal behaviour of staff and the features of the environment contribute? Walk round hospitals, clinics or pharmacies and see how they make you feel, and what it is that gives you a good or bad impression.

Second, learn about your own non-verbal behaviour:

- Heighten your awareness of your interaction with people: watch yourself for a time; notice what you do with your hands, how you stand, whether you have nervous habits, what you do when talking to a group – and everything else.
- Does your non-verbal behaviour convey and reinforce the messages you intend – or is there a conflict between your intentions and your behaviour? Does your behaviour inhibit or distract others?
- Get yourself filmed in action: watch, analyse, reflect and decide what you would like to do differently. Audio recordings of consultations

are also very revealing and useful for analysis and study – they reveal not only the content of meaning, but also the tone and style of the encounter, which may be at least as influential in determining the outcome.[48] You may be surprised how you sound!

- Ask trusted colleagues to observe you in action over a few days and make notes on what they see – what you do well, what is distracting or unhelpful; then discuss their observations with them.

Third, decide what non-verbal behaviour you think will improve your professional practice. For example:

- To listen more carefully, and adopt helpful listening behaviour
  - — turn towards the patient
  - — give good eye-contact
  - — give undivided attention
  - — try to sit or stand still.
- Slow down movement and speech, however much under pressure.
- Be prepared for people and information that will shock or upset; anticipate and practise how to maintain eye-contact and attention without reacting unhelpfully facially or physically.
- Remedy distracting habits: stop tapping your pen on the desk or shifting files around on the desk.
- Pay more attention to patients' non-verbal behaviour and interpret its meaning; use it constructively (by interpretation, comment and discussion).

And in the immediate environment:

- Reduce interruptions to an absolute minimum (the files for the next patient should be brought in with the previous patient, not in the middle of the consultation; divert all except emergency calls).
- Provide a more comfortable chair for patients.
- Place the chair where there is no physical barrier in front of the patient (in cultures where this is helpful).
- Place a sign on the desk with your name and job on it.
- Provide a quiet, private place for conversation in a busy public environment (in a pharmacy, for example).

Go through the list of desirable behaviour you developed in your observation of others and of yourself.

Intelligent observation

Listening and watching are two of the skills which a busy schedule always puts at risk, but they are probably the most valuable communication tools an HCP has. By listening attentively to the verbal content of a patient's communication, paying close attention to all the non-verbal aspects, and observing their total physical presence (stance, posture, clothing, movement, gestures, eye-contact, restlessness and so on), an impression will emerge which may have a determining influence on understanding a patient's symptoms and needs.

As you gather this evidence, you can use it to clarify issues, perhaps taking the discussion deeper than the patient might voluntarily manage. This is the skill of managing the process of relationships (what is going on under the surface) as well as the content (what appears to be happening on the surface) (see also Chapter 11).

There are thousands of combinations of verbal and non-verbal clues that will, in infinite variety, be expressed by patients and colleagues (and family and friends). Observing, interpreting and responding to such clues, to both the obstacles and the opportunities they represent, will advance and enrich every relationship, especially where issues are sensitive. The key is in recognising the verbally unexpressed feelings, taking them silently into account in your responses, or bringing them explicitly into the open. Accurate and insightful connections made on this basis are profoundly powerful tools for helping people express facts and feelings that are problematic for them and for forming relationships that are productive and strong.

Echoing and mirroring

When someone is angry with us, or shouts at us, our instinctive response is usually to respond in kind – to get angry or shout back and take up an aggressive physical stance (a mistake in public service – see Chapter 13). We may be led along by the feelings of others in less dramatic ways – by exuberance, cynicism, sadness or depression – finding our mood and the direction of our conversation echoing or following. We need to be aware of the effects of such unintended or manipulative influences, and keep a degree of separateness in perception and judgement, while remaining empathetic and concerned.

Behaviour expresses emotions, but emotions are also, to some extent, led by behaviour – it is impossible to be aggressive if your body is relaxed (much more so when seated rather than standing); it is quite difficult to be angry or hurtful if you are genuinely smiling; it is difficult to be practical and decisive if you are slumped in a chair. The skilled professional uses this kind of knowledge to introduce elements of behaviour to progressively alter the mood and behaviour of an aggressor or anyone else. Similar practice might be used to lift (although perhaps not remedy) a mood of depression or anxiety, guilt or regret; a physical change may alter an emotional state in oneself or in others.

Mirroring

When two (or more) people are in some kind of harmony, their non-verbal behaviour is often mirrored: they may be sitting in similar poses (maybe one ankle resting on the knee, an arm loose on the arm of a chair, or hands clasped behind the head); they may move or make the same gesture at the same time.

Knowledge of this is also professionally important. If a patient is imitating your body posture, then you may assume that they are on at least a similar wavelength to you and amenable to some degree of open conversation. In order to demonstrate the same degree of openness to what a patient is saying, you can unobtrusively mirror their behaviour. A tense patient may be influenced unconsciously to relax and imitate you, by your adopting a relaxed body posture, but if their tension is mirrored in your posture, and you don't recognise the imitation, then progress may not be easy.

Touch

Of all non-verbal behaviour, touch is among the most powerful and the most problematic: powerful, because any intended physical contact between two human beings can have a considerable emotional impact; problematic, because it can be misinterpreted as a sexual gesture, or experienced as a culturally offensive act (see also Chapter 14).

In some cultures, physical contact between adults in public is rare, even taboo. Even in cultures where physical contact is common (friends hugging and kissing one another, for example), there are strict boundaries beyond which touch is hazardous.

> Touch seems to be as essential as sunlight.
>
> *Diane Ackerman*

In cultures where it is permitted, touch can be a compassionate and healing act which gives comfort and strength to those in pain or distress; touch can make contact between two people at a level beyond words. (Therapeutic massage is an activity that combines both the professional healing touch and, in its pure form, the reassuring contact of another person's physical being.)

The touch required for physical examinations is a specialised professional tool (see Chapter 14), requiring sensitivity and skill; the touch required for comfort and reassurance is no less demanding, not least because it is discretionary, and because it must be offered entirely for the wellbeing of the patient rather than for the gratification of the giver.

A healthcare environment in which no patient was ever touched spontaneously would be frigid and sterile indeed. It may seem artificial, ridiculous even, to list the kinds of touch that might be acceptable, because, most of the time, it will be so obvious and so instinctive that little thought is needed – the guiding hand on an elbow, the comforting touch on a shoulder, the reassuring holding of hands, the massage of a foot, picking up and hugging a distressed child – all so obvious, natural and humane. For some people, touch will be unacceptable, even frightening, or will have a unique scary, ambiguous or positive meaning, so an HCP has to be very clear that they are not crossing some sensitive boundary which will distress or mislead the patient. That requires a degree of empathy or rapid responsiveness – either to know in advance whether touch is safe or not, or to retreat quickly from initial touch if there is any sign of withdrawal or distress.

Too often we underestimate the power of a touch, a smile, a kind word, a listening ear, an honest compliment, or the smallest act of caring, all of which have the potential to turn a life around.

Leo Buscaglia

Perhaps the most serious issue is to understand the potential sexual ambiguity of touch, especially in the minds of those who've been abused or who are, for one reason or another, poorly reconciled to their bodies or overly reactive to physical stimulation. Touch can awaken bad memories as well as stimulate good feelings, possibly inappropriate ones. Never use touch in a way that is ambiguous, lingering or remotely flirtatious or could be interpreted as such. Never use touch when the urge is anything but the expression of your wish to comfort and reassure the patient.

The message of this chapter is the power and importance of non-verbal behaviour, and the extent to which management of it and observation of it can greatly enhance the quality of relationships and improve therapy. Poor communicators pay very little conscious attention to non-verbal behaviour, and their relationships suffer greatly as a result.

A light, tender, sensitive touch is worth a ton of brawn.

Peter Thomson

Revision, discussion and application (3)

A. Revision and discussion

1. What do you feel are the primary aspects of your experience and of you as a person (and of other people too) which shape how personality develops and expresses itself? Are there some clear, major elements, or is the picture more complex? What are the ways in which these elements influence relationships in general and with patients? What are the reasons for developing self-awareness and a measure of control in forming professional relationships?
2. Using Box 9.1, 'Characteristics of others' (p. 49) as a basis, examine your personal positive or negative prejudices in relation to the list of qualities, and consider other positive or negative prejudices you may have. What are the origins of these sets of feelings and what explanations can you find for them? What prejudices do you see among your colleagues and patients and what impact do they have on relationships and therapy?
3. Think about an occasion when your perception or the perception of someone else was narrowed in such a way that understanding of the situation was prevented or compromised – perhaps an argument or discussion with your partner or child, a colleague or manager or with a patient or their family. What habits of emotion or thought caused perception of the real world to be deficient? Was the failure due to blindness to fact or evidence, to the perspectives of others, self-centredness or something else?
4. While still getting on with your job, spend a day or two examining the non-verbal behaviour of the people around you. Examine the ways in which non-verbal behaviour: (a) supports or conflicts with verbal messages; (b) reveals information about how a person is feeling, irrespective of what they are saying; (c) affects the emotions and behaviour of others. (Other means of studying non-verbal behaviour are mentioned in Chapter 10.)
5. What do you feel are the most powerful kinds of non-verbal behaviour? What are the habits we should foster in the pursuit of positive professional relationships – both things to do and things to avoid?
6. What advice would you give to a new entrant to one of the healthcare professions about touch?

B. Application

1. What are the major influences in patients' lives that affect their relationships with HCPs? What are the elements that you see most frequently? What are some of the insights and communications in this area that are essential to managing relationships with patients sensitively and successfully?
2. How would you recognise and deal with the positive or negative prejudices of patients in relation to your role and personal characteristics if they are having an adverse effect on the professional relationship? What would you think and what would you say?

3. During a day's work, pay special attention to communications from others which appear to mean more than they say or which are 'loaded' in as much as they hint at a range of thoughts or feelings that are not being made explicit. Decide on each occasion whether it is appropriate to ask a question or share your insight. Develop your skills in perceiving and dealing with such communications and integrate them into your practice.
4. Make a particular study of how patients express pain or discomfort non-verbally: what are the ways in which they hold or carry their bodies? How do they protect vulnerable areas and try to reduce discomfort? What are the non-verbal aspects of verbal communications about pain? What are the verbal and non-verbal messages about their feelings about pain?
5. Spend some time observing how patients react to touch, both in necessary examination and other procedures (a bed-bath, for example) and in informal gestures, such as shaking hands, helping a patient from an examination couch, settling a patient on a gurney, a comforting hand on the arm and so on. Make an inventory of the minor and major reactions patients have and refine your approach to know sensitively how and when to use and avoid touch.
6. Ask for your patients' opinions about the environment in which you work and in which they are treated: what do they like and dislike? What would make them feel more relaxed and comfortable?

Commentary on many of the questions and issues appears on the publisher's website, in Online Resources at www.pharmpress.com.

Part E

Foundation knowledge and skills for effective communication

The first chapter considers the direct practice application of all the background thinking and knowledge that has been reviewed so far. A small number of critical areas of knowledge and skill – caring, helping, empathy, listening and more – underlie all healthcare communications practice and these are examined in detail, illustrated with specific examples of interactions with patients.

The second chapter discusses broad issues that are relevant across healthcare relationships – the effects of becoming a patient, bedside manner and home visiting, sustaining long-term relationships, among others – which cut across all categories of patients and healthcare communications, and exert their own special demands.

For those who would like an introduction to a more methodical, structured approach to examining basic skills, Appendix 3 provides the core material from the remarkable work of Silverman, Kurtz and Draper, which will extend and enhance the reader's understanding of the issues that are dealt with more discursively in this book.

Ὁ βίος βραχύς, ἡ δὲ τέχνη μακρή, ὁ δὲ καιρὸς ὀξύς, ἡ δὲ πεῖρα σφαλερή, ἡ δὲ κρίσις χαλεπή.

Ars longa, vita brevis, occasio praeceps, experimentum periculosum, iudicium difficile.

Acquisition of the unending art and craft of medicine is a task that is interrupted by death; life is short; opportunity fleeting; experiment (or experience) treacherous; judgement (or decisions) difficult.

Hippocrates

[Translation and interpretation rendered by the author with help from diverse sources.]

11 Core concepts and skills

A small number of areas of core knowledge and skills will equip HCPs to be effective, compassionate communicators who can understand their patients and the complexities of their lives more accurately and quickly than those who are less knowledgeable and skilled. The primary aspects of the core skills include empathetic attention to patients, active listening and the ability to elicit useful facts and information through sensitive questioning. HCPs need to care about their patients and show that they do, as well as helping them in ways that meet their felt needs. Explanation is a skill that requires careful thought; checking understanding at every stage is a critical process to ensure messages are fully understood.

Caring

Caring lies at the heart of all effective work and relationships with patients – and, like so many of the concepts and skills in this book, at the heart of humane and moral behaviour in any situation at all. The word and the concept sometimes seem to lack 'muscle', to be sentimental, and used so commonly as to have been weakened and devalued. It doesn't help that the word is part of 'health*care*'.

With its linguistic roots in 'suffering' (as in 'the cares of the world'), *care* is a powerful concept in its meaning of concern, worry, caution about the welfare of a person or activity; commitment to nurture or development; dedication to the prevention or relief of suffering or danger; protection from harm – a safe place – and the provision of hope. Implicit in the notion are compassion, commitment, goodwill and, in its essential sense of kindness and generosity, charity. *Patient care*, in its widest sense, includes the physical environment and all kinds of other arrangements and the extent to which they appear to be provided by people who care and make patients feel cared for in the present and over time.

Box 11.1 'They don't really care'

> In the eyes of patients, there are few more damning conclusions about a hospital, clinic or an individual HCP. Whatever the truth, patients' confidence and trust will be damaged if they feel they are not in the hands of people who *really* care about their jobs and their patients. Caring means making the object of care the number one priority, showing sustained seriousness, warmth and concern, the opposite of just 'going through the motions', which some behaviour can suggest. You have not only to care, but also to make it clear to your patients that you do. This requires all the skills we discuss in this book, along with the occasional explicit, genuine statement: 'I do care about what happens to you, so I really hope we can find a solution together.'

Caring is a specific, intentional, active commitment to serve the welfare and nurturing of others: it may manifest itself in the shortest of encounters (perhaps a brief exchange in a community pharmacy, or in the waiting area of a hospital). It may be in a sustained relationship in which the patient is taken care of, looked after in one way or another over a longer period: examples include the best pharmaceutical care, or the relationship of a physician and team with a young patient with inflammatory bowel disease, or of a midwife with a mother through her several deliveries, or of a community practitioner with a family over many years.

Kindness is the language which the deaf can hear and the blind can see.

Mark Twain

Care of patients has always been at the heart of nursing and it remains critical to the purpose and integrity of the vocation, but nurses cannot carry the entire burden of care for patients – cannot and should not – and their priority commitment should not be an excuse for others to care less, or delegate the burden of caring to them. Arrogant behaviour reveals that the HCP has missed the central point of what they are supposed to be doing: that is, *caring* for patients through the exercise of their talent and skill – being *careful* (full of *care*) in every aspect of their relationships and practice, with patients and colleagues alike. Caring originates in the mind and the heart, and is expressed through behaviour and communication. Those cared for feel they are in the safe, reliable and healing hands of dedicated professionals (see also Chapter 15).

Box 11.2 Bitter experience

A psychiatrist reports his experience of seeking help for his elderly mother.[51]

'The great man *[the consultant]* couldn't manage it. He had the cufflinks but not the questions. He had the style but not the substance. . . It doesn't matter what you do because the "carers" do not care. It does not matter what you say, because they do not listen.'

It is a good thing for a physician to have prematurely grey hair and itching piles. The first makes him appear to know more than he does, and the second gives him an expression of concern which the patient interprets as being on his behalf.

A. Benson Cannon

Helping

Some years ago, a social science writer dryly described a social work 'client' (as they were then known), as: 'a person who receives what the social services call help and who lives with the consequences of that help'.[52]

In the past, and even now in many places, we could characterise a patient as someone who, 'receives what the doctor/hospital/HCP calls treatment and who lives with the consequences of that treatment.'

There are two critical elements:

- One is the risk that help or treatment is defined in terms of the provider's frame of reference or available resources, and not in terms negotiated with the patient and matching their wishes and needs.
- Help or treatment always has consequences which may not truly be taken into account at the point of diagnosis and treatment, and may sometimes be serious and/or long term. Helpers or HCPs may not recognise these, nor feel or take any responsibility, nor plan for them.

This book is an argument against the imposition of any decision or action that does not take full account of the patient's needs and wishes, and that does not have their consent. The point about consequences also relates to a vital issue in this book: the patient as a whole person beyond the healthcare encounter. This forces our attention not only to the depth and breadth of a patient's existence in its complex context of the here and now, but also over time and into the future.

A physician is obligated to consider more than a diseased organ, more even than the whole man – he must view the man in his world.

Harvey Cushing

It is too easy to find a neat solution or to carry out a procedure which appears to deal with immediate needs (even with the patient's consent), without adequate consideration of what the implications are for the patient's safety, welfare and happiness to come, and how they are going to cope in the future. The dispensing of a drug without discussion of the possibility of adverse reactions and what to do about them is perhaps the simplest and commonest example. Discharge from hospital, operations for back pain, lifetime medication, or the birth of a disabled child are other examples, where potentially serious problems or long-term consequences may be quite unclear to the patient and perhaps to the HCP as well.

Patient consent needs to be consent to consequences across their whole life, as far as they can be defined and anticipated. Moreover, HCPs have an obligation to see that the patient has the resources, or has access to the resources, to manage the consequences of any event or intervention. In other words, responsibility does not stop at the point of treatment, discharge or the conclusion of a consultation: effective helping and caring demand that the longer perspective is considered and reviewed as well – that risks and needs are assessed – even if an HCP is unable to provide much in the way of future direct, practical help.

If I knew for a certainty that a man was coming to my house with the conscious design of doing me good, I should run for my life.

Henry David Thoreau

Everything an HCP does might be described as help, and many ancillary services are non-medical help. We need to be clear what the aims of helping are, and to be sure the patient's needs, wishes, dignity and autonomy are at the heart of our intentions. Patients often have ideas about what needs to be done, what help they require. Although we may be broadening their horizons about what is possible, we constantly need to draw out of them what they think is best, what they believe they can do. To the patient's question, 'What should I do?' the best response is, 'What do you feel the choices you have available are, what do you think will be the best answer for you, and how can I help you achieve it?'

Caring for people expresses itself in the compassionate activity of helping them towards good decisions and supporting them in carrying them out; achieving reconciliation with life as it is and is likely to be; protecting their independence; and managing the consequences of the process.

Give a man a fish and he will eat for a day. Teach him to fish and he will eat for a lifetime.

Confucious[53]

Empathy

Empathy is central to everything you will think and do in healthcare relationships and communications.[54–56] It is a skill that can be practised and refined; it arises from a disposition of openness and humility in the face of complexity.

This much-misunderstood, sometimes derided, concept lies at the heart of effective relationships and communications of all kinds.

Empathy is the capacity, experienced even if only for a split second, of understanding what it is like to be someone else; an accurate and transforming insight.

Box 11.3

In its purest form, empathy is not:
- feeling what it would be like for you to be in someone else's shoes *(it is being them in their shoes)*
- feeling sympathy for the suffering of others *(an outsider's, third-party response)*
- imagining how you would feel if the same happened to you *(you are not them)*
- drawing parallels with your own life experience.

The act of empathy requires:
- attention to every aspect of another person's presentation of themselves and their thoughts and emotions
- head, heart and imagination that are temporarily emptied of noise, interpretation, commentary, memory, emotions, ideas and responses
- senses that are perfectly attuned to the reception of complex information from another human being's inner life
- the ability to respond accurately and usefully when appropriate, either spontaneously or on reflection, in ways that absolutely match the reality of the other person's own emotions and understanding of their own life, and which they recognise as the truth about themselves when you show it to them – in short, accurate insight.

Why is empathy so important? Empathy allows us to perceive and to respond accurately and effectively to the otherness of a human being, by seeing them as they are, as they see themselves. It is transforming, because it takes us out of ourselves, if only for a fraction of a second, and allows us to see and feel as if we were not ourselves.

> Could a greater miracle take place than for us to look through each other's eyes for an instant?
>
> *Henry David Thoreau*

Although the definition above describes the nature of empathy (the out-of-self understanding), there is also the broader capacity for empathy. This is the ability and willingness always to try to understand what is behind the words, behaviour and motivation of others, to seek how the world looks and feels to them. What is behind the behaviour of this irritating and disruptive child? Why is this nurse so brisk and cold with patients? Why is this patient constantly failing to adhere to treatment? What does how they are behaving feel like for them?

> Observe, record, tabulate, communicate. Use your five senses. Learn to see, learn to hear, learn to feel, learn to smell, and know that by practice alone you can become expert.
>
> *William Osler*

A crude parallel may help: suppose you meet someone to whom you talk in your native language, not realising that they do not understand or speak it: it is obvious that communication will fail because you did not have one piece of vital information about the other person.

The language that someone speaks is a simple fact to discover and does not require empathy. But, if instead of language, you think about, say, their experience of, and feelings and opinions about disease or injury – then you need to grasp much more than facts and try to perceive and feel what life is like for them, in order that what you say will be in the unique language of their feelings and experience.

Unless we have an accurate understanding of another person, we cannot tailor our communications and plans to fit that individual's needs. To take the example of emotions about disease or injury: an HCP might be perplexed by the anxious or negative reaction of a patient to a treatment plan or proposals for an operation – they are reluctant, uncooperative, don't turn up for appointments, postpone decisions: what is going on?

Box 11.4 'If I were you . . .'

> This phrase is on Hugman's 'Do Not Use' list*, because it is usually the preface to advice that will entirely miss the point, and may seriously upset the recipient. 'But you're not me . . .' is the instant response, with the corollary that what you'd do is probably of little or no relevance at all to what I should do. 'If I were you' denies empathy and stands in the way of finding solutions that arise out of the reality of the patient's life. Even if the offered advice is sound, and based on true understanding of the patient's life, the form of words is alienating in its implication that decisions *I* would make in my life are the kind of decisions *you* should be making in yours.
>
> *The more authoritative Joint Commission's 'Do Not Use' list is on p. 185.

There are three options:

- Struggle to deal with the difficult behaviour as it is presented, arguing the case for the treatment, persuading, cajoling and so on, which may or may not have any positive effect.
- Ask direct questions which may or may not be answered (the patient may not know what is driving their own responses).
- Listen and watch with empathy; suspend judgement; pick up and interpret hints; try to feel what underlies the patient's superficial presentation; gain insight into the buried problem and deal with that, which then releases the patient to collaborate.

Asking direct questions may not produce anything – especially if very strong or repressed feelings are attached to the problem in the patient's mind, or the patient doesn't know the answer anyway.

With a patient who is resistant to treatment, for example, the empathetic HCP might have a moment of insight, and say: 'I have the feeling that you're frightened by this and I don't really understand why. Can you tell me?'

If the HCP has got it right, and 'frightened' is the exact emotion that the patient is feeling, then a powerful connection is made, because the HCP has shown that they are in touch with the patient's emotions, which may not have been remembered or be clear even for the patient.

Such an accurate insight can lead to a moment of release and/or insight for the patient, and they can then explore what's holding them back. For example:

'Yes. You're right. It's all flooding back. I hadn't realised I'd buried the feelings and that they were still so strong. I don't like to think about it, but both my parents died in hospital and mother, especially, had a terrible time. She had an operation and was at home afterwards, in real pain for months, and I had to look after her while I was working. It was the worst time of my life and I was on the edge of collapse. The mention of an operation just brings back all those bad times and overwhelms me.' (See Table 11.1 for a continuation of this dialogue.)

Now the difficulty is out in the open, and the HCP can begin to deal with it directly, rather than trying to manage only its symptoms – the lack of willingness to consider the possible operation. Certainly the HCP should express concern for the past suffering of the patient, but it is not the HCP's job to provide some kind of psychotherapy for the problems and their enduring effects. What needs to be done is to take account of the past problems and factor them into the negotiations for the present situation.

Table 11.1 is a compact version of how an HCP might respond empathetically to what has been learnt about this patient, distilled from what would be a much longer interaction.

It is obvious that treating this patient simply as difficult, without understanding why they were being difficult, probably won't solve the problem,

Table 11.1 A compact version of how an HCP might respond empathetically to what has been learnt about this patient, distilled from what would be a much longer interaction

'I'm really sorry to hear about that.'	A genuine expression of concern.
'It must have been a terrible time for you and the family.'	Showing empathy and understanding and recognition of the patient's suffering. Using the same adjective (terrible) that the patient used.
'Operations can seem frightening, especially when you've got memories like that.'	Acceptance of the patient's perspective and the validity of the reasons for it.
'Though it may be hard for you to accept this, I do think your situation is different.'	Transition: making a separation from the bad experiences of the past; focusing on the new situation. Here feelings are being respected and managed while a bridge to firmer, less emotional ground is built.
'You're young, healthy and strong and there are usually very few complications with this procedure.'	Providing reasons that the current situation is different; focusing on positives and the low risk; leading the patient away from fear.
'I'd like you to meet the surgeon, hear what she has to say and then make up your mind.'	Transition: practical proposal for cautious, exploratory next step; reassurance that the patient remains in control; drawing thoughts about the operation away from fantasy to reality – the person who would do the job.
'In the end it's entirely up to you.'	Confirmation that the patient is in charge.
'What you need to balance is the very small risk of the operation against the probability that the condition [maybe a knee injury] will get worse in the future, and may be quite painful.'	Input of professional judgement: frank exposition of the issues – risks and benefits – on which the patient has to decide.
'Can we take that first step before you finally make up your mind?'	Seeking permission to move things cautiously forward; restating the patient's freedom to choose.

and may result in a damaged relationship and a lost opportunity. This applies to hundreds of different circumstances, where, for various reasons something is:

- interfering with the honesty of a patient's communication
- preventing a patient from managing their disease or adhering to therapy
- damaging the effectiveness of relationships with HCPs
- provoking difficult or uncooperative behaviour
- distorting a patient's perception of other people, plans or suggestions, therapeutic options and so on.

Many of the experiences and emotions that may influence patients' behaviour are discussed in Chapter 9. You don't need an explicit, verified list of the details of a patient's inner life, nor to provide feedback on your impressions to the patient, but you need to be picking up the clues, asking yourself questions, and making choices. There may be occasions when an HCP might acknowledge, with a gentle touch, the patient's predicament, as a way of throwing a lifeline to the heart of the problem. This would not be to put pressure on the patient to open up or discuss the issue (although that might happen), but rather to show the extent to which the HCP perceives and values the whole person and has empathy for their trouble.

> When we acknowledge a child's feelings, we do him a great service. We put him in touch with his inner reality. And once he's clear about that reality, he gathers the strength to begin to cope.
>
> *Adele Faber*

In the examples in Box 11.5, each item represents an insight into a patient's difficulties and the HCP's decision about the practical consequences. Each item is followed by a form of words that an HCP might use to demonstrate accurate understanding of the patient's pain and to provide caring support – without necessarily intending to open up the entire issue for exploration. Opening the doors to communication, however, is very often what

Box 11.5 Demonstrating empathy

The items illustrate, first, the insight and its practical consequences; second, what an HCP might say if it seemed helpful to share the insight. In these cases, the insights are gained from empathy, not from information provided directly by the patient.

This patient doesn't trust men and me as a male doctor; I'd better offer the alternative of a female colleague.

- 'I think you've had a rather hard time with the men in your life, so perhaps you'd feel more comfortable with a woman doctor?'

This patient is actually a depressed and disappointed husband, but he'll never admit it, so I'll have to factor that into the decision.

- 'I'm sorry things haven't worked out as you hoped at home, but can we think of some practical ways to manage your diet?'

There's a real risk of this patient doing something desperate: I'll have to limit the prescription and ask him to come back in five days.

- 'I'm very concerned about your welfare during this horrible period of your life. Do you need any help? Or can I give you medicine for five days and feel confident of seeing you again next Tuesday?'

This patient is terrified of disease, doctors, hospitals, I need to take this slowly and carefully.

- 'I'm sorry that coming here makes you feel so distressed. Today I don't want to do anything but talk with you and introduce you to the senior nurse. If you feel better after that, you can come back tomorrow and we can go from there.'

This patient won't talk about her abuse as a child and the problems she's having with her own children, so I'll need to treat her disease and then offer her an introduction to the women's group.

- 'I feel you've had a very tough time in one way or another, right from the beginning. We need to deal with your ulcer, but afterwards, I'd really like to introduce you to a friend of mine who's been through a lot and might be able to help.'

Half the health problems of this patient arise from loneliness and self-neglect; what resources can I suggest he might try?

- 'Although it's hard to admit, I think you're suffering from the condition known as loneliness, and it really is affecting your health quite seriously. Do you think we could talk about that problem before we turn to medicine?'

This patient has a whole bundle of deep and unresolved conflicts which are making her life a misery and treatment impossible: how can I find help for her?

- 'I get the feeling that you're so worried and anxious the whole time, that it's impossible for you to think about anything except how unhappy you are. I'm sorry I can't help you much with that, but I do know someone who may be just the person you'd like to meet.'

empathetic concern will do. As well as being a healing process (a relief, an unburdening), it is also risky, especially in opening the flood-gates of misery when an HCP may not have the skill, time or resources to respond adequately. On the other hand, the surprise and trust prompted by the accurate empathy of others can lead to facing, relieving or resolving problems.

Illuminating effects

The discussion so far has focused on empathy as a motivator and means for discovering problems and addressing them. Its importance is also much wider than that.

Understanding the power of empathy and integrating it into the habits of one's life alters how one perceives and experiences every aspect of human beings: they are no longer, to the same extent, inexplicable creatures who automatically stimulate a predefined response in us, but endlessly complex and deeply different from us and from each other, requiring serious attention and study if we are to grasp anything of their real nature. Empathy dissolves barriers of ignorance.

Understanding of others does not imply acceptance or approval, but it does mean that judgements and behaviour can be based on sound evidence and on the reality of people as they are.

Box 11.6 'Mindless violence'

'Mindless', as it is commonly used to characterise perhaps shocking and incomprehensible acts, more accurately identifies the state of the critical faculties of the people commenting on such behaviour, than the state of mind of the perpetrators. No human behaviour is devoid of meaning, even if it is at the boundaries of or beyond our intelligence or empathy to grasp it.

These are profoundly important issues in healthcare, because we are responsible for the health and welfare of people of an almost unimaginable variety, every one of whom, so very different from us, requires us to see them clearly and accurately. If we see them vaguely and inaccurately, or as stereotypes, we cannot know them or respect them, or provide the best care and solutions for them.

Box 11.7 Lightness of touch

In the midst of all this desperately serious stuff, we should mention the extraordinary importance of lightness of touch, of humour, of laughter, of affectionate irony – those aspects of communication that bring a smile to lips or a chuckle to the throat. There are many things we can laugh about or poke fun at (including ourselves) in ways that damage no one but rather uplift spirits and deepen relationships. There will be situations in which humour is utterly inappropriate but many more in which it will warm people's hearts and help in their healing.

In the next section, on listening, we describe how powerful and healing an experience it can be to be given the attention of listening. Empathy comes from, among other things, serious listening, but empathy in action goes much further because it moves from receiving information to showing that it has been received, and received accurately.

> The professional must learn to be moved and touched emotionally, yet at the same time stand back objectively: I've seen a lot of damage done by tea and sympathy.
>
> *Anthony Storr*

Most of us, and most patients, have aspects of our selves which we do not want other people (perhaps especially strangers) to know about, and we'll protect those areas very carefully, even as far as using direct deception. An empathetic individual (a doctor or nurse perhaps) will sometimes get a glimpse of one or more of these hidden areas or sets of feelings and must decide, very thoughtfully, whether or not to pursue or reveal the insight. Empathetic understanding handled carelessly can be very damaging.

Whether you reveal to patients what you know about them is a matter of careful judgement. But what you know about patients, gained from the exercise of empathy, will always enhance your relationships and your practice, whether the insight is shared or not.

Humor is the affectionate communication of insight.

Leo Rosten

Listening

Everybody varies in their capacity to listen effectively and in the amount of information they retain during and after listening. Effective listening requires full attention and concentration on the source of the sound. Few of us have the mental clarity and commitment to do this consistently. The problems are exacerbated in a world full of distractions. However, listening skills can be learnt and practised, to the enormous benefit of all participants. HCPs can improve their skills, while they remain alert to the extent that their patients' listening skills will be highly variable (from zero upwards). Showing your patients that you are listening to them is a further important skill.

I remind myself every morning: Nothing I say this day will teach me anything. So if I'm going to learn, I must do it by listening.

Larry King

Box 11.8 Effective listening

'Effective listening' is the ability to receive (hear), process (interpret) and perceive (grasp and understand) accurately a message in the exact terms the sender transmitted it through their words and paralinguistic attributes (the non-verbal aspects of the sound). The message will include both the intended, voluntary content, and the unintended or involuntary elements. (Most listening is also accompanied by observation, of course, as a part of the essential interpretive process.)

What customarily happens in almost all social and professional situations is that we listen with only part of our brains, the other parts being variously occupied with:

- reacting to what we are hearing and preparing our response
- distracting thoughts about the person speaking, or about work, shopping, family and so on.

The opposite of talking isn't listening. The opposite of talking is waiting.

Fran Lebowitz

Our minds are usually a ferment of emotions, issues and questions, likely to fly off at any moment to some other preoccupation. It is most obvious when we consciously realise we have been briefly totally distracted from listening, miss what has been said, and have to ask for a repetition. Most of the time we don't notice this state of incomplete attention and listening, because we hear enough to continue the conversation coherently, without gross misapprehensions, and to avoid appearing absent minded. However, one of the reasons that we can easily make mistakes (the time and place of an appointment, for example, or the dose or strength of a drug) is that we are actually paying much less attention to the communication than we thought we were or should have been. This is profoundly true for patients who may have many, immediate and serious internal preoccupations distracting them from listening attentively to their HCP.

Listening is a magnetic and strange thing, a creative force. The friends who listen to us are the ones we move toward. When we are listened to, it creates us, makes us unfold and expand.

Karl A. Menninger

The next time you are having a conversation, and are listening to someone, try to notice the number of things going on in parallel (or spiral, more likely) in your head while the other person is speaking (and this exercise has just added another distraction to reduce your attention!) What can be done to reduce the noise and the clutter?

Activate listening!

Good listening has at least one feature common to meditation practice (and empathy): calming and emptying the mind: that is the secret. The moment a patient starts talking to you, you must instantly calm and empty your mind; make it a receptive instrument for listening, by sweeping, as it were, the noise and clutter out of the way, and concentrating, focusing exclusively on what the patient is saying. It is a trick or a tactic that you can learn to execute whenever you recognise that listening is important, in any situation. The internal command is: 'Listening. Switch on.' It becomes easier as you practise, although it may never become entirely foolproof or automatic.

The same tactic of switching on mentally attentive calmness applies to effective visual observation too.

Mass communication, radio, and especially television, have attempted, not without success, to annihilate every possibility of solitude and reflection.

Eugenio Montale

Author's note: Since the Nobel Laureate died in 1981, we should perhaps take the liberty of adding mobile phones, personal sound systems, the internet and computer games as further threats to solitude and reflection.

At the same time as you are focused on listening, what you are hearing has to be stored and retained in a temporary mental 'holding bay', which can release its content when input has ended, and allow you to review it and to respond accurately and intelligently. It is hazardous to form reactions or reach conclusions before the input has ended, because those may become barriers to hearing what follows, or may prejudice better conclusions you would make later on the basis of further evidence. (It can be particularly unhelpful to interrupt a patient's story simply because you have a point you want to make – see below for more on this.) You may need to store some temporary assessments or conclusions if they seem strong, but only in such a way that they do not interfere with hearing what is still to come, and to their being modifiable in the light of later information.

To perform effectively at this level, you also have to be aware of the limits of your attention span, as well as the occasional need to clarify your understanding of what you are hearing. The amount of input any one of us can store in the temporary holding bay will vary greatly, and there is no point at all going beyond its limits and finding you've lost the first half of the patient's communication. As you come to the limit (which you'll come to recognise and which may grow as your listening skills improve) you need to ask the patient to pause, so you can review what has been said and react to it and record it (perhaps in your notes).

Equally if your attentive listening reveals something the patient has said which you do not understand, or is contradictory to something that has gone before, then you need either to store the query for later or to ask them to pause and help you understand what they mean. It is important that such interruptions should not disturb the flow and direction of the patient's story; that they should be made in such a way that they support continuity, not divert the narrative. Repeating the last words or the gist of what the patient said before the interruption is a powerful way of achieving this.

You can't fake listening. It shows.

Raquel Welch

Some exchanges may be quite short, of course, but accurate interpretation of short messages still requires intense concentration: in a rapid exchange there is considerable risk of misinterpretation on either side, and of heading off down a blind alley.

Insensitive interruptions of any kind from any source (mobile phones especially) can be very damaging to attentive listening and, for the speaker, the confidence that what they have to say is important.

Helping patients to listen effectively

Although an HCP's own listening skills must be honed to a fine degree, knowledge of the extent to which a patient is listening is a further vital dimension of this topic. There's more on this in the section 'Checking understanding and seeking feedback', later in this chapter, but there are a few issues that need discussion here.

Most patients will not be familiar with effective listening practice, and will not necessarily pay careful attention to the individual words or phrases or sentences that an HCP utters. They may not be familiar with processing serious, dense messages at all; they may pick up only a general impression of what is being said or the feelings expressed; they may overreact to certain words or phrases and lose the general sense or context; they may miss vital details.

There are many benefits to this process of listening. The first is that good listeners are created as people feel listened to. Listening is a reciprocal process – we become more attentive to others if they have attended to us.

Margaret J. Wheatley

An HCP needs to be closely monitoring the extent to which a patient is listening, and is able to make sense of what is being said. Should a patient be distracted (in a busy pharmacy, for example), or have withdrawn into introspection, or seem to be reading the package or a poster while the HCP is talking, or the patient may be fiddling with their mobile phone, or attending to a demanding child – whatever dilutes attention, then the HCP has to pause, try to remedy the cause of the distraction, ask for feedback about the information already conveyed and find diplomatic ways of demanding the attention necessary: 'I really need you to understand this. It won't take long. Can we go through it again together?'

Effective listening can take place only when a patient is communicating, of course, and the skills of questioning and active listening are those that will increase the chances of your having something to listen to, and something that is relevant and important to the patient and you.

Listening to people keeps them entertained.

Mason Cooley

Questioning

A patient consultation is not a simple encounter between a patient with information they want to give and an HCP who wants to hear it. A patient may not know that they have information that is important for the HCP to know, or they may have information that they are keen to shield from the HCP. Initially, the HCP will get to know only what the patient chooses to tell them, and all kinds of vital information may remain hidden unless it is expertly sought and discovered, overcoming many kinds of possible barriers.[57]

Questions are a burden to others; answers are a prison for oneself.

Patrick McGoohan

Questioning is an intrusion into another human being's life. Conventions in many societies place some degree of obligation on someone asked a question to answer it or appear to be answering it. Questioning, then, can be seen as (and may be), at one end of the spectrum, an intrusive, aggressive act, an assertion of power, whereas at the other, it can be a demonstration of gentle and affectionate concern. We may be only seeking information, but the meaning of that seemingly non-threatening intention may prompt very different reactions from different people. (Teenagers commonly react very negatively to 'simple' questions about what they're up to, and may resist personal revelations very strongly, for example.)

[In personal relationships] . . . beware the man who does nothing but ask you questions about yourself and offers

no information about himself. Not only is he keeping you at bay, he is probably not listening to your answers.
Merrill Markoe

Questioning skills are very important, but not at the expense of listening, of course.

Box 11.9 Illuminating research

Hargie[58] vividly describes a common state of affairs:

West (1983) revealed that of 773 questions featured in the 21 doctor–patient consultations sampled, only 68 (9%) were initiated by patients. Indeed, in a study cited by Sanchez (2001), doctors incredibly managed to ask, on average, one question per 4.6 seconds during consultations lasting little more than 2 minutes each. Patients may even be interrupted in order for a question to be asked. In one investigation, patients got little more than 18 seconds into a description of their symptoms before the physician butted in (Epstein *et al.*, 1993). Summing up this state of affairs, Street (2001, p. 543) noted: 'Research consistently shows that physicians tend to talk more, ask more questions, give more directives, make more recommendations, and interrupt more than do patients.'

The research findings are open to several interpretations (not all of them entirely bad), but none of them can banish the image of the patient as a pretty passive recipient of interrogation and instruction. Although we know nothing about the seriousness of those patients' symptoms, and have no evidence about levels of patient satisfaction or outcome success, the picture is stark enough: these patients were not partners in their healthcare.

There are several kinds of questions, some neutral in essence, to be chosen carefully for use at particular times, but damaging if carelessly used; others, essentially risky or manipulative, should be largely avoided.

The important thing is not to stop questioning.
Albert Einstein

Open and closed questions

- An open question is any enquiry that simply opens the door for someone to talk about something (the openness stops at the point of definition of the subject, of course, so even that has to be chosen with care, lest it should be off the point)
  — 'How are you feeling today?'
  — 'Please tell me about your symptoms'
  — 'What are your feelings about the treatment?'
  — 'How is the family reacting to the news?'
  — 'Is there anything else you wanted to mention?'
  — 'Are you worried about anything else?'

For clarity, here are the closed versions of the first four questions: assuming that these are the first questions asked, you'll see that the patient's freedom to answer strictly in their own terms is limited, and that a degree of assertiveness is required to answer more than 'yes' or 'no' or challenge the assumptions embedded in the questions:

— 'Are you feeling better today?'
— 'Are you getting on well with the new diet?'
— 'Are you comfortable with the treatment?'
— 'Is the family upset?'

None of these questions is bad per se, but if they are asked in a rapid sequence and before the patient has identified their feelings or their cause for concern in response to open questioning, there's a risk that their real feelings will be inhibited by the limitations of the closed question; a patient could even get the impression that the questioning is a kind of empty routine and that serious answers are not expected. Such closed questions are fine for discovering more about the issues a patient has already had the freedom to identify as concerning them.

Closed questions will also be useful for diagnostic purposes, when an HCP needs factual information from the patient:

- 'Is the pain worse?'
- 'Is there blood in your urine?'
- 'Do you drink at least a litre of water each day?'
- 'Have you fainted before?'
- 'Is there any history of heart disease in your family?'
- 'Have you had unsafe sex?'

All of these will probably spawn further closed questions until the patient has no more information to contribute.

You mustn't always believe what I say. Questions tempt you to tell lies, particularly when there is no answer.

Pablo Picasso

The doctors who were asking one question every 4.6 seconds (Box 11.9) were almost certainly asking limited, rapid-fire questions:

- 'What's wrong?'
- 'How did it happen?'
- 'How long have you had it?'
- 'How bad is it?'
- 'Have you had it before?'
- 'Do you smoke or drink?'
- 'Are you allergic to penicillin?'
- 'Can you take this prescription to a pharmacy?'

All these questions may generate important facts, but, on their own, they may not provide useful information without further careful enquiry. An HCP who gets into a yes–no question–answer session may not learn enough about a patient, and the patient may not be encouraged to open up with new and useful information. Closed questions tend to generate more closed questions, which take the participants down a narrow and pre-specified track. A narrow and pre-specified track may be exactly where part of the consultation should be heading, but only by specific intention, not by accident or default.

Difficult as it is really to listen to someone in affliction, it is just as difficult for him to know that compassion is listening to him.

Simone Weil

Not every patient will be able to respond usefully to open questions, and may require help or prompting, but this should still be done in a spirit of open questioning:

HCP: 'How can I help you?' *(Just about as open as a question can be.)*
P: [baffled silence]
HCP: 'What made you come here today?' *(This confines the area of questioning to the cause of the visit, but leaves open all response possibilities within that field.)*
P: 'It's my chest.'
HCP: 'Tell me what's worrying you.' *(As open a question as possible.)*
P: 'I have this terrible pain.'
HCP: 'I'm sorry to hear that. Where is the pain?' *(Sympathetic response, followed by the first specific question of the diagnostic investigation.)*

You can see that the HCP's first three questions are open in their form but progressively narrow in scope in response to the patient's ability and needs. Although some patients would simply have declared their chest pain after the HCP's first question, this one needs gentle prompting towards the main point. A similar pattern may apply to any aspect of a consultation.

Leading or manipulative questions

If you have never beaten your wife, the lawyer's unscrupulous question, 'Have you stopped beating your wife?' cannot be answered by yes or no, and the fact that you have never beaten your wife can be declared only by rejecting the assumption in the question. This may seem obvious, but it is a good example of the category of questions that have unscrupulous motives and require some intelligence, assertiveness and mental agility to answer.

The form of a question can exert pressure for a particular kind of answer ('You don't really believe that, do you?') and many people will find it difficult to resist the pressure to give the answer that seems to be expected, or which seems to promise approval or avoid disapproval. This kind of question puts a person into a position where to express their genuine opinion they would have to make an assertive effort to challenge the questioner but may not have the strength or ability to do so.

The largest category of this type is known as leading questions. These are questions where the desired or expected answer is wrapped up in the question, and demonstrate bias and pressure on the part of the questioner:

- 'You don't drink a great deal of alcohol, do you?'
- 'Do the children get at least two good meals a day?'
- 'Have you been taking the tablets exactly as I said you should?'
- 'You won't mind if I examine your breast, will you?'
- 'Can I take it that you've been having fewer headaches?'
- 'I'm sure you'll want to have the operation, won't you?'

The open forms of these questions are as follows:

- 'How much alcohol do you drink?'
- 'How many meals a day do the children have?'
- 'How have you been taking the tablets?'
- 'I need to examine your breast. Are you comfortable with that?'
- 'Have you been getting headaches more or less frequently than before?'
- 'Do you feel you want to have the operation or not?'

Tone of voice is an additional variable in determining the meaning and impact of a question and on the patient's freedom to answer openly.

Influencing memory and perception

There is a further remarkable effect from the way questions are formulated and the assumptions they embody: they can alter how reality is described or remembered.

We hear only those questions for which we are in a position to find answers.

Friedrich Nietzsche

The controversial issue of 'recovered memory' also relates closely to the methods through which information is sought: are memories reliably 'recovered' or can they be implanted by the nature of the investigation? ('The headlight' in the third example in Box 11.10 suggests that there was a headlight which the observer might have seen or missed, and therefore exerts pressure to claim recall of the headlight rather than admit missing it through stupidity or lack of attention.)

Box 11.10 Distortions

In Hargie's summary of research on questioning [59] he reports on research that showed:

- People who were asked the height of a well-know sports figure estimated that he was taller or shorter by a wide margin, depending on whether they were in the group asked how 'tall' or how 'short' he was (the same differential applied to the remembered length of a movie (how 'long' or 'short' it was)).
- In responses to the questions, 'Do you get headaches frequently, and if so, how often?' and 'Do you get headaches occasionally, and if so, how often?' – the reported averages were 2.2 and 0.7 headaches per week for comparable groups of subjects.
- In reviewing a short film of a motor accident, the question, 'Did you see the broken headlight' produced fewer uncertain or 'I don't know' answers than did the question, 'Did you see a broken headlight?'

This is a fascinating area of research which we cannot pursue in any depth here. These are the things we must remember:

- Every aspect of the formulation of a question, and the attitude of the questioner may influence:
  - — understanding of what the question means
  - — willingness to answer the question
  - — capacity to answer the question
  - — adaptation of the answer to what the question appears to mean
  - — adaptation of the answer to how the content of the question is interpreted (e.g. in relation to frequency, seriousness)
  - — adaptation of the answer to gain the approval of the questioner, or not to challenge the questioner
  - — accuracy or mutual comprehensibility of the answer.

Children, and those with learning difficulties are particularly vulnerable to the effects of leading questions, but everyone can be misled or manipulated by intended or unintended elements in the formulation of questions. In dealings with patients we have to make sure not only that we understand what they are saying to us but also that what they are saying is based on an accurate understanding of the purpose and terms of our enquiry, which itself does not damage or interfere with the truth as they see it.

Multiple questions – a string of questions following each other – can be very problematic in terms of getting good responses and should be avoided almost always. Take questioning through a slow, step-by-step progression, dealing with one aspect of each topic at a time.

You can tell whether a man is clever by his answers. You can tell whether a man is wise by his questions.

Naguib Mahfouz

Active listening, prompting, probing

This section includes issues closely relating to everything that has gone before in this chapter. They are linked here, because they are all ways to ensure that, once a patient has started to communicate, they continue to do so and in ways that are relevant and to the point.

Active listening

This involves clear demonstration of the fact that you are listening, through some or several of the techniques in Box 11.11.[60]

Box 11.11 Techniques of active listening

- maintaining visual contact (eye contact)
- head nodding
- furrowing the brow, narrowing of eyes or compressing the lips in concentration (not in scepticism or doubt)
- brief withdrawal of eye contact for absorption of information (a show of concentration such as indrawn breath, head tilted back)
- low-key, supportive or facilitating noises or phrases:
  - 'Uh huh'
  - 'Ah'
  - 'Mmmmm'
  - 'I see'
  - 'Really' (as a quiet statement of acknowledgement, or an expression of surprise, or, if appropriate, incredulity)
  - Changing body posture to one of greater concentration (e.g. elbows on desk, hands linked in front of mouth)
  - Being silent and still, giving space for reflection and formulation of ideas and answers.

All these actions will have a helping effect on the patient's fluency in telling a story. There is, however, one serious reservation about providing positive, encouraging feedback: should the respondent be more interested in giving you an answer that you approve of, than in providing the truth, then your active listening techniques may be seen as approval, rather than active listening, and so encourage the speaker to follow that line of thought even if it is not true. Your first nod of the head will confirm for the patient that you are listening and are happy with what you have heard, although what you have heard may have been a tiny experiment by the patient to see where you stood on the issue, an experiment that would have been abandoned in favour of another had you shown any degree of disapproval. People will often struggle to say what they think others want to hear, and will look for any clue being offered as to how they are doing, even unconsciously (remember the power of non-verbal behaviour and hidden motivation).

Active listening is important to demonstrate that you are paying attention, as long as your mind is calm and empty and you are really listening as well as giving the appearance of doing so.

What honour have we got left, when nobody is listening to us?

Abu Bakar Bashir

Prompting and probing

Prompting is the next stage beyond active listening, when the patient needs more active help to continue the story. In the discovery phase of enquiry, prompting should not take the patient off in a new direction but simply help them to complete what they have started.

These are examples of this kind of neutral prompt:

- 'So, what happened next?'
- 'When did your son get back from the hospital?'
- 'What did your husband say when he found out?'

- 'What happened after you were sick?'
- 'Did the headache come back again then?'
- 'This is important. Please carry on.'
- 'Don't be embarrassed. It's fine.'

Some of these could also be probing questions, but may also simply be helpful nudges to keep the story going.

Every clarification breeds new questions.

Arthur Bloch

Probing a patient's story really needs to come after the story has been told – because probing before the end may take the patient off somewhere new and make them forget the larger shape of what they wanted to say. (Remember the rapidity with which doctors interrupted patients in the study quoted in Box 11.9, 'Illuminating research'.) Probing questions are used to clarify and extend information.

Box 11.12 Probing question types

Hargie[61] lists the following kinds of probing questions, derived from an extensive review of research in the area:

- Clarification/informational probes ('Can you just tell me that again please?'; 'What exactly did you say happened after the accident?')
- Justification or accountability probes (seeking reasons or causes: 'Why was it you stopped taking the medicine?'; 'What did you do when the bleeding started?')
- Relevance probes ('Please tell me how that relates to your stomach pain'; 'How does you son's behaviour relate to your illness?')
- Exemplification (giving specific examples: 'Describe a recent occasion when you felt faint'; 'What are you doing when the pain in your back is at its worst?')
- Extension ('Tell me what happened next'; 'Did the pain get better or worse after that?')
- Accuracy ('Did you say five times a week?'; 'Exactly how many tablets have you been taking each day?')
- Restatement (repeating or rephrasing a question: 'Can I just ask you that question again, to make sure we understand each other . . .?'; 'Is this the question you want me to answer . . .?')
- Echo (repeating a telling word or phrase: 'You said like a hot knife in your brain?'; 'You said you were "terrified" of needles – can you tell why you feel that way?')
- Consensus (finding out if a view or fact is shared or agreed among more than one person: 'Do you both feel the same about this?'; 'Does you daughter agree with you?')
- Non-verbal (raising eyebrows; tilting the head and frowning).

Good probing is vital to achieving good, comprehensive information. It is a process against which there is some cultural resistance in normal relationships because of our wish to avoid seeming intrusive or presumptuous: most people protect sensitive information about themselves and tend to behave in ways that support the protection of others' privacy too.

HCPs must probe until they are satisfied that they have as full a picture as necessary and possible. For every HCP there will be a point when they feel that they are at a sensitive frontier – for themselves or for the patient. At that point the decision whether or not to pursue the issue needs to be made, and, in the event of going ahead, the tone and method need to be chosen to reflect both seriousness and delicacy. In doing so an HCP may have to express regret to the patient about the need to ask such personal or intrusive questions, explain the need for them, and help the patient to overcome such resistance as they may have to answering them.

It is the answers, not the questions, that are embarrassing.

Helen Suzman

Explanation

Diagnosis is not, of course, a communication skill, although it is dependent on expert communication in the gathering of fact and evidence to support it. But explanation of a diagnosis, or of a disease process, or of a treatment plan, and many other aspects of healthcare, all require great skill to explain effectively. They require the HCP to understand the topic clearly and fully, and to be very clear about the abilities and receptivity of the patient.

Many attempts to communicate are nullified by saying too much.

Robert Greenleaf

The purpose of explanation is to nurture understanding. In healthcare, its purpose may also be to lead to action or change of some kind, often adherence to treatment or other kind of plan (exercise or diet, for example).

Box 11.13 Effective explanation

Effective explanation involves at least these steps:
- identification of the topic to be explained
- mastery of the facts of the topic, and the logical structure of the topic
- clarity as to why the topic has to be explained; what outcome is desired?
- clarity about what minimal, essential information has to be explained
- assessment of the patient's general knowledge, beliefs, linguistic ability and existing understanding of the topic (including health literacy)
- explanation of why the explanation is necessary and what it is hoped to achieve
- the choice of a starting point that connects accurately with the patient's abilities and needs – a bridge from the HCP's world of assumptions, concepts, jargon and professional expertise leading exactly to a point of knowledge or experience in the patient's world which they recognise and can respond to
- awareness that the basic terms (language) in which the explanation is being given may not be clear to the patient (enzymes, virus, embolism, stroke and so on)
- clear, logical, progressive presentation of information (structure) in chunks that match the patient's ability to absorb and process them (pace and volume of information)
- use of printed or visual material to demonstrate or clarify the topic or aspects of it
- checking understanding on the way
- seeking feedback about the content and the process
- inviting questions from the patient about the content
- providing supportive materials that repeat or summarise the explanation for later review
- ideally, assessment/evaluation of the effect of the explanation in terms of adherence, action or change over time.

Facts which at first seem improbable will, even on scant explanation, drop the cloak which has hidden them and stand forth in naked and simple beauty.

Galileo Galilei

Most of us will remember one teacher or lecturer whose abilities at explaining were exceptional. Some of their characteristics were:
- the ability to stimulate interest and engage their audience
- the ability to relate a complex topic to familiar or simple aspects of life and to demonstrate the importance of the topic
- the use of anecdotes, metaphors, parallels and questions about familiar, related topics
- the building of a progressive structure of understanding, moving from the simple to the complex
- the active involvement of the audience in building the structure and anticipating the next stages
- enthusiasm and humour.

Good explanation, like all aspects of effective communication, is never routine: it is tailored exactly to the needs and abilities of the particular individual and the task in hand. Sharing knowledge through explanation, about even the simplest of facts or procedures, is a powerful way to establish good relationships and to build trust and confidence in patients. It is also an important way in which to build patients' knowledge and confidence in medical matters (Table 11.2).[62]

All HCPs, along with teachers, lecturers and almost every other professional providing service

Table 11.2 Health improvement processes and outcomes[62]

HCP	Patient	Outcome
Friendly, attentive, creates partnership with patient, encourages, is supportive, explains clearly	Tells own story clearly, is encouraged to ask questions, decide on treatment with HCP, and takes responsibility for own health tasks	Increases probability of positive health outcomes
Cool, distant, non-attentive, interrupts patient, has quick-fire questions, gives several instructions, offers several pieces of advice	Passive, does not ask questions, unduly deferential, superficially agrees to comply	Decreases probability of positive health outcomes

to the public, need to have well-developed skills in explaining. Patients and customers, experiencing critical events in their lives, need to understand what is happening to them if they are to have any measure of control, to make informed decisions, and to be participants and not victims. Good explanation is also a vital element in the extent to which patients will feel satisfied with their healthcare, with all the implications that has for adherence, optimism and general wellbeing (and, it has to be said, the avoidance of litigation).

Having the patience to explain is a sure sign of a great communicator.

Good luck needs no explanation.

Shirley Temple

Checking understanding and seeking feedback

This topic occurs repeatedly in this book, and cannot be emphasised enough as a critical element in effective communications of every kind: unless we have evidence from the audience about the receipt and effect of any communication, the process is incomplete; we can never be sure that the message has been received and understood as intended, nor that is has led to the action or change we hoped for.

Checking understanding needs to be carried out sensitively so that patients do not think their intelligence is being doubted. The checking can be presented, as indeed it really is, as a way of testing the effectiveness of the HCP's communication: 'I need to check that I've made this clear and haven't forgotten anything. Can you just tell me what you think I've said so I can be sure I haven't missed anything?'

The process applies to all communications of all kinds: if your recipient or audience hasn't given you feedback about your message, then you must ask for it. (For a discussion of user opinion and complaints, see Chapter 12.)

Box 11.14 Checking understanding

Done internally and silently or actively with the patient or audience it is achieved through these kinds of action and words:

- assessing the degree of understanding from levels of attention and non-verbal feedback, and from verbal responses
- asking if the message has been understood; 'Is that clear?'; 'Do you understand that?' This is the lowest and least satisfactory level of enquiry, because of a patient's possibly mistaken assumption that they have understood, or possible unwillingness to admit to not understanding, or because the patient wants to get home quickly
- asking for a repetition or rehearsal of the message:
  - 'OK. Please can you just tell me how you're going to take this medicine?'
  - 'Can you tell me in your own words what I've just explained?'
  - 'So what are the foods you must avoid while taking this?'
  - 'What do these test results show us?'
  - 'Can you tell me what has happened to your liver and what we need to do to help it recover?'
  - 'When are you coming back to see the surgeon? And where will you find her?
  - 'I want to be sure you'll know what to do: can you just show me exactly how you'll use it?' (e.g. blood-sugar monitoring device).

Summary

These, then, are core skills of effective professional relationships with patients:

- caring and helping effectively
- the exercise of empathy
- active listening
- accurate and purposeful questioning
- explaining
- checking understanding and seeking feedback.

Deployed with the warmth and compassion that are characterised throughout this book, the improvement of these skills will refine and enhance practice, and lead to mature, effective partnership relationships with patients and other audiences.

There is frequently more to be learned from the unexpected questions of a child than the discourses of men, who talk in a road, according to the notions they have borrowed and the prejudices of their education.

John Locke

12 Special communication needs and processes

This chapter discusses broad topics and circumstances (the impact of being a patient, bedside manner and home visiting, sustaining long-term relationships and motivation, for example) which require special consideration and communications. It provides a starting point for reflection and knowledge building across a wide range of essential topics, which are relevant, in one way or another, to most encounters with patients.

Being a patient

As a patient, you are putting yourself in the hands of others, seeking help from them, expressing need, making yourself vulnerable to their opinions and actions, and this can be extremely uncomfortable, embarrassing, upsetting or frightening for some people.[63] The large number of people, especially men, all over the world who postpone seeking medical help long after it is clear they are sick, indicates what immense psychological barriers there can be. Seeking help itself, at the same time as facing possibly distressing news, can create discomfort, shame and even dread.

Becoming dependent and vulnerable, and even more so putting your children in such a position, within a short consultation or when hospitalised, can have a dramatic effect on self-image and confidence, and can be a cause for stress and unhappiness. It can also precipitate dependence, dependent behaviour or regression (when people become more helpless or distressed than their age or maturity suggest they should), as well as other, less dramatic signs of discomfort or disturbance.

There is something in sickness that breaks down the pride of manhood.

Charles Dickens

The simple fact of being a patient, in itself, may be difficult for some people to live with, especially for self-sufficient, independent people. If the diagnosis is of a lifelong problem such as hypertension, diabetes or HIV, the impact may be much greater. In varying ways, such patients have to come to terms with a quite new view of themselves and their future and adjust to possible permanent status, as they see it, as a patient – as vulnerable and dependent (a deficient person?), reliant on healthcare for the rest of their lives.

At the other end of the spectrum will be those patients who easily accept the implied contract between HCP and patient, and responsibility for their own lives, without distracting responses and feelings.

Helping make the transition

Patients' needs for help in adjusting to their new situation will vary greatly. For each patient:

- the way in which they are received and attended to (their first impressions, especially)
- the sensitivity and accuracy with which their feelings and fears are dealt with
- how news is broken and handled

- the seriousness with which an HCP listens to their reactions

will have a big impact on their immediate and longer-term therapy and on their quality of life, even when symptoms or condition are minor.

Diagnosis of a relatively simple disease, such as genital herpes, following the anxiety of deciding to seek help in the first place, may have a devastating effect on someone who has seen themselves as responsible and 'normal', and lead them to a state of anxiety, self-blame, sexual dysfunction or depression. HCPs cannot work psychological miracles, but, on the other hand, they can avoid doing unnecessary damage by insensitive response to patients' reactions, however disproportionate they may seem.

Moderating patient responses

The HCP's job is to understand and accept the nature of the patient's response, relative to the patient's own personality and feelings and to their view of what society thinks (in as much as they are influenced by that); that is the first stage. If there is a disproportion between the intensity of the patient's feelings and the medical facts or the HCP's opinion (for example, extreme distress in response to a minor, curable infection) then the HCP has to recognise that the facts of the case may have very little influence in changing the patient's feelings about it. The facts may have some effect in moderating extreme emotion, but they may not deal with, that is necessarily reduce or banish, the basic emotional reaction, which is not based on the medical condition, but on feelings about the medical condition.

Such emotions (in relation to any kind of bad news, disfigurement, loss of capacity, becoming a long-term patient and so on) need to be expressed by the patient and accepted, listened to uncritically, by the HCP. The HCP's task is to help the patient slowly and sensitively along the path towards some degree of acceptance of the change in their situation and a response that will facilitate treatment and the recovery of self-confidence. That may very likely take time, several weeks or even months in some cases.

The HCP's communications are critical in all such situations, but there may also be more influential and important relationships and communications beyond the HCP. Websites, virtual communities, support groups, patient organisations and specialist clinics and counsellors all offer resources of support and reassurance for patients newly diagnosed and/or feeling anxious and isolated in their distress. With the usual reservation about the unreliability of much information on the internet,[64] any search engine will turn up many sites in response to entering the name of a single disease. HCPs can help their patients by pointing them in this direction, or to specific sites or resources that they know to be reliable and helpful. Few things provide more reassurance than knowing that one is a member of a wider community, especially at a time of vulnerability, encountering a disease or condition perhaps for the very first time. HCPs always need to be thinking about resources in the wider world and about continuity of support and care once the patient is out of sight.

Nothing illuminates the concerns of patients more than their own stories told to sympathetic outsiders. There is an extraordinary record of patients' experience of illness – both good and bad – with many additional resources at www.healthtalkonline.org. An hour or two spent immersed in that unique material may deeply influence your view of healthcare and the priorities in your own practice. A visit may also be a very reassuring experience for a patient. (There are many references to websites concerned with specific diseases in the notes to Chapter 16.)

Patients with disabilities

Nowhere in this book are the needs of patients with physical disabilities given the attention they deserve. This results from the author's sense of inadequacy in the face of so large and important a subject, and the impression that it needs a book in its own right. If able-bodied patients have multiple challenges in getting the best from healthcare, then those whose sight, hearing, speech, dexterity, mobility or other capacities are impaired in some way, have even more: not only the practical problems (reading, hearing, access and so on), but also the unhelpful attitudes, ignorance, prejudice, impatience and other failures in relationships which are all too common – the dis-abling effects of the social and physical world. HCPs need to study and understand this issue as it affects large numbers of people (perhaps 11 million in the UK, for example), and find ways of reducing inequalities and injustices.[65–68]

Key skills for communication with people with disabilities are, of course, those presented throughout this book for effective communication with everyone: in this case the most significant ones probably being the perception of individuals as whole people (not, 'disabled' people), putting aside stereotypes and prejudices, and accurate understanding of how the world looks and feels through the eyes of the patient.

Self-image

How we see ourselves and what we feel about ourselves – our self-image – is a fundamental part of our relationships with everything and of our hopes and fears about life in its entirety; it is the way we hold ourselves together and present something like a coherent performance in the world. (It is, by the way, something HCPs should spend some time examining in their own lives both during training for practice, and during the entire progress of it.) It is a large and complex part of our being.

A good man often appears gauche simply because he does not take advantage of the myriad mean little chances of making himself look stylish. Preferring truth to form, he is not constantly at work upon the facade of his appearance.

Iris Murdoch

Illness, disability, physical damage or loss, disfigurement or loss of capacity of any kind can seriously damage a patient's self-image, their confidence, optimism and capacity to function well. HCPs have a major role in helping patients come to terms with potentially negative change, to adjust their self-image to accommodate it, and to develop new ways of relating physically and psychologically with the world. This challenge takes the purposes of therapy beyond, for example, the comparatively simple restoration of mobility or the ability to communicate. It takes the HCP's role into some of the densest and most demanding of all communications processes.

Box 12.1 Aspects of self-image

These include:

- our appearance and how we feel about it
- our intelligence and physical capabilities and how we feel about them
- our capacity for relationships and sexual fulfilment and how we feel others feel about us
- how much we are loved and feel worthy of love
- our ability to work and earn money and how others rate us
- our possessions and how we want others to see us
- our inner desires and urges and how we feel about them and how far we can pursue them
- our feeling of confidence and social credibility and others' assessment of them
- our capacity for happiness
- our knowledge of our weaknesses and vulnerabilities
- our tactics, strategies, deceptions, survival manoeuvres
- our levels of hope and optimism
- our view of the purpose of life and the ethics it should manifest.

When I was born I was so ugly the doctor slapped my mother.

Rodney Dangerfield

HCPs need to consider their own self-image, too, both the personality they present to the world (the quality of relationships with superiors and juniors, for example, as well as with patients), and also their physical appearance and behaviour: who am I and how do I want others to perceive me? How can I best express in the external world the person I want to be in my professional life?

Patients and pain

The management of pain is one of healthcare's most important challenges. Patients' general morale and wellbeing, their levels of hope and their view of their HCP and their treatment, and especially their cooperation and adherence may be strongly affected by the degree and quality of pain they experience, and how well they feel it is understood and is being managed.

Here, we can deal with only a few key points in a complex and difficult area which has been researched and written about extensively elsewhere.[69] At London's Great Ormond Street Hospital for Children,[70] for example, extensive work has been done in finding out how to help children describe pain and how to manage it. In other places, similar studies have been done with babies and with those with severe mental disabilities and many other categories of patients. Patient organisations devoted to specific diseases also offer much knowledge and wisdom in this area.

Pain is real when you get other people to believe in it. If no one believes in it but you, your pain is madness or hysteria.

Naomi Wolf

Creative communications

What is apparent from these and many other projects worldwide,[71] is that, at the heart of this speciality, there needs to be great creativity in communications, especially in understanding a patient's pain and its meaning for them. Everyone has different attitudes to pain, different levels of tolerance, and each patient's experience of pain will be unique, even for the same disease or injury which an HCP may see frequently. Almost everyone is afraid of pain (sometimes more than death), and living with chronic pain can be deeply damaging psychologically for some.

Questioning is the primary skill in exploring pain. Here is a list of useful questions and probes, adapted from helpful material on Cancerbackup.org,[72] and applicable to pain in all situations.

Box 12.2 Investigating a patient's pain

The objectives are to discover:
- its location
- its characteristics
- its cause
- its nature and severity as felt by the patient
- its impact and meaning for the patient's daily life and mental state.

Questions to assist diagnosis

- Where is the pain?
  - Is it in one or more places?
  - Does it shift, move or spread at any time?
  - Is it near the surface or deep inside your body?
- What is the pain like?

Box 12.3 Pain descriptors

The following list of words may be useful to help a patient pinpoint how pain feels to them. The list could be adapted for any specific location or language and added to as patients find new descriptions that fit their experience:

aching, annoying, biting, blinding, blunt, burning, cold, colicky (varying but not intermittent), constant, cutting, crushing, dragging, dull, excruciating, frightful, gnawing, hot, hurting, intense, intermittent (comes and goes), mild, miserable, moderate, nagging, nauseating, niggling, overwhelming, piercing, penetrating, radiating, scratchy, searing, severe, sharp, shooting, smarting, sore, splitting, spreading, stabbing, stinging, tender, throbbing, tiring, unbearable, vicious.

For presentation to patients, the list would need to be designed in such a way as to be easily read and used.

- Is the pain similar to anything you've experienced before (toothache, cramps, migraine, burn, injury, etc.)?
- Is the pain constant? Does it come and go? Is it better when you sit still? Is it worse if you move around? Is it worse at night or in the morning? Does it keep you awake or wake you up?
- Does anything make the pain better or worse?
  - Do you feel better standing, sitting, lying down, walking?

- — Does warmth (a hot-water bottle, or taking a bath, perhaps) or an ice-pack help?
- — Does taking anything (food, drink, painkillers) help at all?
- — Do painkillers stop the pain or just reduce it?
- — Can you distract yourself from the pain by some activity you enjoy (reading, television, computer games, conversation)?

Perception of pain and impact on patient's life

- How bad is the pain? This is especially difficult to assess by any objective standard, because the experience of pain is essentially subjective. The starting point, therefore, is to try and make the description of pain as accurate as possible within the patient's own frames of reference.
  - — Compare with pain previously experienced (childbirth, period pains, back pain, sports injury and so on) and to discover how it compares in terms of severity and discomfort.
  - — Rate pain on a scale of 0 to 10, where 0 is no pain, and 10 is the worst ever experienced or imagined.
  - — Pain specialists have developed ingenious and effective rating scales for pain, in collaboration with their patients (children, for example), including scales of facial expressions and many more. There are large resources available on the internet, both information and visual and other materials.
- How does the pain affect your daily life? Does it stop you from doing particular things (bending, stretching, dressing yourself)? Does it stop you from sitting for long? Does it stop you concentrating or doing your work? Does it stop you walking or driving?
- How does it affect your morale and moods? Do you feel frustrated/angry/depressed? Is it affecting your family life and relationships? Do you feel that nothing can be done about it or that it will never go away?

Time to explore feelings

Patients need to be encouraged to explore and talk about their experience as much as possible, not only to contribute to effective diagnosis and treatment, but also to ensure their state of mind is understood and so they can see that the investigation embraces their whole person and the meaning of pain for them. An HCP's observation and interpretation of body language may contribute significantly to this process.

Some patients will be reluctant to admit to pain or to its seriousness, perhaps as a result of a 'grin and bear it' philosophy, or from the misguided notion that complaining about pain shows weakness. Such attitudes are probably commoner among men than women, but whenever they are evident, they need to be drawn into discussion of the legitimacy and importance of accurate characterisation of pain. Among other skills, an HCP needs to convey that the patient's admitting to pain and describing it are important for progress to be made, and for the HCP to fulfil their wish to reduce or eliminate it.[73]

Patients will often know little about the causes and characteristics of pain. HCPs may need to provide information about such things as referred pain; there is sometimes a lack of proportionality between severity of pain and seriousness of disease; conditions such as hyperpathia; and pain caused by stress and other psychological elements.

HCPs need to be alert to the psychological effects of pain, particularly to the risk of depression in chronic pain, and to the potentially disorienting effects of pain of any kind, and the effects of treatment. These are important aspects of the enquiry.

Pain management

Some patients will value pain management methods which give them direct control, responding to peaks of pain as they occur, rather than pre-determined dose schedules. When treatment is based on a series of pre-planned consultations, patients need to be encouraged to return as soon as pain recurs or becomes worse, irrespective of the schedule of appointments. Apart from the diagnostic priority of dealing with pain as it occurs, waiting in pain for the next appointment is a grim prospect. Patients need to understand that the HCP's primary wish is to keep them pain free. Some patients will choose pain over medicine, either on principle or because of unacceptable side effects; others will seek remedies that eliminate pain completely, whatever loss of function or clarity of mind may follow. All these issues require patient and perceptive enquiry.

Pain may profoundly affect morale, with associated risks of damaged family or work relationships. In such situations – as with depression – an HCP's own support and compassion, as well as practical measures (medication; referral (to specialists, HCPs in the community, or a pain clinic, for example); introduction to support groups and so on) will play an important part in helping patients live with pain or move towards recovery.

Researches tested a new form of medical marijuana that treats pain but doesn't get the user high, prompting patients who need medical marijuana to declare, 'Thank you?'

Jimmy Fallon

Bedside manner and home visiting

These two topics are paired because they may be relevant to almost any HCP, and because central to both is the idea of the patient's *territory*: in hospital, the tiny compass of their bed and its margins; at home, the physical centre and foundation of their lives. Visiting both these territories demands, among other things, thoughtful diplomacy and respect. Some of the psychological effects of hospitalisation are included in the discussion. ('Bedside manner' is often used to refer to an HCP's entire range of communications and relationship skills; here it is confined to interactions at a patient's hospital bedside.)

Hospitalisation and bedside manner

Patients in hospital are inevitably stripped of almost all the elements of life that provide a sense of identity, security and control:

- personal possessions and clothes
- preferred food and drink, activities, entertainment
- family and social contact (limited only)
- familiar, personal environment
- control, decision making, freedom to choose, including all aspects of physical activity
- the access of others to them
- movement.

They are largely within the control of individuals and a system that is strange to them, and are a very small part in a large and complex whole. They have a tiny piece of territory (their bed and its immediate surrounding area), where they have almost no freedom or autonomy, and no protective frontiers around them. They are psychologically and physically exposed, on show and vulnerable, with few of the defences that we all take for granted (controlling the access of other people into our territory, for example), and there is nothing but inner resources to express who one is (no clothes, accessories, jewellery, for example).

In addition, there are all the many and complex reactions patients will have to their diagnosis, treatment, level of pain, prognosis, use of communal toilet facilities and so on. Depending on the illness or injury, patients may be deeply depressed, anxious, frightened, bewildered, guilty – the whole range of human emotions. (See also 'Being a patient' above.)

Most patients will have a general understanding of how hospitals work, and what is required, and many will be grateful for the care they are getting. That does not mean, however, that they will understand the direct impact being a patient will have on their psychology, the discomfort and insecurity they may feel, or the behaviour they may display.

A hospital is no place to be sick.

Samuel Goldwyn

Psychological effects

One familiar manifestation of the unconscious response to the relatively helpless state of being a patient is dependence – the patient who more or less takes everything as it comes, agrees with everything and shows a reluctance for exertion or protest or for an end to the comfortable state of being totally cared for. Such patients are often valued as easy and cooperative, but their behaviour means that they may not be taking a truly active part in their treatment and recovery and may, therefore, not get well as quickly or thoroughly as they probably could. The long-term prognosis for such patients' general health is doubtful too, because they will not have learnt how to take responsibility for their own health and may become system-dependent – always looking for others to care for them rather than caring for themselves. This odd collapse into dependence can happen to apparently strong and independent individuals.

'Difficult' patients may be reacting to the diminishing of their usual identity or to the levels of their anxiety by, for example, asserting themselves strongly on even small issues – the only aspects of the hospital environment where they feel they have any chance of control or of expressing themselves. Some will sink into a state of passivity; others will react strongly against loss of identity.

Whatever the apparent response, all patients will be deeply affected not only by their illness or injury, and all that may mean for their lives and hopes, by levels of pain and so on, but also by the very fact of being confined to a bed in a hospital.

Bedside manners are no substitute for the right diagnosis.
Alfred P. Sloan

Supportive bedside manner

How they are treated as human beings in this strange situation, and the extent to which dislocation is understood and taken account of – that is, primarily through empathy and the quality of communications – will greatly affect their morale, their emotions, their behaviour and their health outcomes, for better or for worse. Bedside manner, therefore, is a matter of great importance.

Box 12.4 Bedside tips: verbal communications

- Use the patient's preferred name and style. This confirms and supports their sense of identity.
- When there are visitors or family members with the patient, greet them, include them; check if it is OK with the patient for them to stay; ask them to leave if you have good reason to do so.
- Introduce yourself and your role and restate them every visit until the patient knows who you are – among a dozen or more visitors, names and roles will not easily be remembered, especially by the elderly or confused; being dealt with by anonymous people (no name or role) objectifies and depersonalises patients as well as HCPs.
- Introduce others who may be with you.
- After greetings and introductions, use some simple, bridge-building opening questions, to establish unique contact with *this* person, such as:
  — 'How are you today?' (Do not say, 'How are we today?' unless there are two people in the bed)
  — 'Are we feeding you properly?'
  — 'Is everything OK? Are you comfortable in the ward?'
  — 'Oh! You enjoy reading? What's that one?'

Such remarks needs careful calculation in relation to the mood and character of the patient: for some patients such initiatives could seem intrusive or artificial; for some, they will be a welcome bridge between the whole person and the HCP.

- Move on to the purpose of your visit.
- Explain why you are there and what you need to do, and seek permission to do it.
- At the end, thank the patient.

Only kings, presidents, editors, and people with tapeworms have the right to use the editorial "we."
Mark Twain

Skilled professionals have a multitude of small techniques for putting patients at their ease, with different methods for different ages and personalities, all tailored to the particular individual. With children, for example, it may be preferable to sit on a chair or on the bed, or for the child to have some familiar toy or object to reassure them while the meeting is taking place. Although it may be 'your'

Box 12.5 Bedside tips: non-verbal communication

- Slow down as you approach a patient's bed; approach their small territory with respect, not like a whirlwind; knock if it is a private room.
- Adopt a position in which the patient is not dominated by your physical presence and/or can see you easily (it may be uncomfortable for a patient who is lying down to look at someone at the foot of the bed).
- Give them a few moments of genuine attention (accompanying the greeting and small talk with eye contact, listening and bodily stillness – not examining charts or writing notes as you do so).
- Speak and move calmly, so the patient does not feel that their space and person are being overwhelmed or invaded.
- Take notice of the objects the patient has on their bedside locker or on the bed: lots of gifts and cards? Or nothing personal? A photograph? A book? Food? Make a mental note of the meaning of what you see as part of your information gathering about the patient.

hospital, remember that, for a short while, the bed is the patient's territory and home.

Home visiting

Like behaviour at a patient's bedside, visiting at home requires careful management, especially with regard to recognition of and respect for private territory.

A person's home is a place of unique importance to them, about which privately they will have strong feelings of one kind or another. Exposure to visitors or strangers may prompt a range of feelings from pride to shame or embarrassment. However they may feel, home is a place in which they are normally secure and protected; intrusion by strangers can be uncomfortable and upsetting when the details of private life are detectable or on display.

Many people will be relieved and grateful to see an HCP at their front door, but may also be acutely self-conscious about exposure of poverty, inadequacy, lifestyle or taste, or untidiness of one sort or another. Visitors need to be very careful about their spontaneous reactions – to smell, for example, luxury, or dirt or disorder. There are two main things to think about in relation to this:

- Comments about the physical environment are hazardous if they are intended to draw attention to one positive aspect among many negative ones, however kindly the intention – the occupant may well see that the HCP is struggling to make the best of a bad job; unspoken but evident criticism may be offensive. Unreserved, positive reactions are probably acceptable, but even those imply that the HCP has the right to judge the environment and, by implication, the patient and/or their family.
- Few things are more revealing about a patient and their lives than their home environment: it is an important source of insight and understanding. Specific contributory causes to disease may be evident – alcohol on display, stress (keeping up appearances, for example, or tense relationships), lack of warmth or basic hygiene, damp, inadequate cooking facilities and so on. Some remedies may be possible through advice and encouragement, offered sensitively and non-judgementally; other solutions may require referral to other agencies, with the patient's agreement.

Box 12.6 Taking liberties

A community nurse, sitting for a time in the home of a comatose, terminally ill patient, whose palliative care she was supporting, read passages of the *Bible* aloud and sang some verses of Christian hymns. Unknown to her, this thoughtless act was to outrage the non-religious family when they heard about it, no less than it had upset the patient when he was aware of it, but unable to speak or protest. It was an act of unforgivably arrogant imposition of an HCP's personal values and beliefs on a vulnerable and helpless subject, made worse by the fact that it was in his own home and done without permission.[74]

Visitors' guide

Even on professional visits, the usual rules of hospitality and guest behaviour apply. In any one day, HCPs may need to deal with successive offers of food and drink as they go on their rounds; refusals need to show appreciation and gratitude, bearing in mind that the offer may be very important to the giver, and that, in some cultures, refusal would be seen as discourteous. For some people, the offer of something, however humble, may be an important symbol of their role and dignity as householders. Sometimes acceptance – even of unattractive offers – will be an act of kindness.

HCPs need to be as sensitive to the rules of the house, to cultural and religious habits and taboos, as they are anywhere else (see also Chapter 14).

Sustaining long-term relationships

Every day of their working lives, HCPs are required to make new relationships with strangers, in some respects (especially knowledge of the other person) covering ground which, in normal social relationships, might take weeks or months to achieve, although there are limits to the horizon of professional relationships (see below). In little more than minutes they have to present themselves convincingly as sensitive, capable and trustworthy, often with people they would never normally choose to spend time with, indeed, might well actively avoid. One of the greatest challenges of professionalism is being committed and useful to people with whom you may feel you have nothing in common (beyond the health reason for meeting), may even actively dislike.

Long-term relationships offer great challenges and possible rewards for patient and professional alike, whether in allied health roles or clinical practice. What follows are some of the issues for reflection and careful practice, and some of the risks.

Negotiating pace

In every aspect of the relationship, there may be differences between HCP and patient in perceptions of what the real situation is, what should and can be done, and the pace at which it should happen. This applies equally to the therapeutic activity itself and to the human relationship in which it takes place. Sometimes the patient will push the effort or the boundaries further or faster than the HCP feels is desirable; sometimes it will be the other way round; in both cases a negotiated agreement is necessary.

There is nothing more frustrating for a patient than to feel that less progress is being made than they want and feel is possible: in such a case the HCP must explain and justify taking things slower than the patient wants, or revise upwards their view of what can realistically be achieved and meet some of the patient's wishes. Managing a patient's impatience to make progress requires skill and a realistic assessment and explanation of risk.

Motivation

For some patients – young people keen on sports, for example – a programme of physical rehabilitation with the prospect of full recovery may be its own supreme motivator, with the therapist having only to provide the practical activities and the limits and cautions in the schedule. In that respect, the therapist will be more like a mechanic with a machine (because functionality is the top priority without other distractions), but there will, nevertheless, be many subtle personal and psychological aspects to such a relationship – restraining over-enthusiasm and impatience, for example. The relationship itself has still to be managed – the language used (appropriate for the individual); the tone of voice in which directions, explanations and advice are given; the way in which achievement is rewarded or misjudgements are corrected; the degree of authority exercised; the prudent management of pain; openness to negotiation and joint-decision making.

> To array a man's will against his sickness is the supreme art of medicine.
>
> *Henry Ward Beecher*

But there will be many patients, particularly those who have had a long and debilitating illness, for whom motivation may be the primary need. The inner urges which keep us all going, push us to make our decisions and choices, the things that give us hope and determination, are varied and complex – no two people are motivated by exactly the same desires and urges; no two people have the same levels of confidence, courage or tolerance, and such levels change within an individual from time to time. For medical or physical therapy to succeed, the HCP must understand just what it is that the patient wants to achieve, and how the patient's own barriers to that achievement can be overcome. What the patient wants to achieve may not at all be what the HCP thinks is best.

What keeps people going?

Although the details of our motivations differ greatly, there are some common elements for most people:

- the desire to be healthy and mobile, with functioning faculties
- the desire to do things and go places one wants, including working, earning and taking care of family, and enjoying a social life
- the desire for current problems, discomfort or unhappiness to diminish
- the desire to have good relationships with at least a few people.

Although these may seem obvious and simple, they do not necessarily lead to purposeful action and achievement. There are many potential obstacles and complications rising from the inner lives of people.

Box 12.7 Obstacles to progress

- Some people become stuck in an identity of illness or helplessness, even in the extreme form of consciously or unconsciously willing victim.
- Some will use illness or disability as the cover for avoiding work or other responsibilities.
- Some people's caution or depression or risk aversion makes them accept much less than they are capable of.
- The degree of hope for the future, at its profoundest level, will influence what people will commit themselves to and endure: how optimistic are they?
- The prospect of resolving even minor problems may be alarming to those whose lives have been built on the foundation of tolerating and managing problems; liberation (freedom) from problems can be alarming ('Who am I?'; 'What purpose has my life?'; 'What's to fill the time?')
- Some people will be discouraged by slow progress towards a result they desire.
- Some will accept sub-optimal results rather than endure discomfort or pain.
- Some will be so oriented to the present that long-term prospects will have little influence (this applies most obviously to addictions of one kind or another).

These last two relate to the trade-offs patients are willing to make: short term pain/long-term gain; short-term relief/long-term risk and so on.

If my doctor told me I had only six minutes to live, I wouldn't brood. I'd type a little faster.

Isaac Asimov

Encouraging progress

In the end, it is the patient's willingness, capability and levels of tolerance, hope and optimism that will determine progress, but the skilled HCP will be able to stimulate and facilitate willingness and extend capacity through the quality of their relationships and communications, up to the point acceptable to the patient, of course, and, perhaps, even beyond what they thought was possible.

The paradox of gains

An essential professional insight is that in gaining something valuable (a new ability, for example) a patient may also be losing something they are comfortable with (dependence or the indulgence of laziness, for example). The elderly woman who is taught to cook independently in her adapted kitchen may, at the same time, lose the comfort of having most meals cooked for her by her daughter – and fear that her daughter will visit less frequently as a result. The man whose life may be saved by surgery or therapy for prostate cancer may risk impotence in the future. The shy child whose speech impediment is gradually ameliorated may be frightened by losing the justification for or the habit of usually remaining socially passive. (Of course, such activities may, often do, have quite the opposite result – an excited embracing of change.)

These examples highlight one end of the communication skills spectrum, where the role of physical therapist touches or overlaps with that of a psychotherapist; where accurate insight into a patient's state of mind and emotions, and the ability to use that insight productively for the patient's benefit, will determine how successful the therapy is.

Box 12.8 The process of motivating patients

This involves:

- discovering what it is the patient wants to achieve (including the offer of widened horizons from the professional's experience)
- laying out the options for progress
- finding out what reservations the patient has about the options
- negotiating a plan (including likely timescales), which should meet the patient's wishes and overcome the problems
- anticipating problems and setbacks that could occur (which would be de-motivating if not anticipated)
- providing a framework in which progress can be measured and rewarded
- taking the programme step by step, at the patient's pace (although perhaps a little beyond it for those who can cope with such demands)
- maintaining a sensitive awareness of the effect of change on the patient's life and psychology
- measuring and rewarding progress (including comparing capacity at earlier stages)
- renegotiating the programme when unexpected variables intervene
- asking the patient to contact you a few weeks or so after therapy is completed to let you know how they are doing (continuity, compassion)
- celebrating the end result.

Disclosure

For some patients, regular meetings with an HCP they have come to like and trust will provide a welcome opportunity for conversation apparently unrelated to the task in hand; the personal and professional authority ascribed to an HCP, and the vulnerability induced by physical needs, may lead patients to seek advice, reflect on their problems, even to disclose personal issues. For some, regular quiet time with another attentive person will be a rare – if not unique – experience and may seem to offer the chance of comfort and reassurance not otherwise available in their lives.

The benefits of small talk

HCPs in all areas should not be afraid of so-called small talk: although the topics might sometimes seem small to an HCP in the midst of the dramas of medicine, to a patient, discussion of their pets or their hobbies or their child's school achievements or their garden (and especially evidence that an HCP has remembered some of these details of their lives from previous meetings), may have a profoundly therapeutic effect, reassuring and comforting a patient, and opening them ever more willingly to the influence and wisdom of their HCP. Some HCPs, such as nurses and physiotherapists, have more opportunity to enrich relationships with patients in this way, but it is a technique valuable for all.

The tendency to share information and feelings beyond the medical arena vividly demonstrates the patient's own sense of wholeness (at least of being more than just a patient), beyond the specific purpose of the relationship: 'I may have a broken hip/a speech defect/respiratory or dietary problem – but there's more to me than that.' Such a reaction is the natural response of a person who feels their identity is being limited, diminished to that of a labelled health problem, as well as an indication of personal and social need. When patients offer such aspects of themselves they should be acknowledged and valued, even if they are not followed up in any serious way. Most HCPs won't have much time for such exchanges, but their exclusion, for whatever reason, will diminish the patient and the relationship.

There will be some patients – those more confident, self-assured, perhaps better supported in their private lives – who may not feel this need and will be happy to focus exclusively on the task; many others – less confident or secure, more doubtful of their value and status – will want their personal credentials to be shared and acknowledged to a lesser or greater extent: 'I may be helpless and in pain just now, but in other circumstances I have a tough and busy life and am good at what I do.'

Box 12.9 Patient as object

> One of the most dramatic ways in which patients can be depersonalised is through reference to them solely by their diseases:
>
> 'The gallbladder in bed 23.'
>
> 'Where's the prostate disappeared to?'
>
> 'So you're the new myocardial infarction!'
>
> These result from acceptance of the one-dimensional, disease frame of reference, and that stifling of identity and set of values becomes confirmed as it is passed from one HCP to another. Only slightly less offensive than these are the use of an untitled surname ('Lee?'; 'Singh?') and some of the deeply patronising expressions, such as, "How are we today?' or, 'What did the doctor tell us about eating chocolate?'

Responding empathetically and effectively to this profound need, while not entering an intense and distracting engagement with the patient, requires delicate handling, not least because of the risks of wounding a vulnerable patient and of therefore damaging the therapy in progress.

Disclosure by HCPs

On the whole, HCPs need to exercise restraint in disclosing aspects of their own lives, because promoting one's own feelings, interests or views is largely irrelevant and distracting, except when it is judged important to demonstrate shared, common humanity with a patient, or to refer to some topic of mutual interest. The patient who claims their HCP cannot possibly understand just how dreadful is their suffering or disease may be helped with at least an indication that the HCP has another life in which they may suffer too. 'Even doctors have feelings, you know, and bad things happen to them too.' Occasionally, it may be right to go further: 'I lost my son in an accident three years ago, so I do have some idea what you might be going through.' (Note: 'some idea', 'might' – not: 'I know what you're going through.')

Complaints about an HCP failing to grasp the intensity of a patient's feelings or suffering may arise from failure to give a response that demonstrates real empathy, so leaving the patient with the impression that the HCP has missed the point and has neglected their need. Personal disclosure by the HCP may be a useful technique for overcoming such a problem, but it is much better to deal with it through the sensitivity and strength of the reaction to what the patient has said (after all, no HCP can ever have experienced first hand everything that their patients endure). Sometimes, it may be better to remain reflectively silent in the face of a patient outburst: 'How can you possibly know what it feels like to have cancer?' Alternatively, 'I can't, of course,' is a sound response if it is accompanied by assured professionalism: 'I can't, of course, but you must tell me what it's like and I will do my best to understand it and help you manage it.'

Attachment

Patients may become very attached to their HCPs, and the best HCPs often become attached to their patients, too. Far from being a problem, this can greatly enhance the benefits of the relationship for both parties, on the condition that neither is deluding themselves that this is anything other than a professional relationship, which has specific, limited purposes, and, in most instances, will come to an end. Patients may develop a degree of dependence on their HCPs, but that has to be explicitly moderated and managed as a temporary phenomenon, a stage on the way to separation and independence for the patient. HCPs who are over-dependent on their patients, or who make their patients over-dependent on them, may, between them, hold progress back, reduce expectations, and set inappropriately low goals, in order that the relationship can be prolonged.

> The . . . patient should be made to understand that he or she must take charge of his own life. Don't take your body to the doctor as if he were a repair shop.
>
> *Quentin Regestein*

The dangers of dependence

To meet their own psychological needs, some HCPs encourage dependence in their patients. This is ethically unsound because it diminishes the patient's capacity for independence and self-determination, and it risks damaging the patient who will, in the end, inevitably, find that the HCP cannot deliver the degree and intensity of support that seems to be promised. Such dependence on an individual also compromises relationships with future HCPs. In their gatekeeping capacity, HCPs often have to refer their patients elsewhere, and such transfers can be problematic for patients themselves who have become over-attached to one individual (and problematic for successive HCPs). Strong, vigorous, even intense relationships are fine, but they must be conducted in the mutual knowledge that they are temporary, or are likely to be so. Managing endings is a further skill in this area (Box 12.11).

Communication is a continual balancing act, juggling the conflicting needs for intimacy and independence. To survive in the world, we have to act in concert with others, but to survive as ourselves, rather than simply as cogs in a wheel, we have to act alone.

Deborah Tannen

The professional boundaries

The provision of help and therapy mediated through relationships is a complex phenomenon: it has, and must have, many of the attributes of intimate, personal relationships (trust and commitment, for example), but it is not an intimate personal relationship and mature patients usually do not want it to be so, although they might sense its potential to go in that direction in other circumstances. What they want is a relationship that is effective in dealing with their problems, with all the qualities that requires, but only to the limit of their specific medical and human needs. Helpers or HCPs who go beyond those needs may trespass on unauthorised territory and upset, offend, alienate or even damage their patients.

Box 12.10 Ambivalence

This is the term for mixed, conflicting or contradictory feelings. Its influence is important in many aspects of healthcare, no less than it is in the rest of our lives.

At its extreme, ambivalence may mean having completely opposite or contradictory feelings, simultaneously or sequentially, in relation to a person or a choice of some kind: love and hate; repulsion and attraction; commitment and alienation. Some of these apparent paradoxes seem to be natural constituents of being human (such as transient sadness or depression): those we love the dearest will sometimes be the objects of our intense frustration, anger, fear, even hatred. These feelings can be difficult to live with if the essential relatedness of opposites is not understood (light and dark; up and down; front and back; joy and sorrow and so on. This is a philosophical conundrum, which we cannot pursue here.)[75]

Patients will often have a very specific set of ambivalent feelings about disease or therapy:

- wish for relief from disease and fear of therapy
- protection of privacy and wish for disclosure of troubling issues
- keeping up appearances and wanting to admit vulnerability
- wishing to be strong and seeking submission or dependence
- disliking or distrusting healthcare or hospitals or HCPs *and* needing their help.

In relationships with patients, HCPs need to be sensitive to ambivalence, to understand its elements, to acknowledge and discuss them, to negotiate and provide support in the aspects that are obstructive to progress and achievement of the patient's primary wishes. On occasion, it may be difficult to overcome the effect of the negative side of ambivalence, and necessary to negotiate or wait or to find alternatives that stimulate less obstructive feelings or provide less painful choices. Having mixed or contradictory feelings is essentially normal.

From time to time you will be ambivalent about your work or your patients, hating and loving it and them; resenting demands, enjoying rewards; feeling disdain for patient stupidity and compassion for their suffering – many combinations of contradictory feelings. As long as the negatives are secondary, occasional and transient, then you are probably more or less normal. If the negatives come to predominate, then there is a problem that needs dealing with by a change of attitude and disposition or change of job.

Some HCPs and patients do become friends, but that is a quite separate and explicit development. HCPs and patients should not play at being friends (or be flirtatious or provocative) within the professional relationship: the balance is always towards the meeting of the patient's needs, not the pursuit of improper selfish or mutual social gratification.

Box 12.11 Managing endings

How the parties feel at the end of a relationship, however brief or lengthy, is an important aspect of the total picture and will have some impact on future feelings and behaviour, especially for the patient. A patient leaving a consultation of any kind in a positive and confident mood will pay far more attention to what has been learnt than one who feels they have just been dismissed from a soulless production line.

Badly managed endings of longer relationships (at the end of treatment, or because of transfer to another HCP, for example) may leave a patient with feelings of disappointment, resentment or even rejection. These feelings may negatively affect future relationships, adherence or general wellbeing. Endings do, therefore, have to be actively managed, for the HCP's comfort, too. This requires an understanding of how the patient is feeling, acknowledgement of those feelings, and some negotiation of them – clarity, for example that the ending is not because the HCP does not like the patient or is bored with the relationship. At its simplest, an HCP's message might be something like this:

'Well, I'm sorry we won't be meeting again, but my usefulness for you is really at an end now. I've enjoyed knowing you, but I know you'll find [name of another HCP] kind and helpful, and she's the person you need now. Let me know if you have any problems, and best wishes for the future.'

In other circumstances, reviewing the achievements of the past and looking hopefully to the future is a positive way of rounding off a relationship. For very insecure or vulnerable patients, and especially those who are mentally disturbed, the end of a valued relationship may be traumatic and require very sensitive handling.

The endings brought about by death are discussed in Chapter 21.

Revision, discussion and application (4)

A. Revision and discussion

1. In relation to the seven core concepts and skills in Chapter 11, what do you think are the most psychologically challenging aspects of all of them for becoming an effective HCP? Is there one (or more) which really overrides the rest in importance or do they all have an equal first place? Is there an implicit hierarchy leading from a single concept? How do the skills and values of an HCP in one of the areas affect their performance in others? How is it possible to train new entrants in these skills?
2. Review and describe some of the challenges and pitfalls in questioning. What characteristics of questioning risk not stimulating reliable answers? What psychological elements in questioner HCPs and questioned patients can cloud and compromise the process of gathering and giving good information?
3. Why are checking understanding and seeking feedback so crucial to good communications? Why are these processes so often neglected?
4. In reviewing Chapter 12, what do you see as some of the major kinds of psychological vulnerabilities patients have when they are exposed to HCPs and healthcare? What are the ways in which behaviour and communications can be tailored to address and reduce the vulnerabilities? What are the risks of not taking account of the vulnerabilities?
5. Examine some of the things that motivate you and others around you in different circumstances: how far do you and others share the same motivation in living, seeking pleasure, in relationships and so on? What, if any, are the motives common to most people, and what are some of those which are less familiar and common? What motives do you find among patients in relation to their healthcare?
6. Why is the concept of a patient's *territory* so important in healthcare? What are the ways in which possessive territorial behaviour can be a great stumbling block to collaboration and good service?

B. Application

1. How far do plans for helping patients in your place of work really take account of what patients want and of the long-term consequences of help? Can you think of positive and negative examples of how patients were helped and analyse what was good and bad about them? What pointers are there for good practice in this area?
2. If you can find the time, and a suitable and willing patient, test your skills of listening, observation and empathy more intensively and extensively than you might usually do, and see how quickly and effectively you can come to an understanding of the patient's experience and feelings. Observe

what information you might have missed in other circumstances, and compare your overall knowledge of the patient with what would have resulted from a more superficial encounter.

3. Experiment with careful formulation of questions and active listening, even in very short encounters with patients. Try to develop techniques for gaining essential information quickly and effectively, while still leaving the patient space to choose the direction of the conversation.
4. Pay particular attention to the psychological impact of becoming a patient or of being hospitalised. Identify the effects on patients and their reactions, and develop techniques and communications for supporting patients' dignity, independence and self-image.
5. If you have, or know of, patients who are overly dependent on you, other HCPs, or the facility in general, try to analyse and understand what is driving them and develop some techniques for discussing their problems and alleviating them for patients and you.
6. Observe the ways in which some patients may try to assert their personal and social wholeness in a healthcare setting (in small talk, gift-giving or other ways), and develop ways of responding thoughtfully and helpfully, while still maintaining time limits and sensible boundaries for the relationship. Observe what impact this level of contact may have on patients and on their response to healthcare.

Commentary on many of the questions and issues appears on the publisher's website, in Online Resources at www.pharmpress.com.

Part F

The complexity of humanity

The first chapter reviews many different aspects of human needs and experience, especially those that are problematic or atypical in some way with regard to psychological state (depression, anger, stress and phobias, for example). The discussion provides both basic knowledge and indications of how HCPs can shape their communications to respond most effectively to some of the more vulnerable and difficult people they will meet.

The second chapter provides a brief overview of some of the important issues raised by ethnic diversity. It examines many aspects of communications with patients whose ethnic or religious identity may be critical in shaping expectations and relationships, but much of the material is also relevant to most people and to most patients.

We need to reach that happy stage of our development when differences and diversity are not seen as sources of division and distrust, but of strength and inspiration.

Josefa Iloilo

13 The diversity of patients: disturbances and dysfunctions

This chapter provides a brief examination of some of the most difficult emotional states and disturbances that patients may display (anger, stress, depression, for example). It provides a starting point for reflection and knowledge building across a wide range of essential topics that are relevant, in one way or another, to most encounters and communications with patients.

The personalities and problems of patients have an important impact on their communications needs. The categories in this chapter (such as individuals who have been abused or are aggressive or depressed), are rather artificial because no individual falls exclusively into only a single category (although there may be a predominant condition), and within every category there is great individual variety. Every reader will probably think of further groups, and wonder why they are not here, or feel that the ones included are not dealt with in sufficient depth. This is a starting point only.

The material risks providing over-simplified categories, perhaps even stereotypes, and such labels tend to distance individuals from us, rather than highlighting the commonalities, which may in fact be more important. That is the first reservation.

The second is that there is a large body of literature, for example, about the experience of mental illness and depression, and the material here cannot do justice to the state of contemporary knowledge in those and other fields. These communications signposts will be helpful starting points.

Here is the short agenda:

- the impact and meaning of abuse
- anger and angry patients
- aggression and aggressive patients
- depressed patients
- mentally ill patients
- patients under stress or in crisis
- the worried well
- difficult patients.

I didn't know what to do about life – so I did a nervous breakdown that lasted many months.

Margaret Anderson

The impact and meaning of abuse

Victims of abuse

Several meanings of abuse are relevant to our communications concerns, illuminate the reactions and behaviour of some patients and give us clues as to what we should and should not do and say, and how we can help.

Abuse in childhood

Large numbers of people are or were abused as children, physically, sexually, emotionally. This can leave people with a legacy of emotional damage, which affects their relationships, hopes, health and a great deal more.[76]

For some people the triggering of memories of abuse can be deeply disturbing – even dangerous, if the original trauma has been repressed and has not been dealt with. It is very risky territory for careless or insensitive interventions.

Box 13.1 Abuse

Among the effects may be:
- suspicion or fear of other people, perhaps those reminiscent of past abusers (dominant males, predatory females, etc.), or just of strangers, resulting in what seem like inappropriately hostile, neutral, passive or irrational responses
- unwillingness to trust the good intentions of others
- anxious, even phobic reactions to being touched by strangers or by anyone
- a deep sense of guilt or shame at what they may have come to regard as their complicity in their humiliation (often the case in sexual abuse)
- little understanding of how mature human relationships work or can be found and sustained
- problematic or non-existent sex lives
- a sense of helplessness, of inability to take charge and maintain control
- an abiding sense of anger at their victimisation
- adopting the techniques and behaviour of their abusers, becoming abusers themselves, or dealing with the world in a hostile, defensive or irrational way.

Common humanity

Although those who have suffered terribly as children may show quite extreme versions of some of these reactions, not everyone who has been abused does so, of course. What you may notice also, is that each of the items on this list of reactions to suffering, are on a spectrum which is familiar to almost all of us: our psychology is not necessarily different in kind, but different only in the extent and intensity of the damage done and to which we have the feelings – of insecurity, suspicion of others, self-doubt, uncertainty about sex and so on. Nevertheless, it may be the case that some human experiences are so extreme that it is impossible for others to get close to understanding their reality and impact. Empathy, imagination and art are probably the most promising avenues for understanding. The lasting effects of abuse can trigger the collapse of normal coping mechanisms and cause people to fall through the fragile net of control or ability to manage.

You will get some understanding of patients from explicit information. As you build relationships of trust, patients will tell you more. But you also need to have the ability to register vital clues.

- If a patient is seriously disturbed by being touched, or by removing their clothes in a strange place, then you must:
  - — Acknowledge their distress and regret that you are the necessary cause of it (agree to hold off altogether for the time being, if the response is intense).
  - — Explain very simply and carefully exactly what you have to do and why you have to do it; explain any likely level of pain or discomfort; provide realistic reassurance.
  - — Explore if there are ways of reducing the distress for them (adequate privacy to undress; no risk of interruption; adequate covering for the naked body; choice of same or opposite gender for examination; presence of a third party (same or opposite gender) at any stage).
  - — Constantly seek feedback from the patient about how they are feeling, if they want the procedure to pause, if they need a drink of water, etc.
  - — Talk to them quietly and reassuringly throughout the process.
  - — At the end, thank them and express your appreciation of their cooperation.

This process may take time, but it will not take half as much time as a brisk or insensitive approach which causes the patient to have hysterics or to leave and never return. It is part of the immense process of educating patients, reassuring them and familiarising them with best practice, so that, in the future, they may be less anxious and less demanding to treat. At the heart of what is described here as suitable for a difficult patient, is also, of course, a model of good practice for any patient.

If you have a patient who is truly phobic about being touched, with whom you cannot make progress through quiet, patient discussion of the situation, then you may have to engage the help of a professional counsellor or a psychiatrist. True phobias (rather than anxiety or embarrassment or reluctance) are not amenable to ordinary methods of persuasion: the phobic person really is victim of something beyond their voluntary or conscious control.

You may need to take account of whatever lies behind the nature of a patient's responses, particularly if:

- it makes it difficult to gather information for an accurate diagnosis
- it makes it difficult to understand the patient's lifestyle and associated risks
- the patient is distant, disengaged or non-committal about any aspect of the exchange between you
- you feel you are not 'getting through'.

From time to time, HCPs will be aware of children among their patients who are victims of current abuse of one sort or another. This is so complex and special a problem, and such an enormous social issue, that it is not discussed here.[77]

Domestic violence and abuse

Accident and emergency departments, clinics and pharmacies see endless evidence of domestic violence in their patients. It is usually men abusing women, but sometimes women abusing men, and there are many cases of men or women abusing children or elderly relatives. Institutionalised elderly people and those with mental illnesses are sometimes abused and mistreated too. Abuse is not always violent, physical or sexual, although evidence of psychological tyranny is less likely to present itself explicitly to health workers. Human behaviour is often much worse than we might expect, and we must be alert to the clues.

Knowing what to do

Any healthcare organisation, a lone practitioner or isolated pharmacy, needs to have a clear policy on what to do when there is direct evidence or strong suspicion of any kind of domestic violence or abuse. In many places there are strict, statutory requirements with regard to the reporting of suspected abuse, and although there may be no choice in what action is taken, the way in which it is taken and the associated communications may have a considerable impact on the process and the outcome. With the ethical imperative of protecting the welfare of patients and trying to treat not just the symptoms but the causes of their illness or injury, those who are at serious risk, perhaps even of death, cannot be ignored. (There are some cultures – especially where male 'macho' behaviour is common – where these issues are much more complicated, even dangerous for outsiders to interfere in.)

Although discreet and non-judgemental enquiries can be made, the communications associated with domestic violence are very fragile and demanding, and may, ultimately, end in some measure of conflict, if discussion is permitted at all. The issues with regard to the abuse of children are even more critical, with less room for negotiated outcomes if a child is under any kind of serious threat.

At the extreme, the policy of your organisation or jurisdiction may demand that you inform the police or the social welfare agencies. There is probably no way of communicating this in a way that makes it an acceptable message to any of the parties (although some victims may be relieved that someone is intervening), but you should at least make it clear why you feel you have no choice, and be firm in stating your responsibility for the patient's safety and welfare.

This is a large and complex area of human behaviour and psychology. There are rich resources available for its study.[78–80]

Anger and angry patients

This section provides a basic account of anger, which will help you understand more about your own emotions and about those of patients in many different circumstances. It also provides ways of dealing with anger when it becomes a problem. The challenges of dealing with angry and aggressive patients follow.

The nature of anger

In humans, anger is an intense, basic reaction to frustration, threat, disappointment, the defeat of urgent or significant urges or wishes; evident in babies from a very early stage, and in people of all ages, from brief flashes of anger to wholesale tantrums; an effective and important reaction to any threat to survival or integrity; dangerous and destructive when managed badly or repressed. It differs from being irritated or hurt in that its drive is to destroy or get even with its cause.[81]

Productive anger is caused by and may be a mechanism for counteracting injustice, deceit or wilful error, for restoring order, and seeks to change or remedy the cause; such anger is a spur to change, reform, even revolution. Unproductive, unhealthy anger lashes out at the nearest object or person that provides a 'trigger', without reason or intention (this is often stored or repressed anger that hasn't been expressed directly towards its cause). Everyday, average anger results from being frustrated in one's hopes or plans or feelings by some event or person, where there may or may not be attributable blame or provocative intention (late trains, empty fridge, car fails to start, etc.).

Anger is one of the signs of the vitality of one's inner life, one's alertness to threats of any kind to the comfort and security of one's life and the lives of others. Anger is a mechanism of self-protection, of marking the boundaries, demanding recognition, respect and acceptance, even indulgence occasionally.[82]

'Anger management' has become the topic of training courses, because everyone falls somewhere on the spectrum between the extremes of violent, uncontrolled anger and apparent absence of anger, and there are lots of points at both ends of that spectrum where dealing with anger, expressing and communicating it in ways that are useful and healthy, are real problems for many people. Anger, real or assumed, can be used: to oppress and intimidate people; as a mechanism of control; as a distraction from real problems; as a means of asserting dominance; as a means of gaining attention. But it can also be used productively as a means of challenging lazy thinking, poor practice, sloppy procedures; of 'waking people up'.

To communicate with each other, we got to get mad at each other sometimes.

Hal Holbrook

Managing anger

The simplest advice for HCPs and patients for positively managing anger is: when you're angry, express the feeling in a way that is:

- honest but not disproportionate or destructive
- directed to the person(s) and in the situation where the anger was provoked, or as soon after as possible
- limited to the exact cause (not generalised by wounding assertions such as: 'Typical of your whole approach. . .'; 'Trust you to get it all wrong. . .')
- productive and less intimidating
  - — being protective and moderate, by expressing the fact that you are angry, but not being angry or acting it out – separating feeling from behaviour ('This really makes me angry: can't we sort something out?')

Then:

- accept that the other person may be hurt or angry in response and may have good reason to be; give them space to express their feelings
- take careful steps to avoid recriminatory escalation
- try to move to a discussion of the cause and the reasons for your anger
- listen to what the other person has to say
- seek some negotiated result or resolution
- postpone further discussion if feelings on both sides are heightened.

Afterwards, review your feelings and your behaviour:

- was your anger justified?

- was the expression of your anger proportionate to the event/intention and the object of your anger?
- was the selection of your target just and fair?
- did your management of the situation change things for the better?

This thinking applies as much to the management of your children, as to relationships with colleagues, subordinates or patients – or with anyone.

Positive expressions of anger, which may or may not include angry behaviour:

- 'I'm really very angry about this, after all the time we've spent . . .'
- 'How could you let us down so badly after we listened to you and let you get on with the job?'
- 'Going round in circles like this makes me angry and frustrated; can't we move on?'
- 'This whole situation has made me very angry: you promised me a system that would work and we've had nothing but trouble.'
- 'Angry? I bloody well am angry – you've just put the reputation of the whole organisation at risk.'

Man should forget his anger before he lies down to sleep.
Mohandas (Mahatma) Ghandi

Destructive anger

Expressing anger at work or home is useless and destructive when:

- You are on a short fuse because you are tired and under pressure.
- You are irritable and volatile because you had a bad night, or a bad start to the day, or because your baby vomited on your best suit.
- You are angry with peers or subordinates (or family) because you are actually angry with your boss.
- You have got a hangover and it seems as though the whole world is trying to make your life intolerable.
- You are in a personal corner and are fighting for your survival.

When you get angry with people for any of these fragile reasons, then apologise: it happens to everyone sometimes, and the remedy is simple – explain and apologise. You'll be forgiven. Best of all, recognise the inappropriateness of the feeling before it is expressed, and head in another direction.

Some people have so much anger in them that it precipitates them into violence or mental illness. Anger is a potent ingredient which, stored and denied and accumulated, can distort and damage the personality and almost certainly lead to physical illness, too. (Apathy may be an expression of extreme repressed anger.)

'Healthy' anger dissipates once it is expressed, once it is out in the open; mature people let go of their anger once it is expressed, they don't cling to it, revel in it, return to it, prolong it uselessly or hold grudges.

Anger with patients

There are probably very few occasions when it is appropriate to be overtly angry with patients, because short-term healthcare relationships do not really confer the rights of authority and familiarity that expressions of acceptable personal anger require. Anger is an assertion of power that is more likely to damage a patient's confidence or motivation than enhance them in a relationship that is already, to some extent, unequal. Expressions of frustration or disappointment as levers to bring about change in patient attitudes or behaviour may be appropriate, but even they need to be used with caution: there is usually so little time to recover from the negative impact of such feelings and to rebuild the collaboration.

Angry patients

Managing someone else's anger is as challenging as managing one's own, and equally important for professionals. If you already understand the issues in the section above, then this process will be much easier.

Causes of patient anger

What are some of the characteristics and vulnerabilities of patients that might make them prone to anger? (Remember anger can be a mechanism for

Box 13.2 Managing others' anger

The rules are simple:

- Register the anger of others as soon as it reveals itself; exercise empathy – what's behind this? Take it quietly and seriously.
- Take a quiet, deep breath and control and erase any negative, hostile or angry feelings that might have entered your consciousness.
- Relax your muscles and do not express tension or fear (clenching your fists or jaw, for example).
- Listen carefully and give serious, neutral attention (stillness; eye contact; attentive facial expression of concentration).
- Verbally acknowledge the anger and its degree of intensity; use the person's name if possible.
- Express regret that the patient feels there has been cause for anger.
- Do not express an opinion as to the rights and wrongs of the situation (not yet).
- Ask what the patient would like you to do; offer options (explain to you; speak to someone else; see another doctor/pharmacist; get a second opinion; send a complaint to the boss).
- Take it calmly from there (chances are the level of anger will already have reduced – because it has been recognised and taken seriously).

responding to threats to one's security and integrity.)

- They are in a strange, perhaps frightening environment (strange or formal environments heighten almost everyone's anxiety levels).
- Control has been largely taken out of their hands.
- They may be deeply worried about their illness or their child's or parent's.
- They may have difficult, pressurised lives outside and have been kept waiting.
- They may have memories of previous bad medical experiences.
- They may have been dealt with briskly or unsympathetically.
- A relative or friend may just have been injured or have died.
- They may feel their poverty or illiteracy or scruffiness exposes them to comment or ridicule.
- They may be deeply embarrassed by their disease or its cause.
- They may feel they have not been given the quality of attention or treatment they need or deserve.
- They may be struggling to manage their family, their finances or their primary relationship.
- They may have had an angry dispute at home.
- They may be homeless or jobless, feeling helpless and out of control.
- They may be withdrawing from drugs or alcohol, or be suffering their after-effects.
- They may have been kept waiting to see you for an unacceptable length of time.
- You may not be the HCP they were scheduled to, and expected to, see.

All aspects of disease, medicine, hospitals, drugs and so on, can make some people anxious or irritable. It can take only the trigger of some perceived discourtesy, an unreasonable wait, a sharp word, continuing uncertainty, postponement of an appointment or operation, to let loose a patient's frustration or disappointment in the form of anger.

Acknowledging anger

If we take anger as often a cry for help or attention:

- 'Take notice of me!'
- 'Am I invisible?'
- 'I'm being made to feel unimportant!'
- 'Why don't you all take me seriously?'
- 'Useless staff and stupid rules are just getting in the way of helping me!'

Then the obvious, and most important thing to do: take notice of the person, pay attention to them, listen to their problem. Even if you can do nothing to solve the problem (and that's rarely the case), then say how sorry you are that they're feeling angry and upset.

Saying you are sorry that someone is angry or upset does not mean that you are apologising for the cause of their anger.

Anger that is managed early on is less likely to escalate into serious problems, complaints, a public fuss or violence. And, even more positively, finding out the things that make patients angry gives you important information about how the quality and nature of your service affect patients, and what you can do to improve (see Chapter 23 'Complaints').

Aggression and aggressive or violent patients[83]

Aggression is a fundamental characteristic of most animals, especially males; a qualified benefit in terms of progress and social development, but a serious problem among colleagues and patients. Aggression may, at times, have its virtues, but usually when it is applied to tasks or objectives rather than to people: aggressive marketing, for example.

Aggression (in the sense of the wish to dominate, overcome or destroy others) can take many forms: competitiveness, bullying, oppression or unfair treatment of individuals or groups, over-regimented or controlling systems, shouting and intemperate behaviour, cynicism, ridiculing people, physical violence itself and a host of other manifestations. Many of these are common in institutions of all kinds, and in many private homes.

Sometimes the aggression is naked and unambiguous; at others it is hidden and insidious. Aggression is not always loud or obvious. Either way, it is demonstrated by the behaviour, communications and effects of the aggressive individual, evident to any acute observer. It can be difficult, dispiriting or even impossible to deal with.

Aggression is nourished by submission and intensified by opposition. Aggressors love victims, because they confirm their feeling of power; aggressors love opposition because it boosts their strength and urge to win.

Causes of aggressive behaviour

It is difficult to generalise about aggressive people, but they often fall into these categories, similar to those for whom anger is a typical response to difficulty:

- inadequate, insecure people for whom aggression is a defence against revealing their weakness
- bitter, disappointed people who express their frustration in anger and try to make everyone else as unhappy as they are
- 'alpha' males and females who are driven by the urge to dominate, by display, noise and brute force
- those who were the victims of aggression as children and know no other way of dealing with the world
- those who have no finesse, no social or communication skills or no respect for others.

Dangers of aggression

Communications with aggressive people are very difficult, traumatic even. Play the victim to an aggressor, and the behaviour will continue because it appears that the aggression gets results (submission, compliance, obedience), especially if the victim appears wounded or diminished or undermined. Stand up aggressively to an aggressor, and there's a risk that you'll be damaged, especially if he or she is senior to you, or simply stronger.

> The force of the blow depends on the resistance. It is sometimes better not to struggle against temptation. Either fly or yield at once.
>
> *F.H. Bradley*

Organisational aggression at work is beyond the scope of this book, but it is an important topic that is worth investigating, because it affects the welfare and morale of everyone, and requires cool and skilled communications to deal with. There's a considerable literature on bullying at work and allied issues.[84,85]

> Aggression is the most common behavior used by many organizations, a nearly invisible medium that influences all decisions and actions.
>
> *Margaret J. Wheatley*

Aggressive patients

Aggression of any kind is alarming, but the outcome of an aggressive encounter is usually much more dependent on the response to the aggression than it is on the intentions of the aggressive person.

Whether a potentially dangerous situation escalates into an assault or a fight will be largely determined by the reactions and communications of the object of the aggression. (The exception is with aggressors who are very drunk, high on drugs or seriously mentally disturbed, when quite different measures may be required (see below).)

Best responses to aggression

The techniques for responding safely to aggression are much the same as those for responding to anger (sometimes the early signs of later aggression):

- Remain calm and physically relaxed, while assessing the situation and reviewing what help is available and what escape routes you have.
- Whatever you do, don't
  - — get angry or raise your voice
  - — tense your muscles or clench your fists (not before the very moment you have to resist an actual assault)
  - — look distressed or frightened
  - — let your attention stray for a moment.

In many cultures, women are much better at defusing aggression, because, on the whole, their instinctive reaction is not one of competition or reciprocal aggression, as it often is with males. Across both genders, however, we know that there is a minority of people, in all kinds of exposed occupations, who are assaulted more than once, even frequently, during their careers; equally, there are large numbers of people who are never assaulted. The conclusion must be that most people are good at defusing, diverting, avoiding the aggression of others, whereas some do not have the skills and actually provoke or escalate aggressive or violent behaviour. Any organisation should be on the lookout for such individuals and should provide them with counselling and training (and not blame) to help them.

Box 13.3 Anticipating and reducing the risk of aggressive behaviour

> The general culture, ambience and environment of an organisation will affect the behaviour of visitors for good or ill. Austin Health, an 800–bed teaching hospital in Melbourne, Australia, has a well-developed strategy for setting standards and expectations, and for dealing with incidents when they occur. Their skilful poster (Figure 13.1) is empathetic, collaborative in intent, reasonable and firm. The non-verbal behaviour represented in the picture is very powerful.[86]

Figure 13.1 Austin Heath Poster. Reprinted with permission

Mental disturbance and chemical causes of aggression

Dealing with aggression in those who are highly intoxicated with drugs or alcohol, or seriously mentally ill is a different matter. It will probably be instantly clear if an individual is entirely out of control, or beyond the influence of any kind of verbal communication; certainly you'll get an understanding of that after two or three encounters. If such an individual makes no positive response to simple verbal instructions ('Please sit down', 'Please wait here' and so on), and shows no sign of moderating behaviour, then removal or restraint may be the only options – either having the individual escorted off the premises if they are not bleeding or seriously injured, having them restrained, or calling the police. Every hospital and clinic needs to have effective, rehearsed procedures in place, such as methods of rapidly communicating danger, summoning help and restraining violent people.

Depression and other mental disorders

This is an enormous, complex area of study, and here we can do no more than draw attention to its importance and provide some indicators for good communications practice.[87]

> One in six people suffer depression or a chronic anxiety disorder. These are not the worried well but those in severe mental pain with conditions crippling enough to prevent them living normal lives.
>
> *Polly Toynbee*

Depression

It is thought that around 10% of adults in Western countries experience a depressive episode every year, with twice as many women as men appearing to suffer. Depression can express itself through physical behaviour or symptoms, and may, sometimes, itself be a response to pain or disease. Every HCP will meet many patients experiencing depression of one form or another, and relationships, communications and therapy may all need to be adapted to the reality of the psychological state.

Box 13.4 Symptoms of depression

- feeling sad, hopeless and despairing
- a loss of interest and pleasure in normal activities
- loss of appetite or weight
- loss of sex drive or sexual dysfunction
- sleeping problems, such as inability to get to sleep or early waking
- feeling physically tired all the time
- concentration difficulties
- feeling guilty and worthless
- feeling that life isn't worth living.[88]

Helpful patient information is available in many forms. A good example is the New York City leaflet, *Depression, It's Treatable*.[89]

Transient and chronic depression

Everyone experiences periods of sadness or doubt or pessimism, with more or less dramatic impact on their mood and ability to carry on, sometimes for no apparent reason, sometimes for very good reason (loss of a job, or grief at a death, for example), but such episodes pass and life resumes. Such natural swings are emphatically not medical conditions. For seriously depressed people, the mood does not pass quickly, if at all, and they may lose interest in life, feel 'in a black hole', give up hope, be listless and apathetic, neglect to eat or sleep badly, among many other manifestations of the illness.

Distinguishing between transient misery and a condition needing treatment is not easy, and an HCP's diagnosis may be in conflict with a patient's view. The broad criterion for illness is serious, long-term impairment of the patient's life. However, in the midst of intense transient misery, a patient may well feel that their condition is of that kind and demand relief. The solution, in that case, is a negotiated settlement, in which the HCP demonstrates commitment to helping the patient while not necessarily acceding to their immediate wishes (see script extract, Box 13.5) For depressed patients a safety net of continuing support and planned appointments can be important.

Suicide risk

At its most serious, depression can lead to thoughts of self-harm and suicide, or to actual self-destruction. HCPs may often be the first people to whom a patient mentions or hints at thoughts of suicide, or they may be the first to perceive that a patient is at risk. Early recognition of such risk, and taking urgent appropriate action, is a high

Box 13.5 Counselling a patient with transient depression or depressed mood

The patient has recently had a number of personal losses and problems and insists that their misery requires antidepressant medication. The HCP does not believe that the psychological state should be medicated, but that the patient should be supported in trying to live through the troubled time. This is the essence of the message the HCP might convey during a much longer consultation:

'I'm really sorry you're having such a bad time. Your troubles are enough to make anyone feel depressed, I do appreciate that. Really, your reaction is quite normal, and I'd be more inclined to say you were ill if you weren't so upset. I don't want to start you on drugs for a disease I don't think you have, but I have some ideas which I hope will help you. I'll give you some mild sleeping pills for seven days, because I can see that not sleeping is really making things worse for you. I want to suggest some other non-medical things: talk to someone who will really listen to you and tell them everything you are feeling and worrying about; put aside an hour every day when you do something you usually enjoy – exercise, reading, going out for a drink, watching a film, whatever; try to eat two good meals a day; plan some pleasant things for the future – next week, next month – something that will give you something to look forward to. Come back in seven days, and tell me how you're getting on, what you're doing, what you're planning, how you're feeling. We'll take another look at things then.'

priority. Such situations need expert and purposeful enquiry and handling.[90]

To save a man's life against his will is the same as killing him.

Horace

Recognising and responding to depression in patients

Depression takes different forms and is expressed differently in every individual, and there are major differences in children, adolescents, men, women, older adults and elderly people.[91–96]

Some of the challenges of understanding and communications for HCPs include identifying and assessing the condition:

- Early recognition of depression is important if it is not to become more serious.
- To get a clear picture of the nature, depth and extent of the depression, whether it is presented explicitly or diagnosed.
- To bear in mind that many physical symptoms (especially sleeplessness, headaches, stomach aches, overeating, fatigue, generally poor health, angry or disturbed behaviour in children and so on – which may become the distracting focus of attention) can indicate depression – symptoms that may be diverting the patient from their

Box 13.6 A good suicide?

Although this may seem a perverse notion (in a similar way to a good death, discussed on p. 219), it is necessary to consider it as one end of the spectrum of possible self-destructive behaviour. We need to imagine a person in full possession of their reason and faculties who has deeply considered the nature and quality of their life, and decided that it no longer holds any value for them, that there is no good reason to continue living, and that the negative impact on others (if any) is not sufficiently persuasive to alter their mind. Putting aside considerations of the law and the ethics of killing oneself, that someone might arrive at such a conclusion is a credible proposition. (It comes much closer to home when we consider a patient with chronic or terminal illness, whose quality of life is marginal or negative.) Although an HCP might feel an ethical and humane urge to examine, probe and change such a position, ultimately the decision rests with the individual, and vigorous efforts to restrain them or frustrate their wishes could be unfeeling and cruel.

However, most potential and actual suicides are not like this at all. They are likely to be the intense and despairing reaction to situational or more extended problems; a desperate way of calling attention to their misery; a way of punishing someone for real or imagined grievances; a disproportionate solution to intense but transient difficulties; or a gesture of defiant violence. Many people who attempt suicide are relieved when they are rescued, may even set up their attempt in such a way as to ensure discovery before death, indicating the perhaps manipulative or symbolic nature of the act. Such attempts may be repetitive, too.

Someone whose life is in such desperate straits that they are considering suicide may need help beyond what a non-psychiatric HCP can offer, but the first clues may well be manifested in primary or hospital care. The critical element in an HCP's response is providing a strong, caring, human connection to the patient's misery and a convincing argument, however small, that there is some prospect of change for the better of some kind – even, as a first stage, postponement of the decision to die. The underlying conviction in pursuing this line is the intrinsic value of this particular human being and the possibility that they could recover at least some quality of life in their terms. The details are beyond the scope of this book, but it is clear that effective relationships and communications in healing are critical in the prevention of the careless loss of life.

psychological state or become the focus of their distress.

- To take seriously the depressed patient's view of themselves and the world (empathy) without (a) trying to tell them things aren't all that bad, or (b) being drawn into the often powerfully negative and pessimistic mood of depressed people (maintaining a degree of personal and professional detachment).
- To distinguish transient sadness or negativity from genuine (clinical) depression.

Special communications demands

- Many depressed or mentally ill patients blame themselves for their condition, and may be very reluctant to talk about it to an HCP or to anyone at all.
- This self-protective state of secrecy may also lead to the pretence of coping even in the midst of serious problems; such superficial competence is easily mistaken for the real thing in a hasty consultation.
- To distinguish, and explain to the patient, the difference between symptomatic treatment (e.g. sleeping pills) and treatment of causes – which may require time, psychotherapy, changes in social or lifestyle arrangements, or (possibly) medication.
- Although twice as many women as men appear to suffer from depression, there may be much less disparity between the genders, because men are less likely to admit to depression and often express it in diversionary ways – drinking, drug-taking or burying themselves in work, for example. There may also be a tendency for HCPs to be less likely to recognise depression in men than in women. Freedom from prior assumptions and receptiveness to telling hints and clues are important.
- It is important to pace medication, goal setting and physical rehabilitation within a depressed patient's capacity to deliver results and achievements, and to avoid the risk of any element of failure which may intensify psychological problems (by, for example, asking too much or setting unrealistic goals).
- To treat depressed patients and their families with the same degree of respect, patience and compassion due to all patients.

Practical considerations

- Some depressed patients may need extra support in remembering and keeping appointments.
- Patients with mental disturbances such as depression, may find themselves confused, further stressed, even panic stricken by the prospect or reality of being out of their home or in a professional consultation. Suggestions that patients list their questions and concerns in advance of a meeting, or bring along a member of the family or a friend may be very helpful and reassuring.

Further referral and resources

- Patients with serious depression almost certainly need to be referred to psychological or psychiatric therapy whether or not they are the primary illnesses for which help is sought.
- Although a relationship with a trusted HCP may be valuable and important, community-based support, both professional and informal, may have a vital part to play in treatment and recovery. It is in society where social and psychological disturbance often originates, and support and adjustment within society may be part of the best treatment.

There are many books and good websites dealing with depression, which should be explored to supplement this section.

Other mental disorders

Although depression is a kind of mental disorder (and much of what has gone before applies to other psychiatric conditions too), it is more amenable to description and discussion than many of the other disparate disturbed states of mind which some patients develop. Obsessions, mild paranoia and phobias may be among the common kinds of mental disturbance that HCPs encounter, but there will also be many more profound and complex conditions.[97]

Insanity – a perfectly rational adjustment to the insane world.

R.D. Laing

Non-psychiatric HCPs will not usually be called upon to treat those with any kind of psychosis (and they should not be), but all HCPs need to be aware if what their patients are showing them are its symptoms. Communications may be difficult or impossible, and there can also be problems of physical unpredictability or idiosyncrasy. Although some psychotics undoubtedly hold down jobs (even prominent ones), for most, consistent normal communication or controlled behaviour may be difficult or impossible from time to time. There may be evidence of low levels of moral conscience, recklessness, lack of responsibility for the consequences of action, especially in cases of antisocial personality disorders (formerly known as sociopathic or psychopathic disorders).

Box 13.7 What is psychosis?

In the general sense, a mental illness that markedly interferes with a person's capacity to meet life's everyday demands. In a specific sense, it refers to a thought disorder in which reality testing is grossly impaired.

Symptoms can include seeing, hearing, smelling or tasting things that are not there; paranoia; and delusional thoughts. Depending on the condition underlying the psychotic symptoms, symptoms may be constant or they may come and go; they may express themselves in reckless or dangerous behaviour. Psychosis can occur as a result of brain injury or disease, and is seen particularly in schizophrenia and bipolar disorders, the aetiology of which are still poorly understood. Psychotic symptoms can occur as a result of drug use but this is not true psychosis. Diagnosis is by observation and interview.[98]

Obsessional behaviour (constant hand washing or lock checking, for example), disabling phobias (crowds, confined spaces, animals, for example), extreme swings of mood and feeling (bipolar disorder) or evidence of eating disorders, will all tell part of the story. In these situations, the HCP's everyday perceptions and understanding, or capacity for empathy, will probably quickly detect a mind that is not on a normal wavelength, and with which normal engagement cannot consistently take place. Some patients themselves may be fully aware of the nature of their problem and the degree of their suffering and some will be experts on their own condition, although they may not know how to solve their problems alone.

Box 13.8 What is schizophrenia?

Schizophrenia is a chronic, severe, and disabling brain disorder that has been recognised throughout recorded history. It affects about 1% of Americans.

People with schizophrenia may hear voices that other people do not hear or they may believe that others are reading their minds, controlling their thoughts or plotting to harm them. These experiences are terrifying and can cause fearfulness, withdrawal or extreme agitation. People with schizophrenia may not make sense when they talk, may sit for hours without moving or talking much, or may seem perfectly fine until they talk about what they are really thinking. Because many people with schizophrenia have difficulty holding a job or caring for themselves, the burden on their families and society is significant as well.[99]

Be warned, however! The behaviour and conversation of some psychotic people can appear to be absolutely normal, and may also be very effective in controlling and manipulating others.

Passion, you see, can be destroyed by a doctor. It cannot be created.

Peter Shaffer

Communicating with patients with mental disorders

Non-specialist communications need to embrace:

- gentle, friendly, supportive attitude and tone
- empathetic responses to the patient's suffering, and to what may be bizarre or delusional remarks or feelings (in relation to hearing voices, for example), without endorsing their external reality
- a focus on what is internal and subjective, and what is external and verifiable, and

conversations that support understanding of the distinction
- firm, but courteous requests or demands when appropriate
- focus on physical symptoms and disease when they are the priority
- avoidance of criticism or judgement (which are inflaming to insecurity and paranoia)
- clear, simple communications that avoid being patronising
- compassionately and effectively managed transfer to specialists.

Madness need not be all breakdown. It may also be break-through. It is potential liberation and renewal as well as enslavement and existential death.

R.D.Laing

Family and social support

An important factor to bear in mind is that families often carry a huge burden in living with mentally ill relatives, whose needs may be extremely time consuming, demanding and difficult. At its worst, family life and relationships can be deeply damaged or destroyed. Carers may need support, even medication for such problems as insomnia and stress; where available, access to further supportive resources in the community (groups and home-care services, for example); but above all empathy, appreciation and encouragement in their unenviable duties.

Addiction and substance misuse, in all their varied forms, represent a category of mental and physical disorders, and may give rise to specific conditions such as depression or psychosis. The medical, communications and psychotherapeutic demands for such patients are great, and highly specialised. Readers who want to learn more about these important topics will need to research them elsewhere, as they are beyond the remit of this book.

Insanity is often the logic of an accurate mind overtasked.

Oliver Wendell Holmes

Patients under stress and in crisis

In the frantic and pressurised modern world, many patients will be suffering from stress and stress-related diseases and will be seeking remedy for them. These encompass a wide range of conditions and issues from serious morbidity through to simple, non-medical questions of management of daily life. The communications challenges are to understand the nature and cause of the patient's problems, and to help them understand and manage them, with or without medication.

Distinguishing pressure and stress

Explanation of the nature of stress is an important priority. Discussion of stress is frequently clouded by a basic misconception: pressure and stress are not the same. Stress, or being stressed, is an individual's unique response to pressure of some kind. Other individuals, subject to exactly the same pressure, may not find it stressful and not become stressed. Working in a pressurised environment does not mean everyone will become stressed; indeed some people, up to certain limits, flourish under pressure, even when they feel a degree of stress. There are pressures in everyone's life, and for most people a certain level of pressure is productive – even essential (it is hard, for example, to imagine athletes performing at their best without stress).

The distinction between pressure and stress is important in both analysing and treating a patient's problems (or anyone else's). In examining their stress, which may or may not be their primary presenting condition, we need to understand the pressures to which they react badly, and then the particular ways in which they react badly – the nature of their stressed response. Converting a patient's focus of attention from external to internal factors may be difficult when they seek to apportion blame exclusively to external causes, although, of course, in some situations external factors may be predominant.

The secret of health for both mind and body is not to mourn for the past, nor to worry about the future, but to live the present moment wisely and earnestly.

Buddha

Managing external pressure and stress reactions

If there is a direct relationship between pressure of certain kinds and emotional, cognitive or physical reactions or symptoms, then the first priority is to find ways of reducing the external pressure – shortening or changing working hours, for example; reducing expectations of performing perfectly in every aspect of life (setting realistic goals); rearranging and sharing domestic tasks and so on. HCPs may need to help patients plan their strategy for making change happen.

If the pressures can't be easily changed or managed, then the patient may need to be counselled to manage their reactions to the pressure more positively.

Box 13.9 Measures to help patients manage stress

First, to take care of themselves better (tired, unfit bodies are more vulnerable to stress reactions): eat regularly, take exercise, find specific time to relax, establish regular sleeping habits, avoid alcohol and stimulants, and take time out for social life, pleasure and fun.

Second, to try and manage their emotional reactions to life in general and to pressure in particular: many people remain in a state of high anxiety and psychological arousal for long periods at a time, with peaks of fear or even panic in response to predictable stimuli (the arrival of the boss or meetings with strangers, perhaps) or under unusual pressure (these may manifest themselves in physiological symptoms, of course). Such patients need counselling in self-awareness, relaxation and breathing techniques, recognition and management of stress-inducing situations and stimuli, and support in rational discussion of their behaviour, the damage it does to them and the remedies available. At the extreme, the damaging external pressure may need to be eliminated by, for example, changing jobs. There is a wealth of literature and resources on this area on the internet and in book and music shops.[100–102]

Limits of medication

This account makes it sound all too easy: it is not, and managing stress is not something that can simply be accomplished after a visit to the doctor. It is a complex, specialised field in its own right, much of which really exists beyond medicine – in psychotherapy, in the wisdom of meditation, in learning how to live a balanced and healthy life. Medicating reactions to stress will accomplish little, unless the causes are addressed, or unless the medication is understood to be short-term support through an atypical period. The whole process is a model of the true therapeutic partnership, in which a patient must take responsibility for themselves in changes that the HCP cannot directly effect, but can only support.

For some patients, the simple opportunity to talk about the pressures of their lives will relieve them of much of the stress (and perhaps isolation) they feel, and give them strength to return and deal capably with whatever life throws at them. The healing power of sympathetic listening may be exactly what a patient needs. At other times, much more will be required.

Many ordinary illnesses are nothing but the expression of a serious dissatisfaction with life.

Paul Tournier, M.D.

From stress to crisis

Excessive, unmanaged stress may lead to crisis – emotional or mental breakdown, the phenomenon known as 'burn-out', serious physical illness, relationship break-ups and career problems, and much more. But there are many other kinds of crisis that may deeply affect the health and welfare of patients: deaths, injuries, natural and other disasters, accidents, fires, debt and repossession of goods or dwellings, uncontrollable children, violent partners, criminal activity, prison sentences, alcoholism and so on.

It is not a credible proposition that HCPs should sort out the lives of patients in some kind of turmoil or crisis, but it is their job to be sensitively attentive to their patients' sufferings, and, as far as humanly possible, to shape their relationships and services to what patients need and can cope with. Helping patients grieve is one specific task which may be necessary (see also p. 220). HCPs should focus on medical needs, of course, but in awareness of the whole person and that the patient may need support and resources far beyond the clinic or hospital, and long into the future. A sense of crisis is intensified if there appears to be no way out and no one to listen. HCPs can be a gateway to other resources and to the perception that there is at least someone who listens and cares. Pressing single-mindedly ahead with medical priorities for a patient who is stressed or in crisis may be deeply damaging and counterproductive.

Man needs difficulties; they are necessary for health.

Carl Jung

The worried well

Patients in this category – those who are well but worried or convinced that they or their children are sick – have been growing in numbers in recent years.[103–105] Some estimates suggest that up to as many as 20% of patient visits in some places can be prompted by this kind of anxiety. The worried well, often unknowing victims of media scares, real or unfounded environmental pollution concerns, advertising, dubious internet information, drug marketing, or the medicalisation of ordinary life,[106] can be time consuming and difficult to help, particularly if their worries have got a deep hold on their mind.

Those obsessed with health are not healthy; the first requisite of good health is a certain calculated carelessness about oneself.

Sydney J. Harris

How far should medicine go?

There are serious ethical questions about the medicalisation of common, natural events in life (noisy and troublesome children; teenage depression; menopause; occasional erectile dysfunction; the natural mood swings of a living psyche, and many more), and about the breeding of dissatisfaction with one's body (breast size and shape, penis length and girth, facial features and so on). There are serious questions as to how far scarce medical resources should be allocated to interfering with such natural processes or pampering to such vanity. All that, however, has no impact on those who think they're sick or inadequate and need some kind of medical or surgical attention.[100]

HCPs obviously have to make a very careful assessment of a patient's case to distinguish real symptoms from imagined ones, and genuine risks from fantasies. When the early symptoms of serious disease (meningitis, for example) may be superficially indistinguishable from some common complaint, there is no place for over-hasty judgement. However, once disease has been ruled out, convincing the patient that they are well and should get on with their lives may require some considerable communications skill.

I got so anxious sitting in the make-up chair for hours with my face covered. I had my doctor write a prescription for valium. I couldn't have done it without the pill.

Kim Hunter

Understanding anxieties and delusions

It will be important to understand the particular source of their anxieties and what is driving them.

- First, there may be no true symptoms or evidence at all but a preoccupation with the possibility or risk of sickness (hypochondria) leads some people to spend their lives worrying, and taking an endless succession of vitamins, supplements, alternative remedies, perhaps medications, and visiting their HCP unnecessarily. Such people are likely to be victims of a mild or serious mental or emotional disturbance, with some unusual historical event or series of events influencing them from the past, or some underlying anxiety or imagined threat (perhaps not about health at all) constantly hanging over them. An HCP's enquiries may need to uncover some of these hidden influences, if there's to be any chance of improvement in the patient's condition.
- Second, related to the item above, but more difficult, are people without symptoms who are

convinced that they are seriously ill or at risk, for example, are HIV positive or have cancer, when tests or radiographs demonstrate otherwise. Such people are also likely to be victims of a mild or serious mental or emotional disturbance (see below).
- Third, there are those who have mild symptoms of everyday conditions (slight fever, cough, constipation, headaches or other occasional aches or pains; or who have short-term upset, stress or depression) and believe they need medical treatment or are at risk of serious illness (more or less normal people, except for being unusually anxious or vulnerable); some of these will have researched their worries on the internet or elsewhere, and may come armed with all kinds of supporting 'evidence'; some of them will have been influenced and upset by the latest dietary or herbal or environmental fad or controversy.[107]
- Fourth, there will be those who are experiencing real troubles of some kind (difficult children, teenage depression, pre-menstrual syndrome, menopause, sexual dysfunction of some kind, weight problems, sleeplessness or grief, for example) who are convinced that the only remedy is medical or pharmaceutical.

I never read a patent medicine advertisement without being impelled to the conclusion that I am suffering from the particular disease therein dealt with in its most virulent form.

Jerome K. Jerome, Three Men in a Boat

More serious causes

Among all these patients there may be some who have minor or major psychological problems, such as:
- phobia
- obsessive compulsive disorder
- acute anxiety disorder
- guilt complex
- clinical depression
- bipolar disorder.

Dealing with these may need expert help: no amount of solid, everyday evidence is likely to sway the mind of a deeply obsessed or disturbed person. If their mental condition is not diagnosed, treated and ameliorated, they may well go on a round of HCPs and institutions seeking someone who will share their delusion, or who will collude with it for the sake of a quiet life. If they leave a consultation seriously frustrated, they may do much damage to the reputation of an HCP or institution. In referring a patient to psychotherapy or psychiatry, it is important to make sure you are not giving the impression that you think they are mad and are beyond help (although you might think so), which would just exacerbate their vulnerability, perhaps provoking their anger at your response and their symptoms.

There will be many times when an HCP judges that the symptoms they are seeing do not justify medical therapy. For the average worried well person, clear presentation and explanation of evidence (including the possibly symbolic and practical acts of taking blood pressure and temperature) and expert opinion should be enough to reassure. (Reference to first-class authorities, such as the Amercian Council on Science and Health[107] may also be helpful.) Ordinary, non-medical remedies may be suggested (drink more water, eat more fruit, take a couple of paracetamol, take more exercise, take some time off, get the kids to help you). The promise of the availability of future consultation (should symptoms persist or worsen), or other lines of communication (phone or email for example, or of seeing a local pharmacist), may provide enough comfort to allow the patient to leave satisfied.

Box 13.10 This is the news some patients need . . .

Worried about trace chemicals in the water supply or carbon monoxide in your home? Don't be. From plastic bottles and toys to pesticides used in agriculture and French fries, the world can seem full of quotidian lethal hazards, but many of these alarms are completely bogus, while most of the others represent only negligible risks.[107]

When the patient is entrenched, but not mentally ill, skills of explanation and persuasion will come to the fore. This may require knowing the evidence and argument, of course, so an HCP's state of knowledge and access to reliable information are important factors in success. Seeking a second opinion may also help, although it increases the already significant burden on time and resources.

I used to wake up at 4 A.M. and start sneezing, sometimes for five hours. I tried to find out what sort of allergy I had but finally came to the conclusion that it must be an allergy to consciousness.

James Thurber

Worried well patients are primary targets for education in rational understanding of health and medicines. Where the problem is significant, existing or new support or educational groups may be a useful resource to consider. This is a problem that arises out of the culture and values of modern society, and HCPs should not be left to struggle with it in isolation.

'Difficult' patients

One of the best accounts of the management of difficult patients appeared in the *Journal of the American Board of Family Medicine* in 2006.[108] This section draws on that research by Elder *et al.* In their investigation of the views of 102 physicians, they identified the patient characteristics that most frequently led to feelings of anxiety and frustration for them:

- demanding patients who stay sick (the worried well, too)
- unfocused patients with multiple complaints
- patients with chronic pain who may or may not need narcotics.

The authors observe: 'These patient qualities tend to clash with physician traits that encompass who they are – their professional identity and personal self-worth, their time-management skills and confidence, even their comfort with patient autonomy and trust in the patient.'[109]

In a much older review[110] of patients who were dreaded, Groves listed:

- dependent clingers
- entitled demanders
- manipulative help-rejecters
- self-destructive deniers.

Managing difficult patients

Although the ultimate solution to such troublesome relationships is ending them one way or another, most HCPs would regard that as unsatisfactory except in extreme circumstances. Elder *et al.* suggest a model for managing such relationships, which includes collaboration, empathy and appropriate use of power. Collaboration implies joint definition of problems and goal setting, and the establishing of a genuine mutuality in planning solutions; it may need coaching and teaching to correct misapprehensions or false expectations. Empathy (as readers of this book already know) requires a grasp of the patient's world view, and of what underlies their troublesome feelings and behaviour, followed by effective management of those feelings and motives. Appropriate use of power has to do with limit-setting in terms of clinical discretion and time. Either HCP or patient may use their power inappropriately if the relationship is not heading towards cooperation and mutuality (the patient by manipulation, for example, or the HCP by authoritarian assertion).

A woman tells her doctor, 'I've got a bad back.' The doctor says, 'It's old age.' The woman says, 'I want a second opinion.' The doctor says: 'Okay – you're ugly as well.'

Tommy Cooper

Physicians commented on how important it was to be self-aware, and to manage the often negative and unhelpful feelings that blossomed in the face of difficult patients. Having opportunities for recovery from the demands of clinical practice were also seen as very important (attentive and sympathetic colleagues, support groups, exercise, meditation and so on).

Difficult patients are a big challenge, but the more HCPs understand about human psychology and the effective use of communication, the more able they will be to exercise greater control and manage most, if not all of them, without damage to themselves or their patients.

One has a greater sense of intellectual degradation after an interview with a doctor than from any human experience.

Alice James

14 Communication and the richness of cultural and ethnic diversity

Patients come in thousands of varieties, some of them quite similar to us, but many from backgrounds with values and views of the world very different from our own. This chapter reviews some of the major areas of human variation, particularly related to ethnic and religious diversity, but much of it highly relevant to all patients and their needs. The material provides knowledge about the differences that will help HCPs better understand the range of patients they meet, and so avoid mistakes and misperceptions, and tailor their communications more sensitively and effectively. Most applies to patients from any background.[111]

Introductory review of basic issues

Throughout this book we have emphasised the many ways in which people are different from each other, even when they share such basic characteristics as language, age, ethnic origin and so on. Everyone perceives the world, experiences it and responds to it in ways determined by the unique pattern of their own lives, within their personal, social and cultural contexts. Effective relationships in healthcare are carried out by HCPs who have high levels of self-awareness and are acutely sensitive to the ways in which patients are different from them. At the same time, we have identified fundamental skills in relationships which permit the distances to be bridged:

- empathy
- attentiveness
- listening
- observation.

There are also fundamental qualities that permit the forming of strong professional and personal bonds between participants:

- compassion
- concern
- respect
- warmth and goodwill.

Overview of diversity issues and responses to difference

There is very little in this chapter that is not relevant to the diversity of all patients. However, ethnic and religious diversity provide special cases in the spectrum of human differences because there may be much less common ground – even no common ground – in some of the basic tools or concepts used for experiencing and interpreting the world, for communication, in relationships, health issues and so on. There may be little or no common language; beliefs and practices relating to kinship, family, marriage, child-rearing, touch, gender and gender roles, morality, spirituality, life, disease, death and so on, may all be quite different from those of other groups, and quite obscure to outsiders.

Religious diversity appears, of course, within single ethnic groups where there may be a common language and culture, as well as across cultures. There may be very large differences between even those who speak a common first language such as English, for example in the United Kingdom, America, Africa or New Zealand, and in regions and very small areas within them; between those with Afro-Caribbean, Indian or Asian Pacific origins – and the differences may be much greater than may be at first assumed (frames of reference, vocabulary, structure, intonation, idiom and so on).

Many people have a natural prejudice in favour of their own cultural heritage and upbringing, especially if they are members of a long-established national or majority ethnic group, and 'outsiders' may be regarded as inferior, or less rational or intelligent or viewed with suspicion or hostility. Good communications and effective healthcare require us to be aware of these likely prejudices in ourselves and in others towards us, to recognise and overcome them intellectually and emotionally, and to feel for others the respect we demand for ourselves and our culture.

To work with people of other cultures or faiths requires a degree of humility, because we have to accept that the values and beliefs that others hold have, for them, equal weight and validity to our own. This is a challenge at any time, but particularly when beliefs and rituals oppose or offend our own values or morality, as may be the case with such practices as arranged marriages or refusal of blood transfusions, and belief in the supernatural, for example. Respecting others does not mean agreeing with them, but it excludes any right to demand or impose change, other than when personal freedom, fundamental professional ethics or the law is violated. (Child brides and female circumcision are issues that plunge us into the midst of these complex dilemmas and conflicts.)

Overcoming obstacles and finding common ground

HCPs who have frequent contact with patients of different ethnic backgrounds from their own need, of course, to do their own talking, reading and research to increase their knowledge of and sensitivity to particular groups they may meet frequently (preparing a vocabulary of basic, common terms in a minority language is one practical measure, for example). The same applies to managers who have ethnic minority staff working for them. Contact with local ethnic minority groups, or community leaders may be intrinsically productive as well as demonstrating goodwill and commitment. Some members of staff and patients may be willing mentors, too.

We should, perhaps, mention one criticism that is sometimes made of ideas, like those in this book, which suggest we should pay such extraordinarily sensitive attention to others and modify our relationships and behaviour in the light of their needs. The crudest form of objection comes as: 'Why don't they learn the language and the norms of the culture and fit in?' This is no place to enter that particular social and political debate. What we have to do is face the reality: every society includes minority ethnic groups (including, of course, expatriate white people and immigrants all over the world) and their differences from the majority culture demand that they should be studied and understood (as far as possible), *if they are to be helped*. It is only a more extreme form of the same challenge in understanding people of quite different backgrounds from our own, within a majority culture.

The big issues (assimilation, integration, coexistence, etc.) are quite separate from ensuring that we do the best for *this* patient at *this* moment, whoever they are and wherever they come from. It is also possible with ingenuity and imagination, of course, to help, at least to some extent, someone you don't understand at all or cannot communicate with verbally.

Although our degree of attentive flexibility must be enormous, it does not mean that we cannot make requests, set limits, or require patients, in some circumstances, to respect and follow the procedures or values of the culture or organisation we represent. However, such issues need to be negotiated on the basis of understanding and respect for the patient's starting point in their own culture and needs, and with recognition of their right to refuse.

Although the challenges may look huge when surveyed together, as they are here, we must remember that, although there are enormous differences between people, there are also common needs and emotions that are universal: the needs for shelter, safety and food, of course; the urge to form relationships and families; the need for acceptance and respect; the wish to help and support others, and to be supported in times of weakness or sickness; the causes and meaning of tears; the expression of kindness to others, most obviously in that universal expression of goodwill, the smile. As human beings, we start with a lot of common ground, and that is a positive beginning for healthcare relationships too.

In this chapter we shall review the range of cultural issues that are particularly sensitive or difficult, and provide ideas and suggestions for establishing positive communications and relationships and for avoiding some of the major pitfalls. It covers the whole spectrum of communication from issues of language, through non-verbal behaviour, personal habits and needs, rituals and beliefs, food and personal hygiene, and the physical environment and its impact. The material here is, inevitably, a superficial review of a complex area of study. Any thoughtful reader will see that much of this chapter applies to everyone, irrespective of any labelled differences.[112]

Topics

This section examines:

- perception and thinking
- information and signage
- expectations
- language resources
- language
- names
- time
- gender
- touch
- privacy
- clothing
- hygiene
- food
- family and community
- autonomy
- greetings, courtesy and deference
- treatment
- religious practice
- death and dying
- communication between cultures.

Perception and thinking

The diversity in perception and thinking (cognition) is wide enough within a single ethnic group to complicate communication, but across cultures it covers a huge range.

HCPs need to be aware that anything they take for granted (cause and effect; evidence-based conclusions; the undesirability of pain; the action of medicines; the purpose of life; the nature of family, marriage, parenthood and so on) may be viewed utterly differently by people from other cultures or faiths.

Box 14.1 Bends in perception – medicine and beyond

One: to Chinese and Asian practitioners, whose knowledge and skills are based on thousands of years of experience, the designation of their practice as 'alternative' is, at best, a perception that is entertaining, at worst, deeply offensive.

Two: Weather forecasters on international channels habitually speak cheerfully about bright, sunny conditions and regretfully about rain, as if the rest of the world shared the needs and preferences of their home countries in the north northern hemisphere. Unrecognised, unacknowledged assumptions like these can make one seem foolish and out of touch to different audiences.

Among the most varying and difficult issues are beliefs about the aetiology of disease. Disease may be attributed to:

- processes as understood in Western science and medicine
- the influence of past actions in this or previous lives
- punishment by a supernatural power
- the effects of witchcraft, spells or curses

- possession by a spirit or entity
- disturbances in the balance of *yin* and *yang* in the body
- exposure to, for example, sunlight, bats, snakes or black cats.

(If these seem strange, we should remember that all are to be found in various forms in developed, Western societies, including ancient, ostensible remedies for them, such as exorcism. They are 'primitive' only in the sense that they are very old.)

Patients who have sought out an HCP working in a Western-style, scientific health facility are indicating their belief that they can (or might) be helped, whatever their prevailing beliefs. However, an HCP still needs to have a clear idea of what the patient's primary view of the disease and its potential remedy may be, for it to be factored into the explanations and solutions.

Patients may be experimenting, 'dipping a toe in the water', when they feel other approaches have failed them. This may mean they are not seriously committed, or that they won't understand the rationale of the diagnosis and treatment, or the therapy, and may not adhere to it. They may be under social pressure not to regard scientific medicine seriously and to take concomitant alternatives.

For these tentative patients, and others who may have very strong beliefs counter to scientific medicine's principles, HCPs may need to adopt an approach of explanation, negotiation and collaboration, which does not discount or dismiss alternative perspectives and explanations, but offers Western therapy as an option as safe and reasonable as others: 'The risk of trying this is very small, and I believe it will help you. If it doesn't work, then you can reconsider.'

Most patients, whatever their frame of reference, are familiar with taking liquids or substances as remedy for physical ills, and of supplementing or adjusting diet. In that respect, the HCP's therapy may fall within a pattern of familiar and recognisable cultural habits. Surgery, scans, biopsies or radiotherapy, however, may not be understood or acceptable, and may require quite different kinds of counselling and influencing, if they are to be considered by the patient at all.

Superstition and irrationality are common features of human nature, and although an HCP will be familiar with such aspects in their own culture, new examples will constantly surface. Here are a few examples to add to those in the section on aetiology above:

- Pain or other side effects are indicators of therapeutic effectiveness, or of a 'strong' and effective medicine (therefore dangerous side effects may be tolerated or ignored).
- Vomiting or diarrhoea indicate positive cleansing of the body, or the expulsion of disease or its causes.
- Injections are more potent than tablets.
- Remedies for all ills can be found through natural (i.e. non-manufactured) substances.
- Unpleasant tastes or painful procedures will imply effective therapy.
- Naming a disease confirms it and empowers it (although for some, the opposite is the case: naming a disease confines it and makes it known).
- Hospitals are places where people go to die.
- Surgery 'lets out the evil'.

The HCP has to find a way through all these often hidden complexities to get the best possible idea of the mindset and world view of the patient, and to negotiate the best possible options and decisions, taking account of the cultural elements, questions of safety and of the desired therapeutic outcome. Concessions may often have to be made along the way.

Information and signage

Provide signage and introductory leaflets in the languages of local people and major local visitor or tourist languages.

First-time arrival at a hospital, clinic or pharmacy can be an alarming experience. It can be made far more welcoming and less threatening by the provision of clear, comprehensive signage, and leaflets that can be picked up and taken away for reading even before an actual visit. Local public relations activities and information distribution may be important for raising awareness and access. Where there are minority language speakers available to help patients, publicise the fact and indicate where they can be found. In places where there are large numbers of visitors or tourists, anticipation of some of their language needs will reduce problems when they seek medical help.

Remember that some signage may be incomprehensible even to native speakers/readers, for example: 'Cardiac Catheterisation Laboratory and Outpatient Radiology this way'.[113]

Expectations

Provide leaflets giving specific information about how the healthcare system works and what patients can expect in relation, for example, to preliminary health checks, consultation, timescales, treatment, testing, costs and so on. Simple diagrams and flowcharts about a typical patient's journey will help prepare strangers for their visit. This is an opportunity, too, to express the wish to provide services that are culturally sensitive and to invite people to help and advise you.

Language resources

Have basic language resources available in print or electronic form:

- core vocabulary in main ethnic minority or visitor languages, illustrated with pictures (symptoms, body, organs, bodily functions, levels of pain, procedures, medicines)
- dictionaries
- leaflets on common diseases, treatments, adherence, immunisation, public health issues
- blank, pre-printed proforma cards for specifying drug name, dose regimen, future appointments, emergency contact
- interpreters, where the demand is sufficient or progress cannot be made without them. There will often be a member of staff who can help. Using children or family members as interpreters may be sensitive if the patient requires privacy or confidentiality; there is also the serious question of accuracy in non-expert interpretation (also an issue with professional interpreters). Always ask and test initial agreement to any arrangement.

Language

No common language

Where the HCP and the patient share no language at all, imaginative and creative HCPs will (often do) manage to diagnose and treat patients without having a word in common, including delivering babies or providing emergency treatment, or giving more complex therapy. 'Informed consent' becomes a major issue here. Although the challenges are enormous, they are actually less than those in diagnosis of an infant or an unconscious adult: here there is at least some interaction and feedback. Without an interpreter, some printed or pictorial materials are essential. Expressive physical gestures, miming and facial expressions are particularly useful.

The priorities for communication are:

- use of pictorial and written materials if available
- sensitive observation and use of non-verbal behaviour:
  - — attentive watching and listening
  - — imitation and repetition of patient's gestures and expressions for confirmation/clarification
  - — preparatory miming/acting of intentions (e.g. for patient to lie on examination couch; for HCP to take blood pressure)
  - — setting a gentle pace
  - — expressing warmth and concern (especially facial expression)
- recognition if the lack of verbal communication makes diagnosis too uncertain or risky, and rethinking of the plan, except when emergency action is necessary.

Some common language

Limited capacity in the HCP's language does not, of course, imply limited intelligence or articulacy in the patient's first language (using a limited vocabulary in a foreign language tends to make the brightest person feel and seem stupid).

- The HCP needs to search for the simplest possible vocabulary and sentence structure, checking constantly (verbally and non-verbally) that the meaning is clear in both sending and receiving information.
- Even those with a good command of a second language may be unfamiliar with medical terminology.[114]
- Have basic vocabulary lists available (medical and non-medical).
- Speaking more loudly does not aid comprehension whereas speaking more slowly and clearly can; mere repetition of the same form of words is often unhelpful; reformulate in new ways (paraphrase) messages that are not understood.
- Although the words may be understood, some may have quite different meanings or represent different concepts when translated into the patient's own language; the authority and reliability of a verbal agreement will differ greatly between different people (examples in ref. 115).
- The pace of the exchange may be very slow as the patient seeks to translate the HCP's words, and to find the right words to respond.
- The potential for misunderstandings is great: repetition, reformulation and checking understanding are important.
- Patients may feel under pressure to agree or signal understanding when they haven't grasped what is going on, in order to speed things up or not to appear foolish; HCPs need to be sensitive to this risk (see also 'Saying "no"' below).

Names

To be addressed incorrectly or inaccurately is always upsetting at some level, and such mistakes will inhibit or harm a healthcare relationship. As with all patients, check with them how they like to be addressed.

- There are variations across cultures in the order in which first and other names and surnames appear, in the use of nicknames and titles; always ask.
- This is a sensitive issue in all cultures. Addressing patients by their first name may be seen as a presumptuous intimacy; whereas using only a surname may be officious and alienating; using both with or without a title may not be comfortable for some patients, especially when the name is being announced in public. (Although no one else may be paying attention, to hear one's own name publicly announced can be embarrassing or intimidating.)
- Do not be self-conscious about asking a patient to repeat their name until you can say it accurately; record it phonetically, especially for a language not using the Roman alphabet (the patient may well have a standard spelling which is used on their passport or in the country on formal documents – this needs to be used for medical records).
- Names and titles may be particularly important to show respect when addressing older people or members of the opposite sex.
- In some cultures and/or languages, people will sometimes refer to themselves or to the person being addressed in the third person; for a listener not familiar with the convention (and not paying close attention!) this may cause confusion. Sam (or Mr Kiyato or whoever is speaking), may say: 'Sam (or Mr Kiyato) is feeling much worse today,' or: 'Sam doesn't understand nurse,' (meaning 'I don't understand you'). An HCP who wonders, 'Who's Sam?' may appear unhelpfully inattentive to Sam, the patient who is speaking.

Time

Different cultures have very different approaches to time and the concept of time.

- Punctuality (and therefore 'being late') and 'time is money' are quite foreign to some cultures; this difference can lead to great problems if it is not recognised and managed.
- Scheduling flexibility is necessary to manage appointments with some members of some

ethnic groups who may be quite unfamiliar with tight timetabling and rigid schedules (in many countries appointments may require nothing more than specification of a day, with no particular time).
- HCPs can encourage patients to observe appointment times (postal, telephone or email reminders, for example), but their capacity to keep them will not always be wholly in their control (other demands may be seen as more pressing).
- This issue requires a good deal of understanding, and appreciation of the fact that a late patient may not grasp that they have done anything inconvenient or annoying.

Gender

Every society has a view of the place of men and women in it, and of the way in which relationships between them should be conducted. The rules in some societies (Muslim and Orthodox Jewish, for example) can be very strict, with absolute prohibitions relating to a woman revealing her body or hair; touch between the sexes; participation in public entertainment and so on, although there are great variations within single religions. Some women will not put themselves in a position where the rules are likely to be violated, but HCPs need to be extremely careful about:
- consultations between male HCPs and accompanied or unaccompanied women
- physical examination and revealing any part of the body
- touch (including handshake).

Some cultures regard men as having greater authority and knowledge than women, and a female HCP may have some problems asserting her authority with such patients; physical examination by a female HCP may be highly problematic, if not offensive.

In some cultures, women will need a man's permission for any kind of medical attention or therapy and for payment; HCPs may need special skills to encourage a female patient, accompanied by her husband or male relative, to speak for herself, assuming she is not too embarrassed or intimidated to talk about her symptoms in front of her husband; in the latter case, considerable ingenuity may be needed (perhaps asking a female colleague to talk with the woman, while distracting the man with further discussion of his view of the situation, for example).

There are two basic pieces of advice in dealing with powerful issues such as these (and most of those in this discussion):
- Remain initially conservative in speech and action.
- Ask for guidance and advice on any issue that might be problematic:
  - 'Please tell me if having this discussion with a male/female doctor/nurse/pharmacist is a problem for you.'
  - 'Your chest and stomach need to be examined. How can we do this to keep it comfortable for you?'
  - 'We cannot know what the problem is without examining your penis. Would you prefer me to get a male doctor/nurse to do that?'
  - 'I understand you're Jewish/Muslim/Hindu/ Christian Scientist. Please tell me what I need to know to avoid offending you or any of your beliefs.'

Modesty is a primary value and need for women in many cultures, including attitudes of deference and keeping their heads and bodies covered.

Touch

This is largely covered in the section above on gender, but touch may also be more widely taboo than just between the sexes; although many Asians are familiar with the handshake, non-tactile greetings are often the social norm. (There is more on this topic in Chapter 10.)
- In Latin cultures, physical contact is often taken for granted, and its avoidance will make the person seem aloof.
- Although the guiding hand, the touch on the arm or holding hands, may represent warmth and healing for some, for others it will be an

invasion of their space, disturbing – even offensive.

- In many parts of Asia, touching someone on the head is offensive, as the head represents the higher, spiritual aspects of being, in contrast to the feet, which represent the lowest (hence never pointing your feet at someone or at a holy image).
- On the whole, the taboos apply less strictly to children.

The advice, again, is to be initially conservative and cautious with every patient but not to the extent of failing to be comforting and reassuring through physical touch when it is permissible.

Related to touch is the question of personal space: everyone has a circle of space in which they feel comfortable; the dimensions of this circle, especially the distance between people, varies from culture to culture, and in different circumstances (family, social, business and so on). Asians tend to require less personal space than Westerners, but there are also individual variations within cultures. Don't 'invade' a patient's personal space, except during examination or treatment, when the usual rules are suspended with mutual understanding and agreement; don't back off defensively if someone naturally stands closer to you than you are usually comfortable with. Be aware that many people will be anxious at the close proximity of a stranger.

Privacy

This is an issue for all patients, but especially those from cultures where there is a special value placed on privacy in relation to the body and bodily functions. In some cultures even married couples will never see each other naked or using the toilet; in places of crowded communal living, there are often powerful behavioural and non-verbal rituals (aversion of eyes, turning away of the body, preoccupation with some activity or conversation) which protect an individual (washing or changing clothes, for example) from observation even without physical barriers.

- Hospitals and other communal facilities can be a nightmare for those who fear that their privacy cannot be absolutely guaranteed (shower curtains as the only protection, for example; broken or ineffective locks on toilet doors). This is a sensitive issue, which all HCPs need to take account of in both the physical provisions themselves and the verbal understanding and reassurances offered.
- Privacy, in terms of having time alone, may also be an issue for some patients. Particularly important for those who wish to pray, it may also be necessary for those who need time to reflect on their situation, come to terms with bad news, talk with the family and so on. HCPs can greatly assist patients by finding out about their needs and providing them with safe times and spaces to be alone and undisturbed.

Clothing

Many people feel uncomfortable in back-opening hospital gowns; the provision of shawls or dressing gowns can reduce this anxiety.

- In planning future examinations or tests, it can be suggested that patients bring some item of clothing that will make then feel more secure.
- Ritual or religious items (headscarves, turbans, wigs and so on), should removal be necessary, need to be treated with respect, and carefully and securely put aside or stored. Always ask what is acceptable.

Hygiene

Some patients will need running water (not baths) for washing their bodies and their feet (the latter before Muslim prayer, for example), or their face and their hands (before eating, for example). People from many cultures, including those who are extremely poor, have very high standards of personal hygiene, arguably often higher than those in the West, and may wish to shower frequently.

- Blanket baths may cause real discomfort to some people, not only because of the exposure of the body, but also because of, in their view, the unsatisfactory nature of the cleansing.
- People from many cultures find the use of toilet paper revolting and unacceptable and are

accustomed to washing themselves after defecation (and urination); adequate provision for washing after use of a bedpan is important. (The use of the left hand for this purpose explains why, in some cultures, it is regarded as 'unclean' and is never used in social interaction, for passing food or handing gifts, for example; HCPs (especially left-handed) need to be aware of this taboo.) Provision needs to be made for this important need, ideally with both Western and Asian style toilets (the latter with a usable source of running or static water). Sitting on a Western-style toilet is unacceptable to many people whose cultural norm is squatting (which explains the footprints you occasionally find on toilet seats where there is no alternative).

These are powerful and important issues, which will call up emotions of discomfort, resentment or disgust if they are not understood and provided for. Provisions for such basic needs will affect the quality of relationships and all aspects of patients' responses to healthcare.

Food

This is not the place to provide an itemised list of the taboos and prohibitions relating to food, drink and animal products in every culture. It is necessary to state only that such taboos and prohibitions are fundamental to several faiths (Jewish, Muslim, Hindu, among others) and that transgression of the rules, knowingly or unknowingly, can lead to extreme spiritual and psychological distress; the prohibitions include not only eating certain foods, but contamination by them, for example, in the use of a common serving spoon or inadequately washed cooking pot.

HCPs need to know about these issues, not least also because of the possible animal constituents in medicines and vaccines which may be subject to similar prohibitions as food.

- Where it is not in conflict with medically determined dietary requirements, families may be allowed to bring food in for their relatives, providing comfort and reassurance as well as reinforcing social and community links.
- Some patients may regularly take traditional or herbal remedies or supplements and regard them as part of their daily nourishment; thoughtful discussion and negotiation (and possibly even prohibition) may be necessary.
- The faiths of some patients will require them to fast at certain times. HCPs may need to take account of this in planning therapy and diet.
- Hospital food may seem bland and uninteresting to some patients who are used to highly aromatic or spicy food. They may not eat enough if the problem is not addressed (something as simple as the provision of dried chili or chili sauce may help).

If anybody said that I should die if I did not take beef-tea or mutton, even under medical advice, I would prefer death

Mohandas (Mahatma) Ghandi

Family and community

Cultures vary enormously across the spectrum from individuality/self-sufficiency to complex, extended, inter-related networks and loyalties. In some, the entire extended family will want to visit and care for the patient, and may provide a real challenge to hospital rules and conventions.

- In some Asian cultures, in their own countries, members of the family will bed down next to the patient and stay as long as he or she is hospitalised. How such expectations, wishes and demands are handled may have a big impact on the morale and health of a patient and in the confidence they and their family have in the service offered. The quality of communications relating to all these issues will have a big impact, for better or worse.
- In some parts of Africa, family members will expect to stay with a dying relative during their last days or hours, and to be present for terminal events (including cardiac massage, for example); recounting the story of the death and events leading up to it is part of the ritual of mourning.
- The status of children and their rights differ across cultures; some parents may have quite

specific expectations and requirements about how therapy and relationships are conducted; almost all parents will wish to stay with their children as much as possible.

Autonomy

The autonomous rights of the individual are central to Western concepts of democracy and justice and influence important elements of health-care: informed consent is the prime example, along with the right to information about diagnosis, prognosis and so on. In some Asian and other cultures, the recognised and legitimate rights in a patient's situation may extend to include those of the family or social group, who may expect to have as much, or more influence in decisions than the patient, or to have information before the patient and to decide whether or not to share it; the group may expect to give its consent, with or without the patient's participation. This reflects cultures where individuals take their identity as much from their location in family and social networks as from their own personal characteristics. It is quite different from the Western ideal of assertive individuality. This has very significant implications for how and with whom communications take place: about diagnoses; treatment options; prognosis (including the possibility of death); consent; resuscitation and so on. There will be times when a Western HCP will need to negotiate solutions between the individual and the family/social models, and when both sides may need to make some concessions (see also Chapter 18).

Confidentiality is a primary aspect of protection of a patient's rights in many countries, including strict laws in many places. In some cultures, family members will not recognise the same boundaries and may seek information about a patient which an HCP feels they cannot give. One solution to this is to ask for the patient's permission to give information, privately, or in the presence of the enquiring relative. The reasons for taking such a course need to be explained.

Greetings, courtesy and deference

Greetings vary greatly across cultures. Although the Western handshake is familiar round the world, it is not an acceptable gesture to people from many cultures, especially where there are taboos about touching women or strangers. Do not automatically offer to shake hands if there is the slightest doubt about the acceptability of the gesture (see also 'Touch', above).

- The universally acceptable, minimal, courteous and respectful gesture when greeting, is to stand up, welcome the person, and acknowledge them with a smile and a slight forward inclination of the head. The patient's response can then lead on to any further exchange or gesture.
- Direct eye contact is not a universal habit, and in some cultures is regarded as aggressive and disrespectful. In cultures where deference has a high social value (especially Asian), eye contact may be largely avoided during listening and talking – not as an evasive tactic, but as a way of communicating respect.
- In cultures where status superiors are regarded with respect, there may be a profound reluctance to challenge, and a real unwillingness even to question or seek clarification. An HCP's words might either (a) be taken uncritically as gospel, or (b) silently discounted and ignored if there is no explicit exploration of the patient's perspective.
- Some patients will resist confessing anything that they feel the HCP might disapprove of (non-adherence or taking herbal or traditional medicines, for example) – vital information that an HCP must have the skills to elicit. This is also true of symptoms or feelings that a patient finds embarrassing or shameful.
- Patients from non-confrontational cultures find it very difficult to debate issues or review and criticise options in the presence of a status superior; ostensible agreement may mask difference and so pose a threat to future adherence and therapy.

- In some cultures saying 'no' directly is avoided. Some people may simply ignore the question, change the subject, remain silent, reflect on some minor (and seemingly irrelevant) aspect of the topic, all of which can signal disagreement which may never be made explicit.
- Some women will find it difficult or impossible to talk directly to an HCP and may need a companion to speak for them; some may underplay their symptoms in order not to draw attention to themselves or appear immodestly demanding.
- Patients from other cultures (Hispanics, for example) may be much more open in their communications, and more emotional in their responses, sometimes more demanding than an HCP might find comfortable. Such behaviour has to be seen within the great diversity of cultural norms, and not as a personal assault.

Treatment

The following are some of the therapies and procedures about which some religions (and secular groups) have particular views and rules, which are often non-negotiable:

- blood transfusions
- organ donation
- vaccination and some vaccine products
- fertility treatment
- contraception
- sterilisation
- surgery
- life support
- post-mortems
- abortion
- medicines or products containing substances derived from animals or human foetuses.

These are all issues that a skilled HCP will approach with some delicacy on any occasion (although transfusions might be forgotten as a potentially sensitive procedure for some groups). The first step is always to seek the patient's view of any suggested action, and to take things from there, accepting that the patient may be committed to a view that the HCP believes is misguided or even dangerous. In the end, it is the patient's decision, unless their wish conflicts with the law or non-negotiable professional ethics. In the latter case, the only recourse is to the courts and their authority to act against the patient's or the family's wishes (this has happened, for example, where the alternatives were a blood transfusion or death, and in situations where, for reasons of religious conviction, parents refuse to have their children vaccinated against communicable diseases).

Religious practice

Muslims are required by their faith to pray five times a day, and members of other faiths may have rituals that are equally important to them. Healthcare must not stand in the way of patients having the freedom to practise their faiths, other than when there is a threat to life or limb. Respectful exploration of patients' needs and negotiation of solutions with them will usually cover everything.

Patients may want access to a priest, minister, imam, rabbi or spiritual leader. Such visits are a great opportunity for HCPs to spend a few minutes asking questions and learning about a particular faith and its views on healthcare.

He whom the gods love dies young, while he is in health, has his senses and his judgments sound.

Titus Maccius Plautus

Death and dying

(See also Chapter 21.) Contrary to the balance of opinion towards honest disclosure about death and dying in other parts of this book, members of some ethnic groups may not want to be told if they are dying, or if a relative is dying. Knowledge of such issues needs to be gathered from reading and discussion with experts (perhaps local spiritual leaders) and from sensitive discussion with patients and their families.

Life support provides a range of ethical and spiritual dilemmas for groups who have views about human spirituality and the after-life. The possible use of life-support systems needs to be raised well before the necessity arises so that there is time for reflection and decision. Patients and their families must be given the freedom and confidence to refuse, whatever the HCP's views.

Organ donation and post-mortems are proscribed for many faiths. Here, again, local knowledge needs to be gathered, so that unwelcome approaches are not made to patients or families who might be distressed. Again, when such questions are asked, it must be with the clear declaration of the patient's right to refuse. Should a post-mortem be required by law, extremely thoughtful handling of the situation may be required to take account of what the family may see as a desecration. The presence of a figure of authority from outside may help to bring an acceptable solution.

Customs relating to the dead are varied and usually of great importance to members of faith groups. Here are some issues, relevant to some faiths:

- Cover the body.
- Do not handle the body except with gloved hands.
- Do not remove catheters, drains or dressings that may contain body fluids of the deceased, without consulting the family.
- Do not remove jewellery or religious or ritual clothing or items from the body.
- Give the family the option of washing the body.
- Turn the body to face Mecca (for Muslims).
- Prepare to release the body as quickly as possible for those faiths that require speedy burial or cremation.
- Provide private space for mourning or prayers.
- Place a candle or light next to the body.
- Open windows to set the spirit free.

Communication between cultures

There remain a few issues that do not neatly fall into the previous sections in this chapter.[116] Paralinguistic features are the aspects of language other than the words chosen. They are:

- *Structure:* In most European languages the subject of the message ('I', 'you' 'they') and the topic or purpose of the message usually come at or near the beginning. In some other languages and cultures, the secondary, supporting material may come first, building up to the main message, risking that a listener loses track or misses what it important. (The same process may happen with native speakers, when dealing with something embarrassing or painful.)
- *Emphasis:* Differences in intention and meaning can be conveyed by emphasis on particular words. Consider the many different meanings of the following sentence, depending on which word is given the primary emphasis: 'I don't think you told me anything about the accident.' Such subtle (and not so subtle) shades of meaning may not be apparent to second-language speakers, or may be misinterpreted. On the other hand, they may use extra words, repetition, change in pace or pitch to convey emotion or relevance, which may not be familiar methods to a HCP.
- *Intonation*: Intense concentration is needed to interpret the meaning of this and the behaviour relating to many of the topics in this section.
  - — Questions made from statements by raising the voice at the end, without any formal question words, may be understood as statements and not as questions; for example: 'You haven't taken any other medicines?'). Even inverted word order ('Was your husband . . .?') may not immediately be understood as questions.
  - — Speakers of tonal languages (such as Chinese) customarily have a much larger

Box 14.2 Notes on some of the peculiarities of Westerners

The focus of much of the material in this chapter is on providing Western, native English-speakers with guidance for their relationships with people from other cultures. However, there will also be readers of this book from non-Western cultures where English is not the first language, who will, for one reason or another, be treating patients in or from Western countries, English-speaking or not. Much of the chapter is relevant as it stands, but some of the material will require reverse interpretation of information and advice from a Western to a non-Western perspective. Here are some of the primary issues of interest:

- Xenophobia is not uncommon in the West, and with it comes a lack of humility, respect and trust in the face of strangers, foreigners and the unknown; this is intensified when away from the pack or in a position of vulnerability; some patients may be unduly anxious, demanding, assertive in the face of a system or language they do not understand, and require very patient and forgiving handling.
- Many patients will have made little or no attempt to grasp even the basics of the language in a country they are visiting, especially those with English as their first language, and may be under the (bizarre but common) illusion that by repeating themselves more loudly or emphatically they will make their meaning clear. The availability of basic diagrams and pictures, ideally with vocabulary, will enhance useful communication.
- Some patients will arrogantly assume that they have a right to an HCP who speaks English and will place an HCP in a position of disadvantage from the beginning if communication is a problem.
- Some affluent patients may make a display of their wealth and try to use it as a lever for preferential treatment.
- Where English is the common language for HCP and patient when both are non-native speakers, special care needs to be taken in the accuracy of communication: printed symptom charts and visual materials will, again, be helpful.
- Individual rights, including confidentiality and consent to treatment, are strong Western values and need to be respected as far as possible. Patients may ask many more questions and expect much more information than may be customary.
- Many patients will be accustomed to an almost exclusively pharmaceutical response to disease, and may be uneasy at the suggestion of alternatives (acupuncture for pain management or massage for back pain, for example). There are likely to be major reservations about taking local or traditional remedies.
- Punctuality and timescales are problematic in healthcare everywhere, but patients will be greatly reassured by being kept informed of what is happening, likely waiting times, arrangements being made and so on, perhaps beyond what is normal for the location.
- It is a fact that some non-Western ethnic types remain youthful in appearance into middle age and beyond. To those from races whose appearance of youthfulness usually vanishes in the third decade of life (or earlier), being treated by someone who appears to be of tender years can be unsettling. HCPs need to bear this perception in mind as one possible cause of unease or apparent lack of confidence shown by their Western patients.
- Although medical facilities and services in many parts of the world are first class, and the personnel dedicated and effective, there are places where limited resources mean that clinics and hospitals are not the modern, hygienic, well-regulated places that everyone would desire. For some patients from rich countries, however grateful they are for medical attention, the environment will have a great impact on their confidence and morale: this, too, needs to be factored into assessment of patients' reactions and into how care is provided.
- Many foreigners will have great trouble with squat-toilets or washing with water from a container. The absence of toilet-paper to which they are accustomed (although much less hygienic than washing, of course) will seriously upset and distress some patients.
- Foreigners may be unwilling to eat local food, or have reservations about the hygiene of conditions in which it is prepared.
- Many, however, will be grateful for the expert and compassionate attention they are given, and like so many of the survivors of the 2004 tsunami in Thailand, will tell the world about the excellence of healthcare in foreign places. They, and many more, it is to be hoped, will continue to spread the word, and help reduce some of the misconceptions and anxieties associated with healthcare delivered in cultures different from their own.

range of intonation than native English speakers, and their delivery may sometimes seem over-energetic or even angry or aggressive. Some languages also have a wider range of tonal ways of expressing friendliness, emotion or interest (for example), and such speakers may be confused or offended by the limited range of most native English speakers (especially British English).

- *Negative questions*: the patterns of some other languages give rise to difficulties with negative questions in English: 'You don't smoke do you?' may prompt the answer, 'Yes' – meaning 'Yes, I don't smoke', rather than 'Yes, I do smoke.' Such misapprehensions can be serious. Double negatives are difficult in any circumstances: 'It's not that I don't feel you're trying'; 'You haven't started not taking the pills, have you?'
- *Listening*: in some cultures, attentiveness may be demonstrated by stillness, silence, even looking away, in contrast to more active Western head nodding, eye contact and the use of encouraging noises.
- *Silence*: a vital and positive element in any communication that is being taken seriously by both parties; many cultures do not engage in the cut and thrust style of Western conversation, but adopt a more reflective approach (especially when conducted in a second or third language).
- *Alternation*: strangers with common language and culture may take some time to settle into a relaxed rhythm of exchange after first meeting, but they quickly pick up clues about when to speak, when the other is expecting speech, when interruption is acceptable and so on. For HCPs and their patients there may not be common rules or patterns to pick up, and a more explicit, guided structure may be needed – especially specific invitation to the patient to speak when silence may not be sufficient hint or permission.
- *Volume*: speakers of languages that are relatively loud can sound rude and aggressive, whereas others with gentler habits may be misinterpreted as uninterested or without feeling. HCPs need to understand the meaning of the patient's tone and volume of speaking and adapt theirs in line with the patient's.

Non-verbal behaviour[117,118] includes:

- *Eye-contact*: is variously, potentially challenging and offensive or an indication of positive attention and interest, or in its aversion, respectful and attentive or evasive and defensive. You need to know what's going on!
- *Facial expressions*: mostly a cross-cultural lingua franca (especially the smile), but some cultures are much more restrained in range and intensity than, say, Greeks and Spaniards, and some are quite different: Japanese, for example, may remain straight-faced when happy, and smile when embarrassed or angry; Thais smile as a way of dissipating strong emotions which could have negative consequences if expressed (*Mai bpen rai* ('never mind') is a further mechanism for avoiding anger and conflict); some Africans may giggle when upset or embarrassed. Interpretation of non-verbal expressions may need to be asked for if there is any ambiguity.
- *Gestures*: don't assume that shaking the head means 'no' and nodding the head means 'yes'. In Bulgaria and other countries (parts of Greece, Turkey, Iran, Bengal) it is the other way round; in India shaking the head from side to side in a gentle kind of lateral figure of eight is usually a sign of thoughtfulness, agreement or attention (as well as, perhaps, some less complimentary things). These gestures are so ingrained in us all, that divergences in meaning can go unnoticed, and cause real problems.
- *Posture*:
  - Folded arms may mean different things in different cultures (either defensive and closed, or open and relaxed).
  - In status-conscious cultures, the height of the head is an important indicator of social relations: some Asians, for example, will be uncomfortable sitting or standing with their head higher than the HCP's.
  - Exposing the soles of the feet or pointing with the feet (shod or not), placing the feet on furniture, stepping over objects or food, may all be offensive to some people.

Conclusion

The author acknowledges the relative brevity of this section on so complex a subject, but he hopes that the ground covered is sufficient to help in the development of awareness of the variation in human behaviour and social and religious practice. Many people, in a culture foreign to their ethnic origins, make allowances for the ignorance of their hosts or fellow citizens and are forgiving of breaches of their rules. There can be no doubt, however, that in so sensitive and complex an arena as healthcare, the fewer barriers to communication and understanding there are, the fewer the concessions that have to be made by the patient, the more effective and rewarding will the encounter be, socially and medically.

Revision, discussion and application (5)

A. Revision and discussion

1. What are some of the myriad ways in which human beings can be wounded and abused psychologically, at home, at school, at work, in society at large? What are the different ways in which people respond to or cope with abusive relationships and what effects do they have on their lives in general? What are some of the characteristics of bullying at work? How should knowledge of these affect our perceptions of other people and our communications with them?
2. Chapter 13 offers the proposition that many mental disturbances belong at one end of a continuum, which includes so-called normal or undisturbed behaviour and emotions – that mental illness is an extreme form of experiences that everyone has in some measure, although its expression may be dramatically different. Consider and test this proposition against your own experience of human psychology and your reading.
3. What are some of the influences and pressures in the world at large, which might lead people to be over-sensitive about risks to health and turn healthy people into the worried well, into hypochondriacs or health pessimists? What kinds of changes and communications might help reduce these effects, both at social and individual levels?
4. In reviewing the wide range of differences between people, what do you think are some of the major elements that unite people across all races and cultures, if there are any at all? Do you think there are any common elements in relation to healthcare questions and practice? If so, what are they, and how confident can we be about them?
5. When there may be fundamental cultural or religious differences between an HCP and a patient, how can an effective relationship be established (supposing, in this instance, that they share a common language)? What are the techniques, skills and communications associated with successful negotiation of such differences?
6. What is your attitude to non-Western medicine? Among the many alternatives, which do you feel most comfortable with (or least uncomfortable with), and what is the evidence for your view? Are there any to which you would refer a patient for therapy? What are the alternatives that you believe are unreliable and dangerous, and what evidence have you for that view?

B. Application

1. Consider your past dealings with angry patients and other people. What lay behind their anger? How well did you (or others) deal with the situation? What went well and what went badly? What advice would you give to a young HCP in helping them deal with angry patients?
2. Review the material on depression, and consider whether you might revise your assessment of any of your patients. How many patients have symptoms of depression alongside their other medical

concerns? How many of them are chronically depressed and perhaps in need of help? How far is depression a contributory cause to your patient's illnesses or an obstacle to their recovery?

3. What are the characteristics of your 'difficult' patients? What are the factors in your psychology and/or that of your patients that causes the difficulty? With calm analysis and reflection, can you see how some of those difficulties might arise, and how they might be lessened by different methods of communication?
4. What practical steps can you take in your work situation or facility to improve the level of service and quality of therapy you provide for speakers of minority languages?
5. In thinking about the dignity of all patients and the respect due to them, what are some of the fundamental principles and needs that apply across the board to all people? How far do you or does your place of work manage to uphold those standards of dignity and respect most of the time? What can be done to improve standards and practice?
6. What are some of the special considerations relating to dealing with patients of the opposite sex, from both your own culture and from others? Consider not only the thoughts and emotions of HCP and patient but also how situations may be perceived or judged by others. What behaviour and communications are necessary to ensure there are no ambiguities or offensive elements in the encounter? (The questions, with subtle differences, apply equally, but less commonly, to homosexual HCPs with patients of their own gender.)

Commentary on many of the questions and issues appears on the publisher's website, in Online Resources at www.pharmpress.com.

Part G

Working together

The first chapter reviews the delivery of the best patient care through the relationships and communications within a whole integrated and collaborative healthcare team. Communications practice, knowledge and skills for specific roles other than doctors are reviewed (nursing, pharmacy and physiotherapy, for example). The discussion includes how different roles should relate to each other for effective delivery of service and the importance of non-medical jobs in the overall performance of any healthcare organisation.

The second chapter confronts the problems of limited time or resources, and offers suggestions about how these can be negotiated against the demands of the best medical practice and the most effective communications.

What happens then is like what happens when we separate a jigsaw puzzle into its five hundred pieces: The overall picture disappears. This is the state of modern medicine: It has lost the sense of the unity of man. Such is the price it has paid for its scientific progress. It has sacrificed art to science.

Paul Tournier, MD

15 The whole team and the whole patient

Although the purposes and activities, and the knowledge and skills, across all roles in healthcare differ greatly, and the diversity of patients and their needs demand many different kinds of responses, the basic knowledge and skills of communications are similar and essential to all roles and activities. All healthcare personnel, including support staff, need to share the same ideals of patient-centred care and work in a coherent, supportive organisational culture. This chapter provides specific examples of care within and by the team across different medical and non-medical roles and activities.

Differential demands

The range of specialities among doctors, nurses, pharmacists, allied professionals, managers and non-medical staff is enormous, covering hundreds of distinct, significant roles, each with its own knowledge, skills and demands, each contributing to the health and welfare of patients and their families and carers in one way or another. All of them have a common requirement for excellent communication skills, but they do vary in the nature, depth and extent of communication skills required, and the time available for them.

Some relationships will have a much greater action focus (emergency care and acute admissions, for example), with much less time for communication, but with no less a requirement for brilliantly effective communication, especially the rapid gathering of information and provision of reassurance. Other relationships will be less focused on short-term action and be more concerned with relationship building and maintenance (postoperative and chronic care, and rehabilitation, for example). Some non-medical relationships will be brief (receptionists, telephone operators, porters and security staff, for example) but will, none the less, have a real and lasting impact on patients and visitors.

There is a great need for a positive and collaborative culture within an organisation and the networks that deliver multiple aspects of healthcare. This applies among medical and technical roles as well as those large numbers of people with important, if less highly technical roles: cleaners, catering staff, porters, security and maintenance staff, receptionists, telephone operators, and secretarial or administrative staff who meet patients and/or talk to them, who all have a vital part to play in patients' overall experience of healthcare, and can make a great difference for better or worse.[119]

> Science may never come up with a better office communication system than the coffee break.
>
> *Earl Wilson*

The whole organisation addressing the whole person

The primary focus for all specialities is the welfare of the patient as a whole person, including partner, family, or carers. Although the task in hand may be diagnosis or dispensing, a single technical procedure (such as radiography, taking blood, a scan) or activity focused on a single problem (for example, walking, hearing, wheelchair use, regaining speech), or element of service (such as providing food, receiving newcomers, cleaning the toilets) they affect the whole person.

The word 'team' has become badly degraded in management jargon because of its careless use for any group of people loosely associated for some more or less common purpose, but its true meaning is as relevant to healthcare as it is to premier performance in sport.

Box 15.1 A true team is:

a group of diverse people, committed to a common vision; dedicating their various skills to its achievement; following explicit, shared values, rules and conventions; planning, working, developing and communicating coherently together in complex inter-relationships; helping and supporting one another; sharing a determination to do the best possible and maximise every opportunity for achievement.

Too often there is undervaluation, neglect even, of important participants, often the most junior or least visible, although by no means confined to them. Urban civilisation would collapse without garbage collectors, just as hospitals would close without cleaners and maintenance staff. No organisation can function without receptionists, administrators and financial staff – but how often do they truly feel part of the total enterprise, sharing its goals, involved, supportive and enthusiastic? How often, on the other hand, do they feel separate, ignored, alienated even, sometimes obstructing rather than facilitating progress? Such damaging behaviour can affect whole organisations.

Everyone is important. Internal (corporate, managerial) communications need to be as skilled and empathetic as external communications – staff-centred as intensely as services are patient-centred. The values and practices across an entire organisation need to be coherent, professional, skilled, involving and valuing everyone. There is then some hope of creating a powerful, dynamic team in which every individual is deeply appreciated and engaged.

What can I do about it?

But who has the time for this, and what could be done if there were time? The answer does not lie in accepting less than the best for you and your patients. If your organisation is inefficient or unfriendly, with systems and conflicts that waste time and resources and get in the way of good service to patients, where errors, adverse events or infections are perhaps too common, then the incentive is: change things and *save* time and resources, *increase* staff and patient satisfaction. Identify the problems, find allies and try to improve things, step by step, or on a larger scale. Improved people management and teamwork (processes requiring real vision and skills) may be the answer,[120] or exploring the broader concept of culture change, which many large hospitals have pursued with very positive results, including better financial performance.[121–123] Change is possible and achievable when there is a strong enough vision of a better future. (Holding more productive meetings is one small significant step – see Chapter 25.)

Consultations, tests and procedures

What do these ideas of wholeness and coherence mean?

The everyday activities of consultations, tests and procedures in a hospital or clinic provide a vivid illustration. There is always a risk that short encounters with a succession of HCPs becomes a 'production line', in which the patient feels more like an object than a person – a mere body being sent, walked or wheeled from one department to another like a parcel.

It is here that the imaginative and emotional capacity (empathy) to grasp what it is like for the patient, and to have a view of the whole pattern of events to which the patient is being subjected from their point of view, comes into its own. The risk is that the process becomes automatic: patient in, patient out, next please. What for the professional is a series of familiar, even commonplace activities,

Box 15.2 A case in point: paediatric inflammatory bowel disease

The management of inflammatory bowel disease (IBD) in children is a difficult assignment by any standards. The aetiology of Crohn's disease and ulcerative colitis is not yet understood, and although medication and surgery can provide some amelioration of symptoms, there is no known cure. They are chronic, disabling diseases, affecting a large and increasing number of (mainly) young people in developed countries.

After diagnosis, children and their families may be intensely involved with their specialist healthcare team for years, while experimental, ameliorative therapy or surgery is tested and reviewed, prior to the likelihood of a lifetime of closely monitored medication, and the possibility of disabling flare-ups, distressing symptoms and chronic pain. The confidence and morale of patients and their families are major issues in the whole picture.

The range of contributing specialists is wide, including at least: physicians, psychologists and psychiatrists, social workers, nutritionists, nurses, pharmacists, educators, paediatric surgeons, laboratory and other technicians, clinical researchers. Receptionists, porters, orderlies, catering and cleaning staff, accountants, and administrators are all also likely to touch the lives of patients and their families at some time, perhaps frequently, during hospitalisation and out-patient treatment.

The medical and human challenges are enormous, and include virtually the whole range of communications tasks and skills discussed in this book.

- *Empathy:* capacity and willingness to explore and understand the radical physical and psychological impact of the disease on the children and their families, and to engage with the deep needs and fears aroused by it.
- *Listening, questioning:* observing and interpreting non-verbal behaviour; caring, expressing compassion; finding appropriate language to deal with complex issues; using non-verbal behaviour effectively to deepen and maintain the relationship – and so on.
- *Recognising and dealing with psychological needs:* some patients may be depressed by their situation, even to the edge of suicide, and need serious expert help; many will be reluctant to discuss their disease at school or with friends, and be embarrassed by their needs, for example, for frequent and urgent trips to the toilet; the *whole person* may be distressed.
- *Embracing family and carers:* the patient's suffering and uncertain future place an enormous burden of distress, anxiety and practical demands on parents; they are critical and equal members of the therapeutic partnership, and must feel that their participation is respected and welcomed.
- *Managing uncertainty:* explaining what little is known and how much is not known about the disease and therapy; supporting patients and their families through experimental treatments; maintaining morale through uncharted waters; anticipating and dealing with disappointment.
- *Communicating risk:* the risks of the disease, experimental medication, surgery and so on; negotiating with patients and their families about the benefits and harms of any course of action (e.g. continuing a promising course of medication which has not quickly enough slowed potentially fatal weight loss, as against trying an alternative with uncertain benefits; or the choice between continuing experimental medication and surgery).
- *Informed consent:* in a situation where patients and their families will be desperate for any possible remedy, ensuring that they truly understand the realistic risks and possibilities of any course of action and consent to them; that the implications of involvement in any research or clinical trial are fully understood.
- *Maintaining long-term relationships:* questions of pace and depth, planning and structure; maintaining motivation, confidence and morale; creating a real partnership to face the long-term challenges; the identification of resources beyond the hospital or clinic.
- *Commitment and co-ordination across the whole team:* a deep degree of collaboration; mutual-understanding; shared vision; frequent and effective communications providing perfectly managed therapy and seamless and coherent relationships with patients and their families; behind the front-line team, managers and administrators, and all non-medical support staff, who are equally committed to the vision and understand exactly how their behaviour and communications should contribute to its fulfilment.

There is more but the point has been made: here, in one small specialist field, virtually every page of this book is relevant to the complex tasks facing the whole healthcare team.

This material is based on the work of the Centre for Pediatric Inflammatory Bowel Disease at the Children's Hospital of Philadelphia, a specialist centre treating around 3000 patients a year.[124]

is, for the patient, often an entirely novel and perhaps alarming experience, or series of experiences. This can be greatly reduced by visualising the larger picture of the patient's journey and by simple communications measures, carried out with warmth and concern.

The primary skills in such circumstances are:

- making connections
- assessing immediate emotions and needs
- explanation
- support
- providing continuity.

Making connections

Ensure the patient knows who you are (name and role, simply explained) and knows that you know who they are.

As a patient meets a new HCP for a consultation, or is moved around a clinic or hospital, especially if it is very busy, and as they meet a succession of strangers, there is a risk that they will feel that their identity is slipping away, and even a fear that they will have the wrong test or procedure. This anxiety may be particularly strong if the patient is delivered to a waiting area and left without an introduction to the person or a member of their team who will be dealing with them next, their file simply added to a pile on a desk, visible or hidden somewhere.

Ideally, there should be one person, probably a nurse or nursing assistant, who is managing and overseeing the programme of tests or procedures for each patient, explaining them as they move from one to the other and introducing the patient to each specialist. This, of course, is difficult in a busy hospital or clinic, but the idea of connected, managed continuity for each patient's journey is an important one to bear in mind and to fulfil as far as possible. This does not reduce the need for a strong connection to be made at each department. A porter pushing a gurney can play a significant part in this process if they feel involved and valued, and understand the importance of what they are doing.

Assessing immediate emotions and needs

Different patients will need quite different levels of information and reassurance for their peace of mind and cooperation. An assessment of what an individual patient needs must be made on each occasion, judged from their carefully observed responses from arrival at the start of the journey and throughout their stay – non-verbal behaviour (relaxed or agitated or anxious); words (questions, comments, explicit anxieties or uncertainties).

It is necessary to judge if a patient is frightened by the procedures or anxious about infection; has doubts about being 'experimented on'; wonders whether they might be mistaken for another patient; feels uncertain about hospital hygiene (is everyone washing their hands?) and so on. Each of these requires a specific and explicit response.

Some patients may need to be given more information than they appear to want: a resigned, passive patient may need to be encouraged to take a more active interest so that at least they know what is happening, and have some idea why it is happening (their depressed response may be important to take account of). This would be one of those sensitive and testing situations in which an HCP's words and behaviour are not exclusively determined by the limits of the patient's wishes. That need requires its own assessment and plan.

There is also the patient anxious not to waste professional time, or impose on an HCP's patience, although they have doubts and questions. It is important to recognise such considerate diffidence, to acknowledge it gratefully but to encourage patients to raise their questions or express their concerns.

Explanation

For every patient, every new procedure – so familiar and normal for an HCP – may be a mysterious or frightening event; they may fear needles or pain, be anxious about nudity, be alarmed by some elaborate technology or equipment – at the same time as they may already be worrying about the diagnosis of some serious or disabling disease. Patients need explanation and reassurance delivered with seriousness and compassion: the HCP's knowledge of the simplicity and low risk of a procedure and their familiarity with it will not be shared by the patient unless every patient gets an explanation which provides the facts and satisfies them as far as possible.

Here are some of the basic kinds of explanation. They may be sufficient for the patient or may give rise to questions or the expression of anxieties to which the HCP needs to respond thoughtfully.

- 'We need to check if there's any problem in your lungs/if the infection has cleared up.'

- 'We want to check the electrical activity of your heart for anything unusual.'
- 'We'll be using this blood sample to check how your kidneys are doing, your blood-sugar levels and cholesterol – you know, the dangerous fatty stuff in your blood.'
- 'This scan should tell us if there's anything physical causing your headaches, then we'll know what to do.'
- 'This test will help us identify the particular infection you have and then provide the best treatment.'
- 'Examining your eyes can tell me a good deal about your general health as well.'
- 'Checking your urine will tell us about sugar levels in it and help us find out if you're at risk for diabetes.'

Support

Hospitals and clinics can be confusing and alienating places (not entirely unlike enormous supermarkets), and even the small area of a radiology consulting room can be off-putting: where exactly do I wait or sit or take off my shirt or blouse, and where do I put them? Will I be left standing without my clothes? How cold or uncomfortable will this machine be? Will someone else breeze in while I'm half-naked?

Support is provided partly by explanation, but also by an attitude that recognises the vulnerability of the patient on territory that is alien to them, when it is so familiar to the professional.

Box 15.3 The power of 'welcome'

> Whether spoken, written, or demonstrated in behaviour, this is a concept and a communication that never loses its power to warm the heart and put people at their ease. When we move into the territory of others, we should always be made to feel welcome.

The concept of hospitality is relevant and useful: when strangers or friends come to our house for the first time, we exert ourselves to make sure they have somewhere to put their outdoor clothes, know where the bathroom is, provide them with refreshment, seat them comfortably – and so on. The underlying spirit of welcoming generosity is no less relevant in every aspect of healthcare. Try occasionally to see your work environment through the eyes of a complete first-time newcomer: what does it look like? How welcoming is it? What's off-putting? How does it feel? How could it be improved? How can my communications help to compensate for the physical shortcomings?

Providing continuity

A patient abandoned without explanation in the radiology or pathology department waiting area may be unsettled by the multiple uncertainties of their situation: what's going to happen? How long will it take? How unpleasant will it be? How long must I wait? Will they know who I am? Have I been forgotten?

What is needed is an overall narrative in which each incident can be placed and expectations settled. This has to be provided by the nurse or member of staff managing the patient from the beginning, when the series of tests and/or procedures has been decided and the patient is first informed about what is to happen. Stating the level of uncertainty about waiting times is one important element, and more realistic estimates should be provided by departmental staff from time to time if waiting is prolonged, or when takeover from another department is delayed. Patients need to feel that they are involved in an active process (however slow) which has a beginning and a foreseeable end and during which they are not forgotten – and it needs to be described to them. No patient should be sent off to the next encounter or left in a waiting area if the HCP merely *hopes* that they will somehow be picked up and attended.

Although HCPs generally have a single role within an organisation, sometimes remaining mostly in one place, having certain routines, for the patient it is a succession of new encounters and different places, like going in and out of shops in a big mall – the risks of feeling lost and confused are great.

Nurses' special role in the care of patients – a model for healthcare

Throughout the ages, women, especially, have taken care of the sick and the needy, in all imaginable situations. New Zealand led the world in 1901 with the first national regulation of nursing. Since then, the power of vocation, the call to heroic, altruistic work, has remained strong, while the forces of professionalisation and specialisation have marched alongside, occasionally threatening the vision of care at the heart of nursing. The controversial 'romance with medicine' has put great pressure on the distinct definition of nursing as a complementary but separate speciality. Bureaucracy and economics have come to play an ever-increasing part in the day-to-day life of nurses, as they have in every aspect of healthcare, also putting pressure on the non-utilitarian, humane, caring aspects of the job.

> Nursing is an art: and if it is to be made an art, it requires an exclusive devotion as hard a preparation, as any painter's or sculptor's work; for what is the having to do with dead canvas or dead marble, compared with having to do with the living body, the temple of God's spirit? It is one of the Fine Arts: I had almost said, the finest of Fine Arts.
>
> *Florence Nightingale*

Here, we concentrate on the single core activity of nursing care for patients, and the values, knowledge and skills needed for the very best practice in that vital, but threatened area. Any nursing practice and any nursing speciality must be built on this foundation, but its relevance and resonance reach far beyond only nursing.

Vocational values

At the heart of the best nursing is the belief that those who are sick should be cared for in spirit, body and mind; that their fears and anxieties should be reduced; that their health and happiness, and their capabilities, their relationships and their environment should be nurtured and improved; that they should be given the opportunity of the best quality of life possible in their terms, through treatment, convalescence and rehabilitation, or through incurable or chronic illness, up to the

Box 15.4 Peri- and postoperative care

These activities are a perfect example of the unique and irreplaceable part nurses can play in the delivery of quality healthcare: technical knowledge and skill are essential, both for execution and for briefing the patient about what to expect and about interpreting the experience, but the primary contribution is psychosocial.

Operations can generate acute anxiety in patients and their families, even when the procedure is minor and commonplace (neither of which characteristics means the elimination of risk, of course). Some surgeons have a reputation for being somewhat brisk in their dealings with their patients, but even putting that aside and assuming sensitive and empathetic communication, the time a patient spends with their surgeon is a very tiny part of their whole hospital experience and the remaining 23.75 hours in the day (or 167.75 hours in the week) may be filled with uncertainties, anxieties and questions. It is in this enormous expanse of a patient's life that a nurse can provide almost everything that a surgeon does not and cannot:

- empathetic exploration of the patient's ideas, thoughts and concerns as they evolve
- attentive listening to the patient's feelings and anxieties (perhaps some for which there is no solution or answer, but which are relieved through expression)
- the provision of reliable information and reasonable reassurance (proportionate to the true situation)
- explanation of the procedure and likely consequences, as far as the patient wants to know and it is reasonable to predict
- attention to the patient's wider concerns – impact on family, working life, future health and mobility
- a consistent, predictable, caring presence and relationship throughout the disorienting and alienating experience of hospitalisation (continuity of care)
- the provision of a nurturing human relationship and physical care which protects and enhances the patient's dignity and self-respect, with special attention to the unique characteristics of the individual
- the creative use of resources to provide comfort and reassurance, especially immediately before an operation and during the postoperative period of disorientation.

point of death. This vision is achieved through the combination of technical, scientific and medical knowledge and skills and the driving priority of caring, based on deep knowledge and skills in human relations and communications.

Although this book encourages doctors to view their patients as whole people, and to treat them as partners in the enterprise of healthcare, their contact with patients is necessarily very limited in terms of time (although it need not be so in terms of intensity). It is a real relationship, but structured and condensed for specific purposes, and inevitably excludes broad areas of the patient's life and reality. It largely excludes the opportunity, for example, for reflective exploration or explanation of issues, simply because of the time constraints.

Constant attention by a good nurse may be just as important as a major operation by a surgeon.
Dag Hammarskjöld

Nurses in most specialities have the opportunity for the establishment of relationships that are less constrained by time in terms of length and frequency of contact, although, of course there is constant pressure to reduce contact time and 'get on with the work'. However, seeing or meeting a patient over a period of days or weeks (perhaps much longer) provides the opportunity for relationships of an entirely different quality and depth and the potential for healing of an entirely different order.

Physical procedures

The carrying out of physical procedures of all kinds provides the perfect opportunity for the expression of the core caring values of nursing both in the skill and delicacy with which they are carried out, and, perhaps even more significantly, in the communications that accompany them. What is commonplace and risk free for HCPs will often be unfamiliar and alarming for patients, and although professional confidence will reassure, ignoring, dismissing or disparaging a patient's fears will cause nothing but distress.

Box 15.5 The ideal process for any physical procedure

Preparatory explanation of the procedure:
- its purpose and usefulness
- exactly what will happen
- how long it will take
- possible/likely level of discomfort or pain
- attention to and dealing with patient's response – anxieties, issues, emotions or fears that discussion of the procedure prompts

Carrying out the procedure:
- demonstrating care and caution; not rushing or appearing to be engaged in a mere mechanical operation
- talking the patient through each stage
- seeking feedback about the physical and emotional impact of the activity
- ingenuity in distracting the patient from a focus on pain
- pacing each stage to the patient's level of tolerance
- giving the patient space to respond, talk, express discomfort
- apologising for pain or discomfort; reducing causes where possible
- if there is time, and it suits the patient, chatting, or talking about broader issues the patient initiates or responds to, in parallel to the procedure or as a distraction from it

After the procedure:
- checking out the patient's reaction
- making them comfortable again
- asking if there is something they need (water, visit to the toilet, etc.)
- outlining next steps: when results will be available (if relevant); when the procedure might be repeated; what needs to be done next and so on.

In the manner described, the procedure becomes a shared activity, integrated within an attentive, empathetic relationship, in which the patient does not feel like the object of the nurse's activity, but the subject of the nurse's concern. This applies to any nursing situation:
- delivering a baby
- taking blood or swabs
- bathing a patient
- community clinic nurse immunising children
- preparing a patient for an operation
- providing the narrative for a journey around hospital departments
- talking to parents about what needs to be done for their child

- supporting a patient newly diagnosed with diabetes or hypertension
- counselling in a sexual infection clinic.

Nurses can be particularly sensitive and helpful in areas such as personal hygiene, patients' need for privacy, and negotiating social and cultural differences.

God bless the physician who warms the speculum or holds your hand and looks into your eyes. Perhaps one subtext of the health care debate is a yen to be treated like a whole person, not just an eye, an ear, a nose or a throat. A yen to be human again, on the part of patient and doctor alike.

Anna Quindlen

Patient wellbeing

This is the primary concern of nursing (although it should not, of course, be limited to nurses) and pursuing it will often have little to do with physical procedures and much more to do with the formation of concerned, caring, effective relationships and with the quality of information and communication offered. It also has to do with having a sense of responsibility for – caring about – patients' wellbeing – constantly being alert for those things that are troubling patients or might do so, reacting positively and supportively whenever there is any indication that patients are anxious or uncomfortable or needing to talk. The patient's knowledge and confidence that such resources are reliably available will maintain comfort and morale. Those nurses who, when not involved in specific technical nursing tasks, spend most of their time chatting with each other at the ward station are squandering precious opportunities to get to know and to care for their patients as whole persons.

The purposes of all this are clear:

- to prepare the patient's mind and body to gain maximum benefit from therapy and hasten recovery, reducing or removing whatever obstacles might stand in the way
- to support and cherish the patient on their route to independence and to making the best of their lives through convalescence or rehabilitation and after healthcare
- to include in all these considerations the patient's partner, family, friends and carers as part of the wholeness and fabric of their lives.

Box 15.6 Patient commendation points the way

This is part of the text of a patient's public appreciation of first-class nursing care and its profound impact.

'Gail Benedetti was my nurse in the days and nights immediately following my Whipple procedure (a complex gastrointestinal procedure). After more than 7 hours of surgery, I was in no shape to advocate or care for myself. The surgeon may have saved my life but my nurse made it bearable.

'Gail did everything for me, from painlessly removing my nasalgastric tube to gently giving me a sponge bath. I wasn't her only patient but she made me feel that I was. When I woke up, she was there. When I went to sleep, she was there. Bells and lights went off. Tubes and bags needed changing. Gail was there to make it right. It was uncanny. I didn't have to worry. My nurse was looking out for me. Because Gail took the time to explain each procedure, medication, and piece of equipment to me, I knew what to expect. That shared information was both comforting and empowering to me as a patient. When pain was an issue, Gail made it her priority to advocate for me. She truly was my angel of mercy. The memory of her unflagging compassion and competence still brings tears to my eyes. I will be forever in her debt.'[125]

Familiarity

Nurses, on the whole, like pharmacists, have the immense benefit of being seen by patients as more like ordinary people than are doctors; less distant, existing perhaps in a more familiar, less rarefied world, and, therefore, more approachable, more sympathetic, more likely to take seriously and understand ordinary experiences, emotions and anxieties. This is a very positive starting point for being useful. There are patients (and staff), of course, who regard nurses as inferior, and there are some nurses who are patronising, and there are those (in all roles) who sit around chatting with each other, who achieve far less than they might with more gentleness or commitment.

After two days in the hospital, I took a turn for the nurse.

W.C. Fields

The pharmacist's special role in care of patients

Considering the quality of most pharmacy education and training, and the responsibilities that pharmacists carry, the profession does not seem to have, in many places, the reputation and profile it deserves. Fortunately, things are changing in all aspects: increasingly, pharmacists are seen as having a vital role in patient care and patient safety, and the relatively new speciality of clinical pharmacy is seen as a core contributor to patient welfare and safety in hospitals. Effectiveness in communications has a central part to play in the realisation of these new and important opportunities, as well as in the more traditional responsibilities.

The challenging concept of 'pharmaceutical care' was first introduced in the early 1990s and has been developing since then, including the specialist activity of pharmaceutical counselling, championed, among others, by the International Pharmaceutical Students' Federation.[126] In an early definition, published by the American Society of Hospital Pharmacists,[127] pharmaceutical care was described as 'the direct, responsible provision of medication-related care for the purpose of achieving definite outcomes that improve a patient's quality of life'.

The implications of this for relationships with patients are enormous, particularly in the provision of care (at the highest level of its meaning) and in the degree of personal responsibility that pharmacists are expected to take for their patients and their medical needs. For those working in busy retail pharmacies, some of what follows may seem unrealistic but, against the odds, there are many places where the ideals outlined are being fulfilled day after day. Those who are achieving such great things report not only better business, but greater satisfaction among all parties.[128]

The art of dispensing

In fulfilling a prescription in a community or hospital pharmacy, the requirements are technical/medical/pharmaceutical, of course but, more than ever, they are for an effective, individual relationship with the patient – comparable to that of a doctor or nurse or any other responsible professional. Fulfilling a prescription is not just a footnote to the consultation with the doctor, but an essential, critical element in the safe and effective fulfilment of the whole process.[129] (See also Chapters 17 and 19 for more on safety and risk communication.)

Box 15.7 Dispensing

These are some of the communications demands of the apparently simple process.

- Identify the patient and source of prescription.
- Introduce self and role (to help, support safe therapy, answer questions).
- Check the details of the prescription for legibility and accuracy.
- Check the patient's view of the indication.
- Make an initial assessment of the patient's health literacy and begin to choose communication and materials to match their level and abilities.
- Review appropriateness of therapy for the indication.
- Make an assessment of the patient's level of satisfaction with the medical consultation and the outcome.
- Check the patient's disease and medication history, especially if they have been seeing a succession of different HCPs.
- Ask the patient what they were told (what they remember) about the drug and how they were to take it.
- Add important details that may have been forgotten.
- Ask if the doctor enquired about contraindications and about other medications or substances that might interact.
- Confirm, correct or add to the patient's information.
- Provide information about possible adverse drug reactions (ADRs), risk, seriousness, early signs, and action to take.
- Dispense medicines/devices.
- Ask for patient to review dose, frequency, coping with missed doses, cautions and behaviour to avoid.
- Review essentials again, including the importance of completing the course.
- Provide supporting literature, leaflets, charts, etc., as appropriate.
- Provide name and contact details and invite patient to telephone or return if they have any doubts or problems.

Readers will now be able to identify the skills in operation in such an encounter: establishing rapport, empathy, listening, observing, questioning, explaining, teaching, providing information, seeking feedback, and perhaps persuading and providing emotional support, too.

At the end of such an encounter (Box 15.7), a patient should not only know something more about their disease and their medicines, but also about behaviour to protect their safety, lines of communication for future use, and – most challenging – the sense that they are in the hands of a competent and caring professional, whose interest in them does not end the moment they pay and leave. The best pharmacists keep records of their patients, contact them occasionally, discuss issues with local physicians, and become an integrated part of the patient's experience of coherent and effective healthcare. Some pharmacists run support groups for certain categories of disease, or provide specialised counselling or monitoring services – they have moved beyond the notion of being simply dispensers of pills.[130] Pharmacies may be ideal centres for the dissemination of public health information, advice about reproductive health and family planning, nutrition and much more.

Box 15.8 Keeping cool (or not)

Clarify what is permitted behind what is prohibited

'Do not store above 25°C' (or similar) is a common instruction on medicines packaging. It can be perplexing for those who live in places where such a temperature is occasional or common: 'How can I stop my drugs getting cooked?' It will not always occur to patients that the remedy is to keep medicines refrigerated: statement of the hazard of 25°C does not imply, mean or state that 5°C is safe. The complete message is:

If storage temperature rises to or is likely to rise to 25°C or more, keep the medicine in a normal refrigerator (above 0°C or freezing point).

Even this message is not adequate if protection from high temperatures is critical for maintaining product effectiveness, nor for a patient who worries about details (or does not have a fridge). What happens if the medicine has to be carried for use during the working day in high temperatures? What length of exposure is safe (hours, days)?

When advising anyone what they *should not* do, it is important always to make clear the details of what they *should* do.

First aid

In many places, especially developing countries, for those who do not seek traditional healers, pharmacies are often the major providers of first-line primary healthcare, the first port of call for worried patients. There are enormous challenges in on-the-spot diagnosis, perhaps in a busy environment without the possibility of sophisticated tests or physical examination, and its effectiveness and safety will depend as much on communication skills as on medical and pharmaceutical expertise. Demonstrating a caring disposition in a brief consultation requires all the skills of empathy, attentive observation and listening, effective questioning, explanation and so on, and the strength of a pharmacist's performance will affect health outcomes, confidence in the profession and the further development of pharmacy practice as a major contributor to healthcare in general. This is especially important where healthcare resources are limited or expensive, and pharmacists (or unqualified pharmacy assistants) may be a patient's primary or only option for treatment.

Pharmacists have the opportunity of playing a crucial role in healthcare, and a much wider role than is currently the case, but in order to do so they must communicate their resources and their usefulness effectively to other professionals and to patients. In some places, they must develop so robust a definition of their usefulness (and for example, the effectiveness of counselling) that they will convince funders and insurers to reimburse them for their contribution and their time.

Within hospitals, pharmacists have an equally important part to play in relationships with patients, but also on a wider front in helping an institution rationalise its pharmaceutical policy and practices and improve all elements of safety. Where clinical pharmacists have been embraced within the team, improvements in therapy, safety and economy have been achieved. Overcoming institutional barriers requires very subtle, effective communications, but the rewards for everyone are great when new skills and insight can be added to the whole team.

Physical and rehabilitative therapy

In the league table of contributions to the welfare of humanity, those who help restore or enhance physical capacity and independence to the injured and the sick, and to those with disabilities, must rank among the top few. They rank with the achievements of medicine, because medicine may be only half the remarkable story: bringing a patient back from the edge of death after a stroke is pretty impressive, but without speech or movement the rescue may be of equivocal value to the patient and their family; repairing the shattered body of a road-accident victim may be an exercise in technical brilliance, but without restoring such strength and mobility as are possible to that body, the brilliance may be entirely wasted. Nursing represents the primary stage of restoring patients to such independence as they can achieve; then there are many others who must take over specific aspects of rehabilitation.

The demands on specialists in these crucial areas (physical, occupational, speech, audiology, ophthalmology, diet, social work) are intense, in some respects even more so than the demands on HCPs whose contact with patients is relatively brief: often doctors and nurses must compress their relationships with patients into very short time spans (itself a challenge), whereas other members of the team in allied specialities may need to sustain robust, motivational training or therapeutic relationships over long periods, some home-care specialists (health visitors, midwives) over many years, even decades. And, for them, the patient as a whole person, in their whole social and family context over time, is their inescapable subject.

The challenges of motivating patients and maintaining long-term relationships are discussed in Chapter 12.

The great importance of non-medical personnel

Non-medical staff need to be embraced as essential partners in the whole enterprise, trained in the aims of the organisation, listened to and valued as partners in caring for patients. The vision of this book demands that vital, often low-profile jobs are given space and consideration as genuine contributors to the effectiveness of healthcare. They need to feel that they are partners in patient-centred care if they are to contribute to its realisation and not obstruct it. Doctors, nurses and pharmacists have a real part to play in nurturing relationships with all members of the team.

> Just the act of listening means more than you can imagine to most employees.
>
> *Bob Nelson*

Here are three sections showing how cleaning, catering and frontline roles contribute.

Cleaning staff

Cleaners have a job as important as any other in a hospital or clinic – in some respects more so, because failure to achieve and maintain the highest standards of hygiene and cleanliness can kill and injure people and shut down an entire medical service. Without their work the environment is neither safe nor pleasant for anyone, as we know only too well from the depradations of *Clostridium difficile* and meticillin-resistant *Staphylococcus aureus* (MRSA).

The essential nature of the physical work is obvious, although complex and specialised too. What is less obvious and rarely talked about is the important contribution cleaning staff have to make to the overall reputation of a hospital or clinic, not just for its cleanliness but also for its friendliness, helpfulness and humanity.

Whether in wards or corridors, offices or consulting rooms, waiting areas, toilets, canteens – anywhere – cleaning staff will frequently see patients and their families; be asked questions by them; notice them looking lost or uncertain; have the chance to offer some kind of support or information. Poor or working people or those lacking confidence and social skills, especially, may feel much more relaxed about approaching a cleaner or porter to ask for help, than they would a doctor or nurse.

Box 15.9 Training and orientation

Being able to make a truly helpful response to patients requires at least two, major preparatory organisational activities, largely concerned with communications.

- An organisational culture of inclusion and respect where all staff are valued for the contribution they make to the whole enterprise (creating such a culture, communicating it, living it).
- A thorough induction into the organisation for all non-medical staff:
  - its vision and values (including its patient-centred philosophy)
  - basic communications training (empathy, listening, helping)
  - its physical layout and the specialities it offers
  - knowledge of especially sensitive areas, issues or categories of patients (this includes understanding how disease affects people's behaviour – physical vulnerability, difficulty with speech, for example)
  - basic training in dealing with difficult or aggressive people
  - lines of communication for everyday feedback to managers, as well as for emergencies.

Many non-medical staff have a natural talent for friendliness and will help anyone who comes their way. But it is not easy to feel friendly and confident in every organisation, and, without encouragement, many people will shy away from patient contact.

Box 15.10

'During my second year of nursing school our professor gave us a quiz. I breezed through the questions until I read the last one: "What is the first name of the woman who cleans the school?" Surely this was a joke. I had seen the cleaning woman several times, but how would I know her name? I handed in my paper, leaving the last question blank. Before the class ended, one student asked if the last question would count toward our grade. "Absolutely," the professor said. "In your careers, you will meet many people. All are significant. They deserve your attention and care, even if all you do is smile and say hello." I've never forgotten that lesson. I also learned her name was Dorothy.'

Joann C. Jones

Cleaners and other non-medical staff have the potential to make a great contribution to the social harmony of any location and to the health and welfare of patients. Cleaners are out and about throughout a whole building or site and they notice a great deal of what is happening: what the problems are, where patients get lost, where the signage is confusing, what patients are upset or complaining about, where access is difficult for the elderly or disabled, where the unrecognised safety hazards are – and lots more – and any management should be anxious to hear this kind of front-line intelligence about the operation. The quality of management relations and communications will determine whether the organisation capitalises on such invaluable feedback or ignores it and lets problems persist.

This is a resource that management neglects at its peril – not least because neglected staff do not care about cleanliness or anything else, and may even get in the way of the primary activities of patient care.

Man does not live by soap alone; and hygiene, or even health, is not much good unless you can take a healthy view of it or, better still, feel a healthy indifference to it.

Gilbert K. Chesterton

Catering staff

This is another group of people who play a very important part in making a hospital, nursing home or institution of any kind a pleasant, comfortable place for sick people. Much of the material above on cleaning staff applies equally here. Few things upset people (everyone: patients, staff and visitors) more than a conclusion that 'the food is terrible' or that the catering service is second rate; few things provide a greater boost to morale than for everyone to know that their next meal or snack on site will be a good experience. In the alienating environment of a big hospital, a comforting, welcoming cafeteria can be a blessing for anxious or weary visitors, or simply a relaxing pleasure for anyone.[131]

First-class catering for hundreds or thousands of patients and staff is not easy to achieve, especially on tight budgets but it can be done (is done in many places), and should be a high priority for any organisation.[132,133] Along with the provision of nourishing and attractive food itself, there is the whole realm of service associated with catering: how food is served and presented; availability of snacks and drinks throughout the twenty-four hours of the day; how serving staff address their customers and deal with complaints; how staff behave on wards and in canteens; how far there is motivation to improve customer satisfaction.[134]

First need in the reform of hospital management? That's easy! The death of all dietitians, and the resurrection of a French chef.

Martin H. Fischer

Snacks or drinks for the many people visiting a hospital in a single day should always be available somewhere (preferably not from unreliable, impersonal vending machines) – and, at the minimum, a source of fresh drinking water. Patients and anxious families and fractious children have enough troubles without being hungry or thirsty as well, especially when waiting times may be long. There is a very special contribution to be made in the way in which the needs of patients with special dietary needs or preferences are met.

Box 15.11 Catering priorities

Three obvious aspects of communications activity associated with catering:

- Catering staff should have the same kind of induction into the organisation outlined for cleaning staff, and be capable communicators.
- Catering staff are likely to meet almost everyone in a hospital or clinic, perhaps several times a day; their empathy, goodwill and cheerfulness can significantly affect the ethos of an entire establishment.
- All catering operations should constantly seek the opinions of their customers about the service: what pleases them, what they dislike, what they would like done differently, how things could change for the better. This intelligence is available every time a patient or customer comments – either spontaneously or on request – on any aspect of the catering service, or when food is left on trays – is it because the patient is not hungry or not well enough to eat, or because they do not like what they have been given? Staff should be listening and asking; catering management should be listening to what their staff report and gathering customer opinions on a routine, regular basis.

If our commitment is to take care of the whole person (patients and staff alike), then imaginative, attractive catering and friendly caterers are very high on the list of priorities.

The front line and beyond

A patient's entire impression of an institution or clinic may be shaped or determined by the very first encounter: the gardener on the way in; the security guard; the receptionist; the passing nurse of whom an enquiry is made. It may already have been shaped or determined by the response of the telephone operator during an enquiry prior to visiting or by the tone of a letter sent (more on these aspects in Chapter 22.)

The reception arrangements at even very sophisticated facilities are often appalling – unfriendly, alienating, disorderly. Arrangements such as solid screens distance staff from patients, making communication difficult, and often requiring a volume of speech that destroys privacy. At patients' greatest moment of uncertainty and anxiety and tentativeness, natural humane interaction can be all but impossible. If the only breach of the solid barrier is at counter level, patients are forced into the awkward position of bending down, ruling out relaxed eye-contact and natural exchange. Although such distancing, protective measures may be justified on the basis of staff security, they are utterly alien to the welcoming and reassuring service that reception should offer. They actually invoke frustration and anger. Such physical arrangements speak volumes about the priorities of the organisation, and its lack of creative thinking in finding solutions that are satisfactory and safe for everyone.

A warm welcome

A cheerful, polite, sensitive, efficient security guard at the front door can provide a more effective corporate welcome, and a more uplifting effect on visitors than any number of technical or medical geniuses without heart or soul. A distressed patient will be affected by a moment of compassionate attention as their bags are inspected, or the door is opened, or as they are warmly and genuinely welcomed, and shown where they need to go. And as a patient moves to the reception area, where they are again greeted warmly – good eye-contact, immediate attention, focus on their presence and needs – a real credit balance of positive feeling will be accumulating. That positive feeling will affect everything that follows, including a predisposition to see other people and events positively, and to maximise whatever opportunities and help the organisation can offer. The reverse is equally true: an abrupt or brisk greeting will destroy confidence and goodwill. Any member of staff who encounters a patient in a bad mood should explore to see if the source of the negativity is not a lot closer than they might imagine – perhaps a neglected or disgruntled or bored or inadequate member of the home team. In that case, the diagnosis is clear: symptoms of organisational indifference or sickness.

Conclusion

This is an important chapter, on some topics that you may feel are tangential to the main theme of the book: it attempts, unusually for texts like this, to unite the multitude of healthcare roles in a single vision of patient-centred care and sensitive, effective communications. There is little knowledge and few skills in this area which are not pertinent to every role. When everyone shares the same idea of best practice, and there is genuine mutual support and collaboration in achieving it, there will be a dramatic impact on the health and welfare of patients, on professional satisfaction and dynamism, and on health outcomes.

16 When time and resources are limited

Shortage of time or resources and pressure of numbers mean that communications and even therapy may sometimes be compromised. On the basis of knowing what would be ideal, HCPs have to choose and limit what they say and do on the basis of situational triage – selecting only the absolute priorities and essentials. This requires confidence about the big picture and what must or can reasonably be omitted. Communicating limitations of time or resources and restrictions or denial of therapy to patients requires resilience, skill and sensitivity. In reviewing shortage of time and resources, we need to be sure that we are actually making the best of what is available.

Personal style

There is great variation between HCPs in all settings in gross productivity (throughput of patients). The bell curve of annual patients seen in American Family Practice, for example, ranges from 2000 to 6000, with a median between 4000 and 5000.[135] The determining variables include medical issues (chronic, complex or episodic disease, for example); personal characteristics such as professional, communications and psychological needs and style; and serious questions relating to earnings. Those at the lower end are often under enormous pressure to increase their figures and may be resented by those who work faster and have to pick up unattended patients from their slower colleagues' lists. Similar variations and issues apply across all HCP roles. The solutions come from a sophisticated negotiation between:

- personal preferences
- medical demands and priorities
- patient needs
- human and other resources available
- time and money
- the delivery of optimal patient care, including excellent communications.

Those seeing fewer patients may be spending more time in critical cognitive and counselling elements of healthcare (investigation, thinking, talking and listening) and may be providing a superior quality of care. Reimbursement and time-accounting systems often give little recognition to this, leading to their neglect and so to potentially greater – and more expensive – problems in the future, especially where conversations about disease prevention are curtailed. The number of patients processed does not tell us much about the quality of service offered. An important variable in examining pressure of time and resources is the behaviour, efficiency and motivation of HCPs themselves as well as the target quality of service to be achieved.

Resource triage

Careful matching of patient need with appropriate resources is an obvious and basic provision to increase efficiency. Not all patients need to see doctors or qualified pharmacists, for example. Nurse practitioners and physician assistants, as well as specialist nurses and well-trained medical or pharmacy assistants may be the appropriate (sometimes the only) HCPs to whom patients should or can go.

On the other hand, the clogging up of emergency departments with minor, non-urgent cases is clearly inappropriate and wasteful, as is the filling of a doctor's waiting area with patients who could be dealt with by a nurse or other HCP or counsellor. Researching and matching needs and resources is a complex activity, and involves effective communications in analysis of the problem and in explaining what patients should do and why. Resources and needs will be very different in different settings (remote clinics in rural Africa or South America, for example), but the overall principles remain much the same.

The guiding light of ideals

As was conceded earlier, the visions in this book may seen unrealistic. Who has time for all this?[136]

It's a fair point, and in a few paragraphs we'll talk about how to negotiate the demands of effective communications against the tyranny of limited time. First, a few observations.

This book describes and analyses the ideal, the best that any of us can hope to achieve. The purpose of an ideal is to have a standard against which we can measure what we do, and perhaps improve it. The fact that we rarely achieve the ideal does not invalidate it nor justify cynicism about it. It provides guidance about the best choices to make and the errors to avoid. It may provoke distress when we realise we have fallen short, or when circumstances force us to deliver less than our best, but it then allows us to harness that dissatisfaction and examine our practice to see if we cannot improve and refine it in the future. In all the busy chaos of every day, an ideal provides at least a guiding light.

Knowing what is ideal, in all its detail, also gives us much greater authority on which to decide priorities and make limited choices – both what we can do and what we must omit. If we don't have the big picture we are simply muddling along, driven by the often misleading demands, priorities and clues that happen to be in front of us.

> I am only one, but I am one. I cannot do everything, but I can do something. And I will not let what I cannot do interfere with what I can do.
>
> *Edward Everett Hale*

The credibility of the ideal in healthcare at the heart of this book is corroborated from an unexpected and paradoxical source: patients paying for their healthcare will expect nothing less than the ideal in communications and therapy, and HCPs, with the time to do it, will usually deliver nothing less than the best. Failure is likely to put the HCP's income and career at risk. Cash and time may be the critical elements in freedom to achieve the ideal, but lack of cash and time do not in any way compromise the authority of the ideal, nor justify abandoning its essence in any circumstances. HCPs all over the world already achieve remarkable standards in the most hostile and limited environments.

Box 16.1 Spending does not necessarily solve problems

> According to US Commonwealth Fund research in 2002,[137] per capita spending on healthcare does not necessarily provide quality and value for money in the eyes of patients. The US, spending around twice as much as the other five developed countries in the study, was ranked bottom on four criteria, including patient safety and patient-centredness, although it was number one on effectiveness.

Triage

If you have 60 to 100 patients (or more) to see in a day, you cannot spend 15 or 20 minutes sensitively exploring each one's symptoms and emotions, discussing options and providing thoughtful benefit–risk information and therapeutic options: you must concentrate on the most serious cases, on the essentials and make the most effective response possible in the time available. It is the same for a nurse or pharmacist in a short-staffed, busy ward or hospital department. Such production-line pressure hardly ever results in good healthcare in its ideal sense, but the skilled HCP will be able to exploit even the smallest opportunity and make the best of it for patients' benefit; the careless, resigned, exhausted HCP is likely to miss such opportunities and fail to achieve even the modest possibilities of the situation. What do you do?

Much of what follows requires no time at all during contact with a patient, but the preparatory work will have a dramatic impact on how fruitful the short time is. Much of what follows, but not all, is also relevant to any patient contact with or without extreme time-limits.

First: You need to finish reading this book, believe in it and incorporate its values and practices into your conscious and spontaneous life. If you are basically compassionate, attentive and empathetic this will be clear to everyone, and will impress people, even in the shortest encounter. Rooted empathy, concern, commitment, are evident from the very first gesture or word in the briefest of moments. A grasp of the ideal will also make you more discriminating about what you omit, and so have a clearer grasp of areas in which you may need to exercise caution or reserve judgement before further enquiry and action.

Once the knowledge is absorbed, processed and integrated, and the skills practised conscientiously, much of the communication and behaviour will become more or less automatic, spontaneous. But there will always be a self-critical, internal guardian processing events and relationships, and raising alerts when there is anything doubtful, ambiguous or misleading.

Second: Develop your capacity for professional empathy, especially through listening and observation, so that your intelligence-gathering capacity is heightened to the extent that you are instantly receptive to some of the critical underlying communications that patients make with and without words; so that your receptivity and your perception are acutely alert to the inner world of patients, and that you can respond accurately and helpfully, without the need for lengthy verbal

Box 16.2 Working smarter[138–140]

Any of us who conscientiously examine exactly how we spend our time and carry out our tasks, will find areas where we are inefficient, where we waste time and store up problems. For example, we may regularly waste time looking for papers or files when, by taking an hour or two to set up a decent retrieval system, we could save many hours. We may prolong tasks, and do them less effectively, by allowing ourselves to be interrupted by others or distracted by our own concerns (telephone calls and emails, for example). We damage our morale by letting important tasks (such as paperwork or emails in our inbox) accumulate, instead of having strict routines for dealing with them and getting them out of the way. We unnecessarily handle files and papers several times, instead of dealing with them straightaway – reading, filing or discarding them. We run or attend meetings that are wastefully or inefficiently managed, and which sap people's morale (see Chapter 25). We accept without question or effective protest routines, forms or procedures that are inefficient, repetitive and unnecessarily time consuming. We do not use the techniques of differential faster reading skills to deal appropriately with things that we should scan or read.[141,142] Personal productivity can always be improved – leaving more time for the things that really matter. Time and systems management are worthwhile, fruitful studies.[143,144]

This is a selection of tips for working smarter, *from Family Practice Management*[145]:

- Start your day on time
- Dictate charts, notes, hospital notes
- Keep busy and train staff to keep you so
- Limit or avoid frequent breaks
- Pull only the charts you really need
- Bundle refill requests
- Examine your hospital load (economies of time, scale, travel, etc.)
- Send paperless faxes.

Small things, perhaps, but they accumulate very large numbers of saved minutes every day.

It is also important to scrutinise organisational systems and procedures in which there are often enormous inefficiencies, redundant, repetitive or pointless processes and time-wasting activities.

exploration. Read and study so that you have the knowledge to make sense of the variety and complexity of human nature. Harvest understanding and wisdom about humanity from fiction, films, plays, everyday life. When you shake hands with a patient, collect the rich series of data available to you from that simple, momentary gesture and all the associated non-verbal clues – temperature, skin condition and muscle tone, strength, firmness, degree of reciprocated grip, duration, meaning; the patient's morale, confidence, levels of anxiety and so on.

Third: Develop a range of behaviours and remarks that facilitate effective use of limited time and dilute the potential negative impact on patients. Possible useful behaviour includes:

- Mentally and physically preparing for giving undivided, undistracted attention to the next patient (clearing the mind of preoccupations; relaxing and composing the body – see Chapter 11 'Empathy' and 'Listening').
- Making the greeting and welcome as warm and effective as possible as if it were the first encounter of the day (reassuring, strong first impression).
- Adopting a calm, focused, attentive posture.
- Make an open, enabling enquiry about the patient's reasons for attending (it should sound as if you expect the subject to be the first and most interesting and important thing you will hear that day).
- Timing and structuring the consultation carefully, sharing your intentions with the patient; actively managing the compressed timescale and its demands and involving the patient in the process. This requires a delicate balance of assertiveness and attentiveness.
  - 'Mrs Phillips, we have ten minutes (or five minutes) to get to the bottom of this together and, I hope, to help you. Please forgive the pressure. Now . . .'
  - 'To save time, now I need to ask you some basic questions, then you must tell me if you think I've missed anything . . .'

For some patients, it may not be necessary to mention time pressure at all, if their problem is

relatively simple and is likely to be solved within a short period.

- Use markers or signposts for critical information:
  - 'Now this is very important . . .'
  - 'Please try to remember that . . .'
  - 'I want to be sure you understand this . . .'
  - 'We just have a few minutes left.'
- Managing the time so that there is opportunity for a patient's last minute requests, sometimes critical revelations postponed for one reason or another.

Fourth: Cultivate active listening (see Chapter 11 'Listening', p. 80), even under extreme time-constraints, remembering that you may sometimes get better information from one minute of sensitive listening than from four minutes of rapid-fire questioning. Intensive listening also helps develop the capacity for empathy. Listen and watch intensely with your eyes and your ears, your heart and your mind; probe and follow up. Switch your mind and body into intensive listening mode.

Fifth: Refine your questioning technique so that, for each individual patient, you ask questions which are most productive of useful responses, using closed questions for specific information but carefully composed open questions for the patient to set the scene and for wider enquiries. Monitor the effectiveness of your questions and refine your technique. Don't waste questions. Remember that silence may be an important element in helping a patient to provide accurate, considered answers, especially under pressure. Silence is a powerful tool, and it rarely requires more than a few seconds of stillness (see Chapter 11, 'Questioning', p. 82).

Sixth: Develop techniques for sensitively guiding and focusing patients' responses to issues that are most pertinent for them and for you, avoiding digressions and irrelevancies as far as possible (remembering that sometimes what seem like digressions and irrelevancies to an HCP are central to the concerns of a patient; don't jump to conclusions or make assumptions if there is insufficient evidence for them).

- 'I'm sorry to hear about that, but please would you go back to the pain in your stomach and tell me . . .'
- 'OK. I'm not quite sure why you said that – is it related to your headache?'
- 'Yes. I think you'll need to get some help for your mother. Now, back to you . . .'
- 'Let's take one thing at a time.'

Seventh: Develop the capacity to work quickly without appearing to rush the job or harass the patient. This can be achieved partly by varying the rhythm of the encounter, including, for example, attentive listening at one point and efficient physical examination at another; relaxed physical posture at one point, alert, brisker review of options or information at another. The occasional use of silence will also contribute to enriching the atmosphere. The encounter will be distressing for the patient if it is conducted at a constantly breathless pace, and the impression will be left of an unfeeling production line. A more natural (if calculated), varied rhythm will also be much less exhausting for the HCP. It is perfectly possible to work quickly and efficiently while remaining (certainly appearing to be) physically and mentally relaxed.

Eighth: Within the accelerated pace of short consultations, slow down for discussion and giving of critical information. Although the HCP's brain may be working fast, the patient's may be in quite another rhythm, and some questions will require reflection, some information, time for digestion. When giving critical information and explanation (about options, risk, side effects, dosage, adherence, interactions) slow down, repeat information and check understanding (see Chapter 11, Boxes 11.13 and 11.14 'Effective explanation' and 'Checking understanding').

Ninth: Linked to the last point, ensure that there is time for review of the main issues of the consultation at the very end, so that the patient leaves with a strong memory of what they must do and what they must avoid, and that they have some sense of satisfaction and achievement. (Providing brief notes of the key points, or other material for the patient to take away is a valuable technique.)

Tenth: Especially when consultation time is short, there needs to be good back-up support for the patient to clarify or confirm important issues – notes from the consultation, or leaflets or other material; subsequent contact with a nurse or pharmacist, for example, or through invitation to return for a further consultation (there are some HCPs who actually give their patients a mobile or direct phone number for contact). In a very busy clinic or hospital, it is important for nurses, pharmacists or medical assistants to understand that they have a critical part to play in completing the process of counselling the patient about the disease and the therapy. When time is short, leaflets, pictures, diagrams, charts, reminder cards and other supportive materials are also very useful resources to have at the ready.

It is perfectly possible to have an intense and effective encounter with another person in the space of 10 minutes (even less), although it might fall short of ideal. Its effectiveness will depend almost entirely on the HCP's own commitment and intensity, sense of purpose, experience and communication skills. Although there are great risks in brief encounters in a healthcare setting, especially, for example, with regard to missing symptoms or ignoring social, family and lifestyle issues, useful therapy can be offered, even if sometimes of a rough and ready kind. Although the patient in such a situation can be made to feel like a whole person by the skilled professional, such encounters can never really deal with more than a small part of the whole person and the most obvious and immediate of their health needs. But that does not mean the patient must leave feeling diminished or dissatisfied, especially if the whole team is alert to the patient's needs in the circumstances.

Emergency and urgent care

There are no settings in which there is more pressure on everyone for rapid, effective decision making, action and communications. As in crises or disasters, well-practised procedures and routines are essential for swift treatment, quality and continuity of care and accurate record keeping. The demands affect every member of staff from chief physician to porter and cleaner, any of whom may have contact with people in extreme need of some kind. The additional problem of emergency rooms being flooded with minor, non-urgent cases is a further dimension of the pressures.

Box 16.3 Emergency demands

Some of the particular communications challenges in an emergency department are:

- getting good information quickly from:
  - ambulance paramedics and others
  - patients who may be in extreme pain or shock
  - friends or relatives of patients who may be unconscious or unable to speak
- dealing with intense emotional reactions, including grief, anger, hysteria
- communicating unwelcome news about priorities and waiting times
- handling difficult people (drunks, those high on drugs, aggressive people)
- communicating to the patient what needs to be done
- communicating with and controlling relatives and friends of the patient
- seeking consent for what needs to be done
- communicating bad news (loss of limb, necessity for amputation, death)
- communicating uncertainty
- coordination and collaboration among the hospital team
- sharing information; handovers
- keeping records.

Intense situations, with little or no time for reflection, are the occasions when training is tested to the utmost, when responses need to be close to automatic – in communication skills no less than technical and medical knowledge and procedures.

Intense situations are also those where the underlying disposition and values of the professional are exposed because there is no time for calculation or disguise, where strengths and weaknesses are exposed.

In emergency situations there is little or no time for the explicit and careful management of patients' feelings as there would be in a non-emergency consultation, but the underlying values and attitudes of the attending staff will be clear from the way they handle patients: compassion, goodwill, concern, respect, will be evident or absent, and will affect the course of the treatment and its outcomes. Patients' absolute priority will be for effective medical rescue from their physical emergency, not for psychological gratification, but a distressed patient is more difficult to deal with, so distress does have to be managed and comfort offered.

Box 16.4 Exceptional circumstances

HCPs who find themselves working in the extreme situations of war, major accidents and natural disasters face demands of a very different kind from those of ordinary civilian life. This book does not presume to address relationships amidst such extraordinary events, nor to claim understanding of what is required. There may be some helpful material in this book, but even so, it can go only so far in meeting the needs of those in the midst of chaos, injury and death.

Financial and other constraints

An HCP's capacity to deliver the best medical care for any patient may be determined entirely by non-medical issues, such as reimbursement status or the ability to pay; shortage of personnel, expertise or resources; service may be rationed simply by wealth. In some circumstances, HCPs will face the necessity of refusing treatment, giving partial or sub-optimal treatment, requiring suffering individuals to wait endlessly – falling far short of professional ideals and standards, indeed acting in direct conflict with them. Treatable disease or injury may result in disability or death through such neglect. Such, however, is the impact of political and social policies over which HCPs have virtually no control whatsoever, although they are the people who must make the decisions, explain them, be blamed for them and take the hostile criticism.

A hospital should also have a recovery room adjoining the cashier's office.

Francis O'Walsh

There is a special set of skills for dealing with this unenviable and deeply unpleasant task. We can hope only that one day the necessity for them will disappear, although that seems very unlikely. Here, we are concerned with communicating messages antipathetic to all this book stands for, and to the wishes and ideals of most HCPs. First, some issues for consideration.

Decisions and discretion

Not all decisions about limiting therapy will be clearly defined; there will be ways in which an HCP can be ingenious or creative, can give more than nothing or the very minimum, perhaps even bending the rules a little when the situation demands it. What we need to be sure of, is that when the limit is reached and the patient has to be told, we have genuinely done as much as it is in our power to do. Communicating to the patient that we have reached the limit is quite tough enough, without adding the morally dubious deception that we have done all we can, if that is not the case.

Limits that damage patients

This topic is really beyond the remit of this book, but it is so important it needs to be noted. Rules and regulations, financial constraints and staffing levels, are often determined by politicians, bureaucrats, insurance carriers or managers who may have little or no idea what impact their deliberations will have at the front line: their eyes are on financial statements, not on staff or patients or healthcare quality. The boards of Managed Care Organisations (MCOs) and Health Maintenance Organisations (HMOs), insurance companies, and private health delivery organisations are in the business for profit and shareholder benefit. Although profit derives from attracting customers, gaining a reputation for service and maximising revenue (and this works splendidly when your customers are wealthy), it also depends on maintaining costs at a minimum level and cutting them whenever possible, often, seemingly, without much concern for effects on those who are not wealthy or do not have a voice (the latter often appearing to include staff).

When conscientious HCPs endure imposed rules and limits that compromise their ability to deliver decent healthcare, that damage or kill patients, then they have a responsibility to make them known as far as possible, and to contribute to the public debate which will lead to some productive compromise between individual and social rights and assertive financial and commercial priorities.

If you think you are too small to be effective, you have never been in bed with a mosquito.

Betty Reese

Who's to blame?

For a parent with a sick child, or a patient with an injured leg or an acute disease, their needs are urgent and immediate: their fears, and their hopes and their pain will provoke a fierce and determined, even primitive urge to get help. The interference of financial considerations at such a time will seem like an unimaginable, utter irrelevance. The HCP – physically present and available and with the necessary resources – who refuses to provide such help will inevitably be seen as heartless, brutal and hateful. When the HCP's hands are truly tied by regulations, being in receipt of, let alone dealing with, that degree of hostility and perhaps personal vitriol is a tough assignment. The reaction will be complicated by the HCP's feelings about their inability to help, and by their anger and resentment at being the helpless victim of the frustrating decisions of others.

A degree of restraint, compassionate calm and assertive plain speaking are required.

America's doctors, nurses and medical researchers are the best in the world, but our health care system is broken.

Mike Ferguson

For the HCP, required to deliver unpalatable news, genuine concern and support are essential in the community of colleagues and managers. No one should underestimate the toll that giving bad news, and taking the consequences, exerts on health and morale. Open, attentive, supportive and compassionate communications within an organisation will reduce the damage and the risks.

Twenty-first century medicine must not be confined to a twentieth-century bureaucracy.

Charles W. Pickering

Rational allocation of resources

In understanding the limitations of resources, we need to ask ourselves the question whether the resources we have are being rationally allocated, and what percentage of them are being squandered on problems that should be dealt with in other ways. Having entire populations dependent on healthcare for treating even the slightest ailment or injury does not seem ethically, financially or practically attractive or viable. These issues need to be the subject of long-term, expertly managed social debate.

The issue of empowering populations to take responsibility for their own health is beyond the scope of this book, but there are some local implications for all HCPs and managers in all situations. These relate to practical, medical issues and to communications.

Reducing dependence

In this book we repeatedly emphasise the active involvement of patients in decisions about their healthcare and in its management. We discuss educating patients in basic medical and medicinal knowledge, so that they can be more responsible, intelligent, critical and independent in medical matters. These are the first stages in reducing patient dependence on healthcare, and, it is to be hoped, empowering them to do more for themselves. But it is still at an individual level, and does not address the larger issues of community dependence and helplessness.[146]

One of the first duties of the physician is to educate the masses not to take medicine.

William Osler

That is why the message of a book like *Where there is no doctor*[147] and the example of the South African Phelophepa medical clinic train,[148] and the Jeevan Rekha hospital train in India[149] are so important for the developed world too: it reminds us that responsibility for health not only can be, but should be, felt and exercised in the community and by its members, and that the results will usually be no worse, perhaps even better than HCPs could achieve. If, for example, as part of our daily practice, we find ourselves repeating many of the same messages time and time again to individuals, shouldn't we be seeking ways of planting the seeds of those messages in the community and encouraging them to grow independently?[150] If communities are helpless in the face of minor diseases and accidents, shouldn't we be communicating the knowledge and providing the materials and resources for them to cope on their own?

Identifying how such a vision could influence our own practice or a hospital's activity, and starting to take the focus away from us as the sole providers of services and solutions, and how we would communicate the process, is something for inspired individuals, locally and nationally, to explore in the future. We almost certainly overestimate the extent of our unique importance, underestimate the immense resources in the community, and so waste time and resources doing some things which could be done quite differently, and perhaps better.

Revision, discussion and application (6)

A. Revision and discussion

1. The science of complex adaptive systems (CAS) reveals that activity in one part of a system or by one element in a system has potential and perhaps unpredictable effects throughout the system, and that the changing nature of a system affects how individual elements in it behave and react. Healthcare systems and hospitals are complex systems. How well does the system where you work and the people in it serve the best interests of patients? What aspects of the system inhibit coherent collaboration and communications for the delivery of the best possible service to patients? What individual or departmental behaviour has the same kind of inhibiting effects? What changes need to be implemented? (The inflammatory bowel disease case study exemplifies a healthy, enabling system at work.)
2. In your place of work, how far is the work of nurses valued, and how much scope are they given to develop caring, therapeutic relationships and communications with patients? What limitations are there, and what are their causes and effects? How far do nurses want to take a greater share of responsibility for patients' welfare? How far do they feel they are given too much practical responsibility and not enough time for caring?
3. How integrated a part in patient care do pharmacists play in your part of the world? Are they remote and unknown dispensers of medicines or, to any extent, partners in the bigger vision of excellent healthcare? What can be done to expand their contribution to patient welfare and safety?
4. What are the major constraints and limitations under which you must work? Which of them are largely unnegotiable (national policy and budgets, for example) and which of them are really matters of local management and priorities? Can you identify ways in which better use could be made of limited resources and facilities? Are there, for example, highly qualified staff dealing with minor patient or administrative issues? Take a radical look at what is taken-for-granted in everyday arrangements.
5. What advice would you give to a new entrant to one of the healthcare professions about negotiating the limitations of time or resources while maintaining credibility and effectiveness in the eyes of patients?
6. When an HCP's resources, or those of a health facility are limited, what help and support can be found beyond the usual boundaries, in the locality, for example, or by using volunteers or patient organisations? What creative and practical ways can you find to spread the burden of care and support of patients beyond limited, professional resources?

B. Application

1. What specific measures could you take, or could be taken in your place of work, to increase the coherence of patients' experience of healthcare and the seamlessness of the system to which they are entrusting themselves? What specific changes in behaviour and communications could begin to bring about improvements?
2. To what extent are non-medical, support personnel involved in the ethos of patient-centred care? How open are communications between all roles and levels? How could their commitment, goodwill and usefulness be increased, in terms of patient welfare and facility improvement?
3. Ask patients about their experience of healthcare where you work: how good do they think it is? How much communication and collaboration do they perceive between their various HCPs? How good do they think it is? What is their assessment of the quality and quantity of communications with them on all issues? How committed do the staff seem to be to patient care? Use your questioning skills to get beneath surfaces and the kindly intentions of patients not to criticise.
4. Looking at Box 16.2 'Working Smarter', on p. 163, analyse the points in your working life, and aspects of the system in which you work where time and/or resources are wasted. What are the causes and effects of wasteful procedures and duplication? What time-wasting activities and habits can you identify and try to change?
5. Make a conscious effort to think about and plan how you manage short consultations with patients. What are some of the risks of ill-considered or routine encounters, without meticulous use of the few available minutes? What are some of the vital aspects of behaviour and communications in time-constrained consultations?
6. Think about some of the situations in which you have already had to, or may have to deny patients treatment or treatment options on the grounds of cost, limited resources or other considerations. What aspects of patients' feelings need primary consideration in such circumstances? What kinds of behaviour and communications stand the best chance of reducing distress, disappointment, anger? What are the ways in which you can help patients to accept such bad news without the worst kinds of hurt or damage?

Commentary on many of the questions and issues appears on the publisher's website, in Online Resources at www.pharmpress.com.

Part H

Tough topics

Five complex and demanding topics are presented in considerable detail, all relevant to practice and communications challenges across healthcare roles. They are:

As well as discussion of the background issues and questions, extensive examples of communications with patients are offered as guides to overcoming some of the obstacles and pointing the way to best practice.

17 Patient safety

Besides the multitudes who are helped, there are very large numbers who are damaged, injured or killed in one way or another by medicines and medical interventions. Many of these serious events result from failures in communication in relationships and in complex systems: from safety information which is absent or difficult to access or to understand; from poor verbal or written communications; from poorly designed systems and materials; from faults in labelling and dispensing; from inadequate explanation for patients and their incomplete understanding of therapy; from inappropriate use and low adherence. There are also other causes such as professional errors and environmental hazards such as falls. Analysis of many accidents, errors and injuries reveals how improved systems and communications can reduce the risk of their happening, and contribute to greatly enhanced patient safety and satisfaction.[151–155]

'Effective communication is a cornerstone of patient safety'[156]

More harm than good?

Many patients across the world are injured or killed every year through medical or medication error or by the medicines they are prescribed; enormous numbers who suffer as the result of drug-related problems are admitted to the very hospitals where we know there is a significant risk of further adverse events or infections.[157,158] Large numbers of patients are injured during surgical operations, by faulty use of devices, by infections resulting from poor hospital hygiene, by falls and accidents, and many other causes. Complaints about negligence or malpractice are common. The human and economic costs are huge.[159]

The issues have such a high priority for all healthcare personnel that they are included here in this section of special topics, and because many of the causes underlying the problems relate to communication of one kind or another. This especially applies to adverse drug reactions (ADRs) and medication errors, and so they are given prominence in this account. However, communication issues play a big part in almost every aspect of patient safety, and some of the other issues are briefly dealt with here also.

Box 17.1 Adverse drug reactions in the US

There are:
- over 100 000 deaths per year
- 2 216 000 hospitalised patients experience a serious ADR
- ADRs may be the fourth to sixth leading cause of death.[160]

US medical error

Between 48 000 and 98 000 deaths occur annually from medical error.[161]

ADRs in the UK
- ADRs are the cause of 6.5% of hospital admissions, or 1 040 000 patients (2006).[162]

See also ref. 163 for other recent work in the UK, ref. 164 for India and ref. 165 for Thailand.

In 2000, 2.8 billion prescriptions were written in the US – roughly 10 for every member of the population. ADRs and adverse interactions 'increase exponentially with four or more medications.'[166]

The annual cost of drugs to the UK NHS was £11 billion for 752 million prescriptions in the community (excluding hospitals), about 15 prescriptions per capita of the population.[167]

Safety issues relating to medicines

Drugs are tested in meticulous and expensive clinical trials but usually on relatively small numbers of people, often healthy volunteers, over relatively short periods of time, with strictly controlled variables. Results from such trials cannot be guaranteed to apply to very much larger populations of hugely varying patients in the real world. Very few drugs are tested on children, or pregnant women, or on those with complex disease or co-morbidities. Drugs successfully tested in one country or in one ethnic group may have entirely different safety profiles in other situations; drugs taken for many months or years may have direct or latent effects undiscoverable in short trials.

These, and many other factors mean that the safety of patients is often as dependent on effective communication, observant and critical practice, and monitoring by HCPs and patients, as on research data alone.

> Rogue internet pharmacies continue to pose a serious threat to the health and safety of Americans. Simply put, a few unethical physicians and pharmacists have become drug suppliers to a nation.
>
> *Dianne Feinstein*

Adverse events that occur because of the ignorance, laziness or carelessness of an HCP are not discussed here: failure to read essential information or to keep up-to-date generally; or, of course, the issue of diagnostic errors. Those are not basically communications issues at all, although defective communication may be partly the cause of them.

> The young physician starts life with 20 drugs for each disease, and the old physician ends life with one drug for 20 diseases.
>
> *William Osler*

Box 17.2 Safety problems

These are caused by a wide range of factors:

- known adverse drug reactions (ADRs)
- unknown, unexpected ADRs
- interactions (other drugs, foodstuffs, alternative medicines, etc.)
- patient allergies or genetic predispositions
- diagnostic errors
- prescribing errors, including issues relating to name (brand), dose, form and strength
- dispensing errors
- use of ambiguous terms or terms likely to be misinterpreted
- unclear/ambiguous handwriting
- administration errors (route, particularly)
- non-adherence to some or all advice and instruction (patient error)
- drug quality problems (including those arising from unregulated internet sales)
- counterfeit drugs (including the high percentage of dubious products available over the internet and in many developing countries)
- labelling and storage
- packaging
- medicines reconciliation on admission to hospital

And, some would say, indirectly by:

- marketing pressure from manufacturers on HCPs and patients
- innocent sharing of medicines among family and friends, both prescription and OTC (over-the-counter) products.

Quality, availability and accessibility of drug safety information

Healthcare professionals

A wide range of good quality information is available, in all kinds of publications, on many websites and from most national regulatory authorities and/or health ministries and from many manufacturers. The primary source of specific information about a drug is the official product data sheet (variously referred to as the SPC in Europe (Summary of Product Characteristics), Package Insert in the US, and other terms elsewhere), a comprehensive, technical document, which is a regulatory-approved requirement in many countries. However, these are probably much too time consuming for most HCPs to study, and certainly more or less impenetrable to most patients. In some countries, however, patient leaflets in the local language do accompany many, if not most, prescription and OTC medicines.

The first problem is the large volume of information, which:

- can change in the light of new evidence and knowledge
- no one can possibly have in their heads
- may be available and accessible but is rarely instantly on-hand, standing by at the point of need (the moment of prescribing and/or dispensing).

This is a major, technical communications issue: how to get the best, up-to-date, relevant information to an HCP at the point of prescribing or dispensing. Computer-based prescribing systems, linked to drug information databases offer the best contemporary solution: key information, warnings and alerts are available for instant review before a treatment is specified. However, for now and the future, such systems will be available to only a minority of HCPs throughout the world. The US FDA Medwatch email alert system,[168] along with downloadable video demonstrations and case studies, available anywhere, is a good example of modern, accessible, up-to-the-minute information, but even that does not guarantee that an HCP will have the exact information they need at the point of choice of therapy and prescription (and its use requires an effective internet connection).[169]

In many places, the most direct and specific information HCPs receive about drugs is during visits from pharmaceutical industry representatives. Such one-to-one, face-to-face briefing is, of course, among the most effective communications methods possible, but there are questions about the objectivity of information presented in what is basically a marketing activity, and about the possibility of undue influence on the habits of recipients. In some countries (Sweden, for example) such contact is no longer permitted, and the job of briefing prescribers on new drugs and other medication issues is carried out by state-appointed pharmacists. The Drug and Therapeutics Information Service (DATIS)[170] peer-to-peer academic detailing system, started in Adelaide, South Australia, and in action in Kentucky, USA, is a method of very effective professional briefing and updating for practitioners (and can lead to financial savings too[171]).

> The twenty thousand biomedical journals now published are increasing by six to seven per cent a year. To review ten journals in internal medicine, a physician must read about two hundred articles and seventy editorials a month.
>
> *Phil Manning, M.D. and Lois DeBakey, Ph.D. (written in 1987)*

There is no easy, foolproof solution. What HCPs need is ready access to good information sources (national formulary, clinical guidelines, SPCs, electronic databases, internet resources) and the willingness to use them. That willingness to check information is a sign of professional responsibility, and communicating the reasons for doing so to patients is a necessary skill.

Raising and maintaining awareness of drug safety issues, especially ADRs, is a further communications issue for regulatory and local health authorities, health ministries, professional associations, local hospital and clinic management teams, consumer and patient organisations, the pharmaceutical industry, and all sectors of healthcare education and training. It is very clear that the issue is not currently given the priority it – and patients' safety – deserve. In other words, the safety of medicines is everyone's business, and much of that business involves communication.

Patients

Most patients do not know much about medicine in general and drugs in particular. Regulatory authorities seem to be very bashful about direct communication with patients, so much of the educational burden falls on HCPs who need to engage in teaching about diseases and drugs, about risk and uncertainty with their individual patients and to provide them with supporting information and alternative sources where possible[172] Active, well-informed patients have a large part to play in helping to anticipate and prevent errors and injuries, not least in checking that the drugs they are given are the ones that were prescribed and the ones they were expecting, and reporting back when there are adverse effects or other problems (see also 'Medication errors' below).

The patient information leaflet (PIL) or package insert is the main secondary source of information in countries where it is required, for both prescription-only and over-the-counter medicines. In many places where, for example, PILs are not mandatory, or where drugs are dispensed from bulk supplies, word of mouth may be the primary source of information, along with the dispensing label, if provided. The communications challenge for HCPs in these circumstances is enormous, especially when drugs are dispensed without any original package information, in identical containers (plastic bags, for example), identified only by handwriting or computer-printed label.

PILs are of greatly varying quality and usefulness. Patients and patient organisations find many of them obscure, difficult to read and confusing. They are often presented in tiny type, crowded onto unusual sizes of thin paper, and folded very small for insertion into the pack. Many require a magnifying glass for even those with reasonable sight. They contain a large amount of material, much of it of uncertain value to a patient, with the important things (adverse reactions, interactions, contraindications) often buried among the rest. *Taking your Medicine* is a leaflet produced by the City of New York and is an excellent example of plain, simple advice for patients.[173]

Box 17.3 Dispensing labels

Even something as apparently simple as a dispensing label needs careful planning in terms of its communication effectiveness:

- Is the writing/printing sufficiently large and clear to be legible for the patient?
- Is it in a language understood by the patient?
- Is the writing/printing indelible/permanent? (Ballpoint pen on soft plastic bags or pouches easily rubs off, for example.)
- Does the label include all critical information? (Patient name; drug name (ideally generic and brand); strength; dosage and schedule; specific instructions (before or after meals, for example).)
- Is the label attached to the product in such a way that important information on the original package is not obscured?
- Is the label attached to the outer packaging (which may be discarded) or to the tube or bottle or device itself, where it will remain visible and useful?
- On a very small product container (a tube, for example) is the label attached in flag mode, or crushed onto the surface of the container?

Which audience?

Critics observe that the form and content of PILs may be driven more by regulatory demands and by manufacturers' need to protect themselves from future litigation than by a focused wish to provide helpful information for patients. This may be unduly cynical, but many of them appear to have been written and designed without much attention to the needs and abilities of their audience or consultation with them.[174,175] They do not usually have, for example, a bold section of essential information, in large type and simple language, which might be headed, 'If you read nothing else, read this' (see p. 232 for more on structure in communications). In their description of ADRs, they do not specify risk in ways that are sure to make sense to patients (see 'Risk communication', p. 199); while the sometimes exhaustive lists of even the rarest side effects may be more alarming than helpful. Very few PILs would be comprehensible to the (perhaps) more than 50% of even educated populations with poor levels of general and health literacy. Some PILs have, however, been much improved, often when manufacturers have been required to work in collaboration with patient groups in their preparation.

This is a communications challenge for regulators and manufacturers to address, but the current weaknesses of PILs have real implications for HCPs.

- It is not wise to rely on PILs as the primary source of a patient's information about a medicine; in a busy clinic or pharmacy it may be all too easy to say, 'You can get any more information you need from the leaflet'; in fact, the patient may not be able to read or understand it; may look at it in despair and give up; some of the information or language may be unclear or alarming; the indication for which it has been prescribed may not be obvious or included at all.

- Best practice requires that an HCP – and preferably more than one (physician, pharmacist, nurse) – will go through the essential-to-know safety and other information personally with the patient, particularly with regard to ADRs, lack of effect and so on; an HCP must be clear what the minimum essential information is.
- At the point of dispensing, an assessment needs to be made as to how much the patient needs to have (or ought to have) supporting information for future reference or reflection. Scanning the PIL with the patient will help both parties assess how useful and accessible the information is, and significant points can be highlighted (verbally, or literally with a felt-tip highlighter) and doubts clarified. Other material, such as written notes, diagrams or dosing charts may also be helpful.
- Remember that a quarter or more of patients may be functionally illiterate, and many more will have problems in health literacy.

A drug is that substance which, when injected into a rat, will produce a scientific report.

Anon

Transmission and reception

The difficulties with PILs remind us of the critical fact about effective communication emphasised in the opening section of this book (see p. 15): 'A communication is not complete until there is evidence that its message has been received and understood'.

The provision of PILs, that is the mere transmission of information, is only half the story: the communication is not complete until we know whether or not the recipient has made sense of it, and we have taken remedial action if they did not. Some pharmacies produce simplified versions of PILs, which are printed out, at the same time as the dispensing label, including the patient's name, at the point of dispensing. This has great advantages, not least that the patient will feel that the information has been produced for them individually.

User wisdom

Many patient organisations, especially those dedicated to a single disease or disability, provide leaflets, run websites and hold meetings that are sharply focused on their members' needs for meaningful information (some are sponsored by manufacturers, sometimes the providers of a major drug therapy for the disease). HCPs should know about such rich resources available in their locality, in the country or on the internet and connect patients with them when they can. Such organisations often have much more experience of a particular condition (and of patients' perspectives on all issues) than any individual HCP can ever hope to achieve, and although their views may sometimes be controversial or challenging to conventional wisdom (they are, for example, not unexpectedly, intensely interested in risk), they inevitably help patients to become more confident and informed and – yes, probably – more demanding too! (Worldwide, patient organisations concerned with HIV/AIDS and multiple sclerosis, for example, heart disease and diabetes, and with some orphan diseases, have made great contributions to knowledge, the provision of good information, and the advancement of therapy and patients' quality of life.[176–183])

There are many people and organisations who believe that information made available by regulatory authorities and pharmaceutical companies is often far from transparent and comprehensive. Although some are prejudiced, and some whose judgement is questionable, there are also many whose views deserve very serious attention – not least because they have often been proved right about major problems and absent or misleading information about safety and other issues.[183,184]

The better the quality, and the wider the range of information a patient has, and the better it is communicated, the more there is a genuine social partnership model in developing and implementing healthcare communications, so much greater will be the chances of patients being well informed and critical, and of ensuring the safe and effective use of medicines.

Formerly, when religion was strong and science weak, men mistook magic for medicine, now, when science is strong and religion weak, men mistake medicine for magic.

Thomas Szasz

Patients' expectations of safety

That no drug is completely safe for all people in all circumstances comes as shock to many; that, for example, penicillin can kill, is a disturbing revelation. It is important that all patients should know there are risks and they should be advised:

- how to reduce risks (adherence, avoidance of interactions, for example)
- how to recognise and deal with known side effects
- how to recognise the first symptoms of serious or unexpected effects and what to do if they occur.

Risk communication is a complex and demanding activity in which almost all HCPs must involve themselves and become experts (see Chapter 19 for a detailed discussion). Only if patients understand the risks as far as they are able, define and choose what is acceptable to them, is a course of treatment ethical and viable. This means, of course, that an HCP has to know the risks, when such information is in existence, which returns us to the discussion of availability of good information, and an HCP's willingness to check it out and to communicate it.

No human being is constituted to know the truth, the whole truth, and nothing but the truth; and even the best of men must be content with fragments, with partial glimpses, never the full fruition.

William Osler

Pharmacovigilance and error reporting

Pharmacovigilance is the science and activities relating to the detection, assessment, understanding and prevention of adverse effects of drugs, biologics and other medical products, or any other possible product-related problems. Its primary tools are pharmacoepidemiology and spontaneous reporting, and its application covers everything from early- and late-stage clinical trials during drug development to clinical trials and every aspect of clinical practice. As part of the overall effort to improve patient safety, it is an important activity in which all stakeholders must be involved: manufacturers, regulators, HCPs and patients.[185–187]

Effective and observant HCPs can reduce or prevent injury or death for their own patients, and potentially for many more, by ensuring that:

- patients understand the possibility and nature of ADRs
- patients report ADRs to them, especially if they are serious or unexpected
- their patients' ADRs are communicated to the local or national pharmacovigilance centre and/or the manufacturer (where there may already be similar reports, beginning to show evidence of a pattern and/or a problem)
- the concerns are discussed locally as well, especially in a hospital setting where there may be other similar events
- in countries where direct patient reporting is permitted (the Netherlands and Sweden, for example), patients are encouraged to use the system.

(Countries that are members of the World Health Organization Program for International Drug Monitoring will also send their reports to the WHO's international database in Uppsala, Sweden, where issues of safety can be examined in data from across the world.[188]) Many developing countries are in the early stages of establishing their systems.

Among the many obstacles to reporting is the simple matter of the reporting form: many of these are complex, unimaginatively designed and forbidding in their apparent demands for time and detail. HCPs are rarely consulted on the system and the kind of form that they might be inclined to complete; bureaucracy causes failure in the basic communications activities and skills of knowing an audience, testing materials, seeking feedback, tailoring materials and so on.

Inappropriate use

Antibiotics (the broader the spectrum, the better, it seems) are among the most abused medicines on the planet, being both wrongly prescribed (for colds and other viral infections, for example), and arbitrarily self-administered for all kinds of conditions, in places where regulation is lax or absent, and where they can be bought on the street.

This is another area in which HCPs need to be alert to the assumptions and ignorance of their patients and to educate them in a rational understanding of what specific medicines are for and how they work. Under pressure from patients to prescribe something, we know that many HCPs do just that to satisfy the patient and avoid argument, even against their better judgement. That many minor ills and injuries are self-limiting and best left to nature is a fact that people in drug-dependent, risk-averse cultures are reluctant to accept. (There is a further irrational pressure in some societies for an injection, rather than a pill, for every ill.) Disabusing patients of their sometimes deep preconceptions is not an easy communications task.

To do nothing is sometimes a good remedy.

Hippocrates

Antibiotic resistance is a major, worldwide problem, and we can assume that part of it, at least, results from serious failures:

- in public education about the rational use of medicines (public health communication)
- in the practice and communication of HCPs in their relationships with patients
  - — prescribing inappropriately
  - — not challenging inaccurate expectations and not resisting pressure
  - — not adequately ensuring adherence to therapy, especially completion of a course of treatment.

These all relate to the content and effectiveness of healthcare communications, and to the determination of an HCP to see a broader picture than the individual patient or indication in front of them.

Off-label use is another area in which knowledge, risk communication, and openness with patients provide special challenges.

I will lift mine eyes unto the pills. Almost everyone takes them, from the humble aspirin to the multi-coloured, king-sized three deckers, which put you to sleep, wake you up, stimulate and soothe you all in one. It is an age of pills.

Malcolm Muggeridge, 1962

Adherence

Worldwide, patient adherence is thought, by the World Health Organization and other authorities, to be about 50% – a situation with enormous health and economic consequences.[189] Ensuring that a patient with tuberculosis adheres to therapy and completes the course, or that a patient who is HIV positive is meticulous in observing their antiretroviral regimen, and that patients with less serious conditions take their drugs as prescribed, is not easy when an HCP sees a patient occasionally for a few minutes, for a microscopic percentage of the total weeks and months of their lives. Much the same issue applies to the pregnant woman who is taking warfarin or heparin after a pulmonary embolism during pregnancy, or a patient with epilepsy or hypertension: how can you be sure that emerging risks, inherent in the treatment or relating to adherence, are discovered early enough to prevent damage?

When I was 40, my doctor advised me that a man in his 40s shouldn't play tennis. I heeded his advice carefully and could hardly wait until I reached 50 to start again.
Hugo Black

The first answer is: you can't be sure. Risk, in this case, as in all cases, cannot be reduced to zero. But the risk can be reduced. These are some of the management and communication issues and techniques that may support adherence and reduce risk, all used alongside a thoughtful, empathetic response to the patient's feelings about what is under discussion:

- Explain the arguments and evidence underpinning the requirements of treatment (once the chosen option has been agreed and has the patient's consent).
- Assess the extent to which the patient truly understands and accepts the arguments and evidence without reservation.
- Assess the extent to which you feel the patient is motivated and committed to follow the regimen.
- Backtrack, repeat, explain again, rephrase the arguments, if there is any doubt about the patient's grasp of the facts.
- Explore any doubts you have about their motivation and commitment; accept any obstacles they admit to or hint at, and try to find ways of lessening their impact.
- Where necessary, state the facts of the situation compassionately but strongly: 'You must understand that if you don't do this (take your insulin every day, for example), however much you hate doing it, you may get seriously ill or die.'
- Try to explore and anticipate how the patient will feel in the future, before you next see them, after they've been on their own, taking the drugs for a period without supervision; will their motivation slacken as they either feel no beneficial effects or they endure side effects with or without immediate beneficial effects? Will the force of argument about prevention lose its strength? Will they just get lazy or depressed and take a holiday from the drugs?
- Try to help the patient to anticipate how they might feel (lethargic or constipated, for example), so that when the time comes, they remember the discussion and think, 'Aha! That's just what the doc said I'd feel. I'd better watch myself.'
- Agree to the patient doing some kind of self-monitoring – a daily checklist or diary record of tablet-taking, or self-administered test results, or state of symptoms and health, or even feelings about the treatment, including negative and difficult ones; ask the patient to bring such a record with them next time they visit (this would not be suitable for all patients, by any means, but for some – and literacy itself would not be the main criterion of suitability – it might be just right).
- Where there are partners or carers involved, seek their help and support for the patient in adhering to the treatment regimen.
- Seek the patient's opinion as to how long they feel they can keep going in sticking to the treatment without support; some will say a month, others perhaps, especially in the early stages, only a week or two; some will not know and will value the invitation to return as soon as they feel they have some problem; fix the next appointment to take account of the patient's own feelings about how long they can keep going.
- Be sure to express confidence in the patient's urge to do well, even with reservations about the scale of the challenge: 'It's not going to be easy, I think, but I really feel you want to do it, and I'm sure you can.'
- Be sure to praise evidence of adherence when you have it.
- Make careful arrangements for renewing long-term prescriptions well before the patient's supplies are exhausted.
- Limit prescriptions to the length of time you feel the patient can keep going; never issue

repeat prescriptions in their absence if you have any doubt about adherence, or do not have recent evidence of it.
- Where regular tests are necessary for monitoring effectiveness and safety, good opportunities are provided for checking progress and seeing how the patient is feeling.

Keep a watch also on the faults of the patients, which often make them lie about the taking of things prescribed.

Hippocrates

Medication errors

The standard work *Medication Errors*, edited by Michael R. Cohen,[190] covers this topic in exhaustive detail, and we can do nothing but skim the surface here. However, there are several major communications issues arising that relate intimately to the concerns of this book. Some of the issues have been referred to above, but here is a more coherent summary of some of the most important ones, based on the work of Cohen and his collaborators. In this book, we shall not deal

Box 17.4 Some notes on 'take one tablet', 'after eating' and 'three tablets a day'

Adherence to prescribing advice is dependent on many patient factors (trust, confidence, understanding), but also on the prescriber's clarity of language and anticipation of possible misunderstandings.

The word 'take' (and its equivalent in other languages) will often be understood as 'put in the mouth and swallow', but may also be interpreted as chew or suck (even lick).

The precise action should be made clear:
- Swallow whole: e.g. sustained release and enteric-coated tablets.
- Suck until dissolved: e.g. antifungal pastilles.
  — Here, the instruction 'Suck, do not swallow,' alone, may be interpreted as not swallowing the dissolved constituents of the pastille in saliva (i.e spit them out until the pastille has disappeared).
- Rinse and spit out, do not swallow: e.g. for mouthwash.
- Chew and swallow: e.g. calcium tablets.
- Place between the gum and lip/cheek until dissolved: e.g. products for buccal delivery.
- Place under the tongue until dissolved: e.g. glyceryl trinitrate tablets or spray.
  — With both of these last two, the additional instruction, 'Do not swallow' may be misinterpreted similarly to 'Suck, do not swallow,' above.

Great precision is required if the patient is to understand exactly what they must do. Not all languages have vocabulary to deal with the variations, so more elaborate explanations are necessary; instructions in this area can be ambiguous in any language if not managed well.

A special case of 'take': pessaries and suppositories

Familiar though HCPs are with these medicines, for patients they may be confusing or entirely unfamiliar. Not a few patients have been known to swallow both forms, because their dispenser failed to make their purpose and method of use clear.

There are two issues to be addressed:
- The simple practicalities and associated feelings: insertion – how do you do it and how far in? This may seem obvious, but for anyone using a pessary or suppository for the first time, they may have no idea at all how to do it, and, additionally may be shocked or disgusted at the prospect of such contact with their anus or vagina. This will vary as between people and cultures, but may be a real stumbling block if the dispenser is not very sensitive to the patient's reaction, very explicit and clear about what to do, and does not deal with the emotions.
- The dispenser's feelings: some dispensers, especially in some cultures, may find it very hard to refer at all to anus, rectum or vagina, may avoid explicit mention at all, or couch the instruction in so vague a way as to mislead and confuse the patient. This is a further example of a common communications need which must be anticipated and prepared for, like sexual vocabulary (see p. 210). Every HCP needs to develop a comfortable and practical vocabulary for referring to all intimate and otherwise perhaps embarrassing topics, actions, behaviour, parts of the body and so on. It is not possible to retreat into using technical language (e.g. 'rectum' and 'vagina' may not be known or understood accurately by everyone) and alternatives have to be available to suit every patient and match their own verbal usage.

Patients have been known to insert pessaries or suppositories without removing their wrapping or packaging: this is a risk particularly for suppositories when they are stored in hot climates or conditions without refrigeration and are seen to liquefy. Refrigerated storage is not universally available, or may not be understood to be necessary, so the risk needs to be anticipated and explained.

Box 17.4 *Cont.*

'After meals'

If the regimen requires taking a tablet (say) three times a day, after food, then this requirement needs to be explained carefully.

- Some people do not have three 'meals' a day and may wonder how they are to manage their medicine.
- The instruction 'after meals' may make some people eat more than they are accustomed to.
- 'After eating' may, in some cultures be interpreted as meaning after eating the local or national staple which would normally be eaten only once a day ('eating' being applied only to the serious consumption of a major meal – in Ghana, for example, after fufu, or kenkey and fish).
- The critical communication is not so much 'after meals/eating' (both ambiguous) but, 'not on an empty stomach'. Exactly what is meant by a 'not empty' stomach needs to be explained – is an apple or a cup of coffee enough? – and so on.

Patients may have to change their eating habits in some respects in order to adhere to any 'not on an empty stomach' regimen. That requires explanation and discussion at the point of prescribing or dispensing.

As with so many of these issues, failure to be explicit, to explore the patient's understanding and to ensure accurate grasp of the requirements may lead to poor adherence, ineffective therapy or even injury (gastrointestinal bleeding being one of the most obvious).

'Three tablets a day'

All at once? An hour apart? The ambiguities of this simple instruction are obvious. So: 'Three times a day, at six hourly intervals, take one tablet.' Even, 'Take one tablet three times a day,' could confuse a slow-witted patient who thought that the instruction referred to the *same* tablet, and would wonder how to follow the instruction.

with errors resulting from medical or medication decisions arising from ignorance or carelessness or negligence, except inasmuch as they arise from some failure in communication.

It is important to note that patients may define medication error in a broader way than professionals, including such non-technical elements as communication, responsiveness and quality of life, and that *concerns*, not necessarily actual errors, can affect their perception and satisfaction.[191]

System-based problems

Many errors are system-based – that is they are not simply attributable to the faulty behaviour of an individual, but rather to systems in which weaknesses increase the chance of errors occurring. Root-cause analysis of errors which have occurred will usually reveal multiple factors that have contributed to the occurrence of the error: it can be seen, in some respects, as an accident waiting to happen.[192] Its cause can stretch back to the manufacturer and product formulation or labelling or packaging; to procurement decisions; local lack of information and training and so on. That analysis does not absolve the individual of responsibility for vigilance, but it places the error in a much wider context where responsibility and cause may lie far beyond the individual.

Box 17.5 Principal areas of systems in which errors arise

Errors come from failures of one sort or another, most of them involving communications issues[193]:

- lack of information about the patient
- lack of information about the drug
- communication and teamwork failures
- unclear, absent, look-alike drug labels and packages, and confusing or look-alike or sound-alike drug names
- unsafe drug standardisation, storage and distribution
- non-standard, flawed or unsafe medication delivery devices
- environmental factors and staffing patterns that do not support safety
- inadequate staff orientation, ongoing education, supervision and competency validation
- inadequate patient education about medications and medication errors
- lack of a supportive culture of safety, failure to learn from mistakes, and failed or absent error-reduction strategies, such as redundancies (successive layers of safety measures which come into play as primary ones fail)
- an ethos in which vigilance is compromised (by pressure, tiredness, interruptions, for example) and the fundamental need for double-checking and cross-checking is not an established priority ('Have all the swabs and instruments been removed and counted?' 'Is this absolutely certainly the medication prescribed for this patient by the physician?')

In recent years there has been an immense amount of work done in identifying errors and their causes, and much progress has been made (in anaesthesiology, for example, and in specific, dangerous practice such as the inadvertent intravenous administration of concentrated potassium chloride); some packaging and labelling have been improved; 'high-alert' drugs with the potential, used incorrectly, for great damage have been identified; bar-coding and other verification processes have been introduced; insistence on the use of both generic and brand names for any prescription; the promotion of standardised abbreviations and so on.[194]

The Joint Commission of the Accreditation of Healthcare Organisations (known as the Joint Commission), has a wealth of useful material on its website.[195]

Checking and repeating

Nevertheless, wherever the printed, written (especially handwritten), or spoken word is used, there remains a possibility of misunderstanding or misinterpretation. Both the sender of the message

Box 17.6 A radical new approach

For some time, there has been a revolution taking place in how learning and social and other complex systems are understood and how effective models of partnership, citizenship and democracy can be nurtured for progress in many fields (including air traffic safety and the nuclear industry, for example). A dramatic vision of how these ideas might apply in healthcare was described by Vogt (2002).[197] Outlining how old methods and systems were failing, she drew eight principles for the future from her analysis.

- There cannot be a safer drug until there is a safer system.
- All stakeholders are equal partners and have an equal voice in all deliberations.
- Paternalism must be eliminated.
- The expertise for determining acceptable benefit and risk is dispersed throughout society.
- Patients and all stakeholders serve as both teachers and learners.
- All stakeholders are involved in the identification of their learning needs, processes and evaluation of outcomes.
- In a complex adaptive system all individual actions are connected.
- Patients must be involved in the continuous feedback and redesign of the evolving drug safety information system.

Ambitious although all this is, it is perfectly in line with the vision and intention of this book, and with the conviction that patient safety, and healthcare relationships of all kinds, would be transformed by moving towards this active, inclusive, participative model.

Table 17.1 The Joint Commission's official 'Do not use' list[196]

Do not use	Potential problem	Write instead
U (unit)	Mistaken for 0 (zero), the number 4 (four) or cc	unit
IU (International Unit)	Mistaken for IV (intravenous) or the number 10 (ten)	International Unit
Q.D., QD, q.d., qd, (daily)	Mistaken for each other	daily
Q.O.D., QOD, q.o.d., qod (every other day)	Period (full stop) after Q mistaken for I and the O mistaken for I	every other day
Trailing zero (X.0 mg)*	Decimal point is missed	X mg 0.X mg
MS	Can mean morphine sulfate or magnesium sulfate	morphine sulfate
MSO_4 and $MgSO_4$	Confused with one another	magnesium sulfate

Applies to all orders and all medication-related documentation that is handwritten (including freehand computer entry) or on pre-printed forms.

*Exception: A 'trailing zero' may be used only where required to demonstrate the level of precision of the value being reported, such as for laboratory results, imaging studies that report size of lesions, or catheter/tube sizes. It may not be used in medication orders or other medication-related documentation.

Additional abbreviations, acronyms and symbols which can give rise to mistakes, and may be included in future JC 'Do no use' lists: <; >; abbreviations for drug names; apothecary units; @; cc; µg.

and the recipient have great responsibilities to ensure that there are no errors in the process: the sender to ensure the clarity of every detail, and the recipient to check back that there is not the slightest doubt. In receiving oral instruction by telephone (especially mobile phones with the risk of weak signal and poor reception) the details should be repeated, drug names even spelt out, to ensure there is no possible mistake. Messages received on answering devices may require a return call to clarify details. Manually faxed orders can sometimes be less than distinct and may require clarification. Electronic ordering systems are no less prone to human input error and every detail requires checking.

A blame-free culture of openness

It is important that all healthcare systems and organisations should nurture a culture of safety and that everyone should be encouraged to discuss problems, risks, near-misses and mistakes, in an open and unthreatening atmosphere. A blame culture, in which people are afraid of revealing problems and mistakes serves no one's interest. Creating a positive, open, learning culture is a considerable management challenge, but it is clear that the impact on patient safety and staff morale can be significant.

Box 17.7

> The UK government and the medical profession have called for an end to the blame culture of the NHS in a joint statement that aims to raise standards of care.
>
> The document calls for the NHS to be more open in the way it deals with medical mistakes and to 'recognise that honest failure should not be responded to primarily by blame and retribution, but by learning and by a drive to reduce risk for future patients'.[198]

Falls and accidents

Injuries to patients and healthcare staff from poor lifting practices, faulty methods of using lifting devices, poorly maintained equipment, falls caused by wet or irregular floor surfaces or dangerous obstacles, are depressingly common in healthcare institutions, when there is a lack of focus on physical activity and the physical environment as sources of hazard. Here there is a need for effective communication and training about procedures and their safe execution; about maintenance and cleaning standards; about the safe stowing of gurneys, carts and other movable objects, but also for vigilance among every member of the whole healthcare team, active communication of hazards when they are spotted, and urgent remedial action. Cleaners, porters and security staff have a particular role to play in this as they travel around a building complex, observing the environment and the people in it.

Expert patients

In the last decade, this concept has been developed into highly effective programmes for groups of patients living with chronic conditions, including pain.[199] The aim is to support greater independence and self-management by increasing knowledge, skills and confidence through training and group work. Participants' opinion shows substantial empowering effects, including lessening dependence on HCPs but much improved relationships with those who are consulted. This is a very powerful way of pursuing the vision of independent, critical, well-informed patients, making a real contribution to their own safety and health, and perhaps a course some of your patients would greatly value.[200]

Conclusion

In addressing the question of patient safety, we need to look at the nature of the systems that constitute healthcare and increase their coherence and focus. The Joint Commission's assertion that, 'Communication is a cornerstone of patient safety', is relevant for every aspect of healthcare, at almost every moment of every day. It underlines the message of this book: medical and technical expertise without effective communications will not, on their own, serve the best interests of patients, and, indeed, run a real risk of damaging them.

18 Informed consent

It is a fundamental ethical requirement, and in some places a legal obligation, that patients should understand and explicitly consent to any intervention, however minor, and however small the risks may be. Explaining interventions and their benefits, harms and risks, and reaching informed consent require patience and the exercise of a cluster of sophisticated communication skills. Negotiating informed consent for participation in research and clinical trials is particularly important and complex.

Essential and difficult

This important topic needs attention, because fulfilling the requirements of informed consent is, among other things, an ethical imperative and a complex exercise in effective communications. There are also serious issues relating to the possibility of patient dissatisfaction or litigation if informed consent is neglected.[201]

The common term 'consent' is used in this context, although the process of discussing therapeutic options may legitimately lead to informed *dissent* – disagreement or refusal. The process is two-stage: making an informed choice (including perhaps an informed rejection of other choices), and then consenting to it in the knowledge of its implications.

At its simplest, informed consent is 'an agreement for a proposed medical treatment or non-treatment, or for a proposed invasive procedure. It requires (HCPs) to disclose the benefits, risks, and alternatives to the proposed treatment, non-treatment, or procedure. It is the method by which fully informed, rational persons may be involved in choices about their health care.'[202] Participation in clinical trials or other research also requires formal consent, often in relation to very complex issues.[203]

Obtaining informed consent is a legal requirement in many countries, but it also has the deeper ethical basis that everyone has a right to control what happens to their own bodies and the risks to which they are exposed, and to be protected from manipulation or exploitation. (Serious developments in this area[204] began after revelations of medical experimentation in Nazi concentration camps and Japanese units in China at the end of World War 2, and was later accelerated by projects such as the appalling Tuskegee syphilis trial, which went on into the 1970s.)[205,206]

Gaining patient consent should never be a mere token gesture, nor seeking open-ended consent to anything that might happen. In some hospitals in some parts of the world patients are asked to sign a generic consent and disclaimer when they are admitted, covering anything at all that might happen to them while under treatment. That is not consent in any ethically acceptable sense, and certainly not informed consent.

If you think of a sliding scale of treatments and interventions of increasing complexity and risk, there is a point on that scale beyond which nothing should happen without detailed explanation and genuine informed consent. The location of that point needs to be the subject of debate and guidelines within the professions and in ethics and other forums. Before that critical point on the scale, there is still a requirement that no patient should be subjected to anything to which they do not agree, or to risks they do not understand, but the pressures of practice will mean that the process will sometimes be carried out perfunctorily, minimally or perhaps neglected altogether. When this happens, the decision should be conscious, even when the intervention appears to be elementary and relatively risk free.

Reaching agreement

There are five critical stages in moving towards informed choice and consent:

1. HCP: Setting the scene for the patient, explaining the process, helping them to engage in the process and make an informed choice.
2. HCP: Providing the patient with comprehensive information.
3. Patient: Processing and understanding the information.
4. Patient: Making an informed choice.
5. HCP and patient: Jointly confirming the agreement verbally or as a signed contract (in both cases with a record in the patient's notes).

These are discussed in detail below.

Every stage is fraught with challenges, complications and pitfalls. At worst, failure to manage the process well may result in serious legal and professional consequences, so a highly precautionary approach is needed.

1. HCP: Setting the scene for the patient to engage in the process and make an informed choice

Not all patients will expect to be fully involved in decision making, but they and even those who do, may need some explanation of how seriously the HCP takes the process and how it will take place. Some, impatient or simply trusting the HCP, will dismiss the need and say, 'Just get on with it'. There are two important reasons for not following that advice:

- For the best outcomes, patients need to understand what is happening to them and to take active responsibility for their therapy (not to be simply treated as objects).
- Should anything go wrong in the future, and it could be claimed or shown that the active, informed consent of the patient was not obtained, the HCP may be in considerable trouble.

This is a distilled version of what an HCP might say:

'I want to explain to you what I think the problem is and what choices we have to deal with it. There are a couple of ways we could treat this, and I want you to tell me if you are willing to accept either of them and, if so, what you would prefer. I'll also explain what I think will happen with no treatment. Then we can agree together what we'll do. If you choose a treatment, it will work much better if you really understand what's happening and are happy with the way we are going.'

For serious and/or complicated therapy or procedure, or participation in research of some kind,[207] when a consent form is judged necessary, an HCP would add:

'Because this is so complicated, and there are some risks involved, if we agree on what we are going to do (and it is genuinely up to you), then I'll ask you to sign a form recording that you understand the decision we make and have agreed to it. But you are absolutely free to disagree and refuse if you choose. We'll need to go carefully through the form together later.'

2. HCP: Providing the patient with comprehensive information

Areas for discussion usually include[208]:

- HCP's conclusions about the problem and level of certainty about the diagnosis

- implications of no treatment and of treatment being postponed for various periods
- the range of available diagnostic or treatment options
- costs that patients would personally incur and, where relevant, the extent of public or private insurance reimbursement for each option
- the benefits of each option
- the possibilities of diagnostic false results or treatment failures
- the risks (harms) and discomforts of diagnostic or treatment options even when successful
- short-term injuries that diagnostic or treatment failures may cause
- long-term effects of diagnostic or treatment options, favourable and unfavourable, separating probabilities from possibilities
- the level of uncertainty in each element of the information; strength of evidence; 'best guesses'; conflicting opinions
- the HCP's preferred option, presented in a balanced way with its rationale and benefits and risks (this may be postponed until the patient has had time to consider the information up to this point).

The more radical, complex or invasive the therapy under discussion, the more information is likely to be needed. However, although this list looks intimidating, it does not imply that the entire contents of medical textbooks have to be unloaded on patients – indeed, very far from it. The sophisticated skill required is to select such information as is strictly relevant to the particular patient, their disease, their understanding of risk, the demands of their lives, and their wishes and hopes.

After selecting the information, it then has to be presented in ways that the particular patient can understand and process, taking accurate account of their emotional state, general mental and intellectual abilities, and their health literacy in particular. Even the same patient, at different times, will have a quite different capacity to pay attention to information and process it, depending on their levels of anxiety, stress, or other factors, so the patient's emotional state is a major consideration is how information is presented and at what pace.

Discussions about informed consent may not be productive immediately following a diagnosis which has made the patient distressed, shocked or angry, when they will be preoccupied with their emotional reaction and have little energy or attention for information and decision making. Forced to make decisions in such circumstances, patients may later question or regret choices they made under pressure, so postponement (for an hour or a day or a week) is sometimes the best course.

Taking blood[209] may be one of the simplest of minor procedures, but even this should not be done without permission and explanation: the purpose of the procedure; usefulness of results and when they will be available; the level of discomfort and possible temporary, minor injury at the site; when the wound will heal. Consent may be easy and rapid, but it must be obtained, nevertheless. (It is salutary to remember that in many legal codes, touching another person without consent itself constitutes the offence of assault, and that an assault of that class, coupled with an injury of some kind, is even more serious.)

When the issues are much larger – options in oncology, for example – the pace at which information is given may need to be very much slower, even spread across days or weeks, depending on the patient's responses. Demanding rapid answers, except in emergencies, may be very damaging to a patient's morale and to their subsequent satisfaction with the decision made. They may wish to discuss issues with their partners or families without the presence of the HCP and to make choices which are genuinely considered. Arriving at an informed choice should be seen, in all circumstances, as a process, not an event.

The communication of risk and uncertainty, in relation to all the elements in the list above, requires considerable skill. These topics are discussed in detail in the next chapter.

To provide useful information about the options under discussion, the HCP may find that a degree of medical teaching is necessary if the patient is to understand the choices on offer. It may be that the functions of organs, or the mechanisms of pharmaceuticals, or the features of diseases, or the nature or cholesterol or insulin or other substances, and many other things, are unknown to a patient, and without that knowledge they are unable to understand the discussion. Issues such as evidence, risk and uncertainty may need elucidation. Patients may have misconceptions or superstitions about such matters, and believe they understand when they don't.

The skills of empathy, assessing mental and emotional state and educational health literacy levels, explaining, listening, questioning, seeking feedback, checking understanding, observing and interpreting non-verbal communication, are all vital at this stage.

3. Patient: Processing and understanding the information

The process must be an interaction, in which the patient is positively engaged – genuinely receiving, absorbing, processing and making sense of information; asking questions, raising doubts, seeking clarification and so on. It must leave the patient in no doubt as to the basis on which a decision is made, *and that the process took place.*

In the definition of informed consent quoted above, reference is made to the patient as a 'rational' person. This signifies that valid consent can be given only by someone capable of doing so, or, in addition, permitted to do so. People with serious mental disabilities or illness may not be capable of giving consent, and, under legally defined ages, children may not be permitted to do so. In these cases, authorised officials or guardians, partners or family members will be those making the decision, and with whom an HCP will have to talk. (There are some cross-cultural complexities in confining consent to the word of an individual, even the patient: see Chapter 14 'Autonomy', p. 136).

4. Patient: Making an informed choice

The patient makes a choice, which they genuinely and wholly understand and accept. Should any signs of doubt or anxiety appear at this stage, then the HCP needs to cover some of the ground again.

5. HCP and patient: Jointly confirming the agreement verbally or as a signed contract

Patient and HCP review the choice. In a complex situation, the HCP should itemise the elements of the agreement, especially mentioning the risks and the level of uncertainty about outcomes, checking that they remain acceptable. If there is a consent form, then it should be reviewed line by line, demonstrating to the patient that the contents are exactly what they have agreed to, and that there are no hidden conditions, risks or waivers. Should variations be needed for the particular patient, then those need to be recorded and signed by both parties too. Some patients may want to take their form home, study it further or discuss it with others.

When there is a form, there are good arguments for having a third-party HCP present it to the patient, perhaps discuss it further, and witness the signature. This allows patients to ask questions they may have overlooked or, for one reason or another, could not ask their primary HCP. Third-party endorsement of the satisfactory completion of the process is also powerful evidence that all possible care has been taken.

When there is no form (as will be the case most of the time for most HCPs), then a careful record of the process must be made in the patient's notes.[210]

The way in which the whole process, particularly this last stage, is conducted, and the clarity of the memory of the process in the patient's mind, are extremely important. When all goes well, informed consent may well be forgotten, but when things go wrong, it may be pivotal in determining a patient's morale and their confidence in healthcare; more worryingly, it may also play a big part in allegations of negligence or malpractice or in litigation. Those who are injured in some way, and claim they did not consent to the treatment, or were not told the risks, may be able to present a strong and damaging case. Hence, the vital necessity of the process itself, and of detailed recording of what was discussed and agreed.

Box 18.1 Note on consent forms

Many consent forms (especially those for clinical trials) are many pages long, printed in small, dense type, and full of often incomprehensible technical detail. They (like some other materials in healthcare) are often designed and written by lawyers for the protection of the company or institution involved, rather than primarily for the interests of the patient, or with the priority of clear communication in mind. Vital details (like the patient's right to opt out of a project) may be buried and effectively invisible in the text. This is an issue of great concern in the field of patients' rights. Any HCP forced to use unsuitable forms should protest and seek reform but, given the necessity to use a bad form: (a) pay meticulous attention to highlighting (verbally or on the paper) all the significant information for the patient; and (b) spend as long as it takes to make sure the patient really does have all the critical information they need. Forms, here and elsewhere, are communications instruments that are often designed without much attention to good practice, and undermine their purposes through their regrettable deficiencies.

Conclusion

Although the process of gaining informed consent may seem elaborate, and, to some, unnecessarily so, the requirement is ethically and professionally sound in every aspect, whether the law requires it or not: none of us should be subjected to any interference with our body or our health without our informed agreement; no HCP (or any other official or person whatsoever) has the right to impose upon us anything that affects our body or our health without their having ensured that it has our full understanding and explicit consent. Therapy based on decisions made willingly by a patient on the basis of good information is likely to be much more beneficial than therapy delivered without adequate discussion and genuine consent.

19 Risk communication

Understanding of risk is not well developed in society and is subject to many irrational influences. Many people are unaware of the fact that any medical intervention carries some risk, however small, and that there is often a degree of uncertainty in scientific and medical judgements. There is poor understanding of risk factors associated with health and disease. There are problems about the availability and intelligibility of information about medical risks. Communication of risk to patients is a complex activity and requires considerable skill. The process demands careful consideration of the language and concepts used. It can be helped by the creative use of visual aids and other resources.[211,212]

For patients, few things are more important than sound information about their disease, their medications and procedures. For HCPs, few things are more challenging than the effective provision of that information and the balanced communication of risk and benefit. Such knowledge as we have about this area shows that it is one of the highest priorities for patients and one that causes some of their deepest dissatisfaction and frustration. This topic embraces surgery, medication, physical therapy, and all activities wherever there is any measure of risk or outcome uncertainty.

For our purposes, *risk* means the chance or probability of something bad happening; *hazard* refers to the inherent danger in something (a tank of flammable liquid, for example, a polluted work environment, smoking or excess alcohol consumption), but not to the *likelihood* (risk) of accidents or injury occurring. The term *harm* is used to characterise the nature of the negative event, its severity and duration.

If you resolve to give up smoking, drinking and loving, you don't actually live longer; it just seems longer.

Clement Freud, The Observer, 27 December 1964

Risk factors

This chapter is primarily concerned with the communication of the risks and benefits of therapy, but we must also consider the challenge of communicating about the risk factors in patients' lives, too. The risk factors associated with, for example, heart disease, are clear and unambiguous in medical knowledge, but the top-line threats (high blood pressure, high low-density lipoprotein levels, smoking, diabetes), and the hidden ones, such as familial hypercholesterolaemia, are not widely known among populations. Even when well known they do not necessarily influence behaviour and lifestyle; even when diagnosed and treated, there are problems with commitment and adherence, especially in the young.

I drive way too fast to worry about cholesterol.

Anon

Across all comparable diseases, there is an enormous challenge in public health education, and in influencing individual patients to appreciate the risks, to modify their behaviour to reduce them, and to adhere to medication and lifestyle change. Many of the issues that follow are as applicable to this area of communication as to that of the risks and benefits of therapy itself. The difference is that in communications about pure prevention, before the onset of disease, patients have to be convinced of the nature of the hazard, the reality of the risk and the seriousness of the potential harm.

If you are young and you drink a great deal it will spoil your health, slow your mind, make you fat – in other words, turn you into an adult.

P. J. O'Rourke

The problem of good information

There are great problems in the availability, accessibility, quality and usefulness of data about risk and benefit, particularly about adverse drugs reactions (ADRs), their probability and seriousness. On the whole, there is good data from clinical trials about effectiveness and safety within the very narrow range of trial subjects, but rather general and unhelpful data about adverse drug reactions (ADRs), sometimes listed in their dozens in patient information leaflets and formularies. There is almost no good data about dose-related effects in relation to both effectiveness and harm (a 'one size fits all' being the usual approach to dosing). We should note the distinction between *data* (the statistical, numerical facts) and *information* (the translation of the statistics into something useful and meaningful for patients, usually having to be done by an HCP).

Box 19.1 Communicating risk information to HCPs

This is a major concern across the world, as regulatory authorities and manufacturers struggle to communicate complex and changing data and information to HCPs effectively. The issue is discussed in Chapter 17, Patient safety.

Nevertheless, there is still a great deal of data and some information about drugs and devices and their ADRs, especially older drugs, and about risks in anaesthiology, surgery and many other interventions. It is a sad fact that many of the injuries and deaths resulting from medication, known interactions included, could have been prevented if only the prescriber or dispenser had researched the data at the time and been more conscientious about keeping abreast of new data. Many useful drugs have been withdrawn because of the apparently unmanageable prevalence of preventable harm to a minority of patients, resulting from careless or irrational prescribing. This sometimes results in useful drugs being lost to large numbers of people for whom they are beneficial.[213–216]

These important background issues, belonging to the field of risk management, cannot be dealt with in any detail here, but every HCP needs to spend a good deal of time investigating known data about the risks of any therapy or procedure being contemplated. Our concern is how to communicate available data effectively – turning it into useful information for the patient; how to manage therapy where the risks are uncertain or not known, and how to help patients and their families make the choices and decisions which are acceptable to them and best for them in every sense. (There are similar challenges in public health risk communication, which we do not deal with here: among them, transforming public health risk statistics into patient-specific risk messages.)

Risk: knowledge and attitudes

That no drug is completely safe for all people in all circumstances is a truth that is not commonly recognised or understood. Even well-educated people are sometimes shocked to learn that there is a risk of serious, even fatal, adverse effects from common, usually benign drugs such as aspirin. Many, probably most, patients start from this position of ignorance and their expectations of therapy are based on it. They also start from a belief that science provides definite answers to questions, and find it very hard to accept that in medicine there is often a high level of uncertainty. Both of these misconceptions provide huge obstacles to effective communication and patient satisfaction if they are not recognised and carefully and explicitly dealt with. (Of course science and the scientific method provide answers and strong probabilities in relation to many issues and processes, but it is far from always being the case, especially in complex situations with multiple variables, and in medicine in particular.)

Box 19.2 Social amplification of risk

The most insubstantial gossip or rumours about risk or harm can quickly escalate into major crises if they take hold in the minds of the public or the media, without any evidence. In 2007, in northern Ghana, a speeding ambulance taking a traffic-injured child to hospital was interpreted as rescue of a child supposedly injured by the national de-worming programme taking place in the locality that day. Hundreds of panicked parents besieged the schools and clinic and withdrew their children from treatment.[217] Similar fiascos have happened in many countries, most commonly in relation to controversial and unresolved issues in vaccine safety. Scientists require evidence for a causal link; popular opinion requires strong evidence *against* a plausible link. There is commonly an *over*-estimation of dramatic or rare events and an *under*-estimation of common killers or risks.

A lie can travel half way around the world while the truth is putting on its shoes.

Mark Twain

All of us are a bundle of contradictions and illogicalities in relation to risk; in general, our perception of risk is filtered through emotion as much as through fact:

- We choose to do things that we know are risky, sometimes very risky – rock-climbing, paragliding, motor racing and lots more (including smoking and having unprotected sex).
- Daily, we take risks that, although we know them to be very high, are almost invisible because they are so familiar – especially driving motor vehicles and travelling in them, riding motorbikes and bicycles, crossing the road; some people greatly increase even those already high risks by drinking and driving, or using their mobile phones while driving; we are also careless about the very high risk of accidents in the home.

Box 19.3 Accident statistics

In the UK in 2002, more than 2 million accidents occurred in the home, of which most were falls. In 2005 (estimates), more than 3200 people were killed on the roads; there was a total of more than 28 000 serious injuries and 238 000 slight injuries. In 2005/6 more than 30 000 workers were killed or seriously injured at their place of work (212 deaths), and there were 328 000 reportable injuries.[218]

- We are extremely sensitive to even very low, remote – even unproven – risks that result from the actions of others, which are imposed on us, even more so if they involve our children (vaccination, food additives, mobile phone use, radio masts and power lines, factory pollution, public transport, and lots more).
- Although we often put ourselves voluntarily at high risk, we are deeply outraged by organisations or governments (or anyone) whose action or neglect put us even at very low risk (broken pavements are an example).
- Like everything in our lives, our perception of 'facts' is filtered through emotion and the legacy of our life experience, and all of us react differently to different facts, especially to those that are familiar and those that are novel or unexpected; those that derive from a trusted source and those that come from a stranger.

Box 19.4 Everyday risks

Just on plain statistics, during 2005, UK residents had 671 chances in 60 million of being killed as a pedestrian in a road accident – that is one chance in around 90 000. Even then you have a better chance of avoiding such a fate if you do not belong to one of the groups most at risk: children and old people . . . but in the UK, you are more than four times as likely to die as a result of an accident in your own home than in crossing the road.[219]

As an example to others, and not that I care for moderation myself, it has always been my rule never to smoke when asleep, and never to refrain from smoking when awake.

Mark Twain

We live in an era in which there is an expectation that planning and regulation should not just decrease risk but reduce it to zero: 'We must ensure that such an event never happens again' – says the minister or the CEO or head of the drug regulatory agency after some accident or crisis, vainly echoing popular and media demands for an entirely impossible level of safety – a life of absolute security, without risk. Patients will often share this fantasy and will need a lot of help to abandon it.

From caution to adventure

Responses to the inevitability of risk in life in general, and medicine in particular, fall between two extremes:

- Those who espouse the precautionary principle in its purest form, which means essentially that you do nothing until it has been proved to be as safe as it is possible to prove anything (which is actually a very long way from 100% – it is impossible to demonstrate the absence of possible future harm – and much further from 100% than the rhetoric suggests) (see also Box 19.12 'A postscript on evidence and uncertainty', p. 206)
- Those who believe that only by taking risks, rationally managed, will progress be made and will benefits accrue. (In the financial markets and other commercial sectors, risk takers have been admired and hugely rewarded when they're successful and sometimes brutally punished when they fail.)

All growth is a leap in the dark, a spontaneous, unpremeditated act without benefit of experience.

Henry Miller

Patients will hold opinions somewhere between those positions, from the highly cautious to the very adventurous; from those who need a great deal of detailed, definite and reassuring information (as far as it is possible), to those who want a responsible overview opinion and are much less frightened by risk. An individual patient will view risk differently at different times depending on their disease or level of pain, on their perception of the balance of risk and benefit, or on their current life situation. What we can be sure of is that the patient's emotional and rational perspectives of risk will be different, perhaps dramatically so, from the HCP's, and it is those gaps that have to be bridged in risk communication. Attitudes to risk and the nature of acceptable and unacceptable risk really need to be the subject of open public debate.

The American Council on Science and Health (ACSH) publication, *Weighing the Risks and Benefits of your Medications*, is a first-class example of honest, straightforward information about benefits and risks, although too dense and complex for those with anything but advanced literacy skills.[220]

Box 19.5 The language of risk and benefit

Risk and benefit are commonly paired together in characterising drugs and procedures, but it is an inaccurate coupling, because *risk* tells you the odds of something happening, and *benefit* tells you what good things might happen (not the chances of their happening). Even if we use the pair, we need to remember the accurate definitions of those and related terms:

- *risk:* the odds of something (bad) happening
- *effectiveness:* the chances of a beneficial outcome in clinical practice ('real-world')
- *harm:* the possible injury or damage that might occur
- *benefit:* the possible positive outcome that might occur
- *efficacy:* the level of positive and intended effects in an ideal laboratory or clinical trial situation.

When talking to a patient, describing the harm that might occur needs to be accompanied by a description of the risk of that harm happening; equally, in terms of benefits, what are the chances of their occurring (effectiveness)?

Effectiveness is a very unsatisfactory word for the purpose, but it will have to do until something better is adopted.

Uncertain information

There are basic problems of knowledge in achieving good communication about risk for several reasons:

- There may be no data or information about risk and harm, or none that relates to the profile of a particular patient (use in paediatric practice or in pregnancy are two examples).
- Risk and harm information may be inaccessible or obscure.
- Information about the comparative risks of therapeutic options, or of no treatment may not be available.
- Prognosis for the disease or injury may be uncertain.
- Dose-related risks and harms (rather than risks of the drug itself) may not be known or available (this is particularly true of off-label use in paediatrics).
- HCPs themselves may not understand the meaning and metrics of risk for specific interventions; the picture may be filled with fairly complicated statistics and nuances that do not lend themselves to simple explanation, especially for patients.

Medicine is a science of uncertainty and an art of probability.

William Osler

Risk communication is not only about the benefit and harm of a single therapy, but also about risk-to-risk comparisons of:

- the disease itself and treatment or no treatment
- different therapeutic options.

Box 19.6

'What the TGN1412 case [the clinical trials in March 2006 that caused catastrophic systemic organ failure in the subjects] has shown is that the medical profession has to become better at communicating both the risks and the benefits of its work to the rest of us – and that there is a need for more involvement by independent experts in the regulatory process.'[221]

Consult Dr Paling

Helping Patients Understand Risks, by John Paling,[222] is a splendid book dealing with risk communication in a lively and practical way. Although one of his main purposes is to introduce HCPs to the use of visual aids in risk communication (a practice much to be recommended, see below), he elucidates the whole topic in a book that is itself an excellent example of good communication. This section draws on some of his ideas, as well as other sources.

Obstacles and influences in effective risk communication

- Patients may be distressed or shocked to learn that their medication or therapy carries risks at all.
- They will be influenced by their feelings about the nature of the possible harm irrespective of the risk. (A low risk of something perceived as dreadful may be less acceptable than a high risk of something less alarming, for example.)
- Few patients understand the complexities of modern medical science and the level of uncertainty inherent in practice.

- They may have been alarmed (or reassured) by the use of relative risk statistics in the media or elsewhere (where a '50% increase' may mean an increase from 2 in 1000 to 3 in 1000, for example, but sounds much more worrying – or comforting, as the case may be – without the absolute figures).
- Patients are often not familiar with statistical expressions of risk and the associated jargon and cannot make sense of them.
- They will be greatly influenced by the opinions of their family and friends, anecdotes of positive or negative experiences, media stories and so on.
- They are likely to respond poorly to risks they feel they do not understand or which are not acceptable to them, or are in some way imposed on them, or by someone whom they do not fully like or trust.
- They cannot, themselves, necessarily translate data into information – that is, into something that they understand and that helps them make decisions.
- Patients use language, especially descriptions of frequency ('low', 'rare', 'common') in ways that may be entirely different from HCPs' use of the terms and will vary greatly from patient to patient, culture to culture, etc.
- They will be influenced by the framing of the risk (negative: 'This operation does not work for 30% of patients'; positive: 'For 70% of patients this operation is a success').
- What is a 'small' risk or a 'small' operation to an HCP may seem quite different to a patient.

The issues in summary

Whether the risks and benefits and harms are known or not (surgical outcomes, specific drug therapy, for example), there are several essential elements in communications with the patient[223]:

- the risks of the disease and the risks/effects of no treatment
- the nature and benefits of treatment options
- the nature of the possible harm from treatment options, described by quality, intensity, and time course (onset, duration, reversibility)
- the probability that harm will occur (risk), including elements of uncertainty and areas where the risks are unknown

Box 19.7 John Paling's seven strategies for risk communication with patients

- Prepare by first learning about the actual difficulties that patients experience in attempting to understand risks.
- Accept the challenge that patients' emotions will invariably filter the facts and cannot be ignored.
- Revise the way you explain probabilities to patients. The most commonly used methods can be greatly improved with small changes.
- Try to avoid speaking to patients in terms of relative risks (especially isolated percentage figures). Ensure you provide context so patients get 'information' and not just 'data'.
- Never give only the negative perspective, but, instead, make sure the positive perspective is always provided as well.
- Explain the risk numbers by using visual aids. These give context as well as achieving understanding for the largest number of patients.
- Realise that sharing aids with patients can serve to reinforce the doctor–patient bond, enhance trust and encourage acceptance of the HCP's message.

Box 19.8 Principles and practices for avoiding the obstacles and managing the influences

- Ensure that the emotional content of the patient's response is taken very seriously and explored.
- Identify the patient's worries and fears, accept their authenticity in the patient's view, then moderate and negotiate them, where possible, in relation to medical reality and known facts.
- Find ways of expressing risk which are absolutely clear to the particular patient; ensure that there is a common understanding of figures and terms; never use relative risk figures without referring to the absolute figures.
- Compare the risks of treatments or no treatment using the same denominators.
- Where helpful, relate the medical risks to familiar, everyday risks.
- Use visual materials where helpful (such as Paling's perspective scale or one of his palettes – see Figures 19.1–19.3 for examples).

- the meaning and importance of the harm to the person experiencing it, and their perception of the relative weight of benefit and harm
- how the benefit can be maximised, or the harm minimised or prevented
- what action to take if unexpected events occur
- ensuring that the patient truly understands the issues and the information on which they must make their choice and decision
- gaining the patient's voluntary, informed consent (see also Chapter 18).

What to do

These methods offer an edited version of John Paling's work, with his permission.

Use visual aids

Paling has developed visual aids to a high degree of sophistication to help patients understand risk.[224,225]

The first useful tool is a perspective scale of particular medical risks and ordinary everyday risks (Figure 19.1). This allows patients to compare medical risks with risks they are familiar with and to have some kind of conceptual context in which to reflect. There are scales which, for example, show the relationship of serious harm from blood transfusion (like this one) or bone-marrow donation with ordinary risks (accidents, illness, heart attack and so on). Such comparative scales could be made for any medical intervention when the risks are reasonably well known.

The second kind of useful tools are Paling's 'palettes', which show large groups of icons of people (Figure 19.2). There may be 100 or 1000 icons, and they may be men, or women, or men and women with or without children. These allow the very graphic demonstration of the statistics, not only of the number likely to be affected within the whole population of icons, but also the additional

Figure 19.1 Probabilities of risks associated with a blood transfusion. This Paling scale offers a comparison of some medical and non-medical risks. The data and contents of such an instrument can be modified to match the needs of a particular patient or group of patients. Not everyone will be able to interpret the logarithmic scale productively but provision of the absolute figures helps comprehension. Comparisons with 'everyday' risks can be very illuminating in placing medical risks in a wider context of understanding. Copyright John Paling (www.riskcomm.com). Reproduced with permission.

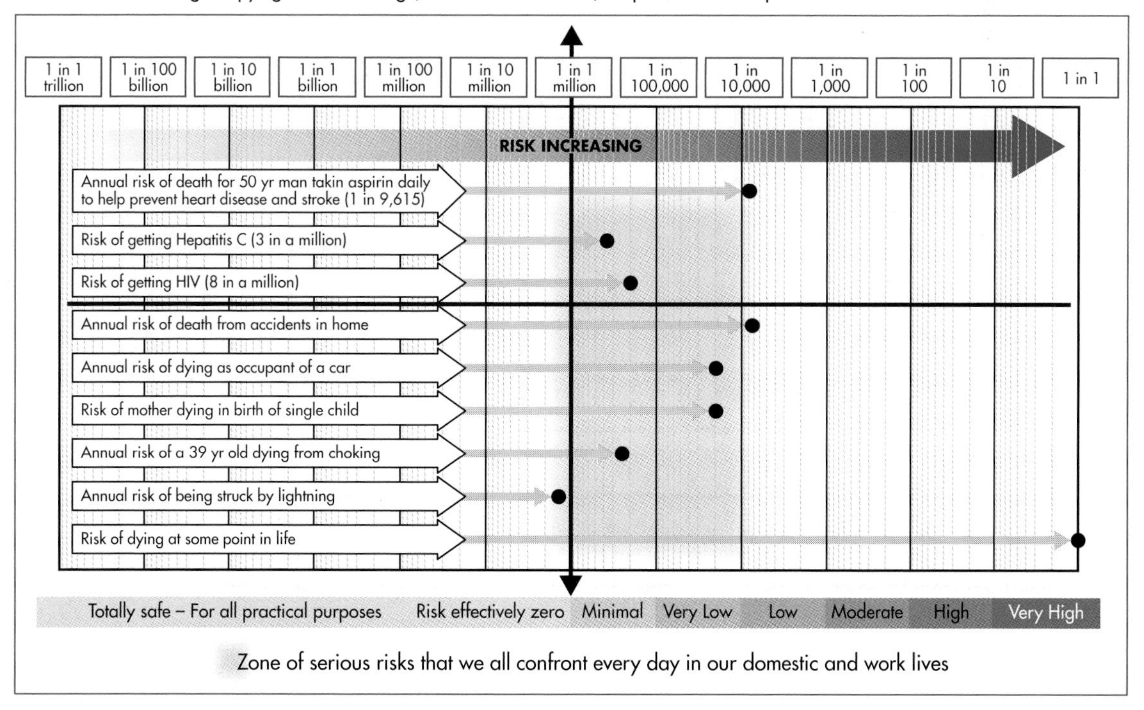

Figure 19.2 Two maternal risks. This Paling palette, with 1000 female icons, provides a striking visual representation for two maternal risks. As would be the case for any risk presented in this way, the at-risk numbers and the safe numbers are presented with equal clarity and balance, in a way that the numbers alone could never do. In addition to other ways of communicating risk, this is a very valuable additional instrument. Copyright John Paling (www.riskcomm.com). Reproduced with permission.

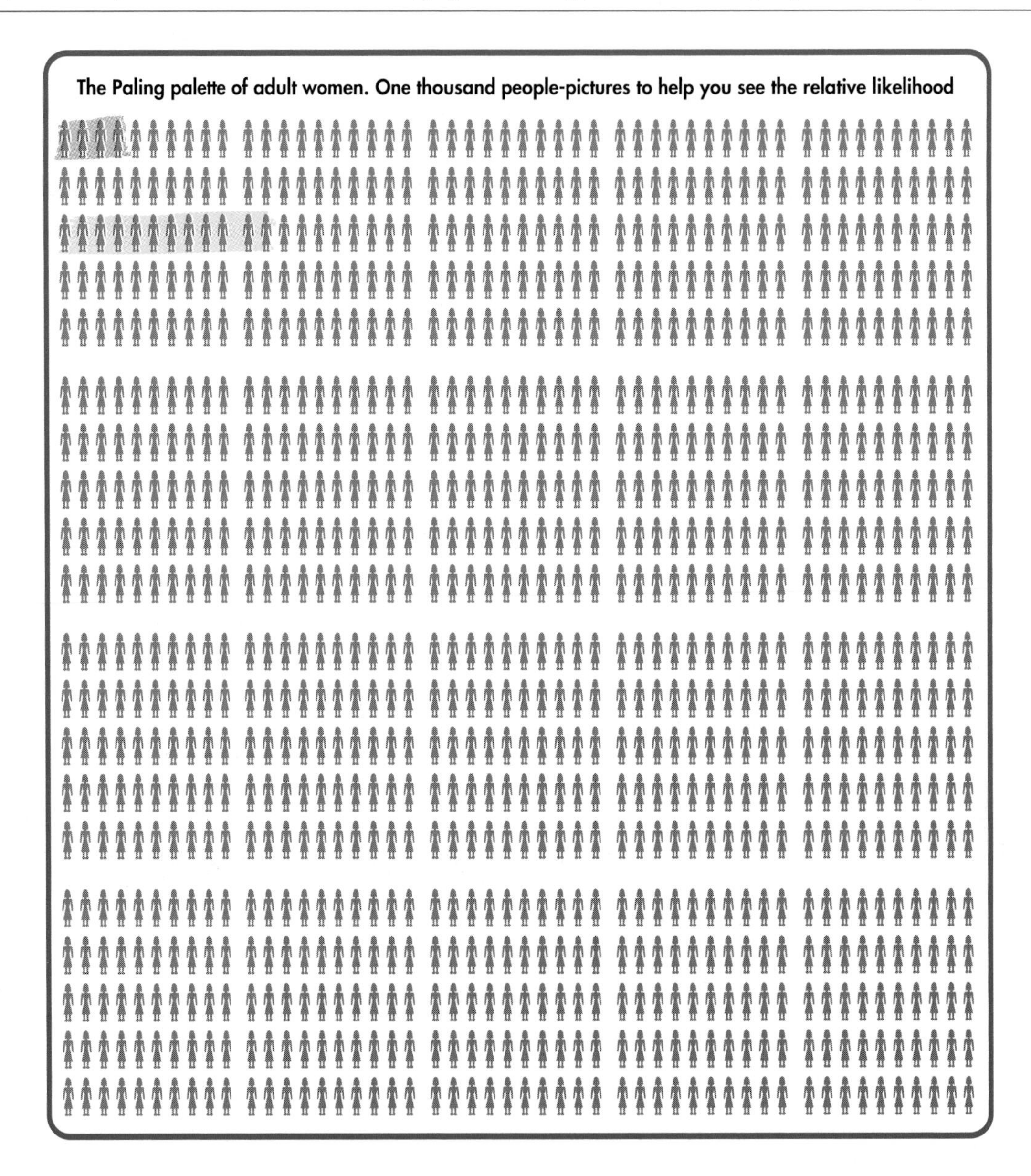

Odds for 39 year old woman producing a child with Down Syndrome or other chromosome abnormality (12 out of 1000)

Odds of a woman having a miscarriage as a result of amniocentesis (4 out of 1,000)

risk brought by additional factors (for example, the risk of breast cancer and the additional risk for those on hormone replacement therapy).

These tools have real benefits as they:

- are simple to understand
- have a common denominator (100 or 1000 people)
- show even-handedly positive outcomes and risks
- are useful in consolidating the relationship between HCP and patient.

You can read more about these and download samples from the website.[226]

Use more than one method

Every patient will make sense of risk in different ways, and require different methods to arrive at a clear understanding of what is involved. The same method will convey different meanings to different patients. Using two or more methods that convey the same information, and checking with the patient as to how satisfied they are with the communication is much the best approach.

Avoid using only descriptive words

Use words like 'common', 'unlikely' and 'rare' only when backed up with some numerical descriptor, when available, supported by visual aids where possible, and ensure the patient shares the meaning you intend. (Rare events, of course, do happen, and a patient who has taken 'rare' to mean 'It won't happen to me' will be very upset should they turn out to be the rare example.)

Use standard vocabulary

Consistent use of terms throughout healthcare, and in the media, would help in establishing at least a common basis of understanding of descriptive terms for everyone. Practice does vary in the US, Europe and elsewhere so it is always important to check the numerical value of any term used in the literature. You can see that the words in column 1 of the table in Box 19.9 could mean very different things to different people, if they were not supported by some kind of numerical qualification. It is probably helpful to relate such terms to everyday risks (injuries or deaths at home or on the road, for example).

Use a standardised numeric definition

Most people are familiar with the '1 in *n*' format of expressing odds, and it is probably the best numeric definition to use. Paling suggests that it is beneficial always to scale up or down to a common denominator, probably 1000 in most cases. (There is evidence that some patients see a higher denominator as a higher risk (e.g. 1 in 300 against 1 in 50.) Using the same denominator for all risks is helpful in making comparisons.

For most of the population, the use of the statistical form (column 2 in Box 19.9) and the frequency bands (column 3) will result in nothing

Box 19.9 Standardised frequency bands

These are the terms for frequency/risk commonly recommended for use in patient information leaflets and other formal communications in Europe.

It is usually suggested that within each system organ class, adverse drug reactions or other risks should be ranked under headings of frequency, most frequent reactions first. The accurate translation of the terms into other languages is a considerable challenge.

1. Descriptive word	*2. Statistical form*	*3. Frequency bands*	*4. Odds*
Very common/very high	>1/10	100–10%	1 in 1 to 1 in 10
Common/high	>1/100, <1/10	10–1%	1 in 10 to 1 in 100
Uncommon/moderate	>1/1000, <1/100	1–0.1%	1 in 100 to 1 in 1000
Rare/low	>1/10 000, <1/1000	0.1%–0.01%	1 in 1000 to 1 in 10 000
Very rare/very low	<1/10 000	0.01–0.001%	1 in 10 000 to 1 in 100 000

When frequency data are not available, the terms "*frequent/ly*" or "*less frequent/ly*" may be used.[227]

but mystification. It is likely that most people will be able to grasp risks in the order of 1 in 10, and 1 in 100 as being within their everyday experience; beyond that (certainly at 1 in 10 000 and above) figures may seem meaningless.

Use of simple percentages – '80% of patients have no adverse effects at all' – is a method that will make sense to almost everyone, when the facts support such a simple declaration.

Box 19.10 Measuring patient and community outcome preferences

> A great deal of work has been done on *health utilities*, which are indicators of the strength of individual preferences for specific outcomes in conditions of uncertainty. Research has used four principal methods: the standard gamble approach; the time trade-off approach; rating scales; and the willingness-to-pay approach. Within scales from death to perfect health, these allow large groups of patients to specify what they most want to avoid or most want to achieve, usually in relation to a particular category of disease or intervention (cancer or anaesthetics, for example) and the probabilities or choices available. Such approaches can be adapted and used informally with individual patients to help them rank their priorities and indicate their therapeutic and quality-of-life preferences.[228]

Avoid relative risk figures alone

Common in health-reporting headlines, relative risk figures are potentially seriously misleading for everyone, even numerically literate people, unless the absolute figures are given real prominence.[229] Generally, relative risk figures should be used judiciously and treated with caution. The Australian HRT crisis in 2002 was partly, perhaps largely, attributable to the careless use of relative risk statistics, when 600 000 women were simultaneously alarmed by the belief that their risk of breast cancer had suddenly doubled.[230]

Frame risk positively

A '70% chance of success' does not mask the 30% risk of failure, but the positive expression of the risk may have a positive impact on the patient's willingness to take the risk and on their confidence. This positive framing does have an inevitably manipulative element in it (as would the opposite). If it is in the genuine interests of the patient to reflect on possible courses of action that will affect their health and welfare, and on the associated risks, then it can be argued that positive framing is justifiable if it does not mislead the patient or disguise the truth. The positive position (chances of success) can always be followed by statement of the inevitably related risks of harm. Use of Paling's palettes largely overcomes this problem.

Avoid complex forms

Complex forms such as number needed to treat (NNT), or number need to harm (NNH), prevention or risk over time (except when essential to the message), as well as the statistical format in column 2 and frequency bands in column 3 of the table in Box 19.9, are all likely to confuse rather than clarify issues for patients.

Uncertainty

Where risks are known reasonably well, methods for their effective communication are relatively simple, although the process for ensuring patient understanding may be anything but easy.

Where the risks are not known, or available information is incomplete or contradictory, or where the known risks are more or less evenly balanced, the challenges are much greater.

'We don't know for sure, but I will try and explain the issues to you,' may not be regarded by patients as the most reassuring introduction to their decision-making processes, but it may have to be the starting point for many discussions of risk. At the same time, patients have to be cautiously counselled in the simple truth that medicine is an incomplete and uncompleted science, and that there are still areas of ignorance and uncertainty. New uncertainties constantly arise in every field, especially with new pharmaceuticals, new disease strains and mutations, resistance, new technologies, new evidence, patient idiosyncrasy and so on.

No professional medical intervention will be proposed or implemented on the basis of no information at all, that is 100% ignorance or uncertainty (or 100% faith): a move in any direction will always be based on some professional knowledge or instinct, however tiny or tentative. Many decisions will be based on more than an absolute minimum, but still falling long short of certainty. HCPs need to have a very clear understanding of confidence intervals and standard deviation and their impact on the strength of any statistic or result on which they are relying.

When there is uncertainty in the prognosis for a disease, in the action of a drug, in the outcome of an operation, in the variables influencing a patient's response, then the HCP has to build from the ground up with what information and evidence there is to make a case for choice and action of some sort, or choices and actions of several sorts. The relative strengths and weaknesses of various courses of action will become apparent through this process.

The case or cases then have to be presented to the patient as responsibly and objectively as possible. The patient may well want the HCP's opinion on the strongest case, even when it falls short of any comforting degree of certainty. This is when the patient's trust in the HCP, and the professional authority and experience of the HCP, are really put to the test. The accuracy and balance with which the known or speculative risks and the areas of uncertainty are presented pose further serious demands. For the peace of mind of both HCP and patient, sometimes a second opinion will be desirable. Patients may need time to reflect on the choices available; immediate decisions will not always be the best, or the ones that patients will feel happy with in the future.

Not all courses of action are irreversible, of course. Uncertainty will be more acceptable if there are progressive stages towards discovery of what the real risks are. For example, prescription of a drug with known serious risks may be accompanied with very careful monitoring to ensure that, at the first sign of any adverse reaction, therapy is reviewed or changed. Patients will be reassured that emergence and management of early, minor, remediable signs will prevent them from being seriously damaged: the risk will seem far less off-putting and overwhelming. This safety net needs to be strongly emphasised.

If the patient is convinced that some kind of action is needed, they will be much more likely to agree to moving forward if they feel they are being accompanied into the unknown or uncertain future by their HCP, not being left to cope on their own. Trust in the HCP's judgement is vital, of course, but so also is the confidence that the patient is not alone and will not be abandoned: a genuine sense of committed partnership, that the risks and uncertainty are, in some sense, shared.

Box 19.11 Patients do not sue HCPs they like

Litigation is the most extreme expression of patient dissatisfaction. It arises more or less as often from failures in communication as it does from disappointing outcomes or even errors.

Patients do not usually sue, who:

- like and trust their HCPs and their health team
- were given satisfactory information, *in their terms*, and realistic expectations about their therapy and its risks.

Pragmatism, then, if nothing else, suggests that good communication is in everyone's best interest (although pragmatism alone willl not ensure good communication).

Conclusion

The ethical and effective communication of risk is one of the high priorities in relationships with patients and one of the most difficult.[231] HCPs need to be able to communicate the truth as far as it is known in ways that really make sense to their patients and do not alarm, deceive or unreasonably reassure. There are specific communications knowledge and skills needed to achieve this, along with the use of helpful visual aids and other resources.

Box 19.12 A postscript on evidence and uncertainty

Evidence is one of those concepts that is commonly misunderstood and can give rise to serious confusion and error in discussions of any kinds, not least with patients. 'What is the evidence?' is an important question to ask in any circumstances, but the answers it produces may be less certain than is often implied or wished. Although this discussion may seem, at first glance, remote from real issues, or wilfully philosophical, it has profound importance for medicine and for making sense of many big contemporary issues.

Evidence is any fact, information or experience that appears to support or challenge an opinion, a hypothesis or a decision. The presence of evidence does not at all necessarily prove or disprove anything *with certainty*, and it is often an unreliable predictor of future events, because it is inevitably based on the past. (And, as we all know, absence of evidence is not evidence of absence.)

There are very few situations in which evidence can claim to prove or disprove a case beyond doubt, other than retrospectively (as possibly in a research project, or a criminal case, for example). Even where past evidence seems convincing, new evidence often emerges to challenge past certainties. The evidence we have may be only a fraction of the evidence there is but which we have not yet discovered. In fact, there are very few matters on which we can be sure that past evidence is reliable: there is no doubt about the evidence that tells us that depriving a human being of oxygen or cutting a major artery will both lead to more or less rapid death. We can trust this as reliable in terms of making sense of past events, and as a predictor of future events.

However, the degree of certainty is much less when you consider, for example, the reaction of a patient to a drug, even when it has been extensively tested and comes with evidence from the testing process. The predictive value of such evidence would be nearer 100% only if the current patient and all variables were, in every tiniest detail, identical to the patient or patients on whom the drug was previously tested. In spite of the control of major variables in the experimental group, all variables cannot be controlled – indeed, all variables cannot even be known in an organism as complex as a human being, and no two human beings are, in any case, ever identical. This dimension of difference applies to the provider as much as the recipient – no two surgeons, physicians, nurses, physiotherapists, any HCP – will ever have an impact on any patient identical either to the impact of other HCPs, or even to their own previous interventions. So the evidence, in the case of any historic study of any medical intervention, however grand or comprehensive, cannot provide us with certainty about the same intervention in the future. It can provide us with likelihoods, probabilities, guidelines, against which we can make decisions, but no more.

> Variability is the law of life, and as no two faces are the same, so no two bodies are alike, and no two individuals react alike and behave alike under the abnormal conditions which we know as disease.
>
> *William Osler*

The most important – and obvious – facts about evidence are that it can take many forms and that its weight and authority are infinitely variable. This applies to the law, science and healthcare – three areas in which evidence plays a formal and crucial part – as much as it does in everyday life – driving, cooking, education, character analysis and so on.

At the lowest level of credibility, evidence may be presented in the forms of:

- anecdote
- hearsay
- personal experience.

'Well, my grandmother ate green vegetables every day of her life, and she lived to be a 103.'

At the highest level is evidence which, in legal and scientific terms, demonstrates a case 'beyond reasonable doubt'. In pure science, this means that an experiment can be replicated again and again, in identical circumstances, and produce identical results. No medical intervention whatsoever can ever be replicated in all its fine detail, so the outcome of any medical intervention is inherently uncertain.

This is an unnerving fact for HCPs and patients to entertain, and it poses a supreme challenge to those who claim that evidence-based medicine is the sole key to safety and effectiveness. Of course there is an enormous amount of useful evidence about almost every possible medical intervention and all HCPs need to be familiar with the evidence about any intervention or therapy they are providing, but they also need to know about the outriders, the exceptions, and the sometimes distorting effects of means and averages, which invite caution and reservation. They also need to know about the multiple variables that may intervene and affect the most meticulous, evidence-based plan: incomplete knowledge of the patient, human error and patient idiosyncrasy are three of the most potent.

The use of algorithms, diagnosis trees and computer-based diagnostics (as examples of the tools of the evidence-based approach) is surely a helpful way to cover a lot of basic questions and information, especially in relatively simple, single-disease cases. But even where the case seems simple, and certainly when there are multiple symptoms or complexities of any kind, an HCP still needs to ask:

Box 19.12 *Cont.*

- What don't I know?
- What could I have missed?
- What other explanation could there be?
- Does this really fit with what the patient is telling me?

Nothing can or should replace the acumen, experience and intuition of the HCP in lively interaction with the patient.

Patients who are told that things are more certain than they really are, or are given the impression that there is no risk are being deceived. HCPs who are overconfident themselves about the conclusiveness of evidence or the safety of their practice are likely to have some very hard knocks.

20 Sex and sexual orientation

Sexuality exercises a radical influence on the lives of most people, whether it is recognised and understood or not. HCPs need to know how sexuality influences their own behaviour and that of their patients, and how it and communications about it affect physical and mental health. Taking a sexual history and communicating about sexual matters are sensitive and difficult tasks. HCPs need to know about those whose sexual tastes and habits are different from their own and how to respond effectively, and to avoid unhelpful reactions or judgements. A differential everyday vocabulary for sexual matters needs to be developed which can be used comfortably with the whole range of patients.

Sex and sexuality

The imperative to reproduce belongs with the search for food, shelter and security as one of the fundamental, defining aspects of all animals; indeed the primary purpose of feeding, finding shelter and staying safe is to ensure favourable circumstances for the birth and survival of the next generation, and so the continuity of the genetic line.

When we look at other animals (and, indeed, almost all organisms) and their behaviour, we can see clearly how urgent and dominant are the instinct and the urge to reproduce.

In understanding human beings we need to take account of this powerful motivation which, as suggested earlier in the book, may have a much greater influence on our lives than we recognise or find comfortable to acknowledge.

Sex lies at the root of life, and we can never learn to reverence life until we know how to understand sex.

Henry Ellis

Human sexuality in its social context is much more complex than sex in the natural world beyond us: among other variables, being liberated from the inevitability of reproduction by drugs and devices. Although the reproductive urge probably still determines the basic pattern, sexual activity has become associated with many other emotions and purposes that do not have reproduction as their aim: on the positive side – pleasure, intimacy, mutuality, excitement, adventure, an end in itself; on the negative side – domination, subjugation, submersion or loss of self, exploitation. Sexual activity may be a way of seeking approval, dealing with loneliness, asserting power, filling time, showing off, manipulating partners; it may be seen as precious and valuable or trivial and commonplace; it may be an obsession, a pastime or a business. And all this is just a fraction of the possibilities in the labyrinth of human motivation and purposes.

Life is a sexually transmitted disease.

R.D. Laing

What has this to do with healthcare communications?

First, in seeking to understand human beings, we have to take account of the influence and importance of sex in their lives and its impact on their psychology and disease patterns.

Psychology The extent to which an individual's sexual needs are being met, and to which they feel themselves to be sexually attractive and/or successful, may have a large influence on how happy or optimistic they are; frustrated or unfulfilled sexual needs can lead to depression, stress-related illness, psychosomatic conditions and to disturbed or criminal sexual activity (rape, for example). Very large numbers of people are troubled, one way or another, in this area of their lives.

Disease or physical problems A range of common infections, as well as specific sexually transmitted infections, can be problematic and distressing; diseases affecting the reproductive system are common and potentially serious or fatal; problems with male or female arousal and orgasm may have psychological or physical origins; many other conditions affect sexual performance and/or confidence; discussion of any of these issues may be very difficult for some patients. The political, social, medical and personal issues associated with HIV and AIDS are enormous almost everywhere.

Second, we have to be alert to the extent to which hidden or apparent sexual motivation (even without any expectation of direct sexual activity), may influence us and our patients in relationships of all kinds, and distort perception and priorities.

Bias Almost everyone reacts more favourably to people they find physically (sexually) attractive – perhaps by giving them more attention, treating them more kindly, being disposed to trust them prematurely, seeking to please them, raising their expectations, perhaps being tempted to touch them inappropriately. Conversely, we are often less than fair to people we find ugly or unattractive, and give them less chance to win our approval.

Flirting This is a specific and dangerous effect of bias. Although in normal social life, flirting is an innocent (or not so innocent) pleasure, unrecognised, it is a hazardous trap for HCPs – either as initiators or recipients. The dangers of flirting arise from the fact that it can imply that there is a deeper level to the relationship, or a different, subversive set of purposes beyond the professional reasons for meeting and so distract from the main purpose. HCPs and patients would be inhuman not to react positively to others they find attractive: we just need to be aware of how far such factors are influencing us and our patients, and manage them so they remain minor and controlled. (There is always a risk of sexual exploitation in professional relationships.)[232]

Third, we need to have the courage and the skill to initiate discussion of sexual matters and to take effective sexual histories when we feel they are relevant to a patient's problems.

Although, in many respects, sex appears to be a commonplace, everyday commodity, for most people the reality of their sexual needs, fantasies, feelings, organs and activity remains intensely private, protected areas of their lives. If disease of the reproductive system, or sexual anxiety is at the base of a patient's problems, they may need sensitive and supportive help to submit to physical examination or to talk about them at all; without such help they may never be mentioned.[233]

Playing it cool There is almost no limit to the range of human sexual fantasy and activity and HCPs need to be prepared (on occasion) to hear things that they might find upsetting or shocking, without betraying their feelings to the patient ('normal' is not really a useful concept in the field of sex). HCPs need to have knowledge of the mechanics and psychology of the whole range of sexual tastes and activity, first to be prepared to react accurately to a patient, and, second to judge when they feel that what they are hearing is genuinely problematic, as opposed to being merely the unnecessary anxieties of an uninformed patient.

Fourth, we need to develop a sensitive, professional framework of communication for sexual matters, and a non-technical vocabulary that is acceptable and familiar to all kinds of patients, and the strength to use it without embarrassing hesitancy. (There are some specific examples in the next section.)

Gay, lesbian and transgender people

Considerable numbers of your patients (and some of your colleagues) will be gay or lesbian, and it is important you should have some understanding of what that means for their lives and how you can communicate most effectively with them, ensure fair and equal access to healthcare and treatment, and avoid unhelpful or damaging assumptions or errors. You will also meet some transvestite and transgender individuals, who may or may not be gay or lesbian. (There are also, of course, many other variations in sexual taste, activity and orientation, some of a quite extreme kind, pursued by hetero- and homosexual people alike. HCPs will certainly come across examples of these specialist minorities, some of which may prompt strong moral or other negative reactions. In some places, unusual sexual practices may be illegal, adding a further inhibiting pressure to sharing of information.)

In this chapter, there is little about heterosexual relationships, because they have been so extensively written about elsewhere,[234–237] and that material is much more easily accessible to readers than discussion of gay and lesbian matters. For heterosexual HCPs, as well as their gay and lesbian colleagues, the author hopes the material here will be illuminating and helpful.

> Does it really matter what these affectionate people do—so long as they don't do it in the streets and frighten the horses!
>
> *Mrs Patrick Campbell*

What does being gay mean?

The primary characteristic of gay men and lesbians is simply that they seek their sexual fulfilment with members of their own gender (the 'homo' in 'homosexual' means 'the same', whereas the 'hetero' in 'heterosexual' means opposite or different).

Homosexual men and women seek intimacy, security, affection and love; may or may not seek exclusive, lifelong partnerships; may or may not set up home together or want to be parents; may or may not find their best social relationships with their own sex. But for what they do in bed, they are not fundamentally different from the heterosexual population. Most homosexuals are not sexually attracted to prepubescent children, any more than heterosexuals are; indeed female children are proportionately at much greater risk from heterosexual paedophiles than male children are from homosexuals (except in certain, specific environments). That homosexuals may be attracted to the sexually mature, young and beautiful only confirms that their general tastes are much the same as everyone else's.

For gay men, the emergence of HIV in the 1980s, and the subsequent death of so many, had a defining effect on gay consciousness and solidarity in some parts of the world. Gay men played a large part in campaigning for the urgent provision of services and medicines, and in promoting safe sex. Some of the challenges and dilemmas remain the same, but the possibility of healthy, long-term survival has changed the landscape and the perception of risk in the developed world.[238]

> I'm homosexual . . . How and why are idle questions. It's a little like wanting to know why my eyes are green.
>
> *Jean Genet*

It is easy to both understate and overemphasise the differences between homosexuals and the rest of the population. On the one hand, being gay or lesbian is an exceptionally important aspect of personality and self-image, and can also be highly problematic; on the other, being gay does not essentially affect anyone's capacity to engage productively and responsibly in any human activity or occupation or relationship.

English culture is basically homosexual in the sense that the men only really care about other men.
Germaine Greer

There is no such thing as a homosexual or a heterosexual person. There are only homo- or heterosexual acts. Most people are a mixture of impulses if not practices.
Gore Vidal

Homosexuality and healthcare

Although the general health needs of gays, lesbians, and transgender individuals are much the same as the rest of the population, some of their social, psychological and healthcare needs, and some of the risk factors affecting their lives do differ in some significant ways from those of heterosexuals. Here are some of the communications and related issues that need special attention and sensitive handling[239]:

- Evidence or fear of discrimination may restrict access to healthcare or inhibit gays, lesbians and transgender people from seeking help. Explicit non-discriminatory polices are needed, along with outreach communications and activity. Creation of a safe and welcoming environment is important.
- All staff, not least non-medical front-line personnel, need to be educated in minority sexuality and in non-discriminatory and non-judgemental attitudes and behaviour.
- First impressions can be highly inaccurate: the media stereotypes of the 'camp gay' man or the 'butch lesbian' are as misleading as all stereotypes in their focus on superficial characteristics: although there may be proportionately more effeminate gay males than effeminate heterosexual men, they are certainly not in the majority, any more than masculine

Box 20.1 Who has homosexual sex?

Considerable numbers of people will have voluntary or involuntary sex with members of their own gender at some time in their lives.

- Those who have an exclusive preference for sex with their own gender.
- Those who have a general, but not exclusive preference for sex with their own gender; those with a more or less equal taste for both; those who occasionally choose to venture out from their customary heterosexuality – all these are, to a greater or lesser extent, bisexual
  - This group includes men who are, by and large, living ordinary, satisfactory, heterosexual married lives, often with children, with few, if any, of their family, friends or colleagues knowing anything about their perhaps occasional double lives.
  - It also includes men and women who know themselves to be thoroughly gay, but have found their way into marriage and family life for reasons of defence against the frightening reality of 'coming out', as a self-deception, as a disguise of who they are, as an attempt at changing their preferences through force of circumstances, or through sheer loneliness; many in this group will have little or no homosexual sex because of their fear of discovery and the collapse of their elaborate camouflage; some people in this group may live lives of reasonable fulfilment and happiness.
- Many adolescent boys and their peers: most will shift voluntarily to exclusive heterosexuality in due course; for some their identity as gay males will be confirmed, with more or less pain on the way; for some it will leave them in a state of confusion and distress, particularly if there is any kind of negative institutional or parental reaction, or if they suffer from the crippling effects of guilt; some will genuinely not know what their real preferences are, as they struggle to respond to the urge to make a decision one way or the other, and avoid ambiguity.
- Many adolescent girls experience intense emotional attachments to other females, both peers and seniors, which may or may not include sexual fantasy or activity. As with boys, these may resolve themselves in one direction or another, with more or less pain and lasting impact on future choices and relationships. In general, such relationships seem to be subject to much less anxiety and social stigma than intimacy between males.
- Some men or women who are deprived of heterosexual sex for long periods in situations such as schools, colleges, monasteries and convents, military establishments or prisons.
- Those who are abused as children by same-sex relatives, friends or strangers, priests or teachers; those who are raped in adult life in open society or in closed institutions such as military camps and prisons.

lesbians are. All labelled groups of human beings embrace enormous variety and inconsistency.

- HCPs may too readily make an assumption of heterosexuality and so miss out on a major aspect of a patient's life and fail to take an adequate sexual history. Such failure and lack of insight may also disappoint or anger a patient who needs help to disclose their sexual orientation and to talk about difficult or embarrassing personal or health issues
- Gender-specific or assumption-laden language ('wife', 'husband', 'married', for example) may be major obstacles if alternatives are not offered. A negative answer to the question, 'Are you married?' ends the possibility of disclosure unless it is followed by the question, 'Do you have a partner?'; this then allows next steps to the identification of the gender of the partner (who may be a hetero- or homosexual non-married partner, of course). Non-homosexual patients may be very disturbed to think that there was any doubt about the gender of their partner, so it may be preferable to say, 'Tell me about your partner' and then to pick up the clues from the use of personal pronouns and other information. In countries where legal civil partnerships are possible, forms and communications need to take account of that formal status.
- Documentation of next of kin is very important for gays and lesbians. A permanent partner or friend, albeit without formal legal status, may be the patient's choice. Failure to respect patients' authority and choice in relation to this can be disastrous (insisting on the necessity of recording a (perhaps alienated) blood-relative as next of kin, for example). Inviting participation of a partner on exactly the same basis as you would invite a wife or husband is the proper course of action. (This all has major implications for the design and content of intake forms and other documentation.)
- Be aware of how health risks and healthcare issues specifically relate to lesbians and bisexual women – sexually transmitted infections, common sexual practices, cervical health, reproductive health, mid-life changes, ageing, mental health, and substance-use patterns. Do not assume, for example, that Pap smears are not relevant to lesbians, nor that they are safe from the risk of HIV. Do not assume that lesbians have not been pregnant or do not want to have children.[240]
- Be aware of how health risks and healthcare issues specifically relate to gay and bisexual men – sexually transmitted infections, common sexual practices, anal and testicular health, ageing, mental health, and substance-use patterns, and more.
- Members of sexual minorities are almost certainly at higher risk of alcohol, tobacco and substance abuse than some other groups, and may need as much support or more in managing lifestyle issues (diet, exercise, drinking and so on) as other members of the population.
- Depression may be a particular problem for those who are not well-adjusted to their sexual orientation or are subject to any number of pressures and problems because of it.
- Many of the issues above are relevant to transgender people, but, being an often misunderstood, even despised, small minority within a minority, their problems may be much greater. HCPs (and the whole team from front-line in) need to be especially careful about reacting negatively or judgementally. The questions of preferred name and pronoun are important. Sexual and medical history may be complex, including past surgery or the possible use of legitimate or illegal drugs for body enhancement. A transgender individual may have difficulty in choosing an icon-identified toilet or be subject to harassment if someone is offended by their choice. 'Gay' and 'lesbian' labels are not strictly relevant to transgender people.
- This is a field in which there are immense and excellent community and internet resources for HCPs to explore for their education, as well as

for patients to be referred to for their own investigation.[241] HCPs should never be reluctant to ask their patients to help them learn: 'I don't have much experience in this area, so please help me to understand better'.

Our very strength as lesbians lies in the fact that we are outside of patriarchy; our existence challenges its life.

Charlotte Bunch

Language

If you're treating patients in a sexually transmitted infection (STI) or general clinic, then you will need to know all about everything that people do when they are having sex, whether heterosexual or homosexual, especially those activities with risk of infection. You will need to know both what the activities are and the vocabulary customarily used to describe them.[242] Not every patient will understand what you mean by 'penetrative sex' or 'masturbation' and although 'fucking' or 'jacking off' will be the absolutely proper terms to use for some patients, others will find them offensive. But you must have a word for the act, otherwise you cannot talk about it, and are very likely to be misunderstood (perhaps later ridiculed) if you use some euphemistic turn of phrase for that activity, or anything else. Not knowing or using the appropriate vocabulary is a real threat to the credibility of an HCP in the eyes of patients. Following a patient's lead is one way to address this problem.[243]

Box 20.2 Physical and sexual vocabulary

Activity:
This is a task you might like to pursue on your own or with colleagues (a group brainstorm would be instructive and amusing): list all the parts of the body and all the activities and equipment associated with sexual behaviour, and find a range of acceptable, everyday words which you can use differentially with a wide range of patients, including teenagers and elderly people, those with higher or little education, the shy and conservative, those (ostensibly) in the mainstream and those outside it and so on.

Select a core list of words that you think will be most useful to you and practise using them clearly and unselfconsciously.

(The same caution applies to an HCP's use of 'gay', 'lesbian', 'queer', even 'homosexual' and so on: sexual behaviour is not necessarily a determinant of a person's self-image (although it often is), nor a reliable indicator of how they would describe, wish to be described or recognise themselves.)

If you're dealing with a gay man, then knowing that he has anal sex itself is not enough, because you also have to know about roles ('Are you top/active or bottom/passive or both?') and, therefore, who's at risk of what and who should be using the condom (although it is a joint responsibility, of course). (Even the use of the word 'passive' may be an inaccurate description of what some partners feel and how they see themselves.) It is important to remember also, that not all gay sex is about penetration and that some gay men do not have anal sex in either role. Gays and lesbians do not always play an exclusive stereotypical male or female role in their lives or relationships, although some do.

Some heterosexuals feel threatened by gays and lesbians of their own gender, fearing that they will be subject to sexual advances or harassment. This results from the myth that homosexuals are somehow more irresponsible (and promiscuous) than everyone else, and perhaps from some degree of insecurity in the sexual identity of the person who fears being a victim. HCPs who are aware of any serious level of negativity in their reactions to gays and lesbians really need to tackle and resolve their own problems, or refer their patients to a more sympathetic colleague.

As with ethnic minorities, it is obviously enormously helpful if gay or lesbian colleagues can be openly embraced as valued members of the team, not only for their professional knowledge and skills, but also for the important extra contribution they can make to both team education and patient care.

Conclusion

Sex and sexuality are powerful aspects of human personality and motivation. Psychological, social or physical dysfunction in relation to sex can have

Box 20.3 Do you measure up?

The pressures on women to look good – sexy, attractive, glamorous (and, in the West, usually thin) – are persistent and aggressive from dozens of sources: media of all types, the cosmetics and fashion industries, peers, inner desires, and many more. Although ideal types vary considerably from culture to culture, the drive for conformity is much the same everywhere. The impact (positive and negative) that this may all have on a woman's self-image is an important element of personality we must understand if we are to deal sensitively with women's bodies and their feelings about them. Such pressures can lead to bulimia, anorexia, stress-related disease, and other disturbances of health and behaviour.

The pressures on men are considerable too: to be smart, handsome, muscular, sexy – and to have big penises. The author receives a couple of hundred spam emails a day stating that men with small organs are not to be taken seriously and will never make their partners happy. It is just another example of the promotion of dissatisfaction and unhappiness by those wanting to make a quick buck for legitimate and dubious products.

Few people are immune to these subversive and damaging messages, so very effectively and frequently communicated. Some reactions and needs and some diseases of some of your patients will have their origins in this kind of propaganda. Effectively countering it is a real challenge, and may require the help of specialist counselling or psychotherapy.

profound effects on morale and health. For a wide variety of reasons, people may be defensive or secretive about their sexual needs and activities and HCPs need to be sensitive and skilled both in learning about their patient's problems and in finding satisfactory ways of helping them solve them. The quality of communications will have a determining effect on the success of healthcare relationships in this sensitive and complex area of human need.

21 Dying and death

Helping patients and their families deal with dying and death, and loss of other kinds, involves sensitive communication skills as well as emotional strength and personal wisdom. HCPs need to find some measure of internal reconciliation to death and understanding of its meaning for themselves, so that they can be most helpful and supportive to others at their times of need. The quality of a patient's death and the impact of it on those remaining can be greatly affected by HCPs' responses and actions.

If I had my life over again I should form the habit of nightly composing myself to thoughts of death. I would practice, as it were, the remembrance of death. There is no other practice which so intensifies life. Death, when it approaches, ought not to take one by surprise. It should be part of the full expectancy of life. Without an ever-present sense of death life is insipid. You might as well live on the whites of eggs.

Muriel Spark

The end of life is such a common reality in healthcare everywhere, and communications about it so sensitive and so important, that all HCPs need to consider it and reflect how they deal with it for themselves and for patients and their families. This chapter cannot be a comprehensive account of death and the demanding communications associated with it, but it will raise some of the major issues and questions that are likely to affect HCPs from day to day.[243–248]

Responding to death

Understanding of death and its meaning varies enormously across cultures and among individuals. Few generalisations are very helpful, but we may risk some, with the reservation that each individual's death is unique, and the responses of loved ones, across age, location and culture, are immensely varied.

Some thoughts:

- Most (but not all) people are afraid of death itself or the manner of death (pain particularly), for themselves and others.
- Most people find it hard to accept the certainty of their own death, and to be reconciled to it when it approaches.
- Many people fear speaking of death at all; many will use euphemistic phrases like 'pass on,' 'pass away' and so on, to cushion and divert the harsh reality. HCPs need to find their own language for death and dying which they can use comfortably and confidently.
- For many, there is a taboo (a set of irrational, spiritual, religious, psychological (even magical) beliefs and feelings) associated with death, which may lead them to avoid or deny the subject altogether or approach it with particular dread.
- Failure to think about and prepare for one's own death and the death of others (especially sudden death) can make the occasion of death especially painful and difficult.
- For some, death is associated with an extensive scheme of religious beliefs which may invest it with special meaning and importance (and optimism or dread), and may require special rituals.

- For some, the postponement of death – length, continuity of life – at any cost of quality of life, is the priority for themselves or their loved ones.
- For some, death is preferable to some unacceptable (or prohibited) procedures (e.g. blood transfusion, abortion).
- For some, in some circumstances, death will be welcome, and they will accept it willingly, or at least with willing resignation for themselves or their loved ones.
- For some, death is preferable to resuscitation and return to a life of suffering (a life in which the patient believes they have no quality of life, or quality so negative that it is insupportable).
- Many people already know if they are going to die, or if their loved ones are going to die, even if the fact has not been mentioned or discussed.
- There are few more traumatic events for anyone than the sudden death of a loved one, particularly for parents of a child, whatever the child's age.
- The death of a loved one can prompt a wide range of intense and sometimes damaging feelings: as well as grief, there can be regret, anger, guilt, resentment, despair, even hatred and fury.

Dying is something we human beings do continuously, not just at the end of our physical lives on this earth.

Elisabeth Kübler-Ross

Being ready

When a patient dies, or is certainly going to die, HCPs need to prepare themselves, not only to deal sensitively and helpfully with the patient and their friends or relatives, but to cope with the sometimes intense feelings they will have themselves – patients they have become fond of; patients they have seen through difficult times; patients they have perhaps brought back from the brink of death before; young patients who should have bright futures ahead of them; all patients to whose life and health they are committed. Sometimes there will be self-doubt – did I really do everything possible and do it well enough? And there will be times when the decision of life and death rests with the professional, in one way or another. Facing such emotional drama requires a strong heart and a secure personality – and strong personal, professional and social networks for support.

Health is merely the slowest way someone can die.

Anon

To communicate helpfully in these circumstances, an HCP needs to have some view about the meaning of life and death, or at least some structure of thought and forms of words that can be tapped when support or advice is needed. Everyone will have a different view, some deeply influenced by their religious faith. The death of a patient is, of course, not the time to impose one's own values on anyone, or even share them, unless invited to do so, but having some inner frame of reference will provide an HCP with an anchor amidst the often turbulent emotions surrounding death. (The references at the beginning of this chapter provide rich resources for exploration.)

Here are some thoughts that may provide useful starting points for personal reflection and stimulate readers to develop and clarify their own ideas, as well as providing some basis for communications with patients. They are offered in the hope that they will be thought provoking, but with no other credentials than that they are the personal views of the author.

The reality of death

One of the Buddha's teachings is that his followers should 'look death in the eye' every day; that nothing should distract them from accepting the inevitability of death, and its constant presence everywhere. There is great wisdom in this, because to avoid such reflection means that we shall never be prepared for death, but always surprised, shocked, frightened, overwhelmed by the fact of it, aside from the emotions that we may have about a particular instance of death. (HCPs, of course, encounter death much more frequently than the general population, and some measure of self-protection from repeated distress is a necessary survival mechanism. This technique should not, however, disconnect an HCP's experience and emotions from the weight and meaning of death for others; not make them distant, callous or indifferent.)

Live today in the knowledge that it may be your last: for a percentage of the human race, today will be their last day, and one day (perhaps tomorrow) it will be our turn; if you love someone, tell them today; if someone has hurt you, forgive them today; if you have a dream, start following it today – because there may never be another chance; even in our last, perhaps weak and suffering days, there may be things that we should not postpone.

For those who seek to understand it, death is a highly creative force. The highest spiritual values of life can originate from the thought and study of death.

Elisabeth Kübler-Ross

Quality of life

We all need to have some clear idea of what we want from life: everyone wants a long and happy life, but it is really only the extent to which we are happy over which we have any control at all: nature is ultimately in charge of length, assisted by self-harm, recklessness, accidents, luck and so on. Some will say, with absolute certainty, that they would much rather have a short, intense, fulfilling life than any length of moderate or disappointing life. Where do we stand on this? Are we trying to live a life of quality, making it happen, in our own terms, now, or somehow postponing it, or just hoping that it will come along? What is needed to give us the quality of life that will make us feel satisfied, that we have not wasted our time, when we consider it at the moment of its ending, whenever that occurs? What quality are our patients looking for in sickness and in health, and how can we help them achieve it?

Unfinished business

Whether we find ourselves dying at an age of 15, 38, 63 or 91, even if we've conscientiously lived life to its fullest, there will be things we've overlooked, loose ends we haven't tied up, things we haven't said (at 91, fewer, it is to be hoped, than at 38). Reflecting on such things, talking them through, perhaps even remedying some of them (reconciliation with an estranged child, forgiveness of an old enemy), may make a big contribution to the acceptance and peacefulness of our dying. Such conversations and support for patients may be very helpful. (Talking through achievements and happy memories may also bring great comfort.)

The bitterest tears shed over graves are for words left unsaid and deeds left undone.

Harriet Beecher Stowe

What is a good death?

Even someone in their youth can be said to die well, and that quality of death will often have a lot to do with how they are cared for and loved while they are dying. A good death is one where there is a degree of peace and reconciliation at the end, in the heart and mind of the patient, and in those who love them. In cynical mood, one might ask what does it matter how someone dies? – they'll be dead shortly and that will be that. But, of course it does matter, although the arguments are philosophical, imaginative, emotional, aesthetic and beyond cool reason: for the patient, because such quality of life as can be enjoyed, such peace, such lack of suffering, such comfort, such human company, such love, should ideally be the experience of the last minutes of life, whatever you or they may believe follows death in terms of immortality or reincarnation, or whatever; for the living, quality of death will bring a greater chance of eventual and real reconciliation with the inevitability and finality of loss, the transition to whatever they believe may follow, and freedom from regret, whatever the grief.

Letting go

For HCPs, the point at which they cease struggling to revive or save a patient is determined, to a large extent, by clinical criteria, and by familiarity with the physical reality of death (there is, of course, a big emotional and human dimension to the decision too). For fearful, ever-optimistic, despairing relatives and friends, acceptance of imminent or actual death may take a much more tortuous path. While there is oxygen in the lungs and a beat in the heart, however sustained, some will cling and cling to the life that is fading, or has already gone. For a patient who is conscious and dying, such fierce refusal by a partner or relatives to accept the fact can be an obstacle to their freedom to let go and die peacefully. A good death is, among other things, one where the patient has, as it were, the permission of their nearest and dearest to die; they have let go, said goodbye, and the patient can then do so too. Helping in this process is a valuable gift for HCPs to offer, when it is the right path for the situation. It is one that will be familiar to members of palliative care and hospice teams, but one that should not be exclusive to them.

Dealing with the extreme emotions of others

At the moment a death is announced, or a major disease or disability revealed, HCPs may witness outbursts of extreme emotion which can be very disturbing and uncomfortable. In general, the best advice for HCPs in such a situation, is to be quietly supportive and to let the emotion run its course and resist the urge to calm people down or moderate their behaviour: perhaps lead them gently to a quiet area, offer a seat, provide tissues, sit quietly with them for a while, ask what they want, or leave them with members of the family or friends for private time; say you'll be back in 10 minutes, or whatever period seems suitable. Most people will recover, at least temporarily, and engage in whatever discussion and paperwork may be necessary – but such tasks should be requested with the greatest delicacy and regret at their necessity.

Those who have the strength and the love to sit with a dying patient in the silence that goes beyond words will know that this moment is neither frightening nor painful, but a peaceful cessation of the functioning of the body.

Elisabeth Kübler-Ross

Dying is a process, not an event

Although the moment of death is an event, dying itself, except in the case of sudden death, is not, because it takes place over time (some would say over one's entire life), and because it involves a constant succession of physical and psychological change. Given that we all die only once, and that, even in a world in which there is so much death, any partner or family may have relatively little experience of it, HCPs have a great contribution to make in helping patients and their loved ones deal positively with dying and in managing it well – a role in which many HCPs are already deeply compassionate and effective.

Life is pleasant. Death is peaceful. It's the transition that's troublesome.

Isaac Asimov

Box 21.1 Assisted suicide and other deep dilemmas

There are strong ethical and philosophical arguments for patients to have control over their last days (through advanced directives and living wills, for example), and even over the manner and time of death. However, the extent to which an HCP should assist a patient to die remains a matter of social and legal controversy. Requests by patients for help in dying require sensitive and thoughtful responses, and they demand that HCPs have carefully considered their position with regard to their own principles and the provisions of the law in their country or local jurisdiction. The issues of physician-assisted suicide, euthanasia, terminal sedation, withholding or withdrawing life-supporting treatments, pain medication that may hasten death, will confront many HCPs who will need to be well prepared to deal with them[249–251]

Loss and mourning

Helping someone mourn (like helping someone die peacefully) is often much more to do with being present and compassionate than it is about being active and clever. Encouragement to share feelings, attentive stillness, and acceptance and endorsement of the patient's emotions are the hallmarks of good grief counselling. The urges to cheer people up, jolly them along, distract them, are almost always hurtful and damaging. On the other hand, the HCP must be alert to the points at which a patient has reached the end of one stage of mourning, and is moving towards another or ready for it – from disbelief and anger to despairing contemplation of the effects on their life, for example; from thinking of what they have lost to reflection on what they can still achieve – and so on. For many people the time comes when they have grieved enough, and they are ready to move on but may need help, permission, to do so.

When we lose anything, even a minor possession we are fond of, we go through a period of more or less intense sadness, anger, grief, disbelief, hope, disappointment, and then slow detachment and resignation and acceptance. It is a reduced version of how most people react to a death. Grieving is common to all loss; mourning, the process through which we come to accept that things will not change and, in most cases, through which we resume some kind of continuing life. In facing an approaching death, the mourning process may start early, as patient and loved ones together recognise and negotiate the loss they are about to face.

Although much of healthcare practice is about restoring health after temporary setbacks, disease and accidents often result in irrecoverable loss of one kind or another – an ability or capacity, an eye or a limb, mobility, fertility, strength, independence, hope for a long life and so on – all of which are, in some respects a small version of death for the patient and perhaps their family and friends too. The experience of major loss and of death itself are, in some ways analagous, and the concept of mourning is entirely relevant. Patients sometimes need to be helped to understand what is happening to them in emotionally foreign territory, and supported through the process.

Conclusion

In staying alongside others through their grief and suffering, in offering our attention, support and compassion, we are probably doing as much as is possible: we must not delude ourselves into thinking we should or can carry or remove the emotional pain of others. Usually, they must live with it and endure it. An HCP's task is to make sure that patients do not feel their suffering is ignored, unimportant or tiresome, that they are not alone and that they are in the hands of people who care.

Revision, discussion and application (7)

A. Reflection and discussion

1. In the entire system of healthcare, including drug development, there are multiple points at which patient safety may be protected and promoted, or down-played or overlooked; the same applies in the relationships, interactions and communications within the system. What are some of the critical points at which you feel change is needed to improve safety? What do you understand by Vogt's assertion that 'there cannot be a safer drug until there is a safer system'[197]?
2. In terms only of patients and their medication, what do you feel are the greatest threats to safety and what practical, remedial measures and communications need to be used by HCPs and others to reduce those threats and improve safety?
3. What are the arguments in favour of informed consent? Subject those arguments and their strength to hostile analysis, on the basis of its being an unnecessary indulgence, a waste of time and an impractical ideal (and so on). How strong a case can you make?
4. What do you see as the major challenges in the effective communication of risk to patients? What elements in the data and information available, and in the patient's knowledge and psychology make it a particularly difficult task?
5. What are some of the illogicalities and inconsistencies in understanding risk among many populations? Why is it, among other things, that some serious risks are paid little attention whereas minor ones are exaggerated? What impact does the source or cause of the risk have on perception?
6. What are the some of the positive and negative effects that sex and sexual orientation can have on individual psychology and health? What are the particular aspects that impinge on healthcare relationships and therapy?
7. What are your attitudes to gays and lesbians? If you feel any measure of anxiety, disapproval or rejection, what is the source of those feelings? What are the techniques of dealing with negative feelings about patients of any kind in a professional relationship?
8. What is meant by the idea that 'dying is a process not an event'? How does this affect our understanding of death and the ways in which we might approach a patient who is dying? How can you help a patient have a 'good death'?
9. What are the ways in which HCPs can protect themselves from personal damage from exposure to the suffering and death of patients, without losing their capacity for responsiveness and compassion?

B. Application

1. Make a checklist of priority actions for improving patient safety in your area of practice. What are the minimum items you must check and communicate with every patient?
2. Examine the systems, procedures and communications in your work environment and identify points at which you feel there are threats to safety (lookalike drugs, confusing labelling, non-standard procedures, inadequate training, poor patient information and so on). Make a list and try to address some of the problems.
3. Review your approach to patient consent and decide if there are improvements you can make, perhaps in the focus of communications with patients, or in the recording of consent. Are there circumstances in which you can ignore consent without risk?
4. Are consent forms in your part of the world (for complex or risky therapy, clinical trials) simple and acceptable? If not, how can they be improved to make easy sense to patients, to highlight primary issues, to ensure they lead to genuine understanding and informed consent? How can the procedures and communications around consent forms be improved to make the process as transparent and open as possible? What can you do directly to improve available forms?
5. Write down you own protocol for communicating risk to patients: what are the main issues you must remember and the pitfalls you must avoid? What is the minimum information that must be given? How is that going to be communicated? What resources and materials should you have at hand to use or refer to when needed?
6. What is your approach to discussing uncertainty with patients? How would this vary according to different patient types? What techniques would you use to reduce the negative impact of uncertainty for some patients?
7. Building on the exercise in Chapter 20, spend some time thinking about the language you use for discussing sexual matters and other related topics that might be difficult or embarrassing for you or for patients. Scroll through the range of sexual activities, organs and functions (and so on) which you will have to refer to, and select the range of exact words you will use with different patients. Test them in real life, and refine and develop your list.
8. Reflect on the way in which you and others manage dying patients and the actual time of death, and assess if you feel that things are being dealt with as well as they can, or if improvements could be made. How could both practical matters and communications with patients and their families be changed to reduce unnecessary distress and increase comfort?

Commentary on many of the questions and issues appears on the publisher's website, in Online Resources at www.pharmpress.com.

Part I

The broader communications picture

HCPs engage in a host of communications activities (emails, letters, phone calls, writing leaflets and so on) which do not involve face-to-face relationships with patients, but will often have a considerable impact on patients and the public, and on their perceptions and feelings. Many activities belong to the ordinary routines of professional life (record keeping, making presentations, teaching, attending meetings, writing reports and much more) and they can also be sharpened and improved through study and debate.

This final part includes chapters on all the basic communications activities and skills, on complaints and complaint handling, public relations, managing effective meetings, media relations and teaching. Saving time and performing more effectively in any of these areas will improve internal and external relations, boost professional confidence and morale for individuals and whole organisations, and, ultimately, support the development and delivery of much-improved services to patients.

22 Effective written and spoken communication

This chapter deals with the great variety of essential, everyday communications in healthcare, except those directly involving face-to-face contact with patients. It provides general principles that are useful in any situation at all, within and beyond healthcare, and specific guidelines for particular activities – public speaking, letter writing, email management, telephone use, patient information materials and more.[252]

Clarity of purpose

It seems obvious – before starting any communications activity, be sure that you are clear about its purpose:

- exactly what your message is (content)
- who you want to contact
- the result you want to achieve.

Always take a moment to think about these issues and make mental notes or perhaps jot them down on paper, before writing or picking up the phone. Many communications fail in one way or another because the sender, having only a general sense of what they want to do, has not accurately and specifically clarified the details in advance.

Targeting/segmentation

This important issue may sound technical but it is not. It is absolutely essential for anyone wanting to communicate anything.

We can turn again to commercial companies and the media for a model of good practice: they adapt their communications for every different segment of their markets: they know that women and men, children and elderly people, students and tradesmen, all have different tastes, needs, wants and preferences. But it is also much subtler than those crude categories suggest.

We might assume, for example, that the audience segment labelled 'Nurses' was a rational and coherent one, and that we could address all nurses with the same communication content and method. This is highly questionable because (again, obviously) although all nurses share a common professional identity and overall purpose, all nurses are different from each other.

Box 22.1 Audience segments

There are differences in the following dimensions, at least:

- age
- gender
- seniority
- role
- speciality
- education
- country of origin
- ethnicity
- social background
- intelligence
- literacy
- location
- income
- dedication
- job-satisfaction
- attitude.

(The last three elements, and other subjective aspects, are also discussed below, in Audience.)

Within a single hospital, the nursing staff will differ along those different dimensions although they share the same employer and workplace. There are lots of other, subtler differences too, and they relate to the complex dimensions of personality, which further complicate the picture. This applies to any group of people, however superficially similar they may seem.

The point is this: although often used, mass communications, in the sense of effectively reaching everyone, generally don't work. Much of the material and the effort will be wasted because the communications are not targeted, suited, shaped to particular segments of the audience. Successful mass communicators (that is those who do effectively reach masses of people) do so because their message is targeted and shaped to some shared, common denominator among the masses that overrides the differences. (Examples include newspapers, magazines, television shows, internet sites and so on. Even here, however, the changing tastes of the masses mean that communications have constantly to be reviewed and adapted if they are to keep hold of their audiences.) The single common denominator of 'nurse', 'surgeon', 'pharmacist', and so on, may not be sufficient to make a message compelling for every individual within those groups.

A message to 350 nurses in a hospital needs to take very accurate account of the variety within that small group to make sure it has a chance of reaching and affecting most of them: the different specialities; the least and most literate; the enthusiastic and the indifferent; the old-hand and the novice; the most senior and the most junior; the dedicated and the cynical – and all the intermediate stages too. The most effective single communication will take account of as many of those variables as possible in its formulation; at times, the one audience may need to be segmented by some important variable (perhaps by seniority or years of experience or speciality) and a unique message composed for each sub-group.

If you're considering a message to 'Patients' then the variables are even more extensive and challenging, because patients include the entire spectrum of human life in your locality. It is very unlikely indeed that a single format message (leaflet or poster, for example) will reach more than a minority. We must remember the very large numbers of people who have trouble with basic literacy skills, and the larger number for whom health literacy is a big problem, too.

In real life, it is the hare who wins. Every time. Look around you. And in any case it is my contention that Aesop was writing for the tortoise market. Hares have no time to read. They are too busy winning the game.

Anita Brookner

Audience

Beyond taking account of the evident characteristics of your audience, understanding the state of mind of your recipients is also among the most important skills of an effective communicator (see the early chapters of this book for more on this). If a message does not connect with the recipient; if the recipient is not in a frame of mind to attend to the message; if the recipient's feelings are not taken account of in the message, it may fail to have any impact.

Two questions need to be asked and answered:

- What will be the state of mind of my audience when they receive the message?
- What feelings will the message generate when it is received?

These two issues will have as much influence on the effectiveness of a message as its actual content and composition.

Everyone has had the experience of receiving a memo or an email at a time when they were intensely busy, prompting the reaction: 'For goodness' sake! What am I supposed to do with that now?' Or, worse, the message may arrive at a busy time, and not be read at all. Some of the responsibility for such failures must be taken by the sender as well as the recipient: the sender must try, as far as possible, to anticipate and take account of the circumstances of the recipient, if their communication is to have a chance of achieving its aims.

This is even more obvious if you think about the question of language: if the message is not in language that makes sense to the recipient, then the message will not get through at all. At the extreme, sending a communication in English, or Hindi or Spanish to people who do not read that language, obviously will not have much effect. More common is using words or concepts in a common language, but which the recipient cannot understand – bureaucratic, technical, medical or legal jargon for a lay audience, for example; complex, polysyllabic material for illiterate or semi-literate audiences.

Box 22.2 Audience characteristics

Here are some of the general and specific questions about simply reaching an audience that need to be asked by any communicator planning to send out a message:

- What is the state of mind of the audience?
- Where will they be and what will they be doing when the message arrives?
- Will they have time and available attention to notice and respond to the message?
- Where are they and how can I best reach them (the question of method, see below)
- Which language do they read and to what level?
- What is their level of literacy and what degree of complexity of language can they cope with?

Box 22.3 Audience reaction

How will your audience react to the content of the message, and what needs to be anticipated while composing it:

- How will they react to a message from this sender (friendly, hostile, suspicious, irritated)? For example, even an apparently perfectly designed message may fail if its audience perceive it as coming from a source that is not known or trusted.
- How will they react to the content of the message (anger, irritation, relief, amusement, enthusiasm, dismissal)?
- Taking account of their state of mind, what techniques are needed to stimulate a positive, cooperative response (argument, evidence, persuasion, negotiation, instruction, inducement, bribery, humour)?
- Will this message make sense to them in terms of their understanding of the world around them? Do they understand the *context* of the message?

'Where you are coming from' – the starting point for your communication – may not be clear to the recipient. You are in the middle of some intense and complicated situation and you need people to take some action to help move things along. You have a grasp of the whole situation and you know just what needs to be done and how it relates to everything else. The message you send out makes no sense to the recipients because they do not understand the evolution and context of your requirements, and they may ignore what seems to them like a pointless or incomprehensible or irrational request.

Having this intimate knowledge of the audience requires empathy (see p. 75) – a strong imaginative and psychological grasp of what the world of the audience is like for them, for people who are not actually visible to you. It requires a leap of imagination to think and feel what it will be like receiving your message, in order to tailor it accurately for maximum impact.

You need to know your audience, and the most reliable way of achieving such knowledge is constantly paying careful attention to them, and asking them about their habits, tastes and preferences – either talking to individuals or small groups, or using more formal methods such as interviews or questionnaires. All effective organisations do this kind of audience (or market) research on a regular basis, and use the knowledge gained as a central influence in their planning and activities for internal and external audiences.

Method or channel

The method you choose is critical, and it needs to be a method (or, better, methods) that fit with the audience's habits and preferences.

For an individual recipient, or group of recipients, which are the methods best suited to their habits? Not everyone checks email frequently or even uses it at all; for many people, reading is not their favoured or primary source of information about the world (the spoken word is); busy people, overwhelmed with demands on their time, miss or

Box 22.4 Communications methods

The options available, covering every purpose from a public health campaign to making a consultation appointment, are:
- printed document
- personal letter
- leaflet
- home or office delivery
- telephone
- email
- short message (SMS)
- post on a website or blog
- electronic media (CD, DVD)
- advertising
- exhibition or other public event
- multi-method/media campaign
- one-to-one meeting
- small-group meeting
- large meeting.

ignore even important communications – and so on. The hazards are wide-ranging and common!

So the channel of communication must be chosen very carefully to maximise the chances of the recipient seeing and taking notice of the message. Ideally, especially with a large audience, but also for individuals, using more than one method should increase the odds of a message getting through: someone who misses the email will get the leaflet; someone who misses the meeting will get the printed briefing; someone who doesn't see the notice will get the email and so on. One message sent by one method is a fragile communication.

Feedback

Throughout the book this point has been emphasised:

A complete communication is the sending of a message, its receipt and acknowledgement and feedback about it.

Communication is not simply sending a message. The sender has a responsibility to ensure that the message was received and understood, and the communication process is not complete until that has happened.

That is why, for example, putting up a notice is usually such a poor method of communication:
- How do you know who (if anyone) has seen it?
- How do you know if those who have seen it have understood it?
- How do you know if there were any problems in people's understanding of the content?
- How do you know how people have reacted to it?
- How do you know if it has had any effect?

The problem of notices (and posters) is that notice-boards and display areas are often poorly managed, and what is important or current may not be evident among the out-of-date notices. A list of target recipients posted with a notice, and then signed by those who have read it, does overcome some of the problems, but such a procedure is rare and does not answer all the problems.

Recipients have reciprocal responsibilities: their job is to acknowledge communications and report that they have been received and understood, along with any problems or issues that the message has prompted. But the primary responsibility lies with the originator, the owner, of the message. (This also applies to persons passing on or forwarding messages: responsibility does not end until the forwarded message has been received and acknowledged.)

The process is more vividly illustrated by the relationship with an audience in a live meeting: if you are making a presentation, and it is evident that some members of your audience are asleep, then it's clear that your message isn't getting through to them, and that you have to take some action to wake them up and make your communication more effective. With other methods of communication, it's less clear whether or not our audience is, as it were, asleep, but it is sensible to assume that some of them will be unless we take steps to wake them up.

The primary method of getting feedback and checking understanding in all circumstances is actively asking in one way or another. This needs to be done well before the moment when the impact of the message will be spontaneously demonstrated by success or failure (by people turning up (or not) at a meeting, for example, or pharmacists observing (or omitting) a crucial new safety warning on a drug). (See Chapter 11, p. 89, for more on this topic in relation to patients.)

Repetition

Many of you will have had the experience in an airport, railway station or conference centre, when a public announcement was made calling for an individual to report somewhere, or providing information about an event or a delay, or whatever. By the time you are alert to the fact that an announcement is being made (which can take a second or two), you have missed the detail. Even if the announcement includes your name, which gets your attention more quickly, you may miss the detail – unless the message is repeated. Communications professionals repeat messages slowly and clearly, at least once, often more frequently.

This applies to any kind of important communication, whether spoken or written. It is the absolute heart of commercial marketing – endless repetition of the brand, the logo and the message to leave an indelible impression on the mind and memory. Repetition is at the heart of effective public health education (safe sex, immunisation, smoking, whatever).

Many people for whom communications is a core part of their roles believe that once they have sent a message once, their job is done. Sometimes it may be (when there is feedback confirming success), but more often than not, more effort is needed, especially if there is a large number of recipients (the entire staff of a hospital, for example, let alone the population of a town).

One reservation: repetition of exactly the same message in the same form has only a limited life in maintaining effectiveness; after a time the message becomes so familiar, so much part of the taken-for-granted background to everyday life, that it ceases to be noticed. Vital messages about public health, disease prevention, drink and driving, safe sex, hospital hygiene, need constantly refreshing and re-invention if they are to be noticed and to affect people's behaviour. HCPs and managers themselves are not always the best people to do this. (See 'Design', p. 240)

Benefits

Few people will do anything unless they feel there is some advantage to them in doing it. Again, we can see recognition and exploitation of this truth in commercial marketing, when it is not just the features but rather the benefits being promoted: how good this product will make you feel, what it will do for your image, and so on.

The same principle applies to any communication, commercial or not: if I want someone to do something or change a habit, can I identify some benefit that *they* will gain from doing it? For example, if there are to be changes in some hospital routine affecting staff or patients or both, or changes in a pharmacy's opening hours, or new arrangements for physiotherapy, what are the benefits to those who must adapt to the change? Cooperation and goodwill follow understanding and benefit, whereas the same changes may be resented or resisted if they are impersonally announced and imposed.

If, on the other hand, there are no benefits, in fact service quality or working conditions are being reduced, then honest explanation is even more essential, along with acknowledgement of the disbenefit and apology for it. (This is the reverse side of the principle that benefits need to be communicated: when there are none, that fact also needs to be communicated – showing that the sender of the message understands that benefits are a reasonable expectation, and that their disappointment has to be recognised, perhaps regretted as well.)

Disbenefits should not be presented, as they are by some organisations, in the guise of some sort of benefit: 'For the convenience of our customers, our opening hours will change from next week . . .' – when the change is for anything but the convenience of customers, who know only too well they are being disadvantaged and insulted by sneaky dishonesty.

Style, tone, language and structure

Effective communicators adapt their style, tone and language to the content and purpose of the message, and, of course, to their audience.

Box 22.5 Four ranges of style

- Style ranges from dense, elaborate rhetorical, academic or bureaucratic, to everyday conversational and idiomatic; from pretentious to unassuming; from convoluted to elegant simplicity.
- Tone ranges from formal to informal; from aggressive, authoritative or patronising to democratic or collaborative.
- Language ranges from elaborate and complex, to simple, vernacular, colloquial.
- Structure (of the whole message, as well as sentences within it) can range from complex and elaborate, to simple and transparent.

Within the four ranges of style available are a huge variety of possibilities and combinations, most of which will be entirely unsuited to any one chosen audience: for every audience there is a best approach which will have maximum impact. Here, as with all communications activities, guesswork and hunch are poor guides: you need direct feedback about the effect of what you are doing. If it is a leaflet about hospital services – draft it, pilot it, find out what patients and the public think about it, note their comments and opinions, then change the leaflet and start again. Exactly the same process for a new medication form for the wards, or any individual item of communication with anyone. 'Is there any way I can improve this particular item or my other communications with you?' is the enquiry of a mature, conscientious professional.

The best principle for all communications is this: keep everything as simple, elegant and short as possible.

The chief virtue that language can have is clearness, and nothing detracts from it so much as the use of unfamiliar words.

Hippocrates

Structure and economy

This topic overlaps with the previous one, but takes some aspects into greater detail.

Probably the commonest error in written communications is to bury the main point somewhere in the middle or towards the end of a message, where it can easily be missed or undervalued. Where there is some background or history to an issue to be shared, it is very common for writers to spend the first half of the message elaborating such background material which is of only secondary or minor importance. The writer feels it is important, but does not see that the recipient may not, and may be confused and irritated with

Box 22.6 How to do it

- State the main purpose of your message at the very beginning (this is a prime technique in newspapers, where the intention is to grab the reader's interest instantly with the main point of a story).

This has several important effects on the recipient:

- The purpose of the message is immediately clear.
- Grasp of the purpose may motivate the recipient to read the whole message.
- In the light of knowing the purpose of the message the recipient can see the relevance of secondary background, argument or evidence and can follow it.

An ideal message is structured like this:

- main purpose
- summary of argument or evidence
- exposition/explanation of argument or evidence
- restatement of purpose and response/action required
- request for feedback (comment, objections, problems).

In every message there is a hierarchy of importance in the content, more or less like this:

- top priority
- second priority
- moderate importance
- minor importance.

(In some poorly formulated messages, there will also be content of no importance, sometimes lots of it.)

the text when it shows no sign of getting to the point.

The structure and form of the message should reflect that hierarchy with top and second priority standing out clearly and the rest demoted to subsidiary positions. Good practice in writing news releases relegates background information to a 'Note for editors' which follows and is quite separate from the main message and its exposition. This is a good model (see Chapter 24 'Notes on media relations', p. 249).

The discipline is to ask yourself this: 'If the recipient reads nothing else, what are the essentials I must communicate?' This is likely to make the heart of most messages agreeably short. Following that, you can then add the rest of the material in a way, and in a position on the page, which does not clutter perception of the main message and its purpose. (This is a principle from which many patient information leaflets could greatly benefit – see also Chapter 17.)

Box 22.7 More advice on effective writing and communication

- Keep sentences short and their structures simple (12–15 words on average).
- Keep paragraphs short and strictly limited to one point or topic (8–10 lines).
- Keep messages as short as is consistent with effective communication.
- Use the simplest possible language to convey the message.

Visual impression

Stand back and look at your message as it appears on the page or screen: does it look dense and impenetrable? Are the paragraphs long and off-putting? Is the typeface (font) too small? Are the margins too narrow?

Effective communications look good as well as being well-written. There is more on this in the section 'Design' on p. 240.

Emails

One of the transforming miracles of modern life, email offers both rich opportunities and terrible burdens: opportunities, primarily, because it makes communication so immediate, rapid and simple; burdens, because that very ease of communication leads to large numbers of legitimate mailings and overwhelming volumes of rubbish. Few people have not groaned at some time or other to see their bursting inbox with all its unattended contents, which can have a demoralising effect not dissimilar to contemplating the old-fashioned in-tray, piled high with unread memos and papers.

There are a few points worth considering for senders and recipients of email to improve the effectiveness of this major method of communication.

Box 22.8 Principles of good email management

- Make sure your name and the subject and purpose of the message are clear in the information that appears in a recipient's inbox-listing before the message is opened. This increases the chances of a recipient recognising the sender, understanding the purpose of the message, and, therefore, opening it and taking notice of it (it also reduces the chance of the mail being misidentified as spam).
- Keep emails short and to the point.
- Make your emails distinctive.
- Manage your inbox frequently and actively.

For senders:

- Make sure that what appears in the 'From' box or column in a recipient's inbox identifies you clearly, so that an easy decision can be made about the priority of your message. Most people will have no idea how their messages appear on the computers of their recipients, a major blind spot. First and second name is the most direct and obvious option, and this often does not appear, especially in large organisations where combinations of letters and numbers are not unusual: seeing 'from: jtd.pbg21@ws.ac.org' in the inbox list does not immediately provide a stimulating invitation to read the message. This is one of the many useful details of electronic communication that the user can control but many people don't even think about. Seek help if necessary on preferences and other options in the software.

- Make sure that what appears in the 'Subject' box is as clear and specific as possible, particularly if some response or action is required, and to distinguish it from the (often ingenious) formulations of spammers.

Badly formulated subjects:

- 'Reorganisation' – reorganisation of what? What's the recipient supposed to do – read, act, comment? How urgent or important is it?
- 'Pharmacy hours' – is this for everyone, or just pharmacists? Is it a comment or a change or a query? What's the recipient supposed to do?
- 'Patient complaints' – is this a new policy? A record of the month's complaints? A request for ideas? A pat on the back for reduced complaints? What's the recipient supposed to do?

The same subjects, well-formulated:

- Reorganisation of physiotherapy service: comments please
- Changes in pharmacy hours: please note
- Increase in patient complaints: we need to meet.

- Use the flagging options when you want to specify the nature of the message (low/moderate/high importance; personal/private/confidential as the two common sets of flagging options). Use 'high importance' or 'urgent' very selectively and rarely, or they will lose their impact (like antibiotics, their overuse quickly permits resistance to develop).
- Use the 'Request read receipt' option when you want to be sure the message has been seen. Keep a record of the receipts you receive if you've sent the message to many people, and follow up those from whom you have not received one.
- Be aware that spam filters may sometimes intercept your message, especially if it was addressed to a large number of people. This makes follow up even more critical. (Some recipients may need help in amending their spam filter criteria, or specifying you as an approved origin of messages; you may need to check your email authentication protocols.)
- Make sure you have an automatic email signature – details of your name and communications details which appear at the bottom of every email. Few people manage their contacts very efficiently, and having those details on every email means that your contact details are always available: it allows a recipient, for example, to see your phone number and call you immediately in response.
- Make your message short and to the point: follow the principles outlined above about structure and priorities (main point first, summary of argument next and so on).
- Make your emails distinctive: all computers have a vast wealth of options for the appearance of every document you create – type style and size, colour, bullets, and lots more. Most people accept the default settings (those set by the software supplier) resulting in most emails (and other documents) looking more or less the same the world over (Times New Roman or Arial appearing in black) and having little in the way of individuality. Be a little creative, make your emails stand out from the crowd and impress your recipients! (See p. 240 for more on this.)

For everyone:

- Manage your inbox frequently and actively: few things are more overwhelming or demoralising than an inbox with a couple of hundred or more emails in it. It can get to the point where it seems futile to even try and deal with them all. Make a determined effort to do the following:

- Mark as spam anything from any source that you never wish to appear again in your inbox. If you don't have a spam filter, get one! Most organisational networks have a central spam management system; its effectiveness (both permitting access to your important messages and filtering out the dross) is an important issue for monitoring and discussion.
- Delete everything that is not important or interesting.
- Set yourself a target of a maximum number of emails languishing in your inbox (say, 20 as an ideal, but 50 as a concession to reality).
- Read and delete or file in personal folders anything that does not need soon to be looked at again, or needs to be stored.
- Read and respond to anything that requires it; then delete or file the original, or leave it in your inbox if it will be part of an ongoing exchange (it is preferable to file it in another active folder, but there is always a risk that it will get forgotten if it is out of sight.)
- Try to respond to anything of any importance within two days, and if you can't, at least send a very short acknowledgement to the sender and say when you will reply: 'Thanks for the mail. I'll get back to you on Friday,' is a courteous and effective way of keeping the dynamics of communication healthy.

Telephone

Although the telephone has been around for considerably more than a century, the skills for its use, like driving, are still things we all have to learn more or less from scratch and can always improve on.[253–256] Performance varies enormously from person to person.

The telephone (and mobile phones in particular, see below) remains a vital (and growing) element in healthcare communications, particularly in its role as firstline contact for patients with HCPs and healthcare organisations. The way in which people are dealt with on the phone can have deep effects on their feelings and opinions about an organisation and on their disposition towards any future contact.

Most people have so much experience of the telephone (both landlines and mobiles), that they can make very refined judgements about the character and quality of the organisation or person on the other end of the line, and on those who are skilled and competent, or those who are ineffective and irritating. A lot can be learnt just from listening.

Use of the telephone in healthcare is so frequent and varied that we cannot possibly cover all situations, but one or two priorities can be identified and a number of general principles listed.

Frontline and beyond

Those who answer the phone to first-time callers – receptionists, assistants, secretaries, and anyone else who just happens to answer the phone – have an important and demanding job. In a few seconds they have to:

- understand the caller and the nature of their needs
- respond effectively and sensitively
- present a friendly and professional image
- fulfil, manage or negotiate a solution
- wind up the call.

Attention needs to be paid to a number of issues:

- How quickly the phone is answered (this applies to all phones at all times): nothing irritates callers more than hanging on for ages and ages while the telephone rings, and such irritation may transfer itself to the content of the call if it is not dealt with (at least, 'I'm so sorry you've been kept waiting' – which requires the answerer to be aware that the caller has been waiting). What may originally have been a simple reason for the call can be greatly complicated by a perception of neglect. (See more on automatic answering systems below.)
- Every organisation and office should have a target for maximum waiting time – say four

rings (there are places where it is two, and they meet that target most of the time, because it is constantly reinforced as a high priority aspect of service – but callers may be unsettled if the answer is more or less immediate).

- Before answering the phone, clear your mind, relax, put aside the emotions of the moment, particularly if they are negative ones.
- How callers are greeted: this author is not in favour of the pat formulas (of the 'Good morning. This is XYZ hospital. My name's Gaynor. How can I help you?' kind) which get glibly reeled off as if the speaker were actually thinking of something else, and are so obviously a formula and not an authentic greeting. Some kind of agreed, consistent form of words is desirable for any organisation (external communications should be coherent and predictable in content and quality), but they need to be words that are *owned* by the speaker and can be invested with warmth. Spoken in a firm, energetic, warm tone, the simplest form of words has much to recommend it: 'XYZ Hospital. Good morning.' The information is the confirmation that the caller needs that they've got the right number; the greeting, well-delivered, implies the appropriate, courteous, personal welcoming invitation to speak. Further identifying details could be added, of course: 'XYZ Hospital emergency department. My name's X. How can I help you?' and so on.
- Irrespective of the emotional content of the call, many of the skills of face-to-face communications will be needed (listening, empathy, checking understanding, repetition, clarifying detail and so on); the moment before answering a call, the mind needs to be cleared of immediate concerns and distractions, and tone of voice controlled to avoid contamination from busyness or irritation. It is instantly obvious to a caller if they are not being given complete attention (the power of non-verbal communication, again).
- Difficult callers – angry, hysterical, distressed – need the very careful management that would also apply in face-to-face encounters, but with the additional challenge that there is no opportunity for the use of physical non-verbal communication to interpret or support the message, and, therefore, much greater risk of miscommunication: tone of voice is of critical importance here: 'Is this person taking me seriously?' Is the question the caller will be asking and listening intently for evidence that indicates commitment or indifference.
- Smile – you're on the phone. You can 'hear' a smile on the phone, because someone who is smiling sounds different from someone who is frowning. Try it!

Automatic answering systems

Is there anyone who has not, at one time or another, been irritated by a complicated and time-consuming automatic answering system? There are lots of problems: first, that such systems are impersonal and alienating; second, that the options offered do not always match what the caller wants; third, that the lists of options are sometimes so long that a caller will forget which one they needed; fourth, that such systems are time consuming and perhaps expensive for the caller; fifth, that arriving at the end of a list of options and still being number four in the queue (or perhaps number 10), is likely to annoy. Few managers who implement such systems ever use them or test them, and therefore, have any idea what impact they may be having on patients and other callers.

Although it is quite clear that such systems may save money and resources, we have to ask, what is the cost to the peace of mind and goodwill of those wanting to contact the organisation? What price does an organisation put on the importance of easy telephone access from outside? What is the cost of frustrated and irritated callers and the impact on health and relationships?

Managing the relevance and length of calls

This is a set of skills that is useful to everyone in all aspects of their life. What do you do when a caller persists in pursuing an issue or continues beyond what you feel is necessary or tolerable? Solving this requires the skills of both empathy and assertiveness.

First, unless you are prepared simply to put the phone down (an occasionally legitimate option), and so leave the caller frustrated, perhaps angry, you have to recognise and acknowledge the reason for their behaviour, and then perhaps interrupt or intervene firmly:

- 'Mr Daquenta, I understand that this is really upsetting for you and that you want something done. I think you've really given me a very clear picture and I shall talk to the nurse and we shall be in touch with you soon. Can we leave it at that for now?'
- 'Tracie, there's simply nothing we can do just now. I know it's frustrating for you – I can hear just how disappointed you are – but we have to wait for a few days to see what happens. Please call again on Tuesday and we may have some news. If anything happens before then, we'll let you know. Is that OK?'

Or you may simply find an opportunity to curtail the conversation at a point when the caller is just talking for the sake of it rather than pursuing some issue or feeling:

- 'OK. That all sounds fine, then. I need to go now. I hope you have a good weekend. Let's talk again soon.'

Lots of precious time is wasted by calls not being managed. Because the phone is a narrow channel of communication (sound only), some patients will need a lot of reassurance that their message is getting across, and their way of trying to ensure that it does get across will be to talk at length, perhaps repeating things several times. The task is to listen as long as it takes to get the message (much less time than the caller may feel), then effectively feed back the fact that the message has been received and is being taken seriously; then bring the call to a conclusion. Gently assertive management of calls will save a lot of time.

When a caller rambles, talks for the sake of talking or having a listening ear, then they need to be brought back to the salient topic, directly or via a brief response to their digression:

- 'Now, you were telling me about your mother's leg injury: what else do I need to know?'
- 'Well, I hope the kids don't do that again! Let's just get back to the problem with your medicine. Do you need to see the pharmacist again?'
- 'Yes, the trains are terrible, certainly. Have you taken the boy's temperature?'

Repetition (again)

A constant theme in this book: one communication is no communication. This is especially true of the telephone where details are easily lost or forgotten, and there is no visual way of checking out callers' responses. Where critical information is being given – time and place of appointments, advice about medication, suggested treatment for non-serious illness or injury – reception and understanding of the message need to be checked and confirmed.

The usual method applies: ask the caller to repeat the significant information as they understand it and, where appropriate, repeat the information yourself, and check that it is acknowledged (but remember the hazard of people saying 'Yes' just so they do not appear stupid, even when they have not understood or got the whole message). When a call is likely to include times or dates or other detailed information, it is useful to ask the caller to have a pen and paper handy.

Mobile phones

Managing mobile phones in a healthcare setting is an issue that everyone needs to address. Our view is that, in principle, mobile phones (HCPs' and patients') should be switched off, or certainly put to silent or vibrator mode during any kind of consultation. HCPs who must be accessible by phone at all times can select a distinctive (and unintrusive) ring tone for essential calls and ignore others.

There are two reasons:

- First, calls waste precious time during a consultation, especially taken by those who

cannot manage them (a rare, mature response being: 'I'm busy; I'll call you back') and insist on carrying the call through.
- Second, and more importantly, interruptions of this (and any other) kind, damage the thread of communication between HCP and patient, perhaps to the extent that the consultation has to be more or less restarted, if it has not been damaged beyond repair.

Answering essential calls should be preceded by an apology for the necessity, and followed by an accurate resumption of the previous conversation at the point it was interrupted.

Some hospitals and other healthcare locations ask everyone to turn their mobile phones off, probably the best option.

Individual and proforma letters

Much of the material in this section (content priority, structure, presentation and so on) is relevant to both kinds of letters. Letters, like all communications that have some chance of maximum impact, need to appear to be addressed to the individual person receiving them, and to come from some identifiable and credible person.

Box 22.9 Letter management issues

- The form of address needs to be carefully checked. The following mistakes (not uncommon) are crass and upsetting:
  - addressing males as Mrs or Ms, or females as Mr
  - using the generic 'Dear Sir or Madam' (they obviously don't know who I am)
  - addressing couples, when one of them is dead
  - addressing dead recipients

All of these errors, of course, arise from poor data, poor database (or manual record) input and poor maintenance of records. Those activities require serious attention and resources.
- Avoid using forms of words or tone which can reasonably be expected to offend some among the recipients. It is not always possible to avoid upsetting someone, but the risk should be considered as a letter is drafted.

Any document, letter, circular, appointment notification, whatever, should be as personalised as much as it can be, first by getting the recipient's details right, second by other simple techniques when numbers and resources permit:
- On a standard letter or proforma communication, leave the salutation or name line blank and fill it in by hand, in a colour that distinguishes it from the photocopied or printed black.
- Leave the signature area blank, and sign each one individually.

Both of these can be delegated to support staff when there is a lot of mail, but should not be regarded as unimportant tasks.

This clearly is not possible for bulk mailings but, for occasional, even routine, mailing of handfuls or just dozens of items, it is worth considering: it takes the communication beyond a mass-produced transmission to something that the recipient feels was really meant for them. (Printing a signature in a different colour from text is a possibility for mass-mailings, and does lift the appearance of a page from ordinariness.)

Remember that letters can be felt as a crude and damaging way of delivering bad news (results of an abnormal smear test, for example). In such situations letters should be used only to send an invitation for a personal consultation.

Report writing

It is probably the case that few people ever read the full body of most reports of any kind: they look at the executive summary and the conclusions and leave it at that unless they have a special interest, or must show evidence of having studied the whole thing.

When you're writing a report, bear this in mind: few people will be as fascinated by the intricacies of the topic as you will have become, so you need to be very clear about the priority messages for others to consume, and make them very easy to locate and read. The discussion of economy and structure above is useful again here.

This report, by its very length, defends itself against the risk of being read.

Winston Churchill

'I don't know how to start' is a frequent, frustrated feeling for those who have been landed with the task of compiling a report. As with many difficult tasks, the secret is to start small and build; begin with the obvious and move up to the complex.[257,258]

Box 22.10 Questions to ask

- Why have I been asked to write this report?
- What is this report supposed to achieve?
- Who is going to (a) read the report in full and (b) want to know its conclusions but perhaps not read it?
- What questions do I need to answer to write this report?
- Where am I going to find answers to those questions?
- What are the real priority issues and what are the secondary ones?
- How far is the report a straightforward factual account; how far must I argue and persuade, provide evidence and demonstrate to make a case?

When you have answered those questions carefully, you will probably be in a position to start planning the project and structuring the content.

Box 22.11 The basic structure

- Purpose of the report
- Summary of main contents: methods, evidence, results (executive summary, written at the end of the process)
- Description of methods
- *Laying out of evidence and arguments
- *Discussion of evidence and arguments
- Conclusions
- Recommendations

*This pair of activities may be repeated several times for each element of the evidence and arguments.

The plan needs to be made in meticulous detail in advance, and then followed carefully, to avoid the temptation to deviate from the basic structure and logic. Changes should be made only to enhance the structure and logic, not by accident or serendipity.

Choose a style and tone that suits you, the topic and the audience; many people feel under pressure to adopt an unnatural style for professional documents, but report writing does not require an artificial or over-formal style. Keep sentences and paragraphs short; use language no more complex than is necessary; keep the whole thing to a minimum length compatible with doing the job.

Read the text aloud to yourself (a great test of clarity and readability) and get a friend to look it over. Leave it for a day, reread and edit. (Reading aloud is a great test for any piece of writing.)

Public speaking and presentations

Like many of the topics in this book, this is one about which whole books are written, so treatment here will inevitably be superficial. But there are some key points that may help you meet the challenge.[259–260]

Remember that passive listening is a very demanding activity and that few people will remain alert and engaged if they are being addressed for much more than 30 minutes or so. Too many meetings and conferences ignore this simple fact of human psychology as well as the other obvious one: people are stimulated and envigorated by participation (see also Chapter 26).

Whether or not the prospect of a public appearance frightens you, there are things you can do to improve your confidence and performance and elements that should reassure you.

Public speaking is not a kind of private activity taking place on a stage, where the normal behaviour of social communication is simply amplified for a large audience: it is a performance, a small

Box 22.12 Preparing for performance

- Prepare your material meticulously.
- Rehearse on your own (with a mirror if it's helpful) and with a couple of critical friends until you can deliver the material well (do it once or twice in the room or a similar place to where the real thing will happen).
- Try to be confident enough in your material to know that for some (ideally, most) of the time, you will not have to follow your notes (prepare prompt cards if you need them; try not to use a verbatim script).
- Remember that most audiences (especially colleagues) are not naturally hostile and want you to do a good job (it is in their interests too – the better you are, the more they will enjoy and learn from the performance).
- Audiences respond well to speakers who are enthusiastic about their material.
- If you are comfortable and confident in doing so, use verbal or visual humour when appropriate or as an ice breaker at the beginning; it softens the audience, gets their attention, and eases your tension when the audience chuckles or laughs.
- Think less about how you feel than about the job you have to do; concentrate on the delivery of the material.
- Watch others and learn from their skills, tricks, mistakes and shortcomings.

piece of theatre, and it has a completely different set of rules. You will instantly recognise those who are good at it and those who are not: the former, even modest performers, adopt an attitude, a style, a voice, a presence that demands attention from the moment they step on to the stage; the latter, quite common among lecturers and many others, behave more like they were in a small room with a few others, mumbling or reading their script word for word, head buried in the lectern.

It should feel as if you are about to take part in a play, and, as you prepare to climb the steps, you take a deep breath, check your costume, forget your private, personal self, and become the part, ready to *act*, to please and inform your audience – perhaps delight and entertain them too.

Content and structure

Follow the general guidelines given earlier in this chapter under 'Structure and economy' and 'Report writing' – the principles are much the same.

Visual support

Box 22.13 Some suggestions for electronic presentations

- Choose simple layouts and clear colours (some combinations do not work, yellow or purple on a blue background, for example).
- Choose a clear cut, rather than fussy typeface, and one large enough for clarity at the back of the room (26 point is probably the workable smallest).
- Do not overcrowd slides with text (title plus about six to eight lines optimum).
- Use the slides for key points, not for verbatim text of your script.
- Avoid detailed charts or tables which cannot be read – unless such materials are essential, then provide handout copies for reference while you talk.
- Pace the progress of slide material carefully; there is nothing more frustrating to the audience than slides disappearing before they have a chance to digest them or take notes.
- Some audiences (especially international ones) will appreciate having handouts of your slides during the presentation, so they can follow more closely and make notes.

Design

How things look – their design and appearance – is almost as important as what they say or do, and sometimes more so. Opinions, habits, beliefs, behaviour are influenced and changed by varying ratios of substance and appearance, with substance rarely being the clear priority.[261]

> Societies have always been shaped more by the nature of the media by which men communicate than by the content of the communication.
>
> *Marshall McLuhan*

Look around you – at almost any magazine or newspaper; at advertisements and food-packaging; at furniture, cars, the interior design of retail outlets; leaflets, tickets and clothes – and everywhere you will see evidence of the activity of specialist and graphic designers: skilled and usually talented people who create attractive and interesting things that present their messages engagingly or seductively. The world is full of

Box 22.14 Some guidelines for performance

- If there is a microphone on stage, check before your presentation that it is at the right height, and that you know the optimum distance for your mouth to be from it; let the sound technician (if available) or a colleague test the level of optimum amplification for your delivery voice.
- Establish rapport with the audience: greet them, make eye contact.
- Explain what you are going to do, how long it will take, and whether there will be discussion and/or questions at the end.
- Outline the structure of your speech or presentation.
- Speak slowly and clearly (about half the speed of normal speech, slower for a multi-lingual audience).
- Remember that your voice must reach the people furthest from you; if you're in doubt ask if they can hear.
- Go through your material.
- Make sure you keep within the optimal distance from the microphone; it is a sign of amateurishness that will irritate any audience if your voice is constantly slipping in and out of amplification. (If you're a natural mover, it takes great discipline to keep the microphone at the swivel point of your head.) Alternatively hold a roaming microphone and keep it in position.
- Maintain contact with the audience by looking round the whole room from time to time, especially at those furthest from you (do not lock on to one or two people or rows near the front).
- As you look around, check for puzzlement or disagreement, shaking heads, nodding heads, sleepers and so on; *comment on what you see.
- *Pause for or solicit comments or questions if you feel the material or the audience reaction requires them at that point.
- If you are using a projection screen behind you for slides or data, do not turn round and talk to the screen (this is a very common and irritating habit, and additionally so when it means the microphone becomes useless); turn briefly only if you do not have a monitor screen in front of you and you need to check the correct slide is showing; turn if you are using a laser pointer to highlight something, but for only as long as you need to make the point – remembering that when you turn away from the microphone your voice is not amplified (or audible at all, probably).
- Finish with a restatement of the purpose of the presentation and make it clear you've finished.
- Thank the audience for their attention.
- Ask for questions or comments (if that's part of the programme). Repeat questions asked for all to hear, especially if there is no audience microphone but, even if there is, it is a good idea.
- Whether or not there are any questions, thank the audience again and leave the stage.

*These two activities are quite advanced, and should not really be attempted by anyone who does not feel confident and at ease, but they will greatly boost the impact of the show.

Seek feedback from friends in the audience: How could I have done better? Did I speak too fast? Was the argument clear? Was there too much material?

objects (not all of them beautiful, of course) designed by experts.

Sadly, the materials produced by healthcare professionals and organisations do not always equal everyday (and taken-for-granted) standards of quality in design. They often fail to have impact because they are produced by people with no eye for design and simply do not look interesting or attractive. Computers have given us many of the tools of graphic design (typefaces, layout, decoration, illustrations, pictures and so on) but in the hands of inexperienced amateurs, they often produce only amateurish results.

To compete with the massive volume of attractive communications flooding the world, our materials must at least look engaging and interesting, and grab the attention of those we want to take notice of them. Effective design is not what appeals to the taste of the boss or the commissioning client but is what will appeal to the intended audience – that is the sole criterion of effective design. Wherever possible, when planning leaflets or campaigns, or even basic corporate stationery and administrative materials, it is wise to employ a graphic designer and to consult your audience. The initial investment will pay off handsomely almost every time.

When producing materials in-house, there are a few basic principles that will help to lift computer-generated pages beyond the merely ordinary.

Box 22.15 Basic principles of uplifting materials

- Consciously choose an appropriate typeface from the hundreds available, and avoid simply accepting the default typeface (used by millions of others).
- Choose a type size that makes reading easy for all members of the intended audience.
- Ensure that every page has generous quantities of white space (the balance of content and white space is one of the critical aspects of good design: look at advertisements in magazines and see just how much white (or blank) space there often is); have generous margins all round, and don't be afraid to use 1.5 or double line-spacing to reduce the density of the material; you can leave a blank line between paragraphs as well – and keep paragraphs short. (To those who object that such practice wastes paper, it should be pointed out that much more paper is wasted if people do not read materials because they're too dense and unattractive.)
- Use the typographical enhancements of bold, italic and colour – although sparingly – where appropriate, to emphasise important points (underlining for emphasis is a hangover from the days of manual typewriters and is not a good technique for computer-generated typography); use text boxes, similarly, to highlight major points or draw attention to key quotations from the text.
- Use bullet points and lists wherever possible to break up the text and make reading easier.
- Use bold headlines and frequent subheadings to guide readers through your text.
- Hold your pages at arm's length and look at them as design objects: how do they rate in the great scheme of things?

Study graphic design every day as you read your newspaper or magazine or browse through advertisements or the internet, or walk down the street or meander through a mall: how are the effects achieved? What works and what doesn't work? What can I learn and transfer in some way to my communications?

Conclusion

Achieving greater effectiveness in communications of all kinds does not necessarily require large resources of cash or time, but it does require an understanding of the specialist nature of communications as an individual or corporate activity, and of the knowledge and skills that underlie high-quality performance. Many of the messages in healthcare concern matters of the greatest importance to the health and welfare of individuals and society – indeed, sometimes matters of life and death – and we cannot afford to fail in getting those messages across effectively.

Individuals and organisations that approach their communications professionally and creatively will achieve higher public profiles and be more successful in achieving their aims than those that do not, and their patients, clients and customers will, consciously and unconsciously, appreciate the effort and derive much greater benefits from their services.

23 Complaints, apologies and public relations

The welcoming of suggestions and complaints, handling them effectively and being willing to apologise where appropriate, are the signs of a mature and capable organisation. Such good practice will enhance the reputation of any organisation, as will the pursuit of ethical, effective public relations activities. All members of staff need to understand how their communications and behaviour in this area can actively enhance or damage reputation and patient satisfaction.

Learning from patient dissatisfaction

This is an area requiring important skills. Complaints are one of the most direct and accurate ways of learning how you yourself are, or how your organisation or service is failing its customers, either in reality or in their perception (it makes no difference to them).[262] Patients will complain, with or without encouragement, if not to their healthcare providers, then certainly to their friends or to researchers who later ask them their opinions.[263] One of the most powerful ways of improving patient satisfaction and reducing complaints, of course, is to remove their cause, through active research into the aspects of service that are giving rise to patient concern.[264,265]

An organisation that frustrates, diverts or blocks complaints will never learn how to do better, and it will gain a reputation for being hostile to its users. Frustrated complainants go off to tell dozens of their friends about just how badly they were treated, and word spreads fast. An organisation that actively solicits users' views (and that does not just mean leaving forms lying around or routinely handing them out) will be positively perceived and appreciated.

Box 23.1 Crisis at Northwick Park

[After the TGN-1412 clinical trials disaster in March 2006] . . . Even if there was no attributable human error, everyone responsible needed to be clearer, more honest and humbler in stating immediately that they were most sorry for what had happened.[266]

The goal of no complaints is unrealistic: no organisation pleases all its users all of the time, but no half-decent organisation ignores any symptom of user dissatisfaction. In fact, one symptom of a healthy organisation is an increasing level of complaints or suggestions, as users gain the confidence to speak their minds and share their feelings on progressively smaller and smaller issues (as you will already have solved the big ones along the way). Some organisations prefer the language of 'Suggestions' or 'Comments': although comments and suggestions should be actively encouraged in those terms, there is also a manipulative element in avoiding 'Complaints' altogether, skirting round the reality of user dissatisfaction – the hope, perhaps, that if you avoid the word you will avoid the reality.

Research has shown that complainants whose difficulties have been well handled become more loyal to an organisation or a business than those who have never had cause for dissatisfaction. This is explained by the fact that negotiating a complaint with an organisation brings you into closer contact with its staff, requires a more interactive relationship, and you may develop a deeper understanding and appreciation of them when they take you seriously, than you would otherwise have done.

What to do

To handle complaints well:

- Show positively that you want to hear what the person has to say: 'Please tell me.'
- Listen.
- Express your sorrow that the person has cause to be upset (not apologising for the (as yet only alleged/unproven) problem or error): 'I'm really sorry you've been angered/upset/distressed'; 'I'm sorry; it upsets us too when patients have complaints.'
- Show concern for the person, proportionate to the alleged cause or error; respond to their feelings (the underlying script); manage their anger if necessary (see Chapter 13).
- Listen.
- Ask clarifying questions:
  - When did this happen?
  - Who was involved?
  - What did they say?
  - What did they do or not do?
  - Why did they do that?
- Take notes if necessary (almost always, for the record and as a way of showing seriousness to the complainant).
- Take name and contact details.
- If you can deal with the problem yourself, do so; otherwise, follow the procedure in your local complaints policy (see p. 245) and make sure you:
  - Check with the person that you have accurately understood the problem.
  - Ask them what response they want: 'What would you like me/the hospital to do?' (They may want nothing more than to voice their complaint and have it taken seriously; end of story.)
  - Negotiate with them a next step (or a solution) which they can agree to and is within your power (take them to see or give them name and address or phone number of senior manager; arrange an appointment for them to get a second opinion; say the issue will be investigated and they will be contacted within, for example, two days).
  - Tell them exactly what you propose to do, what they can expect and when.
  - Thank them and ask them to let you know how they got on.

In the event of serious allegations of malpractice, error, or improper behaviour, you are likely to need to put the complainant immediately in touch with a senior manager and to make sure the issue is responded to very quickly (there are usually well-established protocols for this). As recipient of a serious complaint, it is your job to nag and harass senior people until they do respond: your responsibility does not stop until the complainant is fully in the hands of another member of staff, and that is actively confirmed by your colleague: 'OK. That's mine. You can leave it with me.' Complainants must not fall into the cracks of organisational life.

Box 23.2 Predicting dissatisfaction in emergency care, avoiding future complaints

In a study of 3152 Israeli patents discharged from 17 acute care hospitals, the researchers came to the following general conclusion:

'Attempts to reduce dissatisfaction with emergency care should focus on caregiver conduct and attitudes. It may also be useful to improve caregiver communication skills, specifically with ethnic minorities and with patients who rate their health status as poor.'[267]

Hovering behind any discussion of complaints and apologies are the anxieties of lawyers and the spectre of liability. Although discovery and admission of liability will always be contentious issues on all fronts, it does not mean that complainants should be dealt with any less respectfully or thoughtfully in the stages before liability is determined, nor indeed afterwards. Although legal concerns may provide specific rules or guidance for staff dealing with patients, they should not in themselves be provocative of further distress or anger, nor inhibit staff from dealing humanely with those who believe they have been mistreated or injured in some way.

'I'm really sorry you feel upset to this extent. The hospital takes complaints very seriously, but I can't make a judgement at this point. Please can you wait to talk to the boss?'

Complaints policy

Every hospital, clinic, nursing home, business of any kind should have a clear complaints policy which is familiar to every member of staff (cleaners and catering staff included, of course), in which they should have some training – and which is publicly promoted to users.[268,269] A basic policy would look like this:

- We welcome complaints, suggestions and comments from our users.
- Complaints and suggestions will be listened to or dealt with as quickly as possible – usually immediately – after they are first brought to our attention.
- Where quick solutions are possible they will be used (no-quibble refunds, replacements, exchanges, alternatives, changes in practice), and an apology given for the cause of the problem or thanks for the suggestion.
- When a complainant reasonably wishes for contact with a senior person it will be arranged.
- Where investigation is required, it will be done quickly (ideally within two days) and the complainant will be kept informed of progress and any likely delay, and regularly informed of any prolongation of the process and the reasons for it.
- Wherever possible (and appropriate) an apology and a remedy will be offered, or feedback about changes introduced.
- Where a negotiated resolution is not possible, after exploring all reasonable possibilities, and as a last resort, a conference of advisers or lawyers will be called.

Box 23.3 The opening message . . .

'We are committed to maintaining the highest standards in all aspects of care. So when patients and visitors offer praise – or criticism – we listen carefully. We review all the comments you make and we use that information to improve our services and facilities even further.

Whatever you want to say, your opinions and comments are important to us – good or bad.'

Spire Healthcare[270]

Complaints sometimes arise because of genuine misunderstandings or misperceptions. Your initial attention to the problem should quickly reveal this, and you then have to inform the person of the facts, and gently try to modify their understanding or perception:

- 'Oh, I'm sorry, I'm afraid the tests always take two days. He should have made that clear.'
- 'No, we have not forgotten you. The doctors have to deal with urgent cases first, and there have been several this morning.'
- 'No, he's not a student, he's an experienced physician, although I agree he does look young.'
- 'No, no; he said you needed to have an X-ray, not radiotherapy.'
- 'I'm sorry, but it just isn't possible to predict how long she'll need to stay in hospital; we just have to wait to see how quickly she responds to treatment.'

Dealing with legitimate, justified complaints is challenging but not impossible. Those complaints that have no real external cause, are more an expression of dissatisfaction with life, anger at disease, disappointment at crushed expectations, or stem from a lonely person's need for attention, can be much more tricky.

Every organisation has those for whom nothing ever seems to be right or who are constantly seeking attention. The danger of dealing with them (and anyone) unsympathetically is that they may then have real cause to be upset; thus might begin a deteriorating spiral of negative encounters. There is a fine balance to be achieved with needy people: you do not want to increase their irritation or hostility but neither do you want to encourage them to take advantage of your good nature. Gently assertive reality testing is one tactic for such persistent complainers: 'I know you asked to see the doctor, but is there really anything you need from her that the practice nurse hasn't been able to give you?' 'The doctor said you should wait for five days now, didn't he? How many days has it been?'

Apologising

Offering an apology for a mistake or a misunderstanding, is a healing, bridge-building communication and a sign of emotional strength and maturity. It is not, as some people feel, a humiliating or self-abasing act, although it does require humility to admit error and ask for forgiveness. Genuinely humiliating and damaging to reputation is the exposure of an error that an individual or organisation refuses to admit and apologise for.

The process of effective apologising takes place in several stages:

- identifying accurately the mistake or misunderstanding, where and how it happened and who was the cause of it (evidence gathering, analysis)
- accepting responsibility, or placing responsibility where it belongs
- apologising, expressing genuine regret (this is like the payment of a debt: it is owed to the victim to remedy, to compensate for the hurt or suffering; at its best it can begin to heal the feelings of the injured person)
- accepting and dealing with negative or hostile feelings (empathy; listening; acknowledging feelings; concern)
- suggesting remedial action, ways out of the dilemma *or*
- explaining the extent of the damage and what action is being taken to reverse it or limit it *or*
- in the event of a critical or fatal error, then attentive, non-defensive listening; bereavement support; full explanation of what happened and why; exploration of what the patient or family wishes to do; offer of access to senior manager; assistance in lodging formal complaint (when the patient wishes).

The full process described here actually goes well beyond the idea of simple apologising and moves into the area of complaint handling and disaster recovery. No number of procedures or protocols to deal with disaster will have a positive impact on the victims of error or accident if they feel that the individual or institution does not take responsibility and is not genuinely sorry for what happened, even when the event could not be avoided.

If there's anything that annoys patients (and most citizens), it is being kept in the dark (deprived of information about anything) and evasion of responsibility. It is these *communications* aspects of healthcare relationships that will drive patients to litigation as much as errors themselves.

Public relations (PR)

Every clinic, shop, hospital or business will develop a reputation among patients, users and customers, and almost certainly, within a much wider community of people who have had no direct contact. This reputation is created whether or not there is any awareness of it or attempt to manage it by an organisation: users will form impressions, make judgements; they will share their opinions with other people, especially if their experience has been negative or exceptionally good (the averagely poor or mildly satisfactory tend to get less attention). As a simple fact, you always have 'public relations' of one sort or another.

Reputation is very important for two principal reasons:

- It will, where there is choice, significantly influence whether people choose to come to you or your organisation at all (this is especially important for any commercially based operation).

- For those who come as first-time or return users, it will significantly influence their expectations (positively or negatively) and, therefore, in healthcare, their confidence and optimism about the service they will receive.

The meaning of good PR

Public relations as a communications and marketing activity has achieved something of a dubious reputation but what we are talking about is the ethical management of reputation in the interests of all parties – patients included.

What any individual practitioner or organisation needs to do first is to make sure that the services provided meet the needs of users, in ways that they find attractive and satisfactory, and that professional aims and user expectations are met. There is no alternative to asking everyone their opinion on these questions (through active research) and to responding positively to suggestions for improvement or development. Complaints are a rich and important source of user opinion. If you are not getting feedback, and encouraging it, then you do not know how you are doing, and your reputation is out of your control.

Reputation will be greatly enhanced where users are asked their opinion, and there is a positive, active response. Reputation will be enhanced when the providers of any service ask themselves how any plan or change will affect users, and set user satisfaction as a primary criterion of change. Reputation will be enhanced when any service provider informs users about what is planned or is happening, along with its reasons.

If you want to grow as an organisation, you have to take active steps to make sure that current users are loyal and supportive, and that potential users know about you. That moves us into the area of proactive public relations – spreading information about your reputation and services widely through leaflets and printed materials, news releases, meetings with local people (including journalists), websites, and other methods. Those are strategic, management issues, which are beyond this book (except see Chapter 24 'Notes on media relations').

The public relations (reputation) of an organisation can be destroyed by one careless, aggressive, rude member of staff; by one badly handled mistake or accident; by any action or behaviour that leaves even a single user or patient aggrieved. Public relations are profoundly important, and every HCP and member of staff needs to understand just how much they can contribute to building or destroying a reputation through everything they do and say.

24 Notes on media relations

Many sophisticated organisations are naive in their understanding of the media and of media relations, and may be resentful victims of media neglect or misunderstanding and also blind to the possibilities of useful collaborative relationships with journalists. Most editors and journalists are responsible professionals and have a real interest in important social, scientific and medical matters. Working as partners in communications about healthcare can be beneficial and productive for all parties, and greatly enlarge the reach of healthcare messages.[271,272]

Essential relations

Effective media relations are an essential aspect of the communications activities of any organisation dealing with issues of social and political interest, especially in high-profile fields such as healthcare, drug safety and public health. Modern media communications, in one form or another, are in touch with most of the population of any country, through television, radio, newspapers, internet, mobile phones or personal digital assistants. Knowing our audiences and their preferred media will help us identify how our media relations should be planned, and which media should be targeted to reach our chosen segments.

Effective media relations do not guarantee that negative or critical stories will never appear in the news media, nor that the message will always appear in the form that we wished or intended. An organisation with an active media relations policy – in contrast to one with no policy at all, or a 'keep them at bay' mentality – can, however, expect these benefits:

- fairer coverage of stories
- more extensive and thorough coverage
- more likelihood of consultation prior to publication
- more likelihood of comment or correction being published
- more understanding of the organisation and commitment to supporting its activities, even if not uncritically.

Don't hate the media, become the media.

Jello Biafra

The essence

As with communications in general, there are whole libraries of books on media relations. Here we can but skim the surface and alert you to the essentials.

People in the news media are, as well as being potential partners, another of our audiences and, if we wish them to take us seriously, we must deal with them as conscientiously as we would with any other audience – doctors, patients, whoever. Most of the problems organisations have with editors and journalists result from the neglect to which these vital, external partners are subjected.

Here are some of the essential truths about media relations:

- The news media owe us nothing; we must earn their interest and attention.

- Editors and journalists are under no obligation to print what we want or say uncritically or at all.
- The publication of news is largely a commercial activity: it is, inevitably, driven by winning and keeping viewers, listeners and readers.
- There are thousands of column inches and broadcast hours to be filled every day: the news media are hungry for stories.
- At the same time, there can be severe competition for space and news value priorities may not include our story, however vital we regard it to be.
- Publishers and broadcasters are interested in exclusives that give them the edge over their competitors. They are likely to give much more time and space to a story they have in advance of others.
- News media work to very short deadlines – print or broadcast schedules – and often need very rapid responses to enquiries.
- With the exception of those in some sectors, editors and journalists are people with principles – honesty, accuracy, balance and the public interest, at least.
- Most editors and journalists will respect the 'off-the-record' convention; it's in their interests to respect it: they know that if they don't they won't get privileged information a second time.
- Most editors and journalists strongly prefer a collaborative relationship, although not conceding their right to independence of judgement.
- It is the business of the news media to expose dishonesty, manipulation, incompetence and misuse of resources.
- Silence or 'no comment' will frustrate, irritate, anger journalists and (naturally enough) predispose them to a negative view or to the suspicion of cover-up.
- If 'no comment' is the policy, and for good reasons, then some explanation should be offered in either diplomatic or off-the-record form.
- Journalists cannot be expected to understand the intricacies of our world unless we make conscientious efforts to inform and brief them; people change jobs quite frequently in the news media, so the process of briefing personnel is a continuous one.
- Journalists cannot be expected to take us seriously if we appear every so often demanding that they do take us seriously; we cannot expect them to take our crises seriously if we are never in contact with them between times and they do not understand the ordinary conduct of our everyday work.
- As with members of any audience, familiarity and trust are essential: these come only through the cultivation of personal relationships with significant editors and journalists on a regular basis.
- Almost all news media have specialist journalists for areas such as health and science. These should be identified and cultivated.
- Beyond the news desk, many publishers and broadcasters have other departments of interest, including features, business, society, environment, health and welfare and so on. They make documentaries, write in-depth pieces on specialist subjects and may be valuable contacts.
- Many printed news media offer the facility of 'advertorials': by buying a certain area of advertising space, you have a similar area for your own copy, photographs, charts, etc. This method, along with the simple expedient of buying straight advertising space, are the only ways that you can guarantee that what you want to say will be printed exactly as you wrote it.
- Organisations need to have a serious schedule of media relations activities, including personal contact; briefings and visits (in both directions), news conferences, information packs, background briefings, regular news release and other information output.

Our most tragic error may have been our inability to establish a rapport and a confidence with the press and television with the communication media. I don't think the press has understood me.

Lyndon B. Johnson

News releases

The subject of news releases deserves its own checklist:

- The regular issue of news releases ensures that the organisation's existence and activities are at least known by editors and journalists, whether or not the content is published.
- Information about the ordinary, everyday activities of an organisation is acceptable and useful for journalists (remember what is ordinary and familiar to us may not be so for outsiders).
- News releases should always include some measure of background information about the organisation and contextual information about the issue in hand.
- They should always carry a named contact with communications details and hours of availability (which need to take account of the working hours of journalists). At times of crisis, availability of contact 24 hours a day must be provided.
- As with off-the-record, an embargo time is likely to be respected by most editors and journalists: those who do not respect it know they will not be likely to get advance information a second time.
- A news release is a briefing for the recipient (first audience) and should not be written in the form it might be expected to appear in the paper (for the second audience): that is the journalist's or the sub-editors's job; discussion with journalists about the form and style in which they would like to receive information is useful.
- Although evidence of wit and originality in news release headlines is not unacceptable, such details are properly the sub-editor's job.
- News releases are sometimes printed more or less verbatim and, for reasons of space, are likely to be edited (cut) from the bottom, in the printed media – so all the critical information should appear very early on.
- Journalists are busy people and are likely to skim the many news releases on their desk or computer screen each day to identify the really interesting ones: a summary statement of the entire release should appear in the first paragraph to ensure yours has a chance of not being discarded.
- News media are not usually in the business of printing materials that are barely disguised advertising.
- 'News values' – remember that problems are often more interesting than everyday achievements; that erectile dysfunction or pink urine are more gripping than a biography of the chairman: learn about the news values of the media and audiences you want to influence.
- The structure of a news release should be: summary; exposition of argument; supporting evidence; elaboration; conclusion.
- It is always helpful if a quote from a named source is included – as senior and/or relevant as possible: this adds life and authenticity to any story. Such a quote may well be followed up for elaboration.
- News releases should never be more than about two A4 pages or equivalent. They should have wide margins and line spacing so that they can be easily read and edited.
- Good photographs or graphics (tables, charts) will enhance the appeal of a story (check editors' preferred formats before sending).
- Most publications and broadcasters will be pleased to receive your information by fax or email; check their preferences.

Active collaboration

In Ethiopia and Ghana (to this author's first-hand knowledge), and perhaps in other places, extremely positive results have come from briefing or training courses laid on by local HCPs for their local media. Few journalists are true health specialists (except in the biggest media outlets), and learning about health facts and issues, especially as they relate to their own audiences, can be popular and productive for both sides. What are to HCPs everyday issues – drug safety, disease control and eradication, counterfeit drugs, and a host of others – may be of consuming interest to journalists who have never been introduced to them. Such issues not only provide stories in their own right but also lead to much greater appreciation of the complexity of healthcare, and to much more thoughtful reporting. The investment of a day or two in such activities, once a year or so, may pay rich dividends.

Conclusion

The most successful businesses and organisations almost always have an active and energetic media relations policy as part of their overall marketing and communications strategy.

Individuals or organisations who are suspicious, hostile or neglectful in their attitudes to the news media, possibly as the result of seemingly negative treatment in the past, fail to understand that the negative treatment may result precisely from their hostility, suspicion or neglect, and that the remedy is within their hands, subject only to imagination and initiative. They completely fail to grasp the enormous potential for their benefit in exploiting the power and influence of the printed and spoken media to reach specialist and mass audiences. News media people cannot ultimately be controlled, but they can be engaged in a mutually beneficial collaboration which, although it has its risks like all communications activities, can be rich and productive when managed skilfully.

25 Notes on managing meetings

Some simple rules and an understanding of the communications processes in groups can help to make meetings productive, dynamic – and short. The skills of the chairperson are crucial to good meetings and those who have the skills should be preferred for the role to those who are simply older or more senior. Participants can also improve their skills as partners in the effort to maximise the productivity of the valuable time set aside for meetings. Enormous savings in time can be made for those who run meetings effectively.[273]

If you had to identify, in one word, the reason why the human race has not achieved, and never will achieve, its full potential, that word would be 'meetings'.

Dave Barry

Conducting effective meetings is an area of communications activity in which performance often does not do justice to the intelligence of the participants. What is often lacking is knowledge and basic skills, which can transform the entire experience of meetings of all kinds from miserable to productive.

How many meetings a year do you attend after which:

- You wonder what has been achieved?
- You resent the length of time it took?
- You wonder if the decisions that were reached could have been achieved by phone or fax or email?
- You wished the person in the chair had better control of the meeting?
- You resented the dominance of one or two people, and their attempts to override everyone else?
- You were irritated by people chatting together while the meeting was in progress?
- You found there was not time to deal with many issues, nor most of the important ones?
- You were not asked to present the materials you had prepared or there was no projector for your slideshow?
- Issues were raised that required preparatory work for which you and others did not have prior notice?
- You feel tired and demotivated?

If any of these items is familiar to you, then you are the victim of meetings conducted by amateurs. As with communications in general, there is a widespread assumption that age, seniority and status somehow confer expertise in specialist activities completely unrelated to their real profession – one of which is chairing meetings. Although many meetings are vehicles for the exercise of authority, they should not be confused with meetings where the purpose is collaborative planning, consultation or problem solving. In such cases what is needed is a skilled facilitator in the chair to liberate the collective intelligence and experience of the participants. Irrespective of seniority, such people should be the most skilled available in running productive meetings.

I don't understand why people whose entire lives or their corporate success depends on communication, and yet they are led on occasion by CEOs who cannot talk their way out of a paper bag and don't care to.

Frank Luntz

Many of you will know that it is possible to have meetings that are brisk, efficient, decisive, productive, and which generate rather than deplete energy.

The critical element in a successful meeting is the person in the chair. The most senior or expert person in the group may not be the best choice:

- They may have no idea at all about how to conduct meetings.
- The prosecution of their case or argument, or the assertion of their authority, compromises their role in the chair as the guardian of the meeting's effectiveness and the welfare of its members. Contrary to common belief, an independent person in the chair, who may or may not know a great deal about the intricacies of matters under discussion, is more likely to conduct a dynamic and efficient meeting.

Meetings are indispensable when you don't want to do anything.

John Kenneth Galbraith

The responsibilities of the person in the chair are clear, although far from simple in execution.

It is their job to:

- Ensure the meeting starts on time.
- Ensure everyone knows all the participants and their interest in the meeting.
- Propose and agree a finishing time (subject to change only by negotiation and agreement in advance).
- Check that the agenda includes all items that require attention, adding new or important items and rescheduling others.
- Assign someone to the job of taking minutes if they are required (see Box 26.1); deciding what kind of minutes they are to be (action points only? Record of points discussed?), to whom beyond the meeting group they are to be sent.
- Allocate and agree time for each agenda item (if this has not already been done prior to the meeting).
- Distinguish between items that are urgent (which may require little time but can easily get out of hand) and those that are important (which may require more time).
- Establish ground rules: one person talks at a time; no mobile phones – whatever is appropriate for focus and good order.
- Identify the purpose of the discussion of each item on the agenda:
  — for information
  — for debate
  — for generation of possible solutions
  — for decision.
- Ensure that the discussion and decisions remain within the remit of the group.
- Identify items that may exclude the majority of the group and propose a separate meeting for the minority – unless it is important that the majority should witness the discussion.
- Ensure individuals are not allowed to dominate the discussion.
- Encourage quiet members to contribute (if they are not contributing, why are they there?).
- Invite contributions from those with knowledge or expertise in the item under discussion if they are not forthcoming.
- Identify and control repetition and circularity.
- Prohibit conversation by sub-groups.
- Be alert to the non-verbal behaviour of members of the group (this will reveal frustration, agreement, dissatisfaction, anger, disappointment, withdrawal and more, any of which may require attention for the welfare of the individual or for the group as a whole).
- Check other aspects of the group process: are members comfortable? Is it too hot or cold?
- Do the smokers need a break? Is it time for a breather and some coffee?
- Recognise the point at which there is actually general tacit agreement (or acceptance) of a decision or conclusion. This is often long before

agreement is explicitly acknowledged or asked for.

- Check opinion round the whole group prior to decisions being formalised.
- Ensure decisions are recorded and read back to check for accuracy and agreement.
- Provide mediation for conflict.
- Suggest alternative solutions if consensus is not possible.
- Identify matters for further discussion and resolution.
- Do not attempt to draft a policy or a document in a full meeting, unless there is really no alternative.
- Seek feedback on all aspects of the meeting – location, timing, refreshments, effectiveness, proposals for doing things differently in future.
- Resolve the problem of the date of the next meeting either by declaring that it will have to be held without all members being present, or leaving the diary negotiations to an assistant to conduct outside the meeting by phone or email or whatever.
- Close the meeting by reviewing its achievements and thanking members for their participation.

Box 25.1 Note on minute-takers and minutes

> This job is often seriously undervalued and dumped on the most junior or least protesting person, or on one of the females present. Where there is not a permanent administrator/secretary to the group, the job should probably be rotated among members. It should be seen as a task of great importance – the accurate historical record of decisions and the basis of future planning and action – not as some low-status clerical task. Minutes should never be taken by the person in the chair as they cannot both conduct and record the meeting effectively.
>
> The exact content and purpose of minutes should be specified and agreed by everyone, so that the document fulfils its purposes, and is not wastefully comprehensive or unnecessarily detailed.

Good meetings do not just happen: they are structured and controlled in ways that are calculated to liberate the members to work effectively together. Few meetings should ever go on for more than one or two hours: in general, meetings will expand to fill the time they are allowed and a meeting that

could have been successfully concluded within a limited timeframe (say, one hour), will stagger on for three hours or more if it is allowed to. Nothing demoralises people than having no end of a meeting in sight.

The least productive people are usually the ones who are most in favor of holding meetings.

Thomas Sowell

There are other considerations:

- clarity about whether or not a meeting is necessary at all
- agendas and meeting papers sent out well before a meeting (ideally no less than a week or 10 days) so that members can prepare
- agendas should not be merely lists of topics, but should provide appropriate information which allows everyone to come prepared to participate fully: notes might include an indication as to why each topic appears, what issues require discussion, who will be responsible for leading on each item, what decisions need to be made
- how long the meeting is planned to last
- who will be attending
- minutes should be circulated within days of a meeting taking place, recording decisions and allocated action points so that amendments can be quickly suggested and the momentum generated is maintained.

Participants also have responsibilities. They should:

- prepare for the meeting
- arrive on time
- concentrate
- take part actively
- not conduct private conversations during the meeting
- declare doubts or reservations openly
- help in solving group problems and resolving conflict
- refrain from anecdote and meandering story telling
- show willingness to compromise if possible
- take responsibility for the decisions of the meeting
- carry out tasks allocated during the meeting by the deadlines agreed.

Most of this applies to any gathering that is not an informal, social event: committees, conferences, seminars, workshops, departmental meetings, focus groups, consultative meetings and so on.

Box 25.2

At any meeting you attend, make sure you ask these two questions (and get answers) if no one else does:

- What is the purpose of this meeting?
- How long will this meeting last?

Adoption of only half of the rules and ideas outlined would increase the productivity of almost any meeting you care to think of. The many hours spent annually in meetings by highly paid professionals round the world would be significantly reduced, and those reduced hours would generate action, energy, optimism and decisive change on a huge scale.

Box 25.3 Are you sitting comfortably?

The way the seats are arranged in a meeting room or lecture hall communicates a powerful message from the organisers about their expectations of the meeting and of the participants, and determines, to a large extent, how the participants will behave:

- Close rows of forward-facing seats imply a passive, dependent audience, focusing on one or more people of superior importance addressing them from the front; forward-facing seats do not encourage any kind of audience participation nor development of audience interaction or solidarity; forward-facing seats are an expression of hierarchy. There are occasions when this arrangement is unavoidable because of numbers, or entirely appropriate for the purpose, but as the unconsidered, default arrangement for all meetings it is extremely limiting. People walking into a room with rows of forward-facing chairs immediately react to what they see as the likely style, purpose and process of a meeting taking place in such an environment; almost all people will avoid the front rows because they fear exposure in a potentially hostile environment. Their general reaction may make them switch off instantly, decide to listen but not participate, put them into cynical mode or any number of other negative frames of mind – all compromising to the purpose of the meeting. Delinquents and sleepers will drift to the back and pay little attention.
- Any seating arrangement that allows participants to see each other (chevron rows, U-shape, round or square tables) reduces the primacy of a single podium speaker or panel and suggests that relationships within the group are also important for the meeting. If the arrangement allows the senior person, or guest speaker, to sit among the group, even at the head of a table, then the sense of potential democracy of participation is further enhanced. Of course these more informal arrangements can result in oppressive, non-participatory meetings under stern management, just as formal rows can be transformed into a lively environment by a talented speaker (this latter is relatively unusual in corporate life, whereas the former is common). In a U-shape or round a table, some people will feel exposed and vulnerable, and the quality of leadership of the meeting will either intensify or alleviate their fears.
- 'Café-style' (round or square tables seating up to 10 people), can be a very positive approach – giving everyone a piece of territory, membership of a transient group, and the easy, non-disruptive opportunity for group discussion.
- Conclusion: if you want a productive, participatory meeting, then make sure the seats are set out in a way that everyone can see each other, and that you have enabling leadership or chairing of the meeting.

26 The challenges of teaching

Teaching is one of the most important and challenging activities in the whole world, and amongst the most complex and demanding. It requires knowledge, dedication and enthusiasm, and a range of sophisticated communication skills. A brief section on the topic is included here because of the vital importance of good teaching in all aspects of healthcare and because it is often done so badly. The issues are particularly important in formal education itself, of course, but relevant also to those aspects of healthcare relationships where patient or public education is the aim.

The good, the bad and the sleepy

What are the characteristics of good teaching?

- Motivating (inspiring) others
  - to learn; to acquire knowledge, skills and competence
  - to ask questions and acquire critical minds
  - to develop personally, socially, intellectually and professionally.
- Providing the means, resources, stimulation and environment for learning and growth.

Don't let schooling interfere with your education.
Mark Twain

Why, in the main, are lectures (and classroom teaching of children) so often inadequate and ineffective?

- They are often simply the transmission of existing knowledge or materials already in print.
- The verbal transmission of such material adds no value to it.
- The length of lectures (sometimes ludicrously up to three hours) ensures that no student can possibly attend to the material for more than a small percentage of the whole time.
- Taking lecture notes is a demanding, mechanical activity allowing for almost no reflection or learning.
- The method does not permit the lecturer or teacher to have any feedback about the impact of the material or the extent to which it is at all useful.
- There is often no provision for students to ask questions or develop critical appraisal of the material.
- Lectures in the least dynamic institutions provide material simply for rote learning and reproduction in examinations.
- The numbers of students (sometimes in the hundreds) mean that none but a handful can ever participate even if there is the opportunity for asking questions.
- Many students dread lectures and see them as a necessary evil to be endured.
- Attendance at lectures is often an important element in term and final grades or qualification, although attendance itself may mean nothing in terms of learning, let alone quality of learning.

- Conscientious, successful students may well achieve their good results as much in spite of as because of lectures and traditional classroom practices.

Education has failed in a very serious way to convey the most important lesson science can teach: skepticism.
David Suzuki

Lectures have a real part to play in academic life, but only with certain conditions:

- The lecturer is an expert or researcher sharing their latest work and thinking with students.
- The lecturer is always fully prepared on the subject matter of the lecture.
- The lecturer is explaining or illuminating existing knowledge or materials, especially complex issues, through commentary and analysis.
- The lecturer is providing an overview or theoretical framework, in which the course or its content can be understood.
- The lecturer is providing knowledge or information or insight of any kind that is not available elsewhere.
- The lecture raises questions as much as it provides answers.
- The lecture does not last more than an hour, or a suitable break is provided for longer stretches.
- There is some mechanism during or after the lecture for the material to be questioned and processed by students (especially through discussion).

The problem with this agenda for lecturing is that it makes the job very demanding and not everyone in academic life is up to the challenge. If, however, we want the best results, that is to say, the most highly motivated students and the most capable professionals, we have to embrace a model of education that throws out rituals and insists on interaction and engagement.

The greatest good you can do for another is not just to share your riches but to reveal to him his own.
Benjamin Disraeli

Students who remain passive recipients of knowledge are very unlikely to:

- develop questioning, critical minds
- be capable of innovation and creativity
- fulfil their personal or professional potential.

In terms of communication skills, students who are trained in institutions that are models of bad practice, will never develop the imagination and the art to become great communicators themselves. Institutions that devalue or ignore the humanity of their students will not produce compassionate, humane health professionals or any other kind of specialist.

Inspiration, engagement and interaction

There are lots of great teachers who excite and stimulate their students, inspire them to learn and grow and engage actively with them in the process. This takes place only in relationships that have many of the qualities of good healthcare relationships, described at such length in this book:

- empathy
- seeing and relating with the whole person
- listening

- skilful use of verbal and non-verbal behaviour
- explanation and clarification
- checking understanding
- motivating and supporting
- enthusiasm for the topic
- repetition
- problem solving
- seeking feedback
- showing care and concern.

A good teacher will make demands of students, push them to greater effort and achievement; will insist that they learn what must be learnt; will engage them in vigorous discussion and debate; will value and encourage their participation; will be open and frank about poor performance; will admit when they do not know the answer to a question, will attempt to obtain it or encourage students to find it for themselves; will appreciate and applaud progress and success. These educational processes are rather stronger and more assertive than those desirable in relationships with patients, but they share many of the qualities of 'tough love' which are common to both professions.

Knowledge can be communicated, but not wisdom. One can find it, live it, be fortified by it, do wonders through it, but one cannot communicate and teach it.

Hermann Hesse

In healthcare, some students will learn from role models they admire and from the professionals they meet during periods of practical work experience. They will learn from each other, as well as from books, and good lectures. The specific behaviour of good teachers in good institutions, and the rich learning culture and environment they foster, mean that students have a solid foundation for the future and the chance of becoming strong, critically minded, happy and effective professionals who will continue to learn and grow throughout their lives.

Box 26.1

There is a wonderful statement about the top ten requirements of excellent teaching at:
http://honolulu.hawaii.edu/intranet/committees/FacDevCom/guidebk/teachtip/topten.htm.

It is from the award-winning Professor Richard Leblanc, of York University, Ontario. The material is so good and so inspiring that this reference for it has not been banished to the notes at the end of the book: do read it!

If education is always to be conceived along the same antiquated lines of a mere transmission of knowledge, there is little to be hoped from it in the bettering of man's future. For what is the use of transmitting knowledge if the individual's total development lags behind?

Maria Montessori

Revision, discussion and application (8)

A. Revision and discussion

1. The concept of empathy is given great prominence in this book in relation to communications with patients. Why is empathy for any audience also important in communications of all sorts? What kinds of subtle information and understanding about an audience must you have which go beyond the categories of audience segments (age, gender and so on) if communications are to be successful? What are the risks of communications without empathy?
2. Review Chapter 22 and draw up a list of your top 10 tips for excellent communications, which relate to almost all communications in a professional setting, excluding face-to-face relationships with patients.
3. Why are comments and complaints so valuable to any service provider? What range of methods and techniques can you think of to make it easy for patients or customers to communicate their dissatisfaction? What proactive methods can you use to discover patient or customer opinion?
4. What are the basic arguments for any organisation in the public eye to have an active media relations policy and to get to know journalists? Keep your eyes on the news media and try to assess which news stories relate to organisations that have good media relations and those whose relations are poor or non-existent.
5. Make a study of some of the meetings you attend, and analyse their strengths and weaknesses in relation to the principles and standards in Chapter 25: is the purpose clear? Is there a time limit? Is the chairperson skilled at the job? What is the morale of the participants? See if you can introduce some improvements in the quality of the meetings you run or attend.
6. Reflect on the issues of teaching and learning, and think about the experiences in your life which have been particularly good or memorably bad. Although there will be different methods for different purposes, what do you feel are the qualities of the best teaching and training in general? Set out some standards for you to refer to when you have to plan some educational activity in the future.

B. Application

1. In relation to the principles set out in Chapter 22, draw up a plan for the production of a patient leaflet, or some other public communication, printed or electronic, paying particular attention to the audience research, testing and feedback issues in the planning stage. Consider how the formulation and presentation of a message is changed as you begin to learn more about your audience.

2. Examine the range of communications materials and activities in your place of work (paper, signage, electronic, voice), and make an assessment of their quality and effectiveness. Where are the weaknesses? What improvements can be made quickly or in the longer term? What needs to be done to stimulate change?
3. How are complaints managed in your place of work? Are there methods and materials for encouraging patients to complain or make comments? How does the organisation respond to complaints? Are there any active methods of soliciting patient opinion of services? What can be done to open up such channels of communication?
4. What is the public image/reputation of your place of work? If you don't know, take some steps to find out from users and non-users and assess how satisfied you are with what you hear. Are there ways in which public image and knowledge of service and service quality in your community could be improved? What simple and more elaborate steps could be taken to start to manage your public relations actively?
5. In meetings that you run or have an influence on, start to introduce some of the behaviour and techniques outlined in Chapter 25. See, at least, if you can bring greater focus to agendas and goals (where they need it) and agreed, shorter time limits. Try to identify those with chairing skills, and get them to manage your meetings. At the radical end of change, see if you can abolish some unnecessary meetings altogether.
6. Examine training and induction activities in your place of work and talk to those who are experiencing them. What do they find useful and what do they find tedious or badly presented? What do they feel is missing and what do they feel is superfluous? Is there enough time, or too much? How can the processes be improved?

Commentary on many of the questions and issues appears on the publisher's website, in Online Resources at www.pharmpress.com.

Appendix 1: Chapter notes and references

Introduction

The book has been written on the basis of the author's lifetime of reading and experience and on the input of many others in the field. Such authority as it has, rests only lightly on specific research and references, and much more heavily on the author's accumulated wisdom and knowledge. As such, it is not a typical academic textbook and may be thought, by some, to be lightweight in that respect. Its intrinsic (rather than attributable) authority will be demonstrated by the extent to which healthcare workers find it useful, stimulating and accurate; by how far its view of the world matches theirs, and helps them to understand theirs better.

The content is basically one person's view of communications, healthcare and the world, and as such is opinionated, but reflectively and intelligently so, your author earnestly hopes. You will be the judge.

In the broadest sense, the author acknowledges the influence on his knowledge and experience of large numbers of writers, colleagues and friends, but very little of what you see here is taken directly from any source other than the author's brain. Where there is another specific source, it is referenced here, along with many other interesting places to visit. The author's larger debt is recorded in the acknowledgements and Appendix 2 lists books and websites and further reading.

This appendix appears in its entirety on the pharmpress.com website, so you can have it open while you read the book and have immediate, live links to the many websites and references mentioned. Even if you do not use the links, you may find it much more convenient to have the notes and references in front of you, rather than having to flip to the end of the book.

Go to: Online Resources at www.pharmpress.com

Part A: Getting Started

Chapter 1 Introduction

1. http://www.dh.gov.uk/en/Publicationsandstatistics/Publications/PublicationsPolicyAndGuidance/DH_065946
2. http://www.dh.gov.uk/en/Publicationsandstatistics/Publications/PublicationsPolicyAndGuidance/DH_065953
3. http://www.dh.gov.uk/en/Managingyourorganisation/Humanresourcesandtraining/Modernisingprofessionalregulation/Professional RegulationandPatientSafetyProgramme/index.htm
4. Find the UK Chief Medical Officer's revalidation proposals at: http://www.dh.gov.uk/en/Publicationsandstatistics/Publications/PublicationsPolicyAndGuidance/DH_086430?IdcService=GET_FILE&dID=144699&Rendition=Web or from this page: http://www.dh.gov.uk/en/Publicationsandstatistics/Publications/PublicationsPolicyAndGuidance/DH_086430

Paragraph 10.3 of the proposals includes the following:

'Patients have an important contribution to make on how well a doctor performs in relation to:

— effective communication, including listening, informing and explaining;
— involving patients in treatment decisions;
— care coordination and support for self-care; and
— showing respect for patients and treating them with dignity.'

These are all topics, among many more allied issues, which will be close to the hearts of those who read this book.

5. http://www.gmc-uk.org/guidance/a_z_guidance/index.asp
6. http://www.who.int/patientsafety/en/
7. http://www.jointcommission.org/PatientSafety/SpeakUp/

Part B: The nature and importance of communication

Chapter 4 What is effective communication?

Materials on communication skills in general appear in Appendix 2.

8. There is an immense amount of information about communication on the internet. Any search will turn up millions of references. One good starting site with dozens of links is: http://en.wikipedia.org/wiki/Communication
9. Notes on non-verbal communication: http://www.minoritycareernet.com/newsltrs/95q3nonver.html
10. Basic discussion of non-verbal communication with good links: http://humanresources.about.com/od/interpersonalcommunicatio1/a/nonverbal_com.htm
11. Givens D B. 'The nonverbal dictionary of gestures, signs, and body language cues.' A remarkable compendium with illustrations: http://humanresources.about.com/gi/dynamic/offsite.htm?zi=1/XJ&sdn=humanresources&cdn=money&tm=18&gps=243_1380_843_614&f=00&su=p560.6.336.ip_&tt=2&bt=0&bts=1&zu=http%3A//members.aol.com/nonverbal2/diction1.htm
12. Wales J [founder of Wikipedia]. Next billion will change the way we think. *The Guardian Weekly*, 20 June 2008, p. 19.
13. See, for example, Robinson R W. *Ancient Greek Democracy*. Oxford: Blackwell, 2003; ISBN-13: 978--06312--3394--7, ISBN-10: 0--631--23394--6.
14. The Plain English Campaign (http://www.plainenglish.co.uk) has a guide to explaining medical terms and a great deal of other useful material to support the continuing battle against jargon, bureaucratic language and ineffective communications. Access to the excellent guide to medical communications, and the list of terms with simplified versions: http://www.plainenglish.co.uk/guides.htm
15. A short list on an excellent site for teenagers living with cancer: http://www.canteen.org.au/default.asp?menuid=78
16. Useful resources from the Medical Library Association: http://www.mlanet.org/resources/medspeak/
17. Excellent commentary on the absurdity and tyranny of jargon: Wolff J. This epidemic of medical jargon isn't good for us. *The Guardian* 1 April 2008. http://education.guardian.co.uk/higher/comment/story/0,,2269627,00.html
18. http://www.netdoctor.co.uk/ate/liverandkidney/ 202569.html

Chapter 6 Communications at the heart of healthcare

19. The Migrant Clinicians' Network provides rich resources about improving services for one much neglected group of people: http://www.migrantclinician.org/?Strangecode=4dc1f35e9a0863065a8bf6d73f3f3369
20. Among many studies worldwide, *Mirror, Mirror on the Wall: An update on the quality of American health care through the patient's lens*, published by the US Commonwealth Fund in April 2006, showed how variable was performance in six developed countries, measured against six

criteria of patient perception and satisfaction. Spending in the US at around twice as much per capita as in the other countries appeared to have no effect on overall results at all. http://www.commonwealthfund.org/publications/publications_show.htm?doc_id=364436. There are more references to patient dissatisfaction studies in Chapter 23.

21. See, for example, commentary by the respected Professor of Risk Management at King's College, London, Ragnar Löfstedt, in the *Independent on Sunday*, 11 December 2005. Available at: http://findarticles.com/p/articles/mi_qn4159/is_20051211/ai_n15918582
22. Brown D. Life expectancy drops for some US women. *Washington Post* 22 April 2008; and Ezzati M, Friedman A B, Kulkarni S C, Murray C J L. The reversal of fortunes: trends in county mortality and cross-county mortality disparities in the United States. *PLoS Medicine* April 2008; 5(4). http://www.plosmedicine.org
23. For example, The World Alliance for Patient Safety: http://www.who.int/patientsafety/en/
24. The most comprehensive and dramatic statement of the problems appeared in the Toronto Consensus Statement of 1991. Though it and its evidence are now nearly 20 years old, and there have undoubtedly been some changes and improvements since then, the situation it describes remains much the same in many places, with new pressures and priorities contributing to the persistence of old problems. This is the opening summary of the position as it was then, with the multiple research references removed:

'Communications problems in medical practice are both important and common. For example, 54% of patient complaints and 45% of patient concerns are not elicited by physicians. Psychosocial and psychiatric problems are common in general medical practice, but these diagnoses are missed in up to 50% of cases. In 50% of visits, the patient and the doctor do not agree on the nature of the main presenting problem. In one study patients were interrupted so soon after they began describing their presenting problems (on average within 18 seconds) that they failed to disclose other significant concerns. Most complaints by the public about physicians deal not with clinical competency problems, but with communications problems, and the majority of malpractice allegations arise from communications errors. Residents or trainees and practising physicians have shown substantial deficiencies when studied. Only a low proportion of visits with doctors include any patient education, and a surprisingly high proportion of patients do not understand or remember what their physicians tell them about diagnosis and treatment. Cultural differences also impede the work with patients.

'Patient anxiety and dissatisfaction is related to uncertainty and lack of information, explanation, and feedback from the doctor. Yet doctors often misperceive the amount and type of information patients want. The language doctors use is often unclear, both as regards the use of jargon and in relation to the lack of the expected shared meanings of relatively common terms.'

This remarkable document goes on to examine the relationship between quality of clinical communication and positive health outcomes, patient satisfaction and adherence. It outlines what is already known about the positive impact of structured training in communications for HCPs and how education can be improved. Their conclusion remains resonant and relevant today:

'Sufficient data have now accumulated to prove that problems in doctor–patient communication are extremely common and adversely affect patient management. It has been repeatedly shown that the clinical skills needed to improve these problems can be taught and the subsequent benefits to medical practice are demonstrable, feasible on a routine basis, and enduring. There is therefore a clear and urgent need for teaching of these clinical skills to be incorporated into medical school curriculums and continued into postgraduate training and courses in continuing medical education. If current knowledge is now implemented in clinical practice, and if the priorities for research are addressed, there may be material improvement in the relationships between patient and doctor.'

Simpson M, Buckman R, Stewart M *et al.* Doctor–patient communications: the Toronto consensus statement. *British Medical Journal* 1991; 303: 1385–1387. A review of progress in a 1998 *British Medical Journal* editorial suggested that, while awareness of the problems had increased since the Toronto Consensus Statement was published, radical changes in practice had yet to be realised and that the issues and challenges remained much the same. See also Meryn S. Improving doctor–patient communication (editorial). *British Medical Journal* 1998; 316: 1922–1930.

25. Joyce Adams on http://www.patientadvocare.blogspot.com/ (a rich and informative source of patient and HCP experiences).
26. A review of 21 studies examining the nature and effects of the quality of physician–patient relationships: Stewart M A. Effective physician–patient communication and health outcomes: a review. *Canadian Medical Association Journal* 152: 1423–1433. http://www.cmaj.ca/cgi/content/abstract/152/9/1423
27. Bunting M. *The Guardian*, 30 June 2008, p. 19.
28. Heisler M, Cole I, Weir D, Kerr E A, Hayward R A. Does physician communication influence older patients' diabetes self-management and glycemic control? Results from the Health and Retirement Study (HRS). *Journals of Gerontology Series A: Biological Sciences and Medical Sciences* 2007; 62: 1435–1442.
29. Tamblyn R, Abrahamowicz M, Dauphinee D *et al.* Physician scores on a national clinical skills examination as predictors of complaints to medical regulatory authorities. *Journal of the American Medical Association* 2007; 298: 993–1001. Also reported by Laura Blue in *Time* magazine, 5 Sept 2007. The research reported demonstrates the particularly interesting fact that HCPs whose communication skills were assessed as poor at the time of qualification, attracted much larger numbers of patient complaints in the succeeding years of their practice than those who showed early signs of competence.
30. Di Blasi Z, Harkness E, Ernst E, Georgiou A, Kleijnen J. Influence of context effects on health outcomes: a systematic review. *The Lancet* 10 March 2001; 357: 757–762.
31. Nick Haslam. Humanising medical practice: the role of empathy. *Medical Journal of Australia* 2007; 187: 381–382. http://www.mercola.com/2001/mar/17/doctor_patient.htm

    Hardee J T. An overview of empathy. *The Permanente Journal*, Fall 2004; 7. http://xnet.kp.org/permanentejournal/fall03/cpc.html
32. Remen R. Recapturing the soul of medicine: physicians need to reclaim meaning in their working lives [editorial]. *Western Journal of Medicine* 2001; 174: 4–5.
33. Di Blasi ZD, Harkness E, Ernst E et al. Influence of context effects on health outcomes: a systematic review. *The Lancet* 2001; 357: 757–762. http://linkinghub.elsevier.com/retrieve/pii/S0140673600041696

Part C: Aims and ideals in healthcare

Chapter 7 Vision at the heart of healthcare

34. The International Alliance of Patients' Organizations has a useful statement of many of the same principles presented in the text. See IAPO Declaration on Patient-centred Healthcare: http://www.patientsorganizations.org
35. The Veterans Administration of the US Government has a powerful, visionary statement of its obligations to its patients and their reciprocal responsibilities: http://www.patientadvocate.va.gov/rights.asp
36. Carvel J. (Social affairs editor.) *The Guardian* (UK), 9 April 2008.

Chapter 8 Ethics in healthcare communications

37. Useful general sources: The centre for ethics and advocacy in healthcare: http://www.healthcare-ethics.org/about/

    The National advisory board on healthcare ethics; http://www.etene.org/e/index.shtml

    Comprehensive coverage of issues from the UK General Medical Council: http://www.gmc-uk.org/guidance/ethical_guidance/index.asp
38. May or may not derive from Hippocrates. The principle *primum succurere* ('hasten to help') may overtake 'do no harm' when responding to cancer with aggressive therapy.
39. The University of Kansas Medical Center. *Hospital Ethics Handbook*, 5th edn (rev. 2002): http://www.kumc.edu/hospital/ethics/ethics.htm
40. Breslin J M, MacRae S K, Bell J, Singer P A. Top ten ethical challenges facing Canadians in healthcare (views of Toronto ethicists). *BMC Medical Ethics* 2005; 6: 5. doi:10.1186/1472–6939–6–5; http://www.biomedcentral.com/1472–6939/6/5. The first five items are by far the most potent issues revealed in this review.
41. Feudtner C, Marcuse E K. Ethics and immunization policy: promoting dialogue to sustain consensus; *Pediatrics* 2001; 107: 1158–1164; http://pediatrics.aappublications.org/cgi/content/full/107/5/1158
42. Goldwater P N, Braunack-Mayer A J, Power R G *et al.* Childhood tetanus in Australia: ethical issues for a should-be-forgotten preventable disease. *Medical Journal of Australia* 2003; 178: 175–177. http://www.mja.com.au/public/issues/178_04_170203/gol10299_fm.html
43. Ross G. How not to communicate risk (from 'flu shots for example). American Council on Science and Health 14 Nov 2006; http://acsh.org/factsfears/newsID.877/news_detail.asp

Part D: Behind the scenes

Chapter 9 Secret life: what drives us in communications?

44. Quoted on http://www.proliteracy.org
45. Joint Commission, 'What did the doctor say?' Improving health literacy to protect patient safety; Quoted on p. 4; http://www.jointcommission.org/NR/rdonlyres/D5248B2E-E7E6–4121–8874–99C7B4888301/0/improving_health_literacy.pdf. (This is an excellent report, full of good examples and practical advice for improving practice throughout the healthcare continuum.)
46. For press release summary see also http://www.jointcommission.org/NewsRoom/PressKits/Health_Literacy/hl_020607.htm

Chapter 10 Beyond words: the power of non-verbal communication

47. http://humanresources.about.com/od/interpersonalcommunicatio1/a/nonverbal_com.htm
48. Givens D B. The nonverbal dictionary of gestures, signs, and body language cues. A useful compendium with illustrations: http://humanresources.about.com/gi/dynamic/

offsite.htm?zi=1/XJ&sdn=humanresources&cdn=money&tm=18&gps=243_1380_843_614&f=00&su=p560.6.336.ip_&tt=2&bt=0&bts=1&zu=http%3A//members.aol.com/nonverbal2/diction1.htm

49. Ambady N *et al.* Surgeons' tone of voice: A clue to malpractice history. *Surgery* 2002; 132: 5–9. This is a remarkable piece of communications research in which surgeons' consultations were audio-recorded then analysed. The authors concluded that: '[The] surgeons' tone of voice in routine visits is associated with malpractice claims history. . . . This is the first study to show clear associations between communication and malpractice in surgeons.' The primary variables rated were: warmth, hostility, dominance and anxiety, without inclusion of content.
50. Ekman P, Friesen W V , Hager J C. Facial *Action Coding System Investigator's Guide; A Human Face*, 2002. ISBN 0–931835–01–1; http://face-and-emotion.com/dataface/facs/guide/FACSIVTi.html

Part E: Foundation knowledge and skills for effective communication

Chapter 11 Core concepts and skills

[Helping]

51. Anon. So, you want to know what's wrong with the NHS? *British Medical Journal* 2007; 335: 994.
52. This description has been attributed to Professor Robert Pinker, but, in a recent conversation with a colleague, the distinguished professor doubted that it came from him. We have been unable to find the original source.
53. I cannot resist adding this cynical variation, from http://www.usingenglish.com, at http://www.usingenglish.com/forum/english-idioms-sayings/6618–teach-man-fish.html: 'Give a man a fish and he'll ask for a lemon. Teach a man to fish and he'll leave work early on Friday.' This results from Western perceptions of fish and fishing, of course, as an indulgence and a recreational sport, rather than as a basic food and survival activity.

[Empathy]

54. Hardee J T. An overview of empathy. *The Permanente Journal* 2004; 7(4). http://xnet.kp.org/permanentejournal/fall03/cpc.html
55. Hojat M. *Empathy in Patient Care: Antecedents, development, measurement, and outcomes.* Springer[AW1]-Verlag, 2007. (for a review, see: http://www.medicalnewstoday.com/articles/64936.php)
56. Larson E B, Yao X. Clinical empathy as emotional labor in the patient-physician relationship. *Journal of the American Medical Association* 2005; 293: 1100–1106. http://jama.ama-assn.org/cgi/content/full/293/9/1100

[Questioning]

57. One of the wonderful texts the author consulted in the writing of this book is: Hargie O, ed. *The Handbook of Communication Skills*, 3rd edn. London: Routledge, 2006. Some of the material in this section draws on Chapter 4 of Hargie's book.
58. Hargie O, ed. *The Handbook of Communication Skills*, 3rd edn. London: Routledge, 2006: 124.
59. Hargie O, ed. *The Handbook of Communication Skills*, 3rd edn. London: Routledge, 2006: 134–135.

[Active listening, prompting and probing]

60. See, for example, Lang F, Floyd M R, Beine K L. Clues to patients' explanations and concerns about their illnesses: A call for active listening. *Archives of Family Medicine* 2000; 9: 222–227.
61. Hargie O, ed. *The Handbook of Communication Skills*, 3rd edn. London: Routledge, 2006: 135–136.

[Explanation]

62. Hargie O, ed. *The Handbook of Communication Skills*, 3rd edn. London: Routledge, 2006: 216.

Chapter 12 Special communication needs and processes

63. One of the richest sources of information from patients about what it is like to be a patient is at the DIPEx Charity: http://www.healthtalkonline.org and http://www.youthhealthtalk.org
64. There are many quality-assured sites such as Health on the Net: http://www.hon.ch
65. Comprehensive information about disability rights and benefits in the UK from the Disability Alliance: http://www.disabilityalliance.org/index.htm
66. Huge resources and numbers of links on all aspects of disability from The Independent Living Institute: http://www.independentliving.org/links/
67. Excellent material for teenagers living with disability: http://www.cyh.com/HealthTopics/HealthTopicDetails.aspx?p=243&np=292&id=2336
68. British Medical Association. Disability equality within healthcare: The role of healthcare professionals, June 2007: http://www.bma.org.uk/ap.nsf/content/disabilityequalityhealthcare. This is a useful introduction to the inequalities and problems faced by people with disabilities in healthcare, with positive recommendations for improvement.

[Patients and pain]

69. An excellent library of evidence-based materials on all aspects of pain is available on Bandolier (along with a thousand other interesting topics): http://www.jr2.ox.ac.uk/bandolier/booth/painpag/index.html
70. http://www.gosh.nhs.uk and http://www.gosh.org.uk; Institute of Child Health: http://www.ich.ucl.ac.uk
71. For example, http://www.ppprofile.org.uk
72. http://www.cancerbackup.org.uk/Resourcessupport/symptomssideeffects/Pain/describingpain
73. Research on this excellent website, Male Health (http://www.malehealth.co.uk), reports how reluctant patients are to ask for pain medication, and that HCPs tend to believe that it is up to the patient to initiate requests: http://www.malehealth.co.uk/userpage1.cfm?item_id=1450

[Bedside manner and home visiting]

74. Incident recorded in the author's own book, *Time to Let Go: A record of the life and death of a young man*. London: 1999: 178–179.

[Ambivalence]

75. The interdependence of opposites is particularly a concern of Taoist studies, but it is familiar throughout philosophy and psychology. 'Every phenomenon consists of a pairing of relative opposites tethered together in a single continuum. This single continuum, this oneness, is Tao. The tethering of relative opposites creates a relationship in which one cannot harmoniously exist without the other; they are interdependent.' http://www.tao.org/CMS827/02._the_rise_of_relative_opposites.html

Part F: The complexity of humanity

Chapter 13 The diversity of patients: disturbances and dysfunctions

[The impact and meaning of abuse]

76. Crosson-Tower C. *Understanding Child Abuse and Neglect*, 7th edn. Harlow, UK: Allyn and Bacon, 2008. ISBN-10: 0–205–50326–8.
77. A good starting point for information about this topic is the MedLine page on child sexual abuse, at http://www.nlm.nih.gov/

medlineplus/childsexualabuse.html with links to the American Academy of Child and Adolescent Psychiatry. Your search engine will provide many more avenues to explore.

78. In many countries, there are extensive public resources of information available about domestic violence and organisations offering advice and help. An good example: http://www.domesticviolence.org/
79. Warning signs and symptoms of domestic violence: http://www.helpguide.org/mental/domestic_violence_abuse_types_signs_causes_effects.htm
80. Comprehensive sources and references on MedLine: http://www.nlm.nih.gov/medlineplus/domesticviolence.html

[Anger]

81. An excellent, discursive account of anger at: http://www.guidetopsychology.com/anger.htm
82. Good stuff on anger for kids: http://kidshealth.org/kid/feeling/emotion/anger.html

[Aggression and aggressive patients]

83. Braithwaite R, *Managing Aggression.* London: Taylor and Francis, 2001. Master eBook ISBN10: 0–203–19391–1.
84. How to deal with bullying at work: http://www.mind.org.uk/Information/Booklets/How+to/How+to+deal+with+bullying+at+work.htm
85. Bullying at work: http://www.workershealth.com.au/facts027.html
86. Forster J A, Petty M T, Schleiger C, Walters H C. kNOw workplace violence: developing programs for managing the risk of aggression in the health care setting. *Medical Journal of Australia* 2005; 183: 357–361. http://mja.com.au/public/issues/183_07_031005/for10203_fm.html

[Depression and other mental disorders]

87. Much work has been done on the question of depression and medication by Charles Medawar, who brings an implacably critical disposition towards the handling of mental illness and medication by governments, the pharmaceutical industry and healthcare. See, for example: Medawar C. The antidepressant web. *International Journal of Risk and Safety in Medicine* 1997; 10: 75–126; Charles Medawar's website: http://www.socialaudit.org.uk
88. From DIPEx Charity. Health: depression and its symptoms. http://www.healthtalkonline.org and http://www.youthhealthtalk.org
89. http://www.nyc.gov/html/doh/downloads/pdf/public/dohmhnews2–06.pdf
90. An interesting study of the relationship between suicide and patient dissatisfaction in a psychiatric clinic, with some methods for predicting level of suicide risk. Richmas J, Charles E. Patient dissatisfaction and attempted suicide. *Community Mental Health Journal* 1976; 12: 301–305.
91. One excellent website is: http://www.helpguide.org/mental/depression_signs_types_diagnosis_treatment.htm
92. National Institute of Mental Health. Depression. http://www.nimh.nih.gov/health/publications/depression/complete-publication.shtml (This is a comprehensive guide available from the website, with many links and references.)
93. http://www.depression.com
94. http://www.kidshealth.org/teen/your_mind/mental_health/depression.html
95. The Mayo Clinic on depression: http://www.mayoclinic.com/health/depression/DS00175
96. The UK National Association for Mental Health (MIND): http://www.mind.org.uk
97. An excellent website on principles and aims in mental health: http://www.schizophreniaguidelines.co.uk/schizophrenia/values_recovery.php
98. Edited from medicinenet.com: http://www.medterms.com/script/main/art.asp?articlekey=5110
99. http://www.medicinenet.com/schizophrenia/article.htm

100. http://www.stress.org/
101. http://www.helpguide.org/mental/stress_signs.htm
102. http://www.medicinenet.com/stress/article.htm

[The worried well]
103. See, for example: http://news.bbc.co.uk/2/hi/health/7001436.stm
104. Diamond F. How to manage the worried well. *Managed Care* 2003. http://www.managedcaremag.com/archives/0306/0306.worriedwell.html
105. In one review of patients physicians regarded as 'difficult', the worried well were one of the largest groups (multiple medical problems was the largest): Elder N, Ricer R, Tobias B. How respected family physicians manage difficult patient encounters. *Journal of the American Board of Family Medicine* 2006; 19: 533–541. http://www.jabfm.org/cgi/content/full/19/6/533
106. The Finnish national advisory board on healthcare ethics: Statement on medicalistion of everyday life (in English); http://www.etene.org/e/documents.shtml or http://www.etene.org/dokumentit/Elamantapal210605en.pdf
107. Miller H. Risky business. *The Guardian* 11 July 2008. Posted on the Amercian Council on Science and Health (ACSH) website: http://www.acsh.org/healthissues/newsID.1711/healthissue_detail.asp. This is a wonderful demolition of many common health scares and concerns, revealing their flimsiness and absurdity. You can sign up for news from ACSH and get regular health information and opinion.

[Difficult patients]
108. Elder N, Ricer R, Tobias B. How respected family physicians manage difficult patient encounters. *Journal of the American Board of Family Medicine 2006;* 19: 533–541; http://www.jabfm.org/cgi/content/full/19/6/533. There is a particularly useful list of 50 references at the end of this article.
109. Elder N, Ricer R, Tobias B. How respected family physicians manage difficult patient encounters. *Journal of the American Board of Family Medicine* 2006; 19: 533–541. http://www.jabfm.org/cgi/content/full/19/6/533, p. 7. There is a particularly useful list of 50 references at the end of this article.
110. Groves T E. Taking care of the hateful patient. *New England Journal of Medicine* 1978; 298: 883–887. http://content.nejm.org/cgi/content/abstract/298/16/883?ijkey=6dd1d1183c40d6ae6fbe18f8169b6d034f1068dc&keytype2=tf_ipsecsha

Chapter 14 Communication and the richness of cultural and ethnic diversity

111. A particularly rich and thoughtful source of information on these issues is at http://www.ethnicityonline.net. The author has drawn on that source, and gratefully acknowledges permission to use it. Copyright © 2003 University of Cambridge, School of Clinical Medicine. See also Fleming M, Towey K. Delivering culturally effective care to adolescents. American Medical Association. http://www.ama-assn.org/ama1/pub/upload/mm/39/culturallyeffective.pdf
112. A useful survey of diversity issues in the US: *Patient Safety: Hospitals, Language, and Culture: A Snapshot of the Nation.* Joint Commission Report, 2006. http://www.jointcommission.org/NR/rdonlyres/E64E5E89-5734-4D1D-BB4D-C4ACD4BF8BD3/0/hlc_paper.pdf
113. Quoted in Joint Commission (JCAHO), 'What did the doctor say?' Improving health literacy to protect patient safety, p. 29; http://209.85.175.104/search?q=cache:YibDv6AKAvsJ: www.jointcommission.org/NR/rdonlyres/D5248B2E-E7E6-4121-8874-99C7B4888301/0/improving_health_literacy.pdf+Joint+Commission+Health+literacy&hl=en&ct=clnk&cd=2

114. The following abstract of a much longer research article highlights some of the profound problems of a vocabulary where the words may be shared but the extent to which they mean the same to both parties will vary from high to non-existent:

 'Analysis of data obtained from prototype definitions responses to a list of 32 medical terms showed that there was a varying amount of semantic overlap between physician or nurse and patient ranging from almost complete overlap to almost zero overlap for some medical terms. Among some of the findings were the following: (1) medical workers have a more general, more inclusive meaning than do lay people for such medical terms as fracture, colic, diabetes, and arteriosclerosis; (2) many medical terms (hypertension, stroke, obesity, prematurity) are not comprehensible at all or are barely so for certain patients, depending upon their backgrounds and experiences; (3) meanings are a result of beliefs and experiences for both males and females; (4) the causes of a disease or condition are less well understood than are the symptoms and results; and (5) lay people operate on a concrete level in understanding medical meanings. In order to improve matches between physician meanings and nurse/patient meanings, physicians need to understand the impact of presuppositions, intentions, beliefs, attitudes, moods, and encyclopedic knowledge in the interpretive processes. They need to lay bare the misleading assumptions common among themselves and nurses that account for difficulties in comprehending medical terms.'

 ERIC, Problems for the Average Adult in Understanding Medical Language. http://www.eric.ed.gov/ERICWebPortal/custom/portlets/recordDetails/detailmini.jsp?_nfpb=true&_&ERICExtSearch_SearchValue_0=ED226336&ERICExtSearch_SearchType_0=no&accno=ED226336

115. One such example is what language scholars call 'false friends' – words in different languages which appear similar in form, but are quite different in meaning, and therefore liable to misunderstandings. Here are half a dozen Spanish words with their English translations: *bizarro*: brave; *complexión*: physiological build; *constiparse*: to catch a cold; *desgracia*: mistake, misfortune; *despertar*: to wake up; *embarazada*: pregnant; *sopa*: soup. And if you are writing dosage instructions for a Spanish-speaking patient, do not write 'once' if you mean one time – 'once' [*onthe/onse*] in Spanish means 11. These examples from: http://spanish.about.com/cs/vocabulary/a/obviouswrong.htm. The German word *scharf* means 'sharp' (as in English) but also 'hot, spicy', and 'sexually attractive'; but a 'sharp' pain is German is *stechend*. In Malay *pening* can mean both headache and dizziness – a hazardous ambiguity if not clarified. *Controllo* in Italian can mean 'control' or 'monitor'.

116. For this section, the author again acknowledges the usefulness of the Ethnicityonline website.

117. Pease A, Pease B. *The Definitive Book of Body Language*. London: Orion, 2006. ISBN: 978–0–7528–5878–4.

118. Cultural values and non-verbal gestures and behaviour: http://www.csupomona.edu/~tassi/gestures.htm#asian

Part G: Working together

Chapter 15 The whole team and the whole patient

119. The Mayo Clinic, working in Minnesota, Florida and Arizona, has a worldwide reputation for medical excellence, based, not least, on its sophisticated vision and organisational culture of collaboration and patient-centred service. http://www.mayoclinic.com; mayoclinic.org; and mayo.edu

120. Leggat S G, Dwyer J. Improving hospital performance: culture change is not the answer. *Healthcare Quarterly* 2005; 8: 60–68. http://www.longwoods.com/product.php?productid=17096&cat=357
121 New York Presbyterian Hospital case study: Anon. New York hospital looks to Six Sigma for culture change. *Performance Improvement Advisor.* Atlanta, GA, USA: National Health Information, 2003. http://www.gehealthcare.com/usen/service/docs/NYPH_pia1103.pdf
122. Hocking Valley Community Hospital: Shifting Cultures, case study: http://www.healthexecutive.com/content/view/1516/
123. Delmarva Foundation, Improving Your Hospital Culture: A Guide to Understanding, Measuring, and Changing your Most Important Asset. http://www.delmarvafoundation.org/providers/hospitals/culture.html
124. http://www.chop.edu/consumer/jsp/division/generic.jsp?id=76600
125. Sixth Annual Boston Globe 'Salute to Nurses' advertising supplement in the May 4 2008 issue. Found on: http://www.patientadvocare.blogspot.com/
126. http://www.ipsf.org/infoEducprac.php
127. See, for example, Statement on Pharmaceutical Care: http://www.ashp.org/s_ashp/docs/files/BP07/Org_St_PharmCare.pdf
128. See, for example: Tindall W N, Millonig M K. *Pharmaceutical care: insights from community pharmacists.* Boca Raton, FL, USA: CRC Press, 2003. ISBN: 1–56676–953–1.
129. The International Pharmaceutical Federation (FIP), for example, has emphasised the role pharmacists have to play in patient safety generally, as well as in the specific activity of pharmacovigilance (identifying and reporting ADRs).
130. For useful skills, see, for example, Evans G. *Counselling Skills for Dummies.* Chichester, UK: Wiley. ISBN: 978–0–470–51190–9.

[Catering]

131. Roosevelt M. Healthier hospital food. *Time* magazine, 15 May 2006.
132. Excellence in hospital catering: see, for example: Better Hospital Food, 2001 UK initiative: http://195.92.246.148/nhsestates/better_hospital_food/bhf_content/introduction/archive.asp, and betterhospitalfood@dh.gsi.gov.uk
133. For a Candian campaigning blog, go to: http://www.betterhospitalfood.blogspot.com
134. There is a good deal of research that demonstrates patient dissatisfaction with hospital food, for example: Anon. Hospital catering survey shows patient dissatisfaction, *Caterersearch News*, 16 Oct 2006. http://www.caterersearch.com/Articles/2006/10/16/309495/hospital-catering-survey-shows-patient-dissatisfaction.html

Chapter 16 When time and resources are limited

135. Gillette R D. Turtles and rabbits: family physicians under time pressure. *Family Practice Management* 1999; 6. http://www.aafp.org/fpm/990400fm/21.html
136. A useful discussion of the pressures under which pharmacists work, and their effects: Smith S R, Golin C E, Reif S. Influence of time stress and other variables on counseling by pharmacists about antiretroviral medications. *American Journal of Health-System Pharmacy* 2004; 61: 1120–1129.
137. Davis K, Schoen C, Schoenbaum S C. *Mirror, Mirror on the Wall: An update on the quality of American Health Care through the patient's lens.* New York, NY, USA: The Commonwealth Fund, 2002. http://www.commonwealthfund.org/publications/publications_show.htm?doc_id=364436
138. Treacy D. *Clear Your Desk!* London: Random House Business Books. ISBN: 0–0917–4850–X.

139. Rith C. Ten tips for keeping your desk clean and tidy. http://www.lifeclever.com/10-tips-for-keeping-your-desk-clean-and-tidy/
140. Anon. How to clean up your desk. http://www.wikihow.com/Clean-Up-Your-Desk
141. Anon. Speed reading. http://www.mindtools.com/speedrd.html
142. Abby Marks-Beale, *Ten Days to Faster Reading*. Clayton, Vic., Australia: Warner Books. ISBN 0–446–67667–5.
143. Anon. Time management. http://en.wikipedia.org/wiki/Time_management
144. Anon. Personal time management guide. http://www.time-management-guide.com/
145. Soper W D. 13 Ways to be more efficient. *Family Practice Management* 1999; 6. http://www.aafp.org/fpm/990400fm/improving.html
146. There are many good resources available for patients and the general public. New York City, for example, has an email alert system for public health issues, and a first-class set of bulletin leaflets on everything from domestic violence to diabetes and finding a doctor. http://www.nyc.gov/html/doh/html/alerts/alert1.shtml. See also Health resources in Appendix 2.
147. Werner D *et al. Where There is No Doctor: A village health care handbook*, 2nd ed. Berkeley, CA, USA: Hesperian Foundation, 2007. ISBN-10: 0–9423–6415–5.
148. Not the main website, but an informative account with links: http://www.canoncollins.org.uk/projects/phelophepa.php; the main website was under construction when this book went to press: http://www.mhc.org.za
149. http://www.impactindia.org/lifeline.htm; http://www.impactindia.org/pdf/llemaual.pdf
150. Staff in the emergency department of Baptist Memorial Health Care, Memphis, felt that there was a lack of understanding of emergency room procedures, among other factors, that was generating patient dissatisfaction. Along with concerns about overcrowding, they took this as an opportunity to educate their community and change their perceptions and expectations. Abstract at: http://findarticles.com/p/articles/mi_hb6488/is_200402/ai_n25823742

Part H: Tough topics

Chapter 17 Patient safety

151. The Joint Commission has extensive material on this topic, including national patient safety goals for hospital and ambulatory care: http://www.jointcommission.org/PatientSafety/

These are also invaluable sites: www.npsa.nhs.uk (The National Patient Safety Agency)

www.who.int/patientsafety (World Health Organisation Alliance for Patient Safety)

www.saferhealthcare.org.uk (division of the NPSA)

Description from the JC's email newsletter: 'Founded in 1951, The Joint Commission seeks to continuously improve the safety and quality of care provided to the public through the provision of health care accreditation and related services that support performance improvement in health care organizations. The Joint Commission evaluates and accredits more than 15,000 health care organizations and programs in the United States, including more than 8,000 hospitals and home care organizations, and more than 6,300 other health care organizations that provide long term care, assisted living, behavioral health care, laboratory and ambulatory care services. The Joint Commission also accredits health plans, integrated delivery networks, and other managed care entities. In addition, The Joint Commission provides certification of disease-specific care programs, primary stroke centers, and health care staffing services. An independent, not-for-profit organization, The Joint Commission is the [US's] oldest and largest standards-setting and accrediting body in health care. Learn more about The Joint Commission at http://www.jointcommission.org.'

152. Many major policy documents have been issued declaring the high priority of patient safety. In the European Union, the Luxembourg Declaration of 2005 is one of the major examples: ec.europa.eu/health/ph_overview/Documents/ev_20050405_rd01_en.pdf
153. Health Action International (HAI) is one of the many rational and credible organisations campaigning on behalf of patients for greater openness about medicines and the giving of a much higher priority to safety in regulatory and legislative activities. There is much of interest on their website: http://www.haiweb.org/
154. The US Department of Veterans Affairs (the Veterans Administration) has done an immense amount of work in increasing the safety of its patients and reducing preventable injury in its more than 150 VA hospitals. It has set up a National Centre for Patient Safety and its website has a great deal of useful information for HCPs and health managers: http://www.patientsafety.gov/
155. Berwisk D M, Leape L L. Reducing errors in medicine – it's time to take this more seriously (Editorial); *British Medical Journal* 1999; 319: 136–137. http://www.bmj.com/cgi/content/full/319/7203/136
156. Joint Commission. *'What Did the Doctor Say?' Improving health literacy to protect patient safety.* Oakbrook Terrace, IL, USA: Joint Commission, 2007. Quoted on p. 4; http://www.jointcommission.org/NR/rdonlyres/D5248B2E-E7E6-4121-8874-99C7B4888301/0/improving_health_literacy.pdf
157. A tireless and virulent critic of modern medicine is the prolific Vernon Coleman, who would not put the question mark after this subheading. His book, *Betrayal of Trust* (*European Medical Journal,* 1994. ISBN: 0-9521492-2-2) is a distillation of his iconoclastic case.
158. See, for example, Day M. *C difficile* infections rise – but MRSA rates drop. *British Medical Journal* 2007; 334: 924.
159. Institute of Medicine. *Preventing Medication Errors.* July 2006. http://www.iom.edu/Object.File/Master/35/943/medication%20errors%20new.pdf
160. Lazarou J, Pomeranz BH, Corey PN. Incidence of adverse drug reactions in hospitalized patients. *Journal of the American Medical Association.* 1998; 279: 1200–1205. In this study there was evidence of a increasing trend of ADRs over the 40-year span of the research. In an accompanying editorial (pp. 1216–1217), David W Bates expressed some reservations about the reliability of these figures, because of the complexity of meta-analyses but confirmed the general importance of the problem of ADRs.
161. Kohn L T, Corrigan J M, Donaldson M S (eds). *To Err is Human: Building a safer health system.* The national Academies, Institute of Medicine. National Academy Press, 2000. Ground-breaking report.
162. Figures from the UK Health Minister Dawn Primarolo, reported by Sarah Boseley, in *The Guardian*, 3 April 2008.
163. Pirmohamed M, James S, Meakin S *et al.* Adverse drug reactions as cause of admission to hospital: prospective analysis of 18 820 patients. *British Medical Journal* 2004; 329: 15–19.
164. Patel KJ *et al.* Evaluation of the prevalence and economic burden of adverse drug reactions presenting to the medical emergency department of a tertiary referral centre: a prospective study. *BMC Clinical Pharmacology* 2007; 7: 8. http://www.biomedcentral.com/1472-6904/7/8 ('The study shows that ADRs leading to

hospitalization are frequent and constitute a significant economic burden.')
165. Hutangkabodee S, Suwankesawong W, Toh M, Thmlikitkul V, Ittiravivongs A, *Incidence of Adverse Drug Reactions in Hospitalized Patients: A prospective observational study in 21 selected Thai hospitals.* Thai Food and Drug Administration, Dec 2007; http://www.fda.moph.go.th
166. Shappet S M. *National Centre Health Statistics*, 1999, Series 13, No 143; National Association of Chain Drug Stores, 2001, quoted in: CDER, Preventable Adverse Drug Reactions: A Focus on Drug Interactions, US FDA Learning Module at: http://www.fda.gov/CDER/DRUG/drugReactions/default.htm#ADRs:%20Prevalence%20and%20Incidence
167. UK NHS Information Centre, April 2008. http://www.ic.nhs.uk/statistics-and-data-collections/primary-care/prescriptions
168. http://www.fda.gov/medwatch
169. Many regulatory authorities provide such services, along with printed materials, drug safety bulletins and so on. The Pharmacovigilance Unit of the Singapore Health Sciences Authority, for example, produces an attractive, regular bulletin of new safety issues for HCPs: http://www.hsa.gov.sg
170. May F. http://www.health.vic.gov.au/aca/conf2003/109datis.pdf; http://www.asapnet.org/Roberts_ASAPJune05.ppt
171. Broadhurst N A *et al.* A before and after study of the impact of academic detailing on the use of diagnostic imaging for shoulder complaints in general practice. *Family Practitioner*. 2007; 8: 12. http://www.pubmedcentral.nih.gov/articlerender.fcgi?artid=1851961
172. There are many useful sites for patient education and information. An excellent one is the Partnership for Safe Medication Use, publishing materials under the flag of the US Center for Drug Evaluation and Research: http://www.fda.gov/cder/consumerinfo/think.htm; for CDER's list of all safe use publications, go to: http://www.fda.gov/buyonlineguide/ensuring_safe_use_text.htm
173. http://www.nyc.gov/html/doh/downloads/pdf/public/dohmhnews7–08.pdf
174. A call for the equality of patients' voices in determining the content of patient safety information is made in: Vogt E M. Effective communication of drug safety information to patients and the public: a new look. *Drug Safety* 2002; 25: 313–321. See also: International Alliance of Patients' Organisations: http://www.patientsorganizations.org
175. The UK's MHRA Committee on the Safety of Medicines produced a useful report on many aspects of good information for patients: *Always Read the Leaflet*. London: HM Stationery Office, 2005. ISBN 0–11–703409–6.
176. HIV/AIDS: National AIDS Manual (NAM) http://www.aidsmap.com
177. Multiple sclerosis: http://www.mssociety.org.uk; http://www.nationalmssociety.org
178. Diabetes: http://www.diabetes.org.uk; http://www.diabetes.ca
179. Heart disease: http://www.americanheart.org; http://www.bhf.org.uk (British Heart Foundation); http://www.childrensheart.org
180. Orphan/rare diseases: http://www.rarediseases.org (National Organization for Rare Disorders Inc); http://www.fda.gov/fdac/features/2003/603_orphan.html; http://www.raredisorders.ca
181. Arthritis in Australia: http://www.arthritisfoundation.com.au
182. The global site for access to all patient organisations: http://www.patientsorganizations.org
183. Health Action International: http://www.haiweb.org

184. Two well-informed campaigning organisations: http://www.worstpills.org (a large resource of first-class information on medicines) and www.socialaudit.org.uk (This website began as an investigation of problems with antidepressant drugs: 'As the problem unfolded, notably between 1997 and 2003, it revealed a glimpse of pharmageddon – a world of sickness created and sustained by exploitation of the fear of disease, indifference to real health needs, dependence on authority, and misplaced trust in the triumph of drug benefits over harm.')
185. This is an enormous field, so two selected references only: Colbert B L, Biron P. *Pharmacovigilance from A to Z*. Oxford, UK: Blackwell Science, 2002. ISBN: 0–632–04586–8.
186. Strom B, Kimmel S E. *Textbook of Pharmacoepidemiology*. Chichester, UK: Wiley, 2006. ISBN-13: 978–0–470–02925–1 (Section II).
187. The international organisation responsible for pharmacovigilance is the Uppsala Monitoring Centre (UMC), which manages the WHO Programme for International Drug Monitoring: http://www.who-umc.org. UMC has a wide range of publications relating to pharmacovigilance, including Viewpoint Parts 1 and 2 which provide details of the science and activities in easy-to-read formats. Download from: http://www.who-umc.org/DynPage.aspx?id=13136&mn=1512#6
188. Pirmohamed M, Atuah K N, Dodoo A N O, Winstanley P. Pharmacovigilance in developing countries. *British Medical Journal* 2007; 335: 462.
189. Described as 'America's other drug problem' by the National Council on Patient Information and Education, in Enhancing Prescription Medicine Adherence, 2007. http://www.talkaboutrx.org/documents/enhancing_prescription_medicine_adherence.pdf

[Medication error]

190. Cohen M R (ed). *Medication Errors*, 2nd edn. American Pharmacists' Association (2007). ISBN: 978–1–58212–092–8.
191. *Joint Commission Journal on Quality and Patient Safety*. January 2007; http://www.jointcommission.org
192. See Gerstein M. *Flirting with Disaster: why accidents are rarely accidental*. New York, NY, USA: Union Square Press, 2008. ISBN-13: 978–1–4027–6183–6. This excellent book looks at a wide range of disasters beyond medicine (Hurricane Katrina, the *Challenger* tragedy and others), and includes a thorough analysis of the Vioxx crisis.
193. Reprinted and adapted by permission from Cohen M R (ed). *Medication Errors*, 2nd edn. American Pharmacists' Association (2007), p. 58. ISBN-13: 978-1-58212-092-8.
194. Among many useful safety guideline publications are: Health Care Association of New Jersey. *Medication Management Guideline*. Hamilton, NJ, USA: Best Practice Committee of the Health Care Association of New Jersey, 2006. http://www.hcanj.org; Hartigan-Go K. *Transforming to a Culture of Safety in the Philippines*. Philippine College of Physicians, 2007; http://www.pcp.org.ph
195. http://www.jointcommission.org/
196. http://www.jointcommission.org/PatientSafety/DoNotUseList
197. Eleanor Vogt. Effective communication of drug safety information to patients and the public: a new look. *Drug Safety* 2005, 25: 5.
198. See, for example: http://www.expertpatients.nhs.uk
199. Wise J. UK government and doctors agree to end "blame culture"; *British Medical Journal* 2001; 323: 9. See also A Commitment to Quality, a Quest for Excellence – available on the Department of Health's website at: http://www.bmj.com/cgi/content/full/323/7303/9
200. See Kennedy A, Rogers A, Bower P. Support for self care for patients with chronic

disease. *British Medical Journal* 335; 968–970.

Chapter 18 Informed consent

201. In recently revised material (2008) the UK General Medical Council has very thorough guidance on this topic, making very clear the non-discretionary obligation: http://www.gmc-uk.org/guidance/ethical_guidance/consent_guidance/how_guidance_applies_to_you.asp
202. *Gale Encyclopedia of Surgery: A guide for patients and caregivers*. Gale Group, Inc. 2005. http://www.enotes.com/surgery-encyclopedia/
203. An excellent summary of the issues, from several sources, can be found at: http://www.answers.com/topic/informed-consent?cat=biz-fin&nr=1
204. Among the very first of these, the Helsinki Declaration remains the basis of global medical research ethics. See http://www.wma.net/e/ethicsunit/helsinki.htm
205. Documents that chart the modern progress of ethical priorities in medical practice and research started with the Nuremburg Declaration; for a time-line of human rights developments since then see: http://www.gwu.edu/~erpapers/humanrights/timeline/timeline6.cfm.
206. See: http://www.infoplease.com/ipa/A0762136.html, or: http://www.tuskegee.edu/Global/Story.asp?s=1207586
207. Consent for participation in clinical trials and other complex projects is beyond the scope of this book
208. Based on Breslow L ed. Gale Encyclopedia of Public Health (eBook version); The Gale Group, Inc.; http://gale.cengage.com/servlet/ItemDetailServlet?region=9&imprint=000&titleCode=M185E&type=4&cf=e&id=190153
209. The principle holds good in all circumstances, even if the way you deal with consent is informal and rapid.
210. 'I [Zurad] include a statement in my note that the procedures, risks, potential consequences and complications, and alternatives have been explained to the patient, understood and accepted in detail (PRCCAEUA)' Zurad E.G. Don't be a target for a malpractice suit. *Family Practice Management* 2006; 13: 57–64.

Chapter 19 Risk communication

211. One of the liveliest and most original thinkers in risk communication in general is Peter Sandman, whose writings cover the whole spectrum of theory and practice across many areas of life, especially public health and environmental and natural hazards and risks. His excellent website can be found at: http://www.psandman.com.
212. Excellent and wide-ranging material can be found in Bandolier's Risk Collection at: http://www.medicine.ox.ac.uk/bandolier/index.html
213. Lyndon B. Withdrawal of useful drugs from the market. *Australian Prescriber* 2003; 26: 50–51. http://www.australianprescriber.com/magazine/26/3/50/1/
214. Whorwell P J. Withdrawal of co-proxamol drug was useful in gastroenterology as well as rheumatology. *British Medical Journal* 2005; 331: 515. http://www.bmj.com/cgi/content/extract/331/7515/515–c; Giacomini K M, Krauss R M, Roden D M, Eichelbaum M, Hayden M R, Nakamura Y. When good drugs go bad. *Nature* 2007; 446: 975–977.
215. See also the great Vioxx controversy – notice of withdrawal: http://www.fda.gov/bbs/topics/news/2004/NEW01122.html. For the controversy and links and references to the serious debate that took place: Jüni P, Nartey L, Reichenbach S, Sterchi R, Dieppe PA, Egger M. Risk of cardiovascular events and rofecoxib: cumulative meta-analysis. *The Lancet* 2004; 364(9450): 2021–2029. http://www.ncbi.nlm.nih.gov/pubmed/15582059

216. http://www.acsh.org/publications/pubID.1183/pub_detail.asp
217. Dodoo A, Adjei S, Couper M, Hugman B, Edwards R. When rumours derail a mass deworming exercise. *The Lancet* 2007; 370(9586): 465–466.
218. Royal Society for the Prevention of Accidents. http://www.rospa.com/factsheets/general_accidents.pdf
219. Terence Hollingsworth, in Notes & Queries. *Guardian Weekly*, 25 Feb–1 Mar 2007. Copyright © Guardian Newspapers.
220. http://www.acsh.org/publications/pubID.1183/pub_detail.asp
221. Ragnar Löfstedt, Drugs trial hospital could have started by saying sorry. *Independent on Sunday*, 9 April 2006, available at: http://findarticles.com/p/articles/mi_qn4159/is_20060409/ai_n16185191?tag=rel.res1
222. Paling J. *Helping Patients Understand Risks*. Gainesville, FL, USA: Risk Communication Institute, 2006. ISBN-10: 0–9642–2367–8.
223. Based on Herxheimer A. Communicating with patients about harms and risks. *PLoS Medicine* 2005; 2: e42. doi: 10.1371/journal.pmed.0020042
224. Paling perspective scale: http://www.riskcomm.com/scales.htm
225. Paling palette: http://www.riskcomm.com/thumbnails.htm
226. http://www.riskcomm.com
227. This table is based on UK MCC 2004; the standards were proposed in CIOMS III (1999): *Guidelines for Preparing Core Clinical-Safety Information on Drugs – Including New Proposals for Investigator's Brochures*, 2nd edn. Council for International Organizations of Medical Sciences (established by WHO/UNESCO); http://www.cioms.ch
228. A starting point is: http://www.evidence-based-medicine.co.uk
229. The BBC's risk reporting guidelines cover many of the issues raised in this chapter, as they apply to journalists: Harrabin R, English S (with Löfsted R). *BBC* 2003; p. 39.
230. Australian Drug Evaluation Committee (ADEC) statement on use of hormone replacement therapy: http://www.tga.gov.au/docs/html/hrtadec.htm and update: http://www.tga.gov.au/docs/html/hrtadec2.htm
231. Komesaroff P A. Ethical perspectives on the communication of risk. *Australian Prescriber* 2003; 26: 44–45.

Chapter 20 Sex and sexual orientation

232. Gabbard G O. *Sexual Exploitation in Professional Relationships*. Arlington, VA, USA: American Psychiatric Publishing 1989. ISBN-13: 978–0880–4829–0–5.
233. In a New York City survey, as many as four in ten men who had sex with men had not disclosed the fact to their HCPs. The figures for black, Hispanic and Asian men were much higher than those for white men, and none of the men who identified themselves as bisexual had disclosed the fact to their HCPs. This has enormous implications for HIV testing and a wide range of other related medical and social problems. Source: New York City Department of Health and Mental Hygiene. http://home2.nyc.gov/html/doh/html/pr2008/pr052–08.shtml
234. For example (four references): http://www.bbc.co.uk/relationships/sex_and_sexual_health/enjsex_index.shtml
235. http://www.thesite.org/sexandrelationships
236. Rouse L P. *Marital and Sexual Lifestyles in the United States: Attitudes, behaviors, and relationships in social context (Haworth Marriage and the Family)*. New York, NY: Haworth Clincal Practice Press, 2002. ISBN: 0–7890–1071–2.
237. Byers E S. Relationship satisfaction and sexual satisfaction: a longitudinal study of individuals in long-term relationships, *The Journal of Sex Research* 2005; 42.

238. For some of the best information about HIV and AIDS, go to: The Terrence Higgins Trust: http://www.tht.org.uk, or NAM at http://www.aidsmap.com; for treatment and practice, visit the HATIP (HIV & AIDS Treatment in Practice) section of the site.
239. An excellent, comprehensive set of guidelines for HCPs is provided by the Gay and Lesbian Medical Association, at: http://ce54.citysoft.com/_data/n_0001/resources/live/GLMA%20guidelines%202006%20FINAL.pdf. There are also other extensive resources on the GLMA site http://www.glma.org
240. This item based on McNair R P. Lesbian health inequalities; a cultural minority issue for health professionals. *Medical Journal of Australia* 2003; 178: 643–645.
241. An excellent, comprehensive set of guidelines for HCPs is provided by the Gay and Lesbian Medical Association, at: http://ce54.citysoft.com/_data/n_0001/resources/live/GLMA%20guidelines%202006%20FINAL.pdf. There are also other extensive resources on the GLMA site http://www.glma.org
242. A comprehensive dictionary of sexual vocabulary, conditions and activities: http://www.sexualcounselling.com/Glossary/Glossarya.htm. There are many resources under Other Links.
243. For some colourful, off-the-street colloquialisms in this area, see Wikisaurus: http://en.wiktionary.org/wiki/Wikisaurus:homosexual#Colloquial_or_slang_terms.

Chapter 21 Dying and death

These first six references provide some rich resources for exploration of issues relating to dying and death, include some well-established classics, and extensive links to other materials.

243. Kübler-Ross E. *On Death and Dying: What the dying have to teach doctors, nurses, clergy, and their own families*. London, UK: Routledge, 2008. ISBN-13: 978–0–4154–6399–7.
244. A good portal for extensive resources about medical and ethical issues and dying and death: http://www.growthhouse.org
245. Kessler D. *The Needs of the Dying: A guide for bringing hope, comfort and love for life's final chapter*, 10th edn. London, UK: Harper Collins, 2007. ISBN 0–06–095821–9. (This author has an excellent website, full of useful advice and information, including titles of the other books he has written himself and with Elisabeth Kübler-Ross: http://davidkessler.org/)
246. *Merck Online Manual of Medical Information: Death and dying*. http://www.merck.com/mmhe/sec01/ch008/ch008a.html
247. *Encyclopedia of death and dying*, 2007. http://www.deathreference.com/
248. Lynne J, Harrold J. *Handbook for Mortals: Guidance for hope facing serious illness*. Oxford, UK, 2001. ISBN-13: 978–0195–1460–1–1.
249. Young R. *Medically Assisted Death*. Cambridge, UK: Cambridge University Press 2007. ISBN-13: 978–0521–8802–4–4.
250. American Academy of Hospice and Palliative Medicine. Position Statement: Physician-assisted death. Feb 2007. http://www.aahpm.org/positions/suicide.html
251. University of Washington School of Medicine. Physician-assisted suicide. http://depts.washington.edu/bioethx/topics/pas.html

Part I: The broader communications picture

Chapter 22 Effective written and spoken communication

252. For excellent materials on all aspects of clear and effective written communications, visit the Plain English Campaign: http://www.plainenglish.co.uk

[Telephone]

253. http://www.legalsecretaries.org/articles/telephone.htm
254. http://www.customerservicepoint.com/telephone-skills.html
255. Farrell T J. *Effective Telephone Skills.* Dryden [AW2] Press, 1989. ISBN-13: 978–0155–2093–1–2.
256. Training resources from: http://www.fenman.co.uk/cat/browse/telephone-skills.html

[Report writing]

257. Excellent general advice from: http://startup.curtin.edu.au/study/writing/report.cfm, and dozens of other website (search term: report writing).
258. For more academic reports, there is good guidance from the University of Canberra: http://www.canberra.edu.au/studyskills/writing/reports

[Public speaking and presentations]

259. The Advanced Public Speaking Institute has free materials on: http://www.public-speaking.org/
260. http://www.mindtools.com/CommSkll/PublicSpeaking.htm. Mindtools.com is an excellent resource of information about all kinds of communications, management and professional issues. It has a regular, free newsletter to which you can subscribe.

[Design]

261. There are some great thoughts on Great Design on Keith Robinson's blog: http://blueflavor.com/blog/2007/nov/28/what-makes-a-great-design/

Chapter 23 Complaints, apologies and public relations

262. A gripping and revealing analysis of 12 000 patient complaints with lots of helpful suggestions about prevention and management from the Joint Commission: Pichert J W, Miller C S, Hollo A H, Gauld-Jaeger J, Federspiel C F, Hickson G B. What health professionals can do to identify and resolve patient dissatisfaction. *The Joint Commission Journal on Quality Improvement* 1998; 24: 303–312.
263. An example of such research from Japan: Kazuyoshi N, Toshiko M, Noriyuki S, Katsuji H, Katsuyasu K, Hitoshi F. Patient dissatisfaction with anesthetic care-direct interviews at an postanesthetic clinic. *Japanese Journal of Anesthesiology* 2004; 53; 1136–1142. Abstract at: http://sciencelinks.jp/j-east/article/200422/000020042204A0738732.php
264. An example of a simple research tool for use in general practice: Steven I D, Douglas R M. A self-contained method of evaluating patient dissatisfaction in general practice. *Family Practice* 1986; 3: 14–19.
265. Several simple patient opinion form samples: http://www.migrantclinician.org/clearinghouse/list.php?file_category_id=23
266. Löfstedt R, Professor of Risk Management, King's College, London, in the *Independent on Sunday*, 9 April 2006. http://findarticles.com/p/articles/mi_qn4159/is_20060409/ai_n16185191?tag=rel.res1
267. Rachel G, Ayelet B, Dan Y, Jochanan B. Predictors of patient dissatisfaction with emergency care. *Israel Medical Association Journal* 2002; 4: 603–606.
268. The UK NHS complaints policy: http://www.adviceguide.org.uk/index/family_parent/health/nhs_complaints.htm. While the content is admirable, the style is long and text-dense.
269. A good example of a simple policy: St Vincents University Hospital Comments & Complaints Policy, http://www.stvincents.ie/Home/Comments_&_Complaints_Policy.htm
270. Another good example with slightly more conviction from Spire Healthcare (UK): http://www.spirehealthcare.com/Treatment-Information/Patient-care/Spire-Healthcare-complaints-policy/

Chapter 24 Notes on media relations

271. Huge resources on the web on this topic; search on media relations skills, for example, Google's ten top tips: http://www.aboutpublicrelations.net/ucgranat2a.htm
272. More on PR: http://findarticles.com/p/articles/mi_qa3984/is_200212/ai_n9151173/pg_1?tag=artBody;col1

Chapter 25 Notes on managing meetings

273. This is a very informative, serious site, with lots of useful organisational topics beyond meetings: http://www.managementhelp.org/grp_skll/meetings/meetings.htm

Appendix 3

274. The Calgary–Cambridge consultation analysis. Reproduced with permission: Silverman J, Kurtz S, Draper J. *Skills for Communicating With Patients*, 2nd edn. Oxford, UK: Radcliffe Publishing, 2006: 22–26. ISBN: 1–85775–640-1.

Quotations

The quotations throughout the book have been drawn from a wide range of sources. Particularly useful were:

http://www.brainyquote.com/
http://www.doctorspage.net/quotes.asp#top
http://www.quotegarden.com/medical.html
http://www.csen.com/anesthesia/quote.htm
http://www.memorablequotations.com/
Sherrin N, ed. *The Oxford Dictionary of Humorous Quotations*, 3rd edn. Oxford, UK: Oxford University Press, 2007. ISBN-10: 0-1928–0657–2.

Appendix 2: Useful books and websites

These books and websites are listed by professional roles and particular topics, but they all offer very interesting material for HCPs across the board. This is an eclectic list of the books and sites the author has read and enjoyed, relating to the topics of this book, and not a comprehensive reading or research list, but it opens the door on some of the best writing and materials in communications and some of the most remarkable authors. The author's top book choices are asterisked. Extensive additional references and resources appear in Appendix 1.

Children and medicine

Kilen Consumer Institute for Medicines and Health. *Children, Youth and Medicines*. Stockholm, Sweden: Kilen Consumer Institute for Medicines and Health, 2006. ISBN: 91–972746–7–4.

Division of Information Development, United States Pharmacopeia. *Children and Medicines: Information Isn't Just for Grownups*. Proceedings of a conference held in Washington, DC, 1996. Rockville, MD, USA: United States Pharmacopeia, 1996.
Communication skills (general)

Communication skills (general)

*Hargie O, ed. *The Handbook of Communication Skills*, 3rd edn. London, UK: Routledge, 2006. ISBN13: 978–0–415–35910–8.

Cartwright R. *Communication*. Mankato, MN, USA: Capstone Publishing, 2002. ISBN: 1–84112–364–1.

Maxwell J C. *25 Ways to Win With People*. Nelson Business, 2005. ISBN: 0–7852–7954–7.

Barker A. *Improve Your Communication Skills*. London, UK: Kogan Page/*Sunday Times*, 2004. ISBN: 0–7494–3262–4.

Communication skills (healthcare)

Berglund C, Saltman D, eds. *Communication for Health Care*. Oxford, UK: Oxford University Press, 2002. ISBN: 0–19–551298–7.

*Silverman J, Kurtz S, Draper J. *Skills for Communicating With Patients*, 2nd edn. Oxford, UK: Radcliffe Publishing, 2006. ISBN: 1–85775–640–1.

*Kurtz S, Silverman J, Draper J. *Teaching and Learning Communication Skills in Medicine*, 2nd edn. Radcliffe Publishing, 2006. ISBN: 1–85775–658–4.

Royal College of Physicians. *Improving Communications Between Doctors and Patients*. London, UK: RCP, 1997. ISBN: 1–86016–054–9.

Counselling

Evans G. *Counselling Skills for Dummies*. Chichester, UK: Wiley, 2007. ISBN: 978–0–470–51190–9.

Tschudin V. *Counselling Skills for Nurses*, 4th edn. Elsevier, 1995. ISBN-13: 978–0–7020–1972–2.

Crisis and crisis communications

Hugman B. *Expecting the Worst: Anticipating, preventing and managing medicinal product crises*. Uppsala Monitoring Centre, 2003 (reprinted 2007). ISBN: 91–631–2971–X.

Gerstein M. *Flirting With Disaster: Why accidents are rarely accidental*. New York, NY, USA:

Union Square, 2008. ISBN-13: 978–1–4027–6183–6.

Death

Immense resources and comprehensive reading list: http://funeralnet.com/info_guide/gri_reading.html

See also notes for Chapter 21 for more reading.

Doctors' practice

*Tate P. *The Doctor's Communications Handbook*, 5th edn. Radcliffe Publishing, 2007. ISBN-10: 1–84619–138–6.

*Groopman J. *How Doctors Think*. Boston, MA, USA: Houghton Mifflin, 2007. ISBN-13: 978–0–618–61003–7.

Ethics

Warnock M. *An Intelligent Person's Guide to Ethics*. London, UK: Duckworth, 1998. ISBN: 0–7156–2841–0.

Pence G. *Medical Ethics: Accounts of the cases that shaped and define medical ethics*. Columbus, OH, USA: McGraw Hill (2007). ISBN: 0–07–292935–4.

Hope T. *Medical Ethics: A very short introduction*. Oxford, UK: Oxford University Press, 2004. ISBN: 978–0–19280282–8.

Healthcare (general issues)

Werner D. *Where There is No Doctor*. London, UK: Macmillan, 1996. ISBN: 0–333–51652–4.

Health information resources

Health on the net: http://www.hon.ch

National Guideline Clearinghouse: rich resources for HCPs to share with their patients: http://www.guideline.gov/resources/patient_resources.aspx

New York City Department of Health and Mental Hygiene: http://www.nyc.gov/html/doh/html/home/home.shtml

NHS Direct: for patients to make telephone enquiries about symptoms and disease: www.nhsdirect.nhs.uk

Medicinenet: huge, reliable resources http://www.medicinenet.com

See also more references in Appendix 1, notes for Chapter 16.

Health literacy

Joint Commission: www.jointcommission.org/PublicPolicy/health_literacy.htm

International Alliance of Patients' Organizations: http://www.patientsorganizations.org/healthliteracy

Management skills and communications

Solomon R J. *The Physician Manager's Handbook: Essential business skills for succeeding in health care*, 2nd rev. edn. Sudbury, MA, USA: Jones and Bartlett, 2007. ISBN-13: 978–0–7637–4603–2.

Hattersley M E, McJannet L M. *Management Communication: Principles and practice*, 3rd edn. McGraw-Hill/Irwin, 2007.

*Heller R, Hindle T. *The Essential Manager's Manual*. London, UK: Dorling Kindersley, 1998. ISBN: 0–7513–0400–X.

Rowntree D. *The Manager's Book of Checklists: Everything you need to know, when you need to know it*. Upper Saddle River, NJ, USA: Prentice Hall, 2005.

Media relations

Henderson D. *Making News: A straight-shooting guide to media relations*. iUniverse, 2006. ISBN-13: 978–1–58348–468–5; 978–0–595–82182–2 (ebk).

Johnston J. *Media Relations: Issues and strategies*. Australia: Allen and Unwin, 2007. ISBN: 978–1–74114 681–3.

Meerman Scott D. *The New Rules of Marketing and PR: How to use news releases, blogs, podcasting, viral marketing and online media to reach buyers directly*. Chichester, UK: John Wiley, 2007. ISBN: 978–0–470–11345–5.

*Allen S. *Media, Risk and Science*. Maidenhead, UK: Open University Press, 2002. ISBN: 0–335–20662–X.

*Levi R. *Medical Journalism: Exposing fact, fiction, fraud*. Studentlitteratur, 2000. ISBN: 91–44–00952–6.

Medication error

*Cohen M R, ed. *Medication Errors*, 2nd edn. Washington, DC, USA: American Pharmacists' Association, 2007. ISBN: 978–1–58212–092–8.

Men's health

http://www.malehealth.co.uk

MedlinePlus: Men's Health www.nlm.nih.gov/medlineplus/menshealth.html

Men's Health Network: www.menshealthnetwork.org

Mental health and disability

Ryan T, Pritchard J. *Good Practice in Adult Mental Health*. London, UK: Jessica Kingsley, 2004. ISBN: 1–84310–217.

Schizophrenia: http://www.schizophrenia guidelines.co.uk/schizophrenia/values_recovery.php

Repper J, Perkins R. *Social Inclusion and Recovery: A model for mental health practice*. Oxford, UK: Elsevier/Baillière Tindall, 2003, ISBN-13: 980–0–7020–2601–8.

Gamble C, Brennan G. *Working With Serious Mental Illness: A manual for clinical practice*, 2nd edn. Oxford, UK: Baillière Tindall, 2005. ISBN-13: 978–0–7020–2716–1.

Laing R D. *The Divided Self: Selected works of R D Laing*. London, UK: Routledge, 1998. ISBN: 0–415–19818–6 (A deeply controversial figure, but a genius in original thinking and his challenge to orthodoxy).

Non-verbal communication

Pease A, Pease B. *The Definitive Book of Body Language*. London, UK: Orion, 2006. ISBN: 978–0–7528–5878–4.

Nursing

Tattam A, ed. *From the Heart: True stories by Australian nurses*. Sydney, Australia: Lothian, 1997. ISBN: 0–85091–846–4.

*Arnold E C, Underman Boggs K. *Interpersonal Relationships: Professional communication skills for nurses*, 5th edn. Saunders/Elsevier, 2007. ISBN: 13: 978–1–4160–2913–7.

Cody W K, ed. *Philosophical and Theoretical Perspectives for Advanced Nursing Practice*. Sudbury, MA, USA: Jones and Bartlett, 2006. ISBN-13: 978–0–7637–4030–6.

Patient biographies/experience of healthcare

Rhys Dent J. *Secret History of a Woman Patient*. Oxford, UK: Radcliffe Publishing, 2007. ISBN-10–1–84619–150-5.

DIPEx Charity: www.healthtalkonline.org and www.youthhealthtalk.org

Patient action and campaigning groups

Health Action International www.haiweb.org

International Alliance of Patients' Organizations, for links to the whole scene: http://www.patientsorganizations.org

Patients (for them, not about them)

Roizen M F, Oz M C. *You: the Smart Patient. An insider's handbook for getting the best treatment*. Florence, MA, USA: Free Press, 2006. ISBN-13: 978–7432–9301–3.

Patient safety

*Vincent C. *Patient Safety*. London, UK: Elsevier Churchill Livingstone, 2006. ISBN: 0–443–10120–5.

Pharmacy practice

Tindall W N, Millonig M K. *Pharmaceutical Care: Insights from community pharmacists*. Boca Raton, FL, USA: CRC Press, 2003. ISBN: 1–56676–953–1.

Tindall W N, Beardsley R S, Kimberlin C L. *Communication Skills in Pharmacy Practice,* 3rd edn. Philadelphia, PA, USA: Lea and Febiger, 1994. ISBN: 0–8121–1633–X.

Berger B A. *Communications Skills for Pharmacists*, 2nd edn. Washington, DC, USA: American Pharmacists' Association, 2005. ISBN-10: 1–58212–080–3.

*World Health Organization. *Developing Pharmacy Practice: A focus on patient care*, 2006. Geneva, Switzerland: WHO/FIP.

*International Pharmaceutical Students' Federation and International Pharmaceutical Federation. *Counselling, Concordance and Communication: Innovative education for pharmacists*. IPSF/FIP, 2005. www.ipsf.org; www.fip.org.

National Pharmacy Association (UK): www.npa.co.uk; www. askyourpharmacist.co.uk

National Pharmaceutical Association (US): www.npha.net

American Pharmaceutical Association: www.npha.com

Canadian Pharmacists' Association: www.pharmacists.ca

Royal Pharmaceutical Society of Great Britain: www.rpsgb.org.uk

Philosophical approaches to healthcare issues

*Groopman J. *The Anatomy of Hope: How people prevail in the face of illness.* Random House, 2005. ISBN: 0–375–75775–9.

Risk, risk management and risk communication

*Paling J. *Helping Patients Understand Risks.* Gainesville, FL, USA: Risk Communication Institute, 2006. ISBN-10: 09642236–7–8.

HM Stationery Office. Communicating about risks to public health. London, UK: HMSO, 1998. ISBN: 0–11–322257–2.

Löfstedt R E. *Risk Management in Post-Trust Society.* Palgrave Macmillian, 2005. ISBN-10: 1403949786.

Bouder F, Slavin D, Löfstedt R E (eds). *The Tolerability of Risk: A new framework for risk management.* London, UK: Earthscan Publications, 2007. ISBN-10: 1–844–07398–X.

Sex and sexual orientation

Nusbaum M, Rosenfeld J A. *Sexual Health across the Lifecycle: A practical guide for clinicians.* Cambridge, UK: Cambridge University Press, 2004. ISBN: 0–521–53421–6.

Minkin M J, Wright C V. *A Woman's Guide to Sexual Health.* Yale, CT, USA: Yale University Press Health & Wellness, 2005. ISBN: 0–300–10594–0.

Spark R F. *Sexual Health for Men.* New York, NY, USA: Perseus Publishing, 2000. ISBN: 0–7382–0206–1.

Clunis D M, Green D D. *Lesbian Couples: A guide to creating healthy relationships.* Seal Press, 2000.

Lockhard J. *The Gay Man's Guide to Growing Older.* New York, NY, USA: Alyson Books, 2002. ISBN: 1–55583–591–0.

Pepper R. *The Ultimate Guide to Pregnancy for Lesbians: How to stay sane and care for yourself from pre-conception through birth*, 2nd edn. San Francisco, CA, USA: Cleis Press, 2005. ISBN: 1–57344–216–X.

Sanderson T. *The A-Z of Gay Sex and The Gay Men's Health Guide.* The Other Way Press, 1994.

Spencer C. *Homosexuality: A history.* Fourth Estate, 1995. ISBN: 1–85702–143–6.

The Gay Men's Health Guide. Health Education Authority, 1996.

For men's sexual health and HIV/AIDS information and support: Terrence Higgins Trust, www.tht/org.uk

Asia:

Totman R. *The Third Sex: Kathoey – Thailand's ladyboys*. Chiang Mai, Thailand: Silkworm Books, 2003. ISBN: 974–9575–26–1.

Dhikav V. *Sexual Deviations: The paraphilias – the hidden aspects of sex in India*. New Delhi, India: AITBS Publishers, 2003. ISBN: 81–7473–227–6.

Jackson P A, Cook N M, eds. *Genders and Sexualities in Modern Thailand*. Chiang Mai, Thailand: Silkworm Books, 1999. ISBN: 974–7551–07–01.

See Appendix 1, notes on Chapter 20 for many more resources.

Small group work

*Beebe S A, Masterson J T. *Communicating in Small Groups: Principles and Practice*. London, UK: Pearson Education, 2006. ISBN: 0–295044956–5.

Social skills

Carnegie D. *How to Win Friends and Influence People*. London, UK: Vermilion, 2006. ISBN: 0–091–90681–4.

Women's health

The National Women's Health Information Center (NWHIC): www.4woman.gov

MedlinePlus: Women's Health: www.nlm.nih.gov/medlineplus/womenshealth.html

National Women's Health Resource Center: http://www.healthywomen.org

Important related topics for further study

The field of communications is enormous. A book of this length can address only a few of the major topics, and deal with even those relatively superficially. There are many other important areas of relationships and communications in which HCPs may be involved and they all have their own realms of specialist knowledge and skills. In all these areas, reading, study and practice will lead to much greater effectiveness.

Here is a short list of some of the areas for further study. Some sources of good information about them appear above and in Appendix 1 but you may want to explore further.

- Counselling
- Crisis management and communication
- Defensive medicine
- Health education
- Influencing and negotiation
- Management communications
- Palliative care
- Public health communications
- Small groups; working with groups
- Video and tele-conferencing
- Website design, development and management
- Working with patients with physical disabilities or mental illnesses.

Appendix 3: The Calgary–Cambridge consultation analysis

Communications process: insight and authority in another book

A first-class framework for analysis

This section introduces one of the most methodical and illuminating books about the detail of consultations in healthcare communications: *Skills for Communicating with Patients* by Jonathan Silverman, Suzanne Kurtz and Juliet Draper. There is an excellent companion volume for teachers and trainers, *Teaching and Learning Communication Skills in Medicine* (see Appendix 2 for full publishing details).

Their first book is a thorough, comprehensive description and analysis of skills in the whole medical consultation process, meticulously documented, well written with extraordinary attention to detail. It primarily addresses the doctor–patient relationship, but it is full of insight and wisdom relevant to most communications in healthcare.

Research authority

One distinctive feature, not shared by the book you are reading now, and which will appeal to those of a studious frame of mind and those in training, is the citing of research findings to support every aspect of good communications practice. Whereas this book relies mostly on argument and assertion, Silverman *et al.* demonstrate, with exemplary thoroughness, that there is good evidence to support almost every detail of good practice; their references to research findings run to several hundred citations.

That is one place you can go if you want to examine a great deal of the evidence that lies behind much of the material of this book.

A clear and helpful framework

Silverman *et al.* have developed a detailed, logical, analytical framework for skills development in the consultation process, called the Calgary–Cambridge Communication Process Guide, on which the entire content of both their books is based. It represents a highly methodical, alternative approach to the one offered in this book, based on the same vision and principles, is complementary, and will provide an enriched and deepened perspective for some readers. Much of our material can be mapped to this guide.

It is gratefully reproduced here with the permission of the authors and publisher, as an additional resource, and as a 'taster' for the quality of the work that it underlies and represents.[274]

Calgary–Cambridge Guides: Communication Process Skills

Initiating the session

Establishing initial rapport

1. Greets patient and obtains patient's name
2. Introduces self, role and nature of interview; obtains consent if necessary
3. Demonstrates respect and interest; attends to patient's physical comfort

Identifying the reason(s) for the consultation

4. Identifies the patient's problems or the issues that the patient wishes to address with appropriate opening questions (e.g. '*What problems brought you to the hospital?*' or '*What would you like to discuss today?*' or

'*What questions did you hope to get answered today?*')

5. Listens attentively to the patient's opening statement, without interrupting or directing the patient's response
6. Confirms list and screens for further problems (e.g. '*So that's headaches and tiredness, anything else?*')
7. Negotiates agenda taking both patient's and physician's needs into account

Gathering information

Exploration of patient's problems

8. Encourages patient to tell the story of the problem(s) from when first started to the present, in own words (clarifying reason for presenting now)
9. Uses open and closed questioning techniques, appropriately moving from open to closed
10. Listens attentively, allowing patients to complete statements, without interruption and leaving space for patient to think before answering or go on after pausing
11. Facilitates patient's responses verbally and nonverbally, e.g. by use of encouragement, silence, repetition, paraphrasing, interpretation
12. Picks up verbal and nonverbal clues (body-language, speech, facial expression); checks out and acknowledges as appropriate
13. Clarifies patient's statements that are unclear or need amplification (e.g. 'Could you explain what you mean by light-headed?')
14. Periodically summarises to verify own understanding of what patient has said; invites patient to correct interpretation or provide further information
15. Uses concise, easily understood questions and comments; avoids or adequately explains jargon
16. Establishes dates and sequence of events

Additional skills for understanding the patient's perspective

17. Actively determines and appropriately explores
    a. Patient's ideas (i.e. beliefs re cause)
    b. Patient's concens (i.e. worries) regarding each problem
    c. Patient's expectations (i.e. goals, what help the patient had expected for each problem)
    d. Effects – how each problem affects the patient's life
18. Encourages the patient to express feelings

Providing structure to the consultation

Making organisation overt

19. Summarises at the end of a specific line of enquiry to confirm understanding before moving on to the next section
20. Progresses from one section to another, using signposting, transitional statements; includes rationale for next section

Attending to flow

21. Structures interview in logical sequence
22. Attends to timing and keeping interview on task

Building relationships

Using appropriate non-verbal behaviour

23. Demonstrates appropriate non-verbal behaviour
    a. Eye contact, facial expression
    b. Posture, position, movement
    c. Vocal cues, e.g. rate, volume, intonation
24. If [patient] reads, writes notes or uses computer, does it in a manner that does not interfere with dialogue or support

25. Demonstrates appropriate confidence

Developing rapport

26. Accepts legitimacy of patient's view and feelings; is not judgemental
27. Uses empathy to communicate understanding and appreciation of the patient's feelings or predicament; overtly acknowledges patient's views and feelings
28. Provides support: expresses concern, understanding, willingness to help; acknowledges coping efforts and appropriate self-care; offers partnership
29. Deals sensitively with embarrassing and disturbing topics and physical pain, including when associated with physical examination

Involving the patient

30. Shares thinking with patient to encourage patient's involvement (e.g. '*What I'm thinking now is . . .*')
31. Explains rationale for questions or parts of physical examination that could appear to be non sequiturs
32. During physical examination, explains process, asks permission

Explanation and planning

Providing the correct amount and type of information

Aims:

- To give comprehensive and appropriate information
- To assess each patient's individual information needs
- To neither restrict nor overload

33. Chunks and checks: gives information in assimilable chunks; checks for understanding; uses patient's response as a guide to how to proceed
34. Assesses patient's starting point: asks for patient's prior knowledge early on when giving information; discovers extent of patient's wish for information
35. Asks patient what other information would be helpful, e.g. aetiology, prognosis
36. Gives explanation at appropriate times: avoids giving advice, information or reassurance prematurely

Aiding accurate recall and understanding

Aims: to make information easier for the patient to remember and understand

37. Organises explanation: divides into discrete sections; develops a logical sequence
38. Uses explicit categorisation or signposting (e.g. 'There are three important things I'd like to discuss. First. . .'; 'Now shall we move on to. . .?')
39. Uses repetition and summarising to reinforce information
40. Uses concise, easily understood language; avoids or explains jargon
41. Uses visual methods of conveying information: diagrams, models, written information and instructions
42. Checks patient's understanding of information given (or plans made) e.g. by asking patient to restate in own words, clarifies as necessary

Achieving a shared understanding incorporating the patient's perspective

Aims:

- To provide explanations and plans that relate to the patient's perspective
- To discover the patient's thoughts and feelings about the information given
- To encourage an interaction rather than a one-way transmission

43. Relates explanations to patient's perspective: to previously elicited ideas, concerns and explanations
44. Provides opportunities and encourages patient to contribute: to ask questions, seek clarification or express doubts; responds appropriately
45. Picks up and responds to verbal and non-verbal cues e.g. patient's need to contribute information or ask questions, information overload, distress
46. Elicits patient's beliefs, reactions and feelings re information given, terms used; acknowledges and addresses where necessary

Planning: shared decision making

Aims:

- To allow patient to understand the decision-making process
- To involve patient in decision making to the level they wish
- To increase patient's commitment to plans made

47. Shares own thinking as appropriate: ideas, thought processes and dilemmas
48. Involves patient:
    a. Offers suggestions and choices rather than directives
    b. Encourages patient to contribute their own ideas, suggestions
49. Explores management options
50. Ascertains level of involvement patient wishes in making decision at hand
51. Negotiates a mutually acceptable plan:
    a. Signposts own position of equipoise or preference regarding available options
    b. Determines patient's preferences
52. Checks with patient:
    a. If accepts plans
    b. If concerns have been addressed

Closing the session

Forward planning

53. Contracts with patient re next steps for patient and physician
54. Safety nets, explaining possible unexpected outcomes, what to do if plan is not working, when and how to seek help

Ensuring appropriate point of closure

55. Summarises session briefly and clarifies plan of care
56. Final check that patient agrees and is comfortable with plan and asks if any corrections, questions or other issues

Options in explanation and planning (includes content and process skills)

If discussing opinion and significance of problem

57. Offers opinion of what is going on and names if possible
58. Reveals rationale for opinion
59. Explains causation, seriousness, expected outcome, short- and long-term consequences
60. Elicits patient's beliefs, raections, concerns re opinion

If negotiating mutual plan of action

61. Discusses options e.g. no action, investigation, medication, surgery, non-drug treatments (plysiotherapy, walking aids, fluids, counselling) preventive measures
62. Provides information on action or treatment offered, names steps involved, how it works, benefits and advantages, side-effects
63. Obtains patient's view of need for action, perecived benefits, barriers, motivation

64. Accepts patient's views; advocates alternative viewpoint as necessary
65. Elicits patient's reactions and concerns about plans and treatments, including acceptability
66. Takes patient's lifestyle, beliefs, cultural background and abilities into consideration
67. Encourages patient to be involved in implementing plans, to take responsibility and be self-reliant
68. Asks about patient support syatems; discusses other support available

If discussing investigations and procedures

69. Provides clear information on procedures e.g. what patient might experience; how patient will be informed of results
70. Relates procedures to treatment plan: value, purpose
71. Encourages questions about and discussion of potential anxieties or negative outcomes

Index